Sibelius

Sibelius

VOLUME I

1865–1905

by

Erik Tawaststjerna

translated by Robert Layton

FABER AND FABER
3 Queen Square London

First published in England in 1976
by Faber and Faber Limited
3 Queen Square London WC1
Printed and bound in Great Britain by
Butler and Tanner Ltd Frome and London
All rights reserved

ISBN 0 571 088325

Abridged version of Vols I and II
originally published 1965 and 1967
by Otava, Helsinki, as *Jean Sibelius*

For Carmen

Contents

List of Illustrations

Translator's Foreword

ERIK Tawaststjerna's study of Sibelius has occupied him for more than a decade. In its Finnish edition it will run to five volumes. The labour of writing a book on this scale in one language let alone two, is Herculean and the Finnish edition, though it has appeared first, is in fact a translation of the Swedish original. The present volume covers the period 1865–1905 and comprises the first two Finnish volumes. It also appears as one volume in Swedish and was published in Stockholm in 1968.

In preparing the present edition I have made a number of changes in consultation with the author consistent with the different needs of the Scandinavian and non-Scandinavian reader. The author also took the opportunity of recasting some sections and making other small revisions so that the edition does not correspond in all respects with the volume published in Stockholm.

There is an oft-quoted saying: 'Translations are like women: if they are faithful, they are not beautiful, and if they are beautiful they are not faithful.' Some women, of course, are both but I would not claim that this translation is either. Professor Tawaststjerna's prose has a special character and personality all its own as well as the elegant flavour of the Swedish spoken in Finland, and is highly admired in Scandinavia. After some struggles I gave up trying to reproduce its distinctive quality and instead concentrated on the sense of what he was saying, attempting to phrase it in the kind of way that I imagined he might, had English been his mother tongue, in the hope that just a little of the personality might come across.

My grateful thanks are due to John Thomson for his invaluable suggestions in reading the manuscript, and to Judith Osborne for her help with proofreading.

In general we have tried to avoid footnotes and I have taken up the large majority of them as well as source references into the main body of the text.

R.L.

Author's Preface

THE successive publication in three languages (Finnish, Swedish and now English) of a large-scale biographical and musical study of a great composer poses special problems. At the time of writing I have been concerned with the third volume of the Swedish edition; at the same time I have been studying a volume of sketches from the period 1914–16 which throws completely new light on the relationship between the Fifth and Sixth Symphonies; and while breaking off to put the finishing touches to the first volume of the English edition, I am grappling with the fourth Finnish volume. Thus, one of the problems is that with every new chapter one's perspective alters; moreover further research reveals new material which has to be worked into chapters that have already been completed in one or other version. Certainly the insights I gained from studying the 1914–16 sketches prompted me to new thoughts about Sibelius's creative processes and to modify my views about the Second Symphony, the discussion of which is entirely different from the Swedish and Finnish editions. I have also had the opportunity of briefly examining some of the material of the first version of the Violin Concerto since the very first edition of that chapter appeared.

During the years immediately after the composer's death, I had the privilege of many conversations with his widow, Mme. Aino Sibelius at Järvenpää. She would receive me in the library of their villa, Ainola, and all the associations and moods conjured up by the atmosphere of the room, the murmuring of the forest outside, the sight of pictures and paintings, would unleash a flood of memories. Her thoughts would range from a painful episode at the time of the Seventh Symphony to the stormy times that so alarmed her during the time he was working—or rather should have been working—on the finale of the Violin Concerto. She would recall her elation in the early 1890s on seeing the first sketch of a theme from *Kullervo* which first opened her eyes to his genius; or her memory would travel further back to their very first encounter in the 1880s; or down to those very last September days in 1957 in the self-same library where he would ask her to sit up with him a little longer, usually until well after midnight. She would speak quietly but with a compelling intensity. Never for one moment did she emphasize her own role in their life together; at times she would reproach herself for some failing, for not having given him sufficient support, and would weep bitterly. It would not help for me to remind her of Sibelius's own diary entry that she had always been behind him and part of his creative work. She was the personification of modesty and dignity. There were rare occasions when her eyes would blaze and her voice assume great firmness; and at such moments I could see something of her background. Her father was a general and so, too, was her mother's grandfather; a portrait of him hangs alongside Kutuzov and other military heroes in the Eremitage while his son's sculpture can be seen on the Anichkoff bridge. At times she would burst into laughter at some other past memory. This did not happen very often but when it did, I felt I could catch a fleeting glimpse of the seventeen-year-old with whom Jean Sibelius fell in love, a character almost from *War and Peace*, meek, poetic, incorruptible, and an aristocrat to her fingertips. Aino Sibelius died shortly before the midsummer of 1969 at the age of ninety-seven. It is only now that I am really conscious of what remarkable evenings these were, for they gave me not only invaluable insights into Sibelius's life and character but brought to life a whole epoch of Finnish history in an extraordinarily vivid way.

Jean Sibelius's daughters have placed every scrap of information in their possession at my disposal: sketches, letters, diaries, contracts, bills; and all this in spite of the relatively short time that has elapsed since his death. My debt to them all cannot easily be expressed in a few words. Mme. Eva Paloheimo, her father's confidante in so many matters, was unstinting in her help; so, too, was Mme. Katarina Ilves, who told me much about his working methods and who is herself a fine exponent of his piano music; Mme. Margareta Jalas, who together with her husband, the conductor Jussi Jalas, have gone to enormous lengths to help me with my researches; Mme. Ruth Snellman who played the role of Ariel to Sibelius's incidental music and Mme. Heidi Blomstedt who have both given me invaluable information about their parents' home and life at Ainola.

It has been my good fortune to have as my translator, Robert Layton, himself the author of a fine study of the composer, for I owe him thanks for invaluable advice and help concerning the reworking of various parts of the book as well as many stimulating discussions. Similarly my thanks are due to my Swedish colleagues, Professor Ingmar Bengtsson and Dr. Bo Wallner for many useful ideas.

During my fourteen years working on this biography a large number of people and institutions have given me their help. Even if I cannot name each and every one in these pages, I have forgotten none. In Finland special thanks are due to Professor John Rosas, Director of the Sibelius Museum in Turku, Professor Jorma Vallinkoski, Chief Librarian of the University of Helsinki, Dr. Nils-Eric Ringbom, formerly Manager of the Helsinki City Orchestra, Mr. Kai Maasalo, Head of Music at the Finnish Radio, Dr. Erkki Salmenhaara and Per-Henrik Nordgren, both of whom gave me secretarial help during their university years. With Joonas Kokkonen, Paavo Berglund and Okko Kamu I have had numerous and fruitful discussions. My Finnish publishers, Otava,

AUTHOR'S PREFACE

and their Head, Mr. Heikki Reenpää, have given me unstinting and loyal support. The Finnish State Commission for the Humanities, the Finnish Cultural Fund, the University of Helsinki, the Wihuri Foundation, the Oflund Foundation, Helander's Foundation, the Finnish–Swedish Cultural Fund have given me scholarships without which much of my work could not have reached fruition.

Elsewhere in Scandinavia my thanks are due to the Royal Academy of Music, Stockholm, Professor Seve Ljungman, Dr. Gunnar Larsson, the Royal Library Stockholm, my Swedish publishers Bonniers Förlag, Stockholm, the Music Department of Sveriges Radio, the Royal Library, Copenhagen, and the University of Oslo Library. In England, Donald Mitchell has given me of his time and ideas and shown an unswerving interest in my work. Several publishers have been most helpful: Fazer, Helsinki, Wilhelm Hansen, Copenhagen, Robert Lienau, Berlin, the Staatsarchiv in Leipzig who possess Sibelius's correspondence with Breitkopf und Härtel as well as a number of autograph manuscripts. My thoughts also go to those persons and institutions in other countries who have been helpful: Professor Carl Dalhaus, Professor H. H. Stuckenschmidt, in West Berlin; Professor Georg Knepler, Deutsche Staatsbibliotek, Berlin (DDR); the Library of the Akademie für Musik und darstellende Kunst, Vienna, Stadtbibliotek, Vienna; Stadtbibliotek, Zurich; the Library of the Accademia Santa Cecilia, Rome; Professor Israel Nestiev, the Lenin Library, the Glinka Library in Moscow, the Library of the Rimsky-Korsakov Conservatory, Leningrad; Professor Leo Normet, Tallinn; Professor Paul Henry Lang, Columbia University; New York Public Library; Library of the New York Philharmonic Orchestra; Library of the Boston Symphony Orchestra, University of Athens (Georgia), Professor Jane Reti-Forbes, and many other colleagues and friends.

E.T.
Helsinki

CHAPTER ONE

Lovisa and the family background

'WHEN I shut my eyes I can picture in my mind a small town with one-storey barracks from the Swedish epoch. It is a late summer's day between five and six in the afternoon some time during the 1820s. The sun is slowly sinking towards the horizon; an officer is visiting a family with two daughters, their mother and brother, and it is obviously not his first visit. They have been enjoying themselves, reading novels, playing the piano; there are geraniums in the window and the house is an old-fashioned one of considerable style. Tea is served and afterwards the party breaks up; they are all fond of each other and there is an atmosphere of real friendship, perhaps love.'

These lines come from an entry in Sibelius's diary for 12–13 April 1915 and in them he sketches a picture of early nineteenth-century Finnish rural life that resembles in certain respects the Finland he himself knew as a child. The little town with the barracks could easily be the garrison town of Hämeenlinna (Tavastehus)[1] in the heart of Finland where he was born and went to school. It could even more readily suggest Loviisa (Lovisa)[1] the idyllic seafaring town where Sibelius often spent his holidays with his grandmother and aunt. In later years he often tried to relive the atmosphere of his grandmother's home and savour the cherished childhood memories of Lovisa. The late summer atmosphere in the picture he draws, lends the scene a touch of melancholy that reminds one of Turgenev, whom Sibelius enthusiastically read in his youth. His aunt's piano playing was for him inextricably linked with these early years and even the geraniums in the window fit into the picture in as much as eighty years later, memories of a visit to a haberdashery in Lovisa were strongly associated with the scent of geraniums.

1. On their first appearance place-names are given in Finnish first with the Swedish form bracketed. After this we have adopted the practice of leaving the name in whichever form seems most natural: thus, Lovisa, which is Swedish-speaking at this time, rather than Loviisa, the Finnish form of the name; Hämeenlinna, the Finnish form, rather than the Swedish, Tavestehus, following the same principle. In certain cases such as Turku (Finnish)—Åbo (Swedish) where the town was predominantly Swedish in the nineteenth century but is now primarily Finnish-speaking, we have chosen the form most likely to be encountered by modern readers, i.e. Turku. Tr

With some slight retouches here and there, this could well pass for a scene from his grandparents' daily life in their Lovisa home on a September afternoon in 1836, some three decades before his birth. Katarina Fredrika Sibelius, the composer's grandmother is sitting in the drawing-room talking to a guest. She is about thirty-five, rather frail in appearance and small of stature. The two daughters of Sibelius's diary entry do not however fit into context. There is only one girl, the four-year-old Evelina who barely comes up to the keyboard of the square piano. A boy of about sixteen, Pehr, is with his mother, and of his three brothers, the eldest has already been to sea as a shiphand, while Christian Gustaf is fourteen and away at school in the neighbouring town of Porvoo (Borgå). A visiting lieutenant bears a letter from Christian to his mother. The younger son, Edward, is in a sulky mood while the head of the house, Johan Sibelius is not in evidence. He is a merchant and a magistrate and rarely has time for social obligations.

Indeed, Johan Sibelius was the first urbanized member of the family which was of peasant origins and hailed from the country north of Lovisa. From the sixteenth century onwards his forefathers had farmed a plot of land at Artjävi (Artsjö) and his grandfather, Matts Mårtensson, the composer's great-great-grandfather, moved in the middle of the eighteenth century to the south, to a neighbouring parish at Lapinjärvi (Lappträsk). Matts' son married into the Sibbe family whose estate was only a couple of miles away and it was here at Sibbe that Johan Sibelius, the composer's grandfather was born. In 1801, when he was sixteen, he left home to become an assistant to a shopkeeper with the name of Unonious and it was perhaps with his new employer's example in mind that he also latinized his name from Sibbe to Sibelius. The change of name is symptomatic of a determination to make a break with the past and with his peasant origins and establish himself in Lovisa.

By 1808 he had been promoted and became the firm's book keeper: that same year in accordance with the provisions of the agreement at Tilsit, Russian troops marched into Finland and one of their first objectives was Lovisa which was only one day's march from their base. Presumably Johan watched as the Swedish–Finnish battalion to whom the defence of the town had been allotted withdrew through the west gates without offering any resistance while at the same moment the Russians marched in from the east. In the spring of the following year Tsar Alexander I and his retinue passed through the town on their way to Borgå where he was installed as Protector and Grand Duke of Finland, thus bringing to an end the six hundred years of union between Finland and Sweden. To all practical purposes the change of status that the Russian Protectorate involved, effected little change in Johan's daily life. He eventually married his employer's niece, Katarina Fredrika Åkerberg and in 1823 was elected an Alderman.

During the period around 1910 when the language dispute between the Finnish majority and the Swedish minority was at its height, the question of Sibelius's family origins was hotly discussed. Did he come from the coastal

Swedish-speaking Nyland or from the Finnish-speaking interior? As is often the case when complex matters of ethnic origin are involved, the problem is not easily resolved one way or the other. Like everyone else in Lovisa, the Sibelius family spoke Swedish and it is clear that both cultures and languages flourished side by side.

So far then, the family background is a typical one for the Swedish-speaking coastal regions. A little further back, however, Matts Mårtensson and his wife were both from a Finnish-speaking parish; Artjävi and names like Pekkala and Lassila, Finnish enough in all conscience, were common there. It is quite possible, though by no means certain, that they were Finnish speaking themselves. In general, the language border is not clearly defined in this part of the world and in his new home Matts was not included on a list of the Finnish-speaking villagers though like the majority of the inhabitants he may well, of course, have been bi-lingual. Moreover, the fact that he and his immediate ancestors were registered in the Swedish form of their names in church registers does not necessarily mean that they were *only* Swedish speaking: it was the custom for the priests to use the official language. Be this as it may, Johan Sibelius and his son, the composer's father, certainly did not know Finnish, and the latter at one time planned a visit to the interior in order to learn some.

Johan Sibelius reflects some of the dynamism and confidence of the period. Throughout the 1830s his home was a meeting-point for the leading families of the town with whom through his wife he had become so closely connected. He was particularly concerned to give his children the benefit of a good education, and in their library, Cicero, and textbooks on Logic and on Geography were to be found side by side. But still, Johan did not forget his peasant upbringing and at Christmas and other holidays he and his sons visited Sibbe to take part in wolf hunting. In some ways, however, his sympathies were with the older generation. His religious outlook, for instance, was sober and rational, unlike so much of the highly charged sentiment of the period. His robustness of spirit and firmness of purpose were inherited, not so much by his own children, but by his grandson, Jean, whose sensitiveness was matched by a strong, unbending will.

Katarina Fredrika brought into the sturdy Sibelius peasant stock a more subtle character for on her father's side the family was musical. Her father, Mathias Åkerberg, was a doctor of Swedish birth, who played both the violin and the cello, while further back in time it is thought that the family had even boasted a viola-da-gamba player. When he moved from Lovisa to Turku (Åbo) he was active in the Music Society but he ended his life miserably in debt. On her mother's side Katarina Fredrika also could claim some musical interest. The family had originally come from Sweden. In her grandfather's home in the last decade or so of the eighteenth century there was a fortepiano, which at this time must have been a rarity for a small Finnish town.

In September 1836, Christian Gustaf, the third of their four sons and the father to be of the composer, was just beginning his schooldays. He did well academically but appears to have had some difficulty in adjusting himself to the new environment away from home. He did not want to participate in the freshmen's party as he was told that new boys were forced to drink. He was bullied by his room-mate and wrestled with his fear of the dark. Tormented by homesickness, he wrote: 'Dear Mamma, write to me often and tell me how you are at home since I am so often thinking of you. There are still two-and-a-half weeks to the holidays which seems to me a very long time, but I will not be impatient but contain myself until Pappa sends word that I may come.' His schooldays, though, were not without some compensation: 'On Friday I saw my dear brother, Janne (the seaman, Johan) who on his way from Helsinki to Lovisa passed through Borgå. A Mlle. Kekoni who lives with Mme. Högvall has taught me a piece for the pianoforte but I would beg you to keep this secret.' Soon after this we learn that Mlle. Kekoni had taught him another piece and that his brother Janne, whose ship was anchored off Borgå, had promised to give him his guitar.

Christian's letters show perhaps a much greater propensity towards melancholia as well as a degree of sensibility than is usual for a fourteen-year-old boy.

From a musical point of view Finland was at a stage in her development where musical activity was predominantly amateur and stimulus was provided by foreign professionals. The leading musical figure in Helsinki was Fredrik Pacius, who came from Hamburg, and taught at the Imperial Alexander University. Shortly after his arrival in 1835 he mounted a performance of *The Last Judgment* of Spohr, whose pupil he had been, relying largely on amateur forces with a stiffening of professional and military-band musicians. But still there were no permanent musical institutions. Finland had never boasted a princely court or anything comparable around which musical activity on any scale could flourish, and there was no counterpart to the Stockholm Royal Academy of Music, although the Music Society was flourishing in Turku.

In Sweden the first manifestation of musical nationalism had appeared as early as 1786 in the opera, *Gustaf Wasa* by Naumann who hailed from Dresden, to a libretto by Gustav III's court poet, Kellgren. It was not until 1852 that Finland made a comparable gesture in the form of Pacius's opera, *King Karl's Hunt*, again the product of a collaboration between an émigré musician and a native poet, in this case Zachris Topelius.

One of the few Finnish-born musicians of the first half of the century with any claims to international attention was Bernhard Crusell, a virtuoso clarinetist and composer. But as a boy he moved to Stockholm and then studied in both Paris and Berlin before becoming an influential figure in Swedish musical life. Apart from Crusell, there were others whose talents never really came to fruition. The most remarkable of them was Erik Tulindberg, whose output included a violin concerto and six string quartets which are surprisingly fresh in invention and thorough in their craftsmanship. He moved in musical circles in Turku but after moving to the north of the country where he worked as an auditor, the creative fires petered out. Much the same happened with

Byström and Lithander, both of them officers. Byström[1] composed early romantic sonatas for violin and piano, and taught the piano in Stockholm while Lithander, a fortification expert, modelled his sonatas on Beethoven. From the sociological point of view they can be regarded as representatives of a dawning national musical interest who did not manage to arouse the right kind of response in their home country. Thus, they either gave up composing like Tulindberg, or went abroad. In the 1830s practically the only composer of native birth active in Finland was Fredrik August Ehrström, whose settings of Runeberg both for solo voice and chorus laid the foundations of the Finnish lyric repertoire.

If in Lovisa the Sibelius family were cut off from the musical life of the capital, they were better served musically than in many other towns of comparable size. The main route from Helsinki to Viipuri (Viborg) and St. Petersburg passed through Lovisa, and on occasion some artists broke their journey there to give concerts.

A quarter of a century later in the autumn of 1861, the shadows had deepened and the pale Biedermeier colourings of the Sibelius home had faded. Johan had died in 1844 and his widow lived alone in the Lovisa home save for the presence of her daughter Evelina who looked after her. Evelina was intelligent and idealistic in outlook; she was an enthusiastic rather than accomplished pianist and a ready duettist though she tended to confine herself to the simpler classical repertoire. Music was certainly a dominating passion in her life and we find her writing to her famous nephew many years later in 1889, 'I could live my life all over again for the sake of music, for although my powers are limited, it is at the piano that I have experienced the mystery of existence.' Outwardly Evelina Sibelius's lot was not much different from the rather shadowy existence of many daughter-companions of the nineteenth century but later she was to play an important role in her nephew's musical development. Very early on in his life Evelina grasped the exceptional nature of his musical talent, and watched its growth with sympathy and understanding.

To her other brother Pehr, the composer's uncle, Evelina wrote of her few concert experiences in Lovisa and asked him for news of musical life in Turku. Pehr Sibelius was a seed merchant there and a keen musical dilettante and amateur astronomer. During the day he saw to his business affairs and assessed the fertility of various kinds of seeds, but by night usually from about two o'clock in the morning until dawn he scoured the heavens with a telescope that he had erected in the garden or played his violin. All on his own he went through the various quartets one part at a time! He also collected instruments and numbered among them three violins, a cello, two horns and two square pianos. As far as music was concerned, Pehr was self-taught but scarcely had

1. Not Oskar Byström, also an officer and composer, but his father, Thomas (1772–1839). *Tr*

he learned his rudiments than he tried his hand at composing. He set a poem, *The Morning*, in the form of a duet and attempted adding a bass part. Another foray into composition was for flute and string quartet. Here a folk-like melody is given to one instrument at a time, the others remaining silent the while. Obviously, the work was intended for the exclusive use of the composer! Pehr Sibelius's work hardly even justifies the epithet amateurish: the remarkable thing is not so much what he wrote but that he wrote at all.

The youngest brother, Edvard was already a victim of tuberculosis while the eldest, Janne, had by now become the captain of a barque called *Ukko*,[1] of which he was part-owner; he sailed to Cadiz and on one occasion heard the music of the Turkish janizaries from the fortresses at the entrance to the Dardanelles. He died the year before the composer was born, either in Havana or on board ship in the Caribbean, as a result of yellow fever. Among his belongings was a packet of visiting cards with the Gallicized form of his name, Jean Sibelius. Both the cards and the name were in due course to be put to good use.

The most talented and at the same time the most disorderly of the family, was Christian Gustaf. As early as the 1840s when he was reading medicine at Helsinki his letters home to his brothers concentrate on two things: hunting and money. He was chronically short of money and was even reduced to borrowing for the fees for his graduation ceremony. He seems to have given up playing the piano though he did continue with the guitar and joined the Academic Choir. His sister served as his intermediary in his numerous and complicated love affairs. During the Crimean War he served as a naval doctor to a Finnish flotilla which protected the Finnish coasts against the Tsar's enemies. His loyalty towards the Tsarist authorities was deeply-felt. In 1855 Christian completed his research thesis in gynaecology and his findings were even drawn on in later gynaecological operations. But he was not able to pursue his scientific researches and ambitions and became a military doctor in the provinces.

At the beginning of the 1860s we find Christian in charge of a crack battalion stationed at Hämeenlinna as well as being the town doctor. He was now in his forties, unmarried and good company; he was in demand at parties in the town and had gracious manners, a pleasant singing voice and accompanied himself on the guitar in the songs of Bellman and Wennerberg. But his colourful way of life absorbed more money than he earned. In spite of the fact that his private practice in the town was growing he did not succeed in making ends meet. He ordered cigars, hunting equipment, cognac, arrack and sherry, mostly on credit, and his debts multiplied. Besides this he was generous to the point of irresponsibility in underwriting loans that he could ill afford.

Even earlier, in Turku, Christian had taken to heavy drinking and in later years bemoaned the fact. He felt that his excessive indulgence had deprived him of some of his capacity for work. 'My father', wrote Sibelius, 'loved his pleasures too much and played cards and so on; we Sibeliuses, once rich are now poor.' Even if this overstates the case a little, for the family was never

1. The name given by the translator of this volume to his cat.

rich, it is still basically true. For all his skill and competence Christian was more strongly at the mercy of self-destructive forces than others in his immediate circle. Admittedly he was pulled in the other direction too: 'It's necessary to do one's duty if you are not to go under', were his words to his sister shortly before his marriage. He did his duty not so much to further his career but rather to prevent any further descent down the slippery slope.

But Christian was by no means an ordinary person. Even if his sister Evelina exaggerated the extent of his musical gifts in a letter to her nephew in 1889, he was undoubtedly musical. His personality, too, had a genuine warmth and impulsiveness that his famous son inherited.

Evelina and her brothers formed a highly individual and widely gifted family; at least four of them showed some kind of creative talent. In Christian's case his scientific gifts were combined with a genuine if limited musical talent; in Pehr's there was a stubborn desire to compose combined with a lively astronomical interest; Evelina's love of music surpassed that of the normal amateur; while even Janne, the sea captain, reveals in his letters a feeling for words that betokens a genuine expressive drive. Among all the brothers there were common traits of melancholia as well as a distinct taste for the unusual. The drive for social status and acceptance that distinguished the father was a good deal weaker in the children. By 1861 seventy-five years had elapsed since Johan Sibelius, the second of ten children, had left farming; and now his five children had all reached maturity but without having families of their own. A few more years and both Edvard and Janne had died; Evelina sat at home with her mother in Lovisa while Pehr spent the years in Turku going grey in expectation of a comet that never came. The Sibelius family was in danger of dying out and a vacuum was created into which the composer was soon to step.

In 1858 we learn that Pehr Sibelius had attended a concert in Turku that had been conducted by the Finnish composer Ingelius. This serves as a reminder of the stride forward that Finnish music had taken over the intervening decades. It was Ingelius who had in 1847 predicted a great future for Finnish music on account of the quality of its folk art. Ingelius's own symphony, the first known example by a native Finn, is for all its dilettantism and lack of polish, a first step towards the foundation of a national art. In it there is a 'scherzo finnico' in a $\frac{5}{4}$ rhythm that suggests runic melodies. The work was not sufficiently accomplished from a technical point of view to cut much ice with as professional a composer as Pacius. Ingelius became something of a tragic Hoffmann-like figure and his miserable end—he was frozen to death in a snowdrift—serves to underline the inhospitable conditions with which Finnish music had to contend.

The 1860s saw a further step forward away from amateurish standards when at the opening of a new Helsinki theatre, the central core of the orchestra comprised Leipzig-trained musicians of quality. J. F. von Schantz conducted his *Kullervo* Overture, the first orchestral piece to be inspired by the *Kalevala*,

7

while Pacius's music to Topelius's *The Princess of Cyprus*, which moves the action of Lemminkäinen's erotic exploits to the island of Cyprus in the days of classical antiquity, made some gesture, albeit feeble, in the direction of Finnish nationalism. But the folk-like elements fit more or less loosely in an imported central European idiom. Several decades earlier Glinka had created a genuinely national opera in Russia with *Ivan Susanin* and *Ruslan and Ludmilla*; Hungary had a national opera in Erkel's *Hunyady Laszlo* while Poland had hers in Moniuszko's *Halka*. But Finland had hardly arrived at the stage where one could speak of folk elements being absorbed into an operatic art, for the Finnish element in Pacius's operas is of little or no significance.

With the erosion of Nicholas I's conservatism by the liberal winds of Alexander II's reforming spirit, a more hopeful atmosphere was reflected in the arts which underwent a thaw. The period of the idyll was over and in the wake of Hegelian ideas of nationality, an intense language conflict began between the advocates of Finnish and Swedish. Since the days of the union of Sweden and Finland, Swedish had served as the official language of the country and was the language of the educated classes. In J. V. Snellman, the philosopher and statesman, the advocates of Finnish as the first language of the country, found a powerful spokesman: although his appeals met some response they also aroused considerable hostility among the educated Swedish-speaking minority. Sibelius's future father-in-law, General Alexander Järnefelt insisted on speaking Finnish in the home but the composer's teacher, Martin Wegelius, was a firm defender of Swedish, having no intention as he put it, either of giving up his native tongue or of emigrating. For the greater part of Sibelius's life right up until the 1940s, the language conflict was a serious divisive force in Finnish life.

However, neither the growth of liberalism nor the language question is touched upon in Christian Gustaf's correspondence with his brothers and sister. So far the Sibeliuses had not emerged from the isolation imposed by the small community in which they lived and thrown themselves into the vital national issues.

Christian Sibelius had talked about women to his Latin master at Borgå, none other than the poet Runeberg. Christian had maintained his ideal woman as simple in her tastes, unaffected and childlike. Perhaps he found these qualities enshrined in the person of Maria Charlotta Borg, a priest's daughter some twenty-two years of age who was the toast of all the students of Hämeenlinna and constantly serenaded by them. In any event they became engaged in the autumn of 1861. According to the local gossip current at the time he seems to have arrived at his choice after an evening of drink spent in the company of the headmaster but even allowing for the fact that he may have noticed the girl earlier, his suit does bear the signs of improvization.

Christian described his fiancée in a letter to his sister Evelina of 5 January 1861, in these terms: 'She is sweet and at times really rather beautiful. She is as tall as I am, but this is not unbecoming in her; on the contrary she looks quite magnificent. It will be strange to see her alongside our aged mother who is so short and thin.' But in general his letters at the time of his engagement do not reflect much enthusiasm at the prospect of marriage. He wrote to his mother earlier in the previous autumn, 'I suppose that at some time or other even I will have to settle down with a companion, for up to now life has brought little happiness with it but rather a sense of emptiness.'

'A child of nature', was how Christian described his fiancée and to a forty-year-old doctor perhaps she did seem unaffected and childlike. Whether she matched his ideals of simplicity, however, is another matter. Certain evidence suggests that Maria Borg was a by no means uncomplicated person. Her son Jean, who was known as Janne at home, was later to testify to her naturalness, gentleness and piety but also her very considerable reserve. At certain times this reserve tended to assume the character of withdrawal into herself and a reluctance to involve herself at all with other people. Needless to say it is difficult to say whether this was an innate or acquired character trait since she was widowed so early in life and thrown back on the resources of her relatives. It is puzzling, for example, to see that she does not sign her letters to her son Janne, 'mother' or 'mamma' but rather 'Maria'; only once shortly before her death did she sign herself 'your mother Maria'. Rather than placing herself on an equal footing of friendship, this practice suggests an unconscious attempt to keep some distance between herself and her nearest and dearest. In one of her letters to her son she asks him to write and tell her all that he was doing, save for the part of one's life that one discloses to no man: 'No, only to God should we and can we speak of all our thoughts!' She was also prey to nervous and oversensitive impulses: once, before Janne's violin developed a fissure, she had a dream that she interpreted as a premonition. Subsequently the dream recurred and prompted her to question him anxiously as to whether he had not had an accident recently. Evelina Sibelius would scarcely have agreed with Jean's view of his mother as predominantly harmonious. On the contrary she saw in her sister-in-law a predisposition to view many things in life, such as her brother's nervousness, with greater pessimism than other members of the family. Maria's religious feeling sometimes assumed a gushing, sentimental character that recalled the evangelism of her cousin, F. G. Hedberg, whose movement was founded to counterbalance the strict pietism of the day.

On her father's side Maria Borg was descended from priests and teachers. Her father had been headmaster at the school in Hämeenlinna and held a similar post in Turku before becoming, like his father before him, a priest. The mother's family, Haartman boasted many well-known academics and government officials including Lars Gabriel von Haartman, a leading political figure of the middle of the nineteenth century. Some of his despotism seems to have characterized Maria's mother, a priest's widow, with a will of iron and a somewhat coarse sense of humour. Sibelius was later to characterize the Haartman family as marked by 'a sense of the realities unencumbered by imagination or grace'.

Maria Borg had some musical ancestors; her father and grandfather were both keen amateur violinists. Maria herself played the piano but does not appear to have kept it up in later years.

Christian Sibelius and Maria Borg were married on 7 March 1862. The bride's earlier suitors foregathered on the steps of the house to sing their last serenade in her honour. One of those present has described the somewhat melancholy moment when the bride, radiant in her youth and bearing, came out to give them her thanks with the rather shorter, corpulent bridegroom twice her age. A year after their marriage Maria bore a daughter who was christened Linda Maria, and on 8 December 1865 they had a son. The father immediately gave his brother Pehr the good news: 'I hasten to inform you that my Maria gave birth at half-past twelve to a healthy boy and that she is in the best of health herself. . . . Dear brother, the Lord has blessed me more than I have deserved.' The child was christened Johan Julius Christian.

From whom did Christian and Maria's newborn son really inherit his musical gifts? His basic musical talent, the sense of rhythm and melody comes out most strongly on the father's side, or so argues Otto Andersson, while feeling and imagination seems to have been dominant on the mother's side. This view however has been challenged by Einari Marvia who has made a comprehensive study of the musical gifts with which the two sides of the family were endowed. In the light of his researches Marvia concludes that the greater part of his musical inheritance came from the mother's side and their related families. But neither Andersson nor Marvia had access to the collection of Pehr Sibelius's 'works' which came to light only after Sibelius's death in 1957. Sibelius preserved these all his life although few of his own manuscripts from the time of his youthful *Water-drops* down to what he wrote of the Eighth Symphony survived the bonfires which warmed his old age. But his uncle's faltering attempts at composition escaped the *auto-da-fé*. In sparing them he made what might to some extent be interpreted as a gesture of pride and solidarity, a hint of the 'we Sibeliuses' mentality which one senses lies behind his assertion of the family's early wealth and subsequent poverty. It is as if he wanted to leave behind him some indication of the Sibeliuses' creativity.

Without doubt the father's family showed genuine creative impulse. The musicality of the mother's family found expression mostly in executive ability and a broad musical culture rather than any creative activity. Admittedly one of the family, H. F. Borg, composed in his spare time and actually published a lullaby while one of the present-day descendants is the singer, Kim Borg who has also composed songs and arranged folk-tunes. But the sensitive, nervous intensity that marked Jean Sibelius undoubtedly came from the Borg family. In his mother it took the form of a capacity for total identification with whatever she did and a keen religious sense; with her sister Julia the nervous intensity and religious fanaticism finally gave way to mental illness. Her brother, Otto Borg, also had to contend with nervous troubles. The pathological elements which are often related to genius are thus present in the immediate family. Later on it emerged nearer to hand in the immediate family circle. Sibelius's elder sister, Linda, developed manic-depressive symptoms when she was forty and never fully recovered but spent the rest of her life in various institutions. After having seen her on one occasion Sibelius wrote in his diary with a characteristic touch of exaggeration, 'I see in her fate my own.' He was conscious of his own depressive tendencies and was horrified whenever he encountered them in a more acute form in his sister. In his own make-up the various conflicting forces resulted in a soundly balanced outlook. The brooding introspection that he inherited from his mother was offset by his father's *laisser-aller* outlook and a disposition that varied from exhilaration to melancholy.

Thus Sibelius's musical genius emerged not so much as a sudden fulfilment of a pronounced musical tradition in his family but rather through a happy combination of musical and other contributory factors. As we have seen, he inherited musicality from both sides of the family but they were gifts of different kinds; from the Sibeliuses, they were primarily creative and from the Borgs largely executive. Sensibility and a capacity for inspiration, in other words the artistic disposition, he derived from his mother. But this in itself is not enough: it was activated by the Sibeliuses' creative drive, intellectual capacity and imagination. Sibelius's musical gift is not a phenomenon that can wholly be explained in terms of heredity. He even seems to have sensed this himself. When in September 1910 he was girding his loins for the last phase of his work on the Fourth Symphony he confided to his diary, perhaps to pluck up his own courage: 'You know your belated artistry, your blood in which widely divergent strains flow—but, none the less, a genius is what you are.'

CHAPTER TWO

Hämeenlinna and the childhood years

WHEN as a young man of twenty-five, he was studying in Vienna, Sibelius wrote to his fiancée, Aino Järnefelt: 'Few can have had so sad a childhood as I have and yet it could have been so happy. I have played with fire and have exulted in its flames; I have never thought of the consequences but have only lived for the moment. One day I will show you a picture of myself as a ten-year-old and then you will see how much I have changed.'

The fire, hardly an original figure of speech to which Sibelius had recourse, could possibly have been inspired by Karl August Tavaststjerna's poem *Liberty* which Sibelius had tried to set some months earlier.

> Burn thyself as I have burned!
> Know thyself as I have learned self-knowledge
> Without a goal in life!

Without actually knowing it, Sibelius reveals a typical attitude current in artistic circles at the time. Like a dreamer he looks into his soul whose dark recesses are lit by Nietzschean fires. His words about his childhood sorrows reflect a common late-romantic preoccupation. Music's greatest depths, as Bruno Walter once said, are not fathomed by those who lead untroubled lives. Without doubt Sibelius did not belong to the species of men into whose innermost recesses of mind one could penetrate. When he calls his brother Christian 'a radiant figure' he hints at the darker recesses of his own make-up. Characteristically, Christian remembered his own childhood and that of his brother as predominantly sunny: 'Think of our childhood so rich in memories' he once wrote when, in the autumn of 1889, Jean was lying ill in Berlin, and he returned to this consoling theme some fourteen years later reminding his brother of their wonderfully happy childhood games! The picture of the ten-year-old Sibelius shows a boy who was just leaving childhood games behind him, indeed when the picture was taken, he had just composed a little piece called *Water-drops* for violin and cello, pizzicato.

Jean, or Janne as he was called by his family, grew up in a fatherless home. As an adult Sibelius had no distinct memory of his father, only the vaguest recollection of his physical presence: he was sitting on his father's lap and looking through a book which had animal pictures in it. Another powerful recollection was of the smell of cigar smoke which adhered to his father's coat as it did to practically everything in the home. Naturally, as a child Janne remembered his father far better than he was to do in later life. Shortly after his father's death Evelina Sibelius wrote to her brother Pehr in Turku: 'Little Janne I hear has said to his mother, "Won't pappa ever come again however many times I call him?" '

The composer's childhood home at Residensgatan in Hämeenlinna was marked by a bohemian atmosphere rather than solid middle-class values. His father had bought books and music instead of bothering about the home; he had hired a fortepiano since he couldn't afford to buy one of his own. A nickel-plated set of drinking vessels and a decanter were among their few luxuries. His death was the indirect outcome of the severe famines that marked the 1860s. During the hungry winter of 1867–8 when epidemics raged all over the country he was in charge of the isolation hospital in Hämeenlinna and the following summer he contracted typhus himself and rapidly succumbed to it. The two-year-old Janne was playing with a hunting horn while his father lay in his coffin in the drawing-room. When the coffin was carried out, the boy apparently started up the children's song 'Run away good reindeer!'

Maria Sibelius became a widow at twenty-seven. She had two children and was expecting a third. With a balance of 12 marks it was she who was left to bear the consequences of her husband's extravagance. During the last six months of his life the doctor had mismanaged his affairs and all his bills were left unsettled. The rent, medicines, the salaries of their servants, the rent for the fortepiano, the provisions and groceries, largely made up of generous quantities of arrack and cognac, were all unpaid. The debts amounted to some 4,500 marks which were partly incurred by sums that the doctor had lost in helping insolvent friends. The estate was declared bankrupt and Maria Sibelius meekly begged to be allowed to keep 'necessary clothes and linen together with two white quilts.' The only steady income on which she could now count, was a widow's pension of scarcely 1,200 marks. As long as the Sibelius family remained part-owners of the barque, *Ukko*, she was entitled to a small part of its profits. But her means did not enable her to maintain a house of her own and she was compelled to move back home to her mother, herself a widow. It is said that after the bankruptcy was declared, she kept her head firmly bowed in her mother's home. In March 1869 the third child was born, the youngest son, Christian.

During Sibelius's early childhood, the bankruptcy was never discussed in the home although it cast an unspoken shadow over the household. With his father's death one of the links which bound Janne to his middle-class origins and way of life was abruptly severed. One would have expected him to develop strong ties to his mother but curiously enough, this did not happen; indeed as an adult he reproached himself on this count. Although he loved her, he was at the same time aware of the absence of a really intimate bond between them. She maintained a kind of telepathic contact with her son and worried about his health and welfare, but at the same time was careful to keep a certain distance between them. Janne was in fact far closer during these years to his aunt Evelina. There was even a certain physical likeness between them and certainly in his aunt he felt a response to music and the things of the imagination that was similar to his own. In his heart she occupied as prominent a place as that of his mother.

The head of the household was Janne's grandmother, whose forbidding glance was tempered by a robust sense of humour. None the less she always felt that she had never really been as strict with the children as she ought to have been. In addition there were two other members of the household, Janne's unmarried aunts. The elder, Tekla, was a hypochondriac and spent a lot of her time in bed; the younger, Julia, was, in Sibelius's words, 'quite nice but a dreadful ninny', a sentiment no doubt inspired by her excessive nervousness and bigotry.

The Borg family, it is said, regarded Maria as having so lively an imagination that her grasp on reality was at times tenuous. Sibelius himself as a child is said to have had difficulty in distinguishing between reality and the private world of his own imagination.

When the summer came, Janne and his brother and sister went to stay with their paternal grandmother and Aunt Evelina. These visits to the Sibelius's old house in Lovisa or their cottage in the archipelago were the high point of their year. The atmosphere in their grandmother's home was harmonious; there were handwoven rugs on the floor; their way of life was a little more gracious than at Hämeenlinna; Janne would kiss his grandmother's hand. His aunt Evelina adored and spoilt him. They rowed together along the shore to a relative who lived near the shipyards where Aunt Evelina went in search of rare French stones down by the wharf, while her nephew launched wooden boats that he had made, watching them sail out of sight. He learned the names of all the sailing ships that anchored out in the harbour while Aunt Evelina told him the story of the hundred-year-old vessel that plied between Finland and Spain, and that was named after her great-grandmother Kristina Juliana. When their boat, *Ukko*, was sighted all the Sibelius family would go down to the harbour to meet it; Janne was first on board and would climb down to the hold where the scent of various spices was powerful and consignments of oranges glistened in their huge nets. Under the trees in their garden Janne played with his friends, the Suckdorffs, the Gyllings and children from other Lovisa families. Aunt Evelina would sometimes take part in their games and even organize puppet shows while the boys would also play along the walls of the old fort nearby where an ancient cannon from the times of the union with Sweden was slowly rusting away. All through the winter Janne longed for the summer to come so that he could escape from Hämeenlinna to Lovisa.

or him the little coastal town was a haven, a symbol of freedom and
appiness.

As a small child Janne used to creep under the square piano when someone
played. He let the music flow over him and related certain keys to colours
that were to be found in the handwoven rugs of their drawing-room. As an
adult he described the way in which he connected colour and key on more than
one occasion. The critic, Karl Flodin, in his memoirs recounts his first meeting
with Sibelius when the latter was a student in the 1880s: 'Before we knew where
we were, Sibelius was juggling with colours and keys as if they were glittering
glass balls, colours were set resounding and keys glowed with light; A major
became blue, C major red, F major green and D major yellow, and so on
like that.'

When he was five, Janne sat at the keyboard and began trying to coax simple
tunes and chords from the instrument. After a couple of years his Aunt Julia
began to teach him the piano but Janne made scant progress. He had much
greater inclination to improvise and go his own way than to learn systematically.
Moreover, Aunt Julia showed precious little understanding of his particular
talents and for every finger slip she rapped his knuckles with her knitting-
needle. Her piano teaching left a lot to be desired and the lessons soon came
to an end. Even later in life Sibelius never developed a really first-class keyboard
technique; 'the piano cannot sing', he told his pupil Bengt de Törne and it is
true to say that he never penetrated its genius. None the less he spent a good
deal of time improvising at the keyboard which became for him a useful
working instrument.

In old age Sibelius advanced another reason that might explain his distaste
for the piano: 'When I was a child we had a square piano at home which was
about three-quarters of a tone flat. This instrument comprised my whole
musical word at the time and when we finally acquired a new one, properly
tuned, I found the change deeply disturbing and transferred my attentions to
the violin.' It is clear from this that even early in childhood Sibelius was
endowed with absolute pitch and that having built up a tonal world based on
an out-of-tune instrument, he found the encounter with the correctly tuned
instrument far more worrying than would a normal child. This does not tell
us what kind of absolute pitch he had at this time: whether at this stage he was
more disturbed by the pitch of individual notes being incorrect or whether it
was the out-of-tune chords that worried him more. Certainly in later years
there is no doubt that he possessed a highly refined ability to note-name and
could even ascribe pitch to birdsong and other natural sounds. Similarly his
violin playing was distinguished by the purest intonation and he was able to
detect the most refined pitch differences.

By the time he was ten he was displaying other evidence of his musicality.
In October 1875 the Swedish harp virtuoso, Adolf Sjödén gave a concert in

Hämeenlinna to which Janne was taken. Sjödén included in his programme the Handel Harp Concerto, as well as his own arrangements of a number of Finnish folk songs. After the concert the boy played quite a number of fragments from Sjödén's programme on the piano at home; some time later he greeted his aunt with a piano improvisation called 'Aunt Evelina's Life in Music', which portrayed incidents from her life. Unfortunately he never committed this embryonic *Sinfonia domestica* to paper. But apart from these feats of memorization and improvisation, he was beginning to feel the need to work over his ideas and put them on to paper. It is presumably from this year, 1875, that his first composition, *Water-drops*, comes:

Ex. 1

In spite of the realistic pizzicato, the piece does not really give the impression of being descriptive. Unlike his exact contemporary, Richard Strauss whose first attempts, the *Schneiderpolka* and *Festmarsch* reflect life in the affable Bavarian capital, Sibelius composed neither marches nor polkas; and even if he, like Mahler and Nielsen, spent his formative years in garrison towns there is no evidence of trumpet reveilles or other martial elements in his music. He lived in an isolated world which forced him in on himself.

It was probably in the autumn of 1872 that Janne was enrolled in Mlle. Eva Savonius's Swedish-language preparatory school. But very soon his musical instincts came into conflict with his schoolwork. His teacher testified to his highly developed imaginative life but found that his thoughts wandered far away from his lessons. He seemed to be listening to some inner music and scribbled the odd musical phrase in the margins of his school books. By way of punishment he was made to 'stand in the corner'; this consisted of sitting under the teacher's desk where he remembered having to gaze at the unappetizing sight of her felt boots.

At the age of eight, he was moved from this school and started afresh in a newly founded Finnish-speaking preparatory school. This change was a response to the transformation that Finnish education was undergoing during the 1870s. In 1873 the first grammar school ever to use the Finnish language as the medium of teaching was founded in Hämeenlinna and at the same time the Swedish-language grammar school was closed. For Janne, as well as the other children of 'the gentry', this meant learning Finnish. The situation wasn't entirely easy for him; even if he lived in a predominantly Finnish-speaking town in a completely Finnish-speaking part of the country, he spoke Swedish at home and with his friends. He spent the summers in a Swedish-speaking area, Lovisa, and thus some measure of preparation in a new school was essential if he was to gain a reasonable command of Finnish. In 1876, then, Janne was enrolled in the first form in the Hämeenlinna Normaalilyseo. The school was the showpiece of the 'Fennomans', the powerful group committed to the dissemination of the Finnish language and culture, and its staff included many well-known figures. It attracted pupils from the length and breadth of the country and the atmosphere was lively, keen, perhaps a bit hearty.

It goes without saying that in a school where musical talent counted for nothing Sibelius was hardly a model pupil. During lessons his attention wandered to the window or withdrew into inner musical reveries that drew the predictable rebukes from authority. Janne was so thoroughly steeped in the cultural traditions of the Swedish-speaking community that his schooling was to be of particular value in opening his mind to the language and cultural traditions of Finnish itself. In the senior part of the school the *Kalevala* was closely studied; Janne had known it only through Collan's Swedish translation. As is so often the case when a poem is analysed to pieces in the schoolroom, the *Kalevala* made little or no impression on him at this stage in his life but he did come to understand the archaic, often subtle language of the Finnish runes and was perhaps subconsciously at least responsive to their magic. It was not until his year in Vienna from 1890 to 1891, that the full realization of the *Kalevala*'s power struck him.

The language barrier presented no problems for Janne and his school-friends. One third of them were from Swedish-speaking homes anyway, and his best friend, Walter von Konow, whose father was a colonel, had been his companion at the preparatory school. Walter was a sensitive and imaginative boy who felt himself misunderstood throughout his life. In spite of his good looks, he made little impression on the girls, which did not surprise Janne who once called him 'a proper old woman'. Walter liked to dance and entertained his friends by adopting various ballet poses. 'You could have danced all these Pavlovas and Lifars off the stage given the chance!', Sibelius told him in his old age.

Janne, Walter von Konow and one or two other chosen companions used to meet on Saturday evenings for amateur dramatics. Janne put together plays from themes taken from Topelius and Hans Andersen and sometimes themes out of his own head. The refinements of the plot were left to be improvised on the spur of the moment and those taking part usually had no idea of how things worked out in the end. As director, author and leading actor, Janne had an excellent opportunity of asserting himself and consoling himself for reverses in school. And when the friends formed their own orchestra consisting of a triangle, mouth-organ, a toy ocarina and a set of chimes, Janne was again the self-appointed leader who conducted from the piano with great abandon and enthusiasm.

Janne was a frequent visitor to the Konow family estate, Lahis in Sääksmäki not far from Hämeenlinna. It was very different from his own home; Evelina called it 'musty', but it would be truer to say that it was stamped with an air of indolence. Inside the house was warm and cosy, the floors were covered with oriental carpets that the colonel had collected while he was stationed in Russia, and in one of the rooms there was a vast wrought-iron spider's web hanging from the ceiling. Walter would tell Janne stories and it was this imaginative side of him that in all probability laid the foundations for their lifelong friendship.

Walter von Konow has described how on their country strolls together Sibelius would people the forests with all manner of imaginary creatures: 'In the dusk Janne would amuse himself by spying all sorts of extraordinary beings in the gloomy forest depths and if the mood took him to be macabre it could be rather eerie to wander through the dark forests by his side peopled by trolls, witches, goblins and the like. At times our imaginations became so fired that when the night closed in all sorts of terrifying shapes loomed out of their dark hiding-places.'

Colonel von Konow had little feeling for music, which he regarded as a suitable occupation for the womenfolk. Nevertheless he appears to have liked Janne and taken him with him on his hunting trips. 'I have been hunting often in Sääksmäki,' Sibelius wrote in a letter of 1891, 'and so I know the forests and countryside well.' He described something of the atmosphere at dawn when on one of these trips: 'The fields, meadows and forests are shrouded in a gentle white mist which covers the whole countryside like a mantle of gossamer. Suddenly a woodcock emerges from the mists. It rises straight up and stays quite still for a moment before going its way. With its flapping wings and long beak it looks bizarre against the white haze of the morning mist. The art is to shoot just at the moment when it pauses in its flight.'

Apart from going to Lovisa during the school holidays, Janne spent some time with other relatives nearer Hämeenlinna. He stayed at Annila which his great aunts owned, as well as at Kalalahti and Kantala. The inland lakes in the province of Häme (Tavastland) where bays, inlets, straits and islands all interlock in an unending complex as far as the eye can see, are among the loveliest in Finland. It was through these waters that Sibelius rowed with his friends all the way from Hämeenlinna to Tampere (Tammerfors). Yet even so he longed to be back in the Lovisa archipelago: 'When the wind comes from the south I can immediately feel the sea; the water has an enormous hold over me.'

After he began playing the violin Janne used to take his instrument with him on his walks in the countryside and improvised out in the open. When in Sääksmäki, he would climb up on a stone by the shores of Lake Vanajavesi and play 'meandering concertos to the birds', while on his sailing trips in the archipelago he stood in the prow and 'improvised to the waves'. He surrendered totally to the fascination of the sea, and sirens and mermaids who lured people to the depths were more to him than just a mere mythological concept.

The most stimulating of his childhood haunts was perhaps his uncle Pehr's home in Turku. His uncle with his pipe and his long beard would tell him about Wilhelm Ernst and all the other great violinists that he had heard in Stockholm and St. Petersburg, and took him to concerts in the town. Janne loved being with him and regarded his nocturnal violin practice and speculations about astronomy as altogether normal. Nor was he worried by Pehr's eccentricity which grew apace with the years. His parsimony went to considerable lengths; in his annual tax return, he even went so far as to estimate the value of depreciation of his old fur hat since he had worked out that he would gain a few pence in so doing. Towards his nephew, however, he was generous: Janne's Steiner violin came from his uncle's collection.

When he was thirteen, Janne's paternal grandmother died and among the Christmas gifts for which he thanked his uncle and aunt in 1879 he mentioned a pillow 'which brings back precious memories of grandmother and which, for this very reason, is the most welcome gift'. In other respects his letter reflects something of the orphan: 'Thank you for your excellent gift of a penknife, gum and lead pencils, dear uncle and aunt; they are all in frequent use. . . . The gloves which you sent were too small. Of my other Christmas presents, Uncle Otto gave me a book called *The Pilot* and Aunt Julia gave me a box of paints; these I think are my best presents. Uncle Axel gave me 5 marks to buy a cap with and among other things I also got two drawing blocks and a bottle of *eau de cologne*.' In other words when relatives gave Janne Christmas presents they concentrated on useful things which other children would have received from their parents during the term in the normal course of events. The Sibeliuses lived in modest circumstances and when their uncles came to visit them, Janne and Christian could not help themselves from admiring their 'princely' possessions.

One of Sibelius's first books was Topelius's anthology of poems and stories for children, on which he drew incidentally for his amateur theatricals. A little later he was to develop an interest in the history of Finland and Sweden in particular in the late eighteenth century with its theatre, literature and Swedenborg. In the first decade of the present century he set the poem, 'Lasse liten' ('Little Lasse') as a tribute to Old Top, as he used to call Topelius, in which the childhood idyll is contrasted with the reality of the world at large. He also avidly read Hans Christian Andersen, one of whose stories inspired a work for chamber ensemble.

The fact that Janne's father knew Runeberg certainly contributed to the cult of the great poet in the Sibelius household. When he was six or seven his mother took him to see the poet at his home in Borgå but he apparently did not remember much of the visit afterwards, apart from the bird-table that stood outside the window! But later on, shortly after Runeberg died in the summer of 1877, Janne went all the way from Lovisa to Borgå for the express purpose of paying homage to the poet, and placing flowers on his grave. For there is no doubt that Runeberg was his favourite poet; his pantheistic outlook harmonized with Sibelius's own, and in later life Sibelius admired the poet's classical restraint, sense of proportion and concentration. But his worship of Runeberg did not stand in the way of his appreciation of other poets such as Stagnelius. In fact during his youth Janne steeped himself in the work of the Swedish-speaking lyrical poets and their influence was a dominating one. He also admired many of the great Swedish poets of the period like Rydberg, and later Josephson and Fröding, but apart from them and his own countrymen, Karl August Tavaststjerna and later Gripenberg, he real relatively little poetry. As far as mythology is concerned, his two main sources of inspiration were Homer and, of course, the *Kalevala*. But if his taste in poetry was confined to the great Swedish lyric poets of the day, his interest both in the theatre and in the novel were perhaps more wide-ranging.

He read Björnstjerne Björnson's short stories and Strindberg's *Red Room* in his last years at school. 'Strindberg tore everything to shreds and I adored this.' He became difficult and a little rebellious; he succeeded in annoying his aunt Julia at the dinner-table with his heretical views. He himself does not appear to have ever undergone any religious crisis. He made the annual trip to church at Christmas with the rest of the family and retained affectionate memories of these occasions later in life. However, when one reads his recollections of his mother and Aunt Evelina, one is left in no doubt that he did not share their views. The nearest thing to religious feeling that he experienced was his awe of Nature. His concept of God was pantheistic, closely related in feeling with Rydberg in his poem 'På verandan vid havet' ('On the balcony by the sea'): 'On shores, and heaven and sea, through all we divine a God.' Nor does he appear to have had much interest in philosophy. Conceptual thinking did not come easily to him; he lived intuitively and thought in concrete terms rather than abstractions. His feeling for nature found expression in one practical form; his collection of wild flowers and fauna was the finest in the class, and during the summers he assiduously gathered all kinds of plants and butterflies. Janne's moods oscillated between the gayest high spirits and the most intense melancholy. He had a lively sense of humour and an infectious laugh. He never behaved shabbily towards his friends although he was something of a tease, and at times was not above making fun of others' weaknesses. During his botany and zoology classes he came into his own; he felt himself on more certain ground and made fun of the somewhat eccentric teacher whose favourite he was. But the most essential characteristic was none the less his 'vein of melancholy, the intense sense of longing and a rare sense of rapture'.

In the autumn of 1880 when he was fourteen, Janne began violin lessons with Gustaf Levander, the military bandmaster at Hämeenlinna, and a new phase in his musical development opened. 'The violin took me by storm and for the next ten years it was my dearest wish, my greatest ambition to become a great virtuoso.' But neither Janne nor those around him quite grasped the extent of the demands made on a violinist of the first order. His virtuoso contemporaries were on their way to stardom. Willy Burmester, to whom he was to offer the première of the Violin Concerto, had already given the Mendelssohn and Bériot concertos in Hamburg, while Busoni, who was a few months younger than Sibelius, had already made several concert tours, had played to Anton Rubinstein and even aroused favourable comment from no less a critic than Hanslick. Janne embarked on his studies at too late a stage. His teacher, Levander, was hardly another Joachim or Auer although he managed to lay the foundations of technique acceptable enough to enable Sibelius to proceed to more advanced studies in Helsinki. But apart from the question of technique, he was not temperamentally equipped for a soloist's career. He suffered from stage fright to such an extent that whenever he was about to play he felt a metallic taste in his mouth, and such was his nervousness that on school speech days it was almost necessary to use force to get him on to the stage at all. On one occasion when he was playing for a small gathering at Sääksmäki he was so overcome by nervous shyness that he played with his back to the public. The after-effects of an accident may also have contributed to his change of plans. When he was thirteen he broke his right arm at the shoulder, and coming as this did in his bowing arm, it proved an inhibiting factor, as he testified in 1914 at a rehearsal in New York.

Together with his brother and sister he formed a piano trio; he played the violin, his younger brother Christian played the cello and his sister, Linda, was the pianist. At first they confined themselves almost exclusively to Haydn, Mozart and Beethoven, so that Janne's grounding in the Viennese classical repertoire was pretty thorough, so much so that when he came to play the F minor Violin Sonata of Mendelssohn for the first time, he could not bring himself to complete his run-through of the piece. But after a while the family trio turned its attention to the romantic repertoire and Janne came to appreciate its riches. As a good chamber music player Janne was much in demand in Hämeenlinna where there was a lively cultural awareness and great store was set by chamber music. Parties given by Dr. Tigerstedt usually turned into chamber music sessions and Janne was often invited there to play and to meet any visiting musical celebrities.

Many of the Russian officers garrisoned in Hämeenlinna were also musical. Janne made friends with Kostia, the son of a Russian colonel, a gentle dreamy child with whom he had much in common and with whom he exchanged confidences. Janne often went to his home and this contact with the Russian way of life was not confined to the caviar and blinis that he eagerly consumed with Kostia.

Another flourishing musical activity during Sibelius's youth was the male-voice quartet and in Hämeenlinna concerts of this kind followed each other in rapid succession. Janne can hardly have escaped making the acquaintance of the typical *Liedertafel* repertoire, mostly Scandinavian and German part-songs together with some folk-song arrangements. In general, however, concerts were rare events; Hämeenlinna had neither a theatre nor an orchestra and when the Turku or Tampere ensembles made one of their infrequent appearances, the repertoire save for some Mozart overtures was mostly light in character. The most memorable events were the visits of leading Finnish singers among whom were Emmy Achté, who was later to take part in the first performance of the *Kullervo* Symphony, and Filip Forstén whom a few years later Sibelius met again in Pauline Lucca's salon in Vienna. Instrumentalists were even less frequent visitors. Sibelius's first encounter with Grieg's F major Violin Sonata as well as some of the viruoso pieces of Vieuxtemps, Wieniawski and Sarasate apparently came from concerts given in Hämeenlinna by A. E. Westerlind. However, when the Helsinki Orchestra and a Music Institute were founded in the early 1880s, the effect was to stimulate concert activity even in Hämeenlinna.

In April 1885 when Janne was preparing for his final school examinations, the higher schools certificate which qualified its holder for entrance to a university, August Wilhelmj whom Liszt had hailed as a new Paganini, gave a recital in Hämeenlinna, and he was followed a few weeks later by Sophie Menter, a famous Liszt pupil whose programme abounded in virtuoso pieces and transcriptions. Sibelius recalled having been at most of these recitals.

In theoretical matters Janne was largely self-taught. His violin teacher, Levander, gave him his basic rudimentary instruction but the greater part of his theoretical knowledge came from a study of Marx's *Die Lehre von der musikalischen Komposition*, which by a curious stroke of fate chanced to be in the school library. 'When I later came to study in earnest at Helsinki. I found that most of what we were learning was familiar stuff', he was later to tell Furuhjelm, laying special emphasis on the exhaustive studies of the classical repertoire that he pursued. Judging from his compositions, at this time, his sense of form was already well developed. Where this was concerned, he felt himself on familiar territory; the actual process of learning was but a verification of something that he already grasped intuitively. It seemed to come more naturally to him and developed more rapidly than his harmonic or contrapuntal skills.

It was for the family trio that Janne composed an Allegro in A minor, which finished in C major. There is a short four-bar introduction which effectively prepares the way for the entry of in the main idea on the piano:

Ex. 2

The closing idea is modelled on the practice of the Viennese masters. In all probability it was to this Allegro or rather the Piano Trio from which it came, that Sibelius was referring in a letter written to his fiancée from Vienna in 1890 in which he speaks of a piano trio that he had composed in 1881, when he would have been fifteen which he thought was quite good considering his age. Another piece to survive but in fragmentary form is part of a movement in E minor for two violins, cello and piano. The $\frac{6}{8}$ metre, the ballad-like melodic line and the tinge of melancholy and restraint suggests the influence of Mendelssohn. But the earliest piece to survive in his own hand is a 'sonata' in five movements for violin and piano which Sibelius later called a Suite.[1] According to Furuhjelm, the Suite was composed some time between 1881 and 1883, although certain melodic ideas scribbled on the cover including a fugue subject from his years in Helsinki, as well as the relatively mature style suggest a somewhat later date.

The opening bars of the first movement breathe an air of Slav melancholy:

Ex. 3

Tchaikovsky's influence can be discerned in certain details; the descending figure in bar nine, for example, immediately imitated in the middle part an octave lower against a sustained D in the upper part. The introduction of such contrapuntal detail as a means of enriching a predominantly homophonic texture is characteristic of such Romantics as Schumann and Tchaikovsky. In the following bar Sibelius uses a chord of the seventh on the augmented fourth, G sharp. This particular chord is typical of Tchaikovsky's harmonic vocabulary and can be found in such works as *The Seasons* and in Lensky's aria in *Eugene Onegin*. It is safe to assume that Sibelius would have come across *The Seasons* during his youth in Hämeenlinna, since they were popular at this time and were to be found on most Finnish piano stands.

The other composer who served as a model for Sibelius in the 1880s was Grieg, whose shadow can be seen in the following movements, and in particular in the rustic fifths in the left hand of the piano part. But the sonority, too, and

1. His change to this effect survives on the original autograph.

the melodic line itself have a colouring strongly reminiscent of the Norwegian master:

Ex. 4

There are imitations of birdsong in the manner of Sarasate, pizzicato and arco at the same time, flageolet and double stoppings; all betray the composer's virtuoso ambitions. Sibelius doubtless wrote the Suite as a bravura study with himself in mind as the soloist. A somewhat less demanding piece from the technical point of view, the Andantino for cello and piano, was similarly intended for his brother.

A string quartet in E flat is dated 31(!) June 1885 and its first movement recalls the evenings of music-making in the family circle in Hämeenlinna and is distinctly Haydnesque in feeling:

Ex. 5

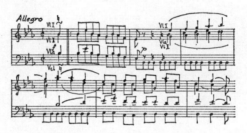

The Andante with its abrupt harmonic turns does however depart from classical models. The Scherzo in B flat minor on the other hand has an unmistakably late eighteenth-century feel about it:

Ex. 6

A movement for string trio of the same period shows considerably greater progress. Sibelius himself gave 1885 as the year of composition but the piece could however be of later origin. It begins with a series of chords on the violin and viola marked with a slow crescendo which is broken off by the cello pizzicato:

Ex. 7

This attack, crescendo and sforzando so familiar from the mature Sibelius assumes a genuine stylistic role in the movement. The use of pedal points and the chord of the sixth is also characteristic of Sibelius's mature style. The tension is resolved in a descending figure which both in shape and rhythm is related to Tchaikovsky's themes associated with Fate and Death:

Ex. 8

In the following idea which anticipates the finale of the Second Symphony there is a triplet of the kind we often encounter in later Sibelius:

Ex. 9

The 'Sibelius triplet' in its most characteristic form assumes the shape of a mordant-like ornament adorning a long sustained note. In this example, too, the harmonic progression, the tonic chord (E flat) followed by the first inversion of the relative minor with an added sixth (A) in the viola part, is highly characteristic. Sibelius conceived the movement as one single whole gradually increasing in dramatic tension. When he arrives at its climax, the 'Fate' theme is adumbrated 'largamente con tutta forza sempre'.

Even if many of these early compositions are relatively primitive, one is none the less struck by their feeling for form and the freshness of their invention and, particularly in the trio movement in G minor, by real traces of individuality.

In his grandmother's home Sibelius's musical talent was tolerated and indeed appreciated but only in so far as it did not encroach on his progress at school. There was no question of it as a career. Indeed for his grandmother the very thought of music as a profession was anathema. If Janne, like Robert Kajanus nine years his senior, later to be the most eloquent Finnish champion of his music, had left school to take up a musical instrument professionally, his grandmother would have regarded it as a social degradation and a comedown. A similar attitude of mind was by no means unusual in middle-class families at this time even in countries with a much stronger musical tradition.

By the time he was twenty Sibelius was still unsure of his musical path. One is tempted to say that his childhood and upbringing militated against his development as a composer but none the less one hesitates to do so. The rapid development of technical mastery is no automatic guarantee for subsequent artistic growth; the case of Glazunov, another exact contemporary of Sibelius, is a good instance of this. His first symphony written at the age of sixteen was acclaimed by Rimsky-Korsakov as 'breath-taking, hair-raising in its precocity'; yet in its very accomplishment one might also detect its composer's limited vision. On the other hand one can well cite the case of Tchaikovsky whose relatively late composition studies did not preclude subsequent mastery. Bruckner again illustrates the relatively slow rate of development of the typical symphonist. In Sibelius's case earlier tuition might have resulted in more polished juvenilia but this is not to say that it would have had decisive long-term effects. Indeed it might be argued that the slow rate of development during these youthful years helped to preserve the powerful untapped forces which came to full fruition in the Fourth Symphony.

The earliest evidence in writing of Sibelius's musicality is to be found in a letter penned by his Aunt Evelina. When she visited Maria Sibelius at Sääksmäki in the late summer of 1883, she wrote to a friend: 'I cannot put into words how close these three children are to my heart. The eldest, the musical boy, Janne takes care of me like a grown man. We have had many memorable times together both from his violin playing and from the harmonium we have out here.' When the summer came to an end and the Sibelius family moved back to Hämeenlinna, Aunt Evelina went too, 'so as to be able to make music with the children for a couple of weeks'. Even in his late old age Sibelius remembered playing the Schubert A major Sonata with her.

After her mother's death Aunt Evelina moved to Turku where she lived with her brother Pehr. For a number of years in succession Maria Sibelius and the family were not able to go to Lovisa for the summer and the house there assumed something of the character of a lost paradise. 'The family still long to go to Lovisa', Evelina Sibelius wrote, 'but how and when will they be able to? Life is hard for them now and the children's upbringing is the principal concern'. High among these concerns was Janne's progress at school; he played the violin so much that he neglected his Latin prose and at the end of the fifth year he was kept down and forced to spend an extra year in the class.

In the spring of 1885 Janne sat for his Studenten.[1] His grandmother has

1. The examination taken on leaving school, roughly equivalent to higher schools certificate, that qualified the candidate for university entrance. *Tr*

described the strain at home before he was to go to the school to hear the results announced. 'Now you can imagine janne is full of himself and is awfully pleased, whatever happens whether he gets through or is ploughed, he plans to slip away to Helsinki with the others, they are going on the evening train. Well, we shall see how it all turns out. . . . He has to have a good head on him if he is to get through that exam. Everybody is rushing about and talking while I am writing and Janne is looking at himself in the mirror.'[1] But unfortunately, the air of expectancy was to be disappointed and the letter continued later: 'Well now they have all been and heard the examination results Mari, poor thing, came back so dreadfully depressed, janne had the poorest results one could have, and she has lost no time in reminding him of this and he, too, seems to have grasped that it is a poor showing, when earlier he had pretended to be satisfied and to my mind the shame he had brought upon himself is well deserved and how things will go with the boy I don't know, I think, he has no ambition in life.'

His grandmother exaggerated somewhat, for although Janne's results were far from brilliant they were by no means wretched. He was placed nineteenth in a class list of twenty-eight. His written papers both in Swedish and Finnish were given credits, while he passed in Latin and mathematics. His essay, 'Gustav II Adolf, founder of Protestantism', shows some historical insight and a good sense of style; his Finnish reads smoothly and contains remarkably few mistakes or Swedish habits of expression considering it was written in the 1880s. But in his aural examinations Janne fared less well. And in history he was given 6 out of 10 though one might wonder, judging from the quality of the essay, on whether his history teacher, the present author's grandfather, had a more knowledgeable pupil in such fields as the Thirty Years' War, the period of Gustav III and the 1808–9 War.

In one respect, however, his grandmother was right: Janne had no special ambitions; he did not want to do anything—except go on with his music, and this was hardly to be countenanced. He made a tentative approach to enroll at Helsinki University and in the spring sought entry to the Faculty of Physics and Mathematics which at this time was the first step towards the Medical Faculty. Perhaps his grandmother had successfully exercised her powers of persuasion and advised the boy to follow in his father's footsteps. If so, it was not for long; in September he had second thoughts and enrolled in the Faculty of Law. In answer to his friends who asked why he had chosen Law he said, 'What else *could* I do?'

1. The letter is not grammatically correct in the original. *Tr*

CHAPTER THREE

His studies in Helsinki 1885–9

WHEN Sibelius came to Helsinki in the autumn of 1885, he came at a time when the gap between the generations, both in taste and ideals, had never been wider. The younger writers reacted strongly against the romantic lyricism of Runeberg and the idyllic plays of Topelius; they read such modern authors as Zola and Maupassant, Ibsen and Strindberg. The Helsinki public was roused from its idyllic slumbers by Ibsen's *Ghosts* and the protest dramas of the Finnish writer, Minna Canth. Those art galleries and salons still dominated by conservative taste came under heavy fire from the younger painters who took the French artists as their models. The rift between the generations was also reflected in the political situation; the young Finnish radicals whose most eloquent exponents included the writers Juhani Aho and Arvid Järnefelt denounced the conservatism and moderation of their elders in the language question.

From his residence on the Southern Esplanade, the Russian Governor-General kept a careful watch on the political cross-currents and skilfully played off the Finns and the Fenno-Swedes against each other. Finland's privileged position within the Tsarist Empire was watched with growing distaste by the Pan-Slav nationalists in St. Petersburg and an anti-Finnish campaign was launched in the Russian press. But Finland itself had been loyal to the Tsar since the days of Alexander II and the menacing rumbles in the Russian press were largely disregarded. In the 1930s Sibelius recalled his four years of study as untroubled by political anxieties: 'No political clouds darkened the horizon, economic problems did not assume the proportions that they came to do in later years, and we thoroughly enjoyed life. There were riotous parties that could go on for two or three days at a time.'

To a boy from the provinces Helsinki seemed to offer a wealth of cultural riches. When later in life he had spent long periods in Berlin, Vienna, Paris and London his perspective was to be somewhat modified: 'How could I have thought of Helsinki as a great city!' he noted in a diary entry.

Busoni who spent two years in Helsinki at the end of the 1880s described the Finnish capital at this time in a letter: 'The town could not be more beautifully situated. It is built on a peninsula and is thus surrounded on three sides by the sea. The harbour is enclosed by a host of small islands, rocks and skerries so that the sea assumes the character of an inland lake. The whole town is scrupulously clean, prosperous and civilized in every respect. The hotels are worthy of any Central European capital you might care to name.' Busoni also comments on some of the Eastern influences in the town: 'Many of their homes are large one-storey villas built entirely of wood (in accordance with Russian usage) and housing one family each,' and he was full of praises for the Finnish smörgåsbord that he was offered in restaurants, with 'its wide variety of delicacies and three different kinds of schnapps to which one can help oneself as much as one likes without having to pay a penny extra; this practice is to be found in Russia, Finland and Sweden.' From a musical point of view however he found Finland a backward country: 'Musical conditions fall far short of the ideal. For my part I need a country that offers the challenge of high standards that must be surpassed rather than one where so much remains to be done before one reaches a standard taken for granted elsewhere.' For all this, however, the development of music in Finland during the 1880s had been enormous. Like other people on the periphery of Europe the Finns were spurred on by the knowledge that they were latecomers.

Two pioneering figures were to emerge during this period, Martin Wegelius and Robert Kajanus. Both of them had studied in Leipzig with Reinecke and Kajanus with Svendsen as well; both had subsequently moved away from the Mendelssohn–Schumann tradition and fallen prey to the powerful spell of Wagner. In 1882 Wegelius founded a conservatoire, the Helsinki Music Institute, and in the very same year Kajanus formed the first permanent symphony orchestra in Helsinki with a hard core of about thirty German musicians and only a few Finnish players. Both were concert-giving organizations which competed for the favours of the comparatively small Helsinki public, and their rivalry soon affected relations between the two men. When Kajanus founded an orchestral school, three years later in 1885 relations deteriorated still further; Wegelius gave his pupils to understand that it was not *comme il faut* to attend Kajanus's concerts. Karl Flodin, the most influential of the Helsinki critics could not refrain from observing that those who suffered most from the animosity that grew between the two organizations were the students, but his pleas for common sense went unanswered. Sibelius himself testified that during his period of study with Wegelius he heard relatively little orchestral music!

The differences between Wegelius and Kajanus were basic. Wegelius, who had the advantage of a university training, argued that every musician should study the other arts and the humanities and should equip himself with a comprehensive theoretical knowledge. Although he never became a composer or conductor of any note, he was an able administrator and a fine teacher. The Music Institute was his life's work, and his theoretical textbooks and his *History of European Music* were the standard works of their time. He attracted to his staff many distinguished foreign pianists; apart from Busoni, he engaged

Pohlig and Dayas, both pupils of Liszt, as well as Melcer, who later won the Rubinstein prize, all of whom made some mark on the international scene. Kajanus, on the other hand, was a practical musician and both a composer and conductor. His somewhat Wagnerian symphonic poem, *Aino*, inspired by the *Kalevala* and written at the beginning of the 1880s, was the most accomplished orchestral piece to have been written by a Finn up to that time; Kajanus also had to his credit a Finnish Rhapsody based on folk songs in the manner of Svendsen. As far as he was concerned the musician required proficiency in the instrument of his choice; nothing else. If in outlook Wegelius and Kajanus had no point of contact, they did have one thing in common; both were despotic. Their mistrustfulness and capacity for resentment deepened the rift between them.

There was still another figure on the musical stage however. After Pacius had retired from his university post he was succeeded by Richard Faltin who was also of German origin. Faltin was a fine musician of enormous vitality; he was active as an organist, composer, conductor, critic, impresario; he ran a piano firm and taught at the Music Institute. He had at one time or another taught both Wegelius and Kajanus, and in the bitter feud between them he maintained a lofty neutrality. All three men were to play their part in Sibelius's life: Wegelius became his teacher and friend and took a paternal interest in his development; Kajanus was to become his champion and interpreter, and at one time his rival; Faltin wanted Sibelius to succeed him at the university though Kajanus's candidature thwarted this plan. But it was in his meeting with Busoni that Sibelius first encountered genius.

As early as the summer of 1885 after Janne had taken his school leaving examination, Evelina suggested to his mother that she and the family should move from Hämeenlinna and make their home in Helsinki. After a great deal of trouble they managed to rent a villa by the shore at Brunnsparken, the southernmost tip of the town and they moved there at the beginning of the autumn term. Evelina joined them so as to help her sister-in-law manage the household, but thought the place 'miserable and expensive'. But the villa was well situated in park-like surroundings and from his window Janne could see the entrance to the harbour; further out in the skerries was the eighteenth-century fortress of Sveaborg, and as at Lovisa there was the fresh tang of sea air to invigorate them. But the economic worries of the family were numerous: a half of Maria Sibelius's pension went on the rent of 600 marks a year; Evelina earned a little money by taking in needlework and making dresses for friends, while Maria's brother Axel, who was a mathematics teacher, bore the cost of Linda's studies. Whether Janne received similar help from his relatives is uncertain. Maria made it a point of honour to live within her means. Sibelius recalled in a letter to his fiancée in 1890 that his mother never borrowed money.

To start off with Sibelius read two subjects, law and music. Once enrolled n the university he felt that he had fulfilled his obligations to his family and in particular to his grandmother. So, on 15 September 1885 he became a pupil at the Music Institute with the violin as his principal study. His professor was Mitrofan Vasiliev, the Institute's most eminent teacher in the subject. By the end of October we find his aunt writing to her brother Pehr in Turku: 'Janne doesn't seem to be able to do the four hours' practice that his professor insists on, but none the less he has made great strides in his playing which has greater power, attack and taste. He is going to play the first movement of a Viotti concerto at the next public concert of the Music Institute, and has been practising it hard over the last few weeks. He seems to be very nervous about this concert even though he appreciates his professor's encouragement and his praise of his talent and diligence. It is rare for a pupil to be invited to take part in a public concert in his first term and the fact that he has, should be seen as a measure of the regard in which his talents are held.' However his appearance had to be postponed on the grounds of 'poor health' which was presumably worsened by his fears of a 'fiasco'. He was likewise prevented from taking part in a drama- tized version of the concert aria, Adelaïde, in which he was to have taken the part of Beethoven no less, which was performed in honour of Wegelius's name day on November 11.

From the very beginning Sibelius seems to have caused something of a sensation at the Institute. One of Wegelius's friends reported his opinion of the boy to Aunt Evelina: 'Sibelius is an exceptional case; his teacher (Vasiliev) says that he has genius, and for my part I cannot think of a future for him except as a great musician.' Janne's first appearance in public appears to have taken place on 14 December at one of the Institute's concerts but it received no press notices as all the critics had gone to the first performance in Helsinki of Tchaikovsky's B flat minor Piano Concerto.

The reports of his musical successes reached his uncle, Axel Borg at Mikkeli and prompted anxious reminders to Sibelius not to neglect his university studies. But his aunt's attitude to his law studies was fairly sceptical. She was confident that Janne would follow his musical star. Uncle Axel's reminders fell on deaf ears; during the autumn term Sibelius took one exam, and that in the Finnish language, not a paper that should have occasioned him any difficulty. (The archives at the Faculty of Law have no record of Sibelius ever taking a Law paper.) When in the spring Sibelius's uncle Otto paid him a visit, he caught sight of an open Law textbook on his nephew's desk that had been untouched so long that the pages were turning yellow from exposure to the sun. Sibelius shut the book and this gesture appears to have been a significant one; in any event, no more was heard of his law studies. The university had an orchestra which Richard Faltin conducted. Sibelius joined it in the spring of 1886 and became its leader shortly afterwards. In March, Faltin auditioned him for the university's musical scholarship and recommended him in strong terms. However, it was not until the following spring, after having been passed over twice, that Sibelius was awarded the scholarship.

At the Institute, Sibelius concentrated all his energies on the violin. In March he again took part in a public concert playing some pieces for three violins by Jakob Dont, whose *Gradus ad Parnassum* was included in the curriculum. Two months later he made a solo appearance playing the David E minor Concerto and won the praises of the critic, Karl Flodin. 'Jean Sibelius possesses a highly developed technique and in general played faultlessly.' This was, incidentally, the very first occasion on which his adopted name 'Jean' appeared in print. He also took part in a performance of Mozart's D major Quartet, K499, during the same spring and at the end of the term Vasiliev evidently entertained high hopes for him. Even though he had not advanced beyond the David Concerto he felt that any technical shortcomings would be more than offset by his pupil's enormous musicality. Undoubtedly Sibelius himself shared Wasiliev's hopes at this time. These were, of course, to be dashed in due course. Five years later in a letter written to Robert Kajanus from Vienna, he said, 'Yes, I still play the violin even now. I even make a little progress but only a little. My talent for the violin is about as much as that of any relatively musical person and not more!' An overstatement, of course, but one that reflects the extent of his disillusion.

Seen in perspective the most important event in his first year was his contact with Wegelius. Wegelius stood in an almost paternal relationship to his hundred or so pupils; he took classes in musical theory, composition, the history of music, singing-at-sight, teacher-training; he conducted the Institute's choral group and also gave piano lessons when the need arose. From the very start he took Sibelius in hand. They spent the autumn on a thorough grounding in musical theory, and in the spring turned to harmony and counterpoint using Bussler's textbook which embraced both strict and free counterpoint. His results at the end of the academic year were very good and, like Faltin, Wegelius made special mention of his good ear and excellent sight-singing. On the other hand, he obviously overrated his prowess at the piano. Subsequently in the autumn term Sibelius got poor marks, though in all conscience, he could plead that he had no piano at the Brunnspark Villa on which he could practise. Towards the end of the spring term pupils and staff organized an outing and picnic during which Wegelius improvised a speech which culminated in his proposing a toast to Sibelius's success. The 'good-for-nothing' who had disappointed his schoolmasters with his lack of ambition had suddenly emerged as the white hope of his teacher.

When the term finished, the Sibeliuses spent the summer in the Houtskär in the south-western archipelago of Finland; Uncle Pehr went with them, complete with his square piano and other musical instruments.

In the autumn of 1886 Sibelius started on his second year at the Institute, this time unencumbered by law studies. He worked very hard at his violin playing during this year and made four appearances as a soloist in such works as Bériot's

Seventh Violin Concerto, Vieuxtemps' *Ballade et Polonaise* and *Fantaisie Caprice*, and at the end of the spring term, the last two movements of the Mendelssohn concerto. In the decisive test, the Mendelssohn, his nerves failed him. Faltin noted in his review the 'somewhat thin tone and not always true intonation' that marred the Andante, while finding his playing in the finale distinguished by 'an eminently respectable technique'. The word 'respectable' stuck in his throat; he did not pass muster as a virtuoso. However, he had been sufficiently well-thought-of to become second violinist in the Institute's string quartet which he joined at the beginning of the spring term.

But apart from his violin playing the creative fires that had lain relatively dormant began to smoulder. As and from the spring term of 1887, Wegelius taught him composition and in common with many other gifted composition students he began to live a double life. He wrote typical student exercises for Wegelius, at least to begin with, but behind the academic façade he composed secretly and took care not to show these works to his master. A short Duo for violin and viola, possibly written as early as 1886, appears to be an exercise but the ambitious Violin Sonata in F major is, on the other hand, one of the most remarkable of his student works. Sibelius himself ascribed the work to the period 1886-7 but the relatively mature style suggests a slightly later date. This is borne out in a letter of Christian Sibelius from August 1889, where he writes: 'Janne has written a violin sonata during the summer.' The main theme of the first movement has a pentatonic flavour and the harmonic support, the tonic chord with an added sixth, has something of Grieg about it; the Norwegian master's sonata in the same key could possible have served as a model:

Ex. 10

But it is in the Andante that Sibelius gives for the very first time some hint of national identity:

Ex. 11

The dactylic rhythm, the fifths in the bass as well as the shape of the melodic line itself all suggest the shadow of a Grieg-like folk melody, but there are also elements that occur in Finnish folk-song; the absence of upbeats, the trochaic repetition of a note at the end of a phrase which on occasion gives way to an ascending note. Though Sibelius's use of the Dorian mode is not in itself specifically Finnish, it does in conjunction with these other factors, and the simple phrase structure of the tune itself, assume a Finnish character. Even the arpeggiated chords in the right hand of the piano accompaniment suggest a kind of stylized writing for the kantele.

This archaic character is reinforced by the insistent monotony of the repeated phrases which move within the compass of a fifth:

Ex. 12

There is an obvious parallel between this and the following idea from *En Saga* (p. 81, bars 13-16, clarinet):

Ex. 13

The Andante is the first portent of Sibelius's national style: the finale opens with an idea in mazurka rhythm. The chord of the seventh on the supertonic over the bass fifths gives the harmony its flavour of Grieg:

Ex. 14

Another work from this period is the Quartet in G minor for piano, harmonium, violin and cello, which in all probability dates from 1887. The use of such a curious combination calls for some explanation: the piece was evidently composed for Sibelius's Lovisa friends, the Sucksdorff family, whose drawing-room housed both a piano and a harmonium. The piece is simple in character and its melancholy has a somewhat Schubertian ring about it compounded with a touch of Nordic romanticism.

All this creative activity unleashed a wave of anxiety and uncertainty in his mind. He wrote of his feelings some time later in the autumn of 1890 and describes how his spirits oscillated between optimism and self-doubt during these years: 'My gift for composition is not of the kind that will ever be "successful". It is far too subjective for that. When I was a boy I thought I would invent an altogether new art (it would be half-sculpture and half-music I thought). I began with sculpture and as you know that turned out disastrously. But I still had deep down inside me a strong impulse to do something creative artistically. I chose music and suffered numerous setbacks until 1886 and that, in spite of the fact that I had as early as 1881 written a piano trio that I thought was quite good considering my age at the time. Afterwards I went to the Institute so as to learn modern technique which doesn't really serve my purposes at all. Things did not work out ideally, although I had some successes, in the absence of any real competition! I think I was almost the only person in Finland who was composing at all during these years (1886–8). At first Martin Wegelius was by no means favourably disposed to my music. You can imagine that my steps were not particularly light as I made my way home of a winter's evening tired and depressed to Brunnsparken. I cannot say how often I wanted to throw in the sponge and live the life of an idiot for which I always have felt myself well qualified. But it was my fate to want to compose.'

If Sibelius gives a one-sided picture of Wegelius's attitude to him, his reports speak for themselves. Wegelius appears to have adopted a somewhat cautious attitude at first and awaited concrete results before giving him the highest marks, which in fact he did in the spring term of 1888. When Sibelius referred to the modern technique that did not suit his ends, he was undoubtedly thinking of the chromatic harmony of Liszt and Wagner, composers whose cause Wegelius enthusiastically espoused.

Wegelius was insistent that his composition pupils should learn to master the traditional disciplines. On one occasion in the autumn of 1889 when Sibelius wrote from Berlin complaining of his German teacher's conservatism, Wegelius replied: 'If he puts you through the mill in strict counterpoint, it is only to enable you to write more freely once that discipline is removed; a lot of the daring things that are now only partially successful in your writing will as a result present no problems for you.' On the other hand, Wegelius was what one might call nowadays a moderate modernist—at least in principle. He was not successful as a composer in realizing his Wagnerian–Lisztian ideals, but he had some considerable sympathy for those of his pupils who were daring and revolutionary in outlook, provided that they went through the time-honoured disciplines. He had little real sympathy for Tchaikovsky or for that matter, any of the Russian composers of the day; nor did he harbour any great admiration for Grieg. Accordingly Sibelius felt little inclination to show him his free compositions such as the Tchaikovskian G minor String Trio or the Grieg-like Violin Sonata in F. Sibelius probably sensed that Wegelius would have found the 'Finnish nationalism' that emerges in the slow movement of the sonata totally alien. In actual fact it was just this particular feature of his style and his absorption in the *Kalevala* that caused his relations with Wegelius to cloud temporarily during the 1890s.

When Sibelius says in his letter from Vienna that as a boy he dreamed of a new art form, a compound of sculpture and music, we have an interesting glimpse of the nature of his thinking. Not for him the mixture of colour and music that was to attract Scriabin, nor of words and music; instead he dreamed of an art form where matter, line and shape would be given life by sound and thus enabled to move. To the three dimensions of sculpture he wanted to add the fourth: time. Sculpture, the supple lines, shape and body it presents, never failed to exercise its fascination for him. In an interview he was once asked if any of his music had been inspired by a painting and he replied that strangely enough, sculpture had always appealed to him more than painting. After visiting a Berlin exhibition he wrote: 'All the galleries were full of battle paintings and portraits of queens; the only real things there were the Ancient Greek sculptures. It's strange the fascination that sculpture has for me.' When in a museum he thought he was alone and unobserved, he would run his hand over a piece of sculpture; touching it gave him great satisfaction and a sense of the movement inherent in the form. In his study at Ainola there were no paintings: the only things were a photograph of the goddesses of Fate at the Parthenon and a sketch by his friend, the architect, Eliel Saarinen, 'Castle of Air' which was the first thing he saw on waking up.

Once again Sibelius spent the summer with his family in the south-west archipelago of Finland, this time in Korpo. Here they were joined by friends, a Dr. Wilenius and his wife who rented a neighbouring property for the summer.

A great many of the long summer nights were spent playing chamber music. Mrs. Wilenius herself was an able amateur pianist and in their large drawing-room, whose windows opened out on to handsome park-like country, she received her visitors, Jean, his brother Christian, and a sixteen-year-old girl, Ruth Ringbom, also a pianist. At these sessions they played the Beethoven and Schubert trios as well as those by lesser lights such as Fesca and Reissiger. According to Christian, Jean composed prolifically at this time and is said to have produced trios, pieces for violin and piano, a concertino for cello and a waltz that Christian himself described as 'very striking'. A minuet and allegro for two violins and cello which was discovered in Christian's music library in 1964 probably comes from this summer at Korpo. The minuet is classical in bearing, while the trio section bears the imprint of Grieg.

Two piano pieces survive from this summer, the Suite, *Trânaden* (*Longing*) written as a kind of *mélodrame* to accompany the recitation of Stagnelius's poem, *Suckarnas mystär*, and a rather Tchaikovskian miniature, 'Au crépuscule', both of which were dedicated to Mrs. Wilenius. The introduction to the suite, in C, and the finale, in E flat, make use of the same theme clothed in heavy chords; the closing bars in E flat minor sound like 'a melancholy sigh, which borne from its source, wanders lost in the labyrinths of time':

Ex. 15

From the autumn of 1887 Sibelius had a new violin teacher, Herman Csillag whose bald-headed figure, fiery temperament, brilliant technique and excessive portamento was to attract Busoni's attention in the following year. The change of teacher had a favourable impact on Sibelius's own playing, and when at the end of the following term, in May 1888, he gave the Rode violin concerto, Faltin wrote of the occasion with much less reserve: 'Herr Sibelius has made gratifying progress during the last year: his tone is much fuller, he seems more secure and composed, while the technical demands posed by the concerto were overcome in a way that did him honour.' Sibelius never came any further than this in his career as a violinist. The most demanding works in the third year course, the Bach solo sonatas, the Paganini caprices, the Beethoven, Brahms and Tchaikovsky concertos, lay beyond his grasp.

In the same spring Wegelius and Sibelius collaborated on a work, the inci-dental music to Gunnar Wennerberg's fairy drama, *Näcken* (*The Water-sprite*), which was first performed on 9 April 1888 before a distinguished audience that included the poet Topelius and the singer Alice Barbi, a friend of Brahms. Sibelius's setting of the poem greeting the water-sprite is a strophic song, free from complexity and laid out for soprano, violin obbligato, cellos and piano. Undoubtedly any comparison between the contributions of master and pupil redounds in the latter's favour; in the scene where the water-sprite is banished by an over-zealous priest, Wegelius's music is unintentionally comic. The last concert of the term included a work by Sibelius, the Theme and Variations in C sharp minor for string quartet. It was well enough received but aroused more good will than enthusiasm. Faltin's unsigned review had prophetic overtones, for he found Sibelius the composer a more interesting figure than Sibelius the violinist.

In the latter capacity, however, Jean continued to play an active part in Helsinki musical life. At the Institute's evening concerts he took part in performances of the Mozart G minor quintet as well as quartets by Haydn and Schumann. When Christian finished school and came to Helsinki to begin his medical studies, the family were able to resume the chamber music evenings that they had enjoyed together in Hämeenlinna. The two brothers formed a quartet with two of their friends in the university orchestra, young Richard Faltin, son of the critic and another medical student, and Ernst Lindelöf, a mathematician. They met once a week usually at the Sibeliuses and during the next two years worked their way through a goodly number of Haydn quartets, the six Mozart quartets dedicated to Haydn, and the Beethoven Op. 18 set. Jean Sibelius was the best violinist but his friends were not particularly enamoured of the idea of his always being leader.

It is not known what music apart from that played at the Institute's concerts or the repertoire they played themselves, Sibelius heard at this time. He took part in the University Orchestra's concerts of course but his attendances at the symphony concerts given by Kajanus were few. Although Wegelius did not encourage his students to attend them, there were exceptions. Sibelius certainly went to hear Svendsen, whom Wegelius had known in his student years, when he came to conduct a concert of his own music. Similarly, it is difficult to imagine that Sibelius would have absented himself when Auer came to play the Mendelssohn concerto or Wilhelmj played the Beethoven. There were opportunities of hearing other celebrities too: the violinist Nachéz, such pianists as d'Albert, Reisenauer, and Grünfeld as well as the singer Amelia Joachim. Opera, however, was something of a rarity. Although there was a lively period in the 1870s when a number of operatic ventures were launched, Helsinki had no permanent opera in the 1880s. An *ad hoc* group of Finnish musicians gave some performances of *Freischütz*, *La Traviata*, *Il Trovatore* and *Carmen* and a visiting Russian company gave Glinka's *Ivan Susanin* (*A Life for the Tsar*) and Dargomizhsky's *Russalka*, but the Mozart and Wagner operas Sibelius first heard were in Berlin.

Sibelius spent part of the summer of 1888 at Wegelius's summer house at

Granholmen in the Helsinki archipelago. These were hardly idle weeks. In earlier summers Sibelius had spent the greater part of his time practising the violin but now he devoted the mornings to counterpoint, relaxing in the afternoons by playing sonatas with Wegelius at the keyboard. When he brought out the music of Tchaikovsky's *Sérénade mélancolique* his host turned up his nose in contempt; 'violinistic drivel', he called it. Wegelius's pedagogic instincts got the better of him in the evenings when he insisted on reading aloud from Gobineau's *La Renaissance* which he translated at sight from the French over a bottle of wine. His wife, who was very fond of Sibelius, saw to it that they were well supplied with food and drink.

The rest of the summer he spent at Aunt Evelina's home in Lovisa where he wrote a piano trio, the so-called 'Lovisa' Trio. The trio has a youthful freshness whose optimism is reflected in the march rhythm of the second group of the first movement, a foretaste of the *Karelia Suite*:

Ex. 16

Later on the writing becomes more contrapuntal. The middle section of the Andante consists of a four-voice fugato, and the finale is built on a *cantus firmus* in C minor with a good deal of contrapuntal writing in quavers and semi-quavers.

At the beginning of the autumn term after a short and difficult time while their home was renovated and decorated, the family returned to Brunnsparken. According to their aunt, the boys threw themselves into the term's activities with great keenness, while Linda left home to begin work as a mathematics teacher in a school in Tampere. During his fourth and last year Sibelius formed a number of valuable friendships. Adolf Paul was one of these newfound contacts; his real name was Georg Wiedersheim and his father who came from Germany to settle for a time in Sweden, eventually moved to Finland where he stewarded an estate. A short thick-set youth with square features, he left the land and his agricultural studies and against his father's wishes began to study the piano. He is said to have had a far from sensitive touch; Wegelius did not care for him. Throughout the whole time he was at the Institute he never once played the piano in public.

Adolf Paul was not the easiest of companions. He worshipped Sibelius and jealously sought to monopolize him and be his only source of help. In his later correspondence with Sibelius he often returned to the theme that they should write some ambitious work in collaboration and enrich themselves on the proceeds. He himself fancied his chances in dealing with contractual matters and, in general, thought of himself as a kind of *éminence grise* in the world of the arts. Sibelius once called him in his diary, 'a comrade-in-arms and an old rogue'.

All his life Paul suffered from an inferiority complex. He dreamed of creating the 'art of the future' together with Sibelius. Several of his novels were published both in Swedish and German and his plays were mounted in Helsinki, Stockholm, Berlin and Vienna. However, he never really gained any measure of longstanding success as a writer and the only books to retain any interest today are the documentary writings: his autobiographical, *En bok om en människa* (*A Book About a Man*), in which one of the characters is based on Sibelius, and the somewhat insensitive *Min Strindbergsbok* (*My Strindberg Book*). As early as his student days, Paul tried his hand at journalism. As a protest against the descriptive writing of Karl August Tavaststjerna, he published a couple of prose poems called *Ur vännen Jeans skissbok* (*From Friend Jean's Sketchbook*), which purport to interpret Sibelius's music in words, and which are prefaced by a short introduction in which Paul presents his friend: '. . . a man of imagination, an eccentric who has greater difficulty than we others in negotiating the pitfalls of everyday life but who none the less really exists and lives his fantasy life here among us realists.'

Even if Paul painted Sibelius as a dreamer in a world of realists, Sibelius regarded himself at the end of the 1880s as a Strindbergian. It was the revolutionary and realist in Strindberg's output that he knew during these student years, books like *The Red Room* and *Giftas* (*Married Couples*). His encounter with these works challenged all the values he had held sacred in the romantic idealism of Runeberg. Yet the change in him took place only on the surface, and through the cracks in his defences, Paul could still glimpse the dreamer and idealist. Together they sought an escape from reality in the world of E. T. A. Hoffmann where Johannes Kreisler, 'Kapellmeister wie auch verrückter Musikus par excellence' disregarded the reality surrounding him. Sibelius must have found Hoffmann's *Kreisleriana* particularly gratifying. He must have felt some response to the passage in which the conductor describes how before sleep overtakes him he feels close relationships between colour, music and smell and how the scent of dark red carnations prompts recollections in his mind's ear of the sound of distant music on the basset-horn.

Incidentally, Busoni played Schumann's *Kreisleriana* at one of his Helsinki recitals in December 1888. The contrasts between the passionate minor sections and the dreamy poetic movements in the major keys mirror the differences between Florestan and Eusebius, the two figures that reflect the opposing forces in Schumann's own psyche. Evidently inspired by Schumann's example, Sibelius set to and composed a little piano suite called *Florestan* in the early spring of 1889, in which the tonal contrasts between G minor and B flat major are the same as in *Kreisleriana*. Again following Schumann's pattern, each movement has a programmatic inspiration and it is clear that Sibelius identified himself with Florestan:

1. Florestan wanders in the forest, depressed and unhappy. There is a strong scent of moss and the damp bark of trees.
2. Florestan comes to a rapids from whose waters, as he watches them, nymphs emerge; there is a scent of water-lilies.
3. One of the water-nymphs has dank, black eyes and bright golden hair. Florestan falls in love with her.
4. Florestan tries to lure her to come to him but she disappears. Downcast and unhappy Florestan returns home through the forest.

Florestan's peregrinations through the woods are pictured in a dolcissimo G minor tune:

Ex. 17

The waves which are transformed into nymphs are represented by a waltz in B flat. The third movement could well pass as an accompaniment for a *pas de deux*:

Ex. 18

As in the Suite for violin and piano we have a melancholy, descending figure which is imitated in the inner parts while again the chord of the seventh on the C sharp has overtones of Tchaikovsky.

During his first years at the university Sibelius moved for the most part in Swedish-speaking circles. He did not leave his Hämeenlinna school with an uncritical passion for all things Finnish. Finnish students usually adorn their student caps with a cockade of a golden lyre; Sibelius's first cockade was one which associated him with the Swedish-speaking community. Like his father and his uncle Edvard he belonged to the predominantly Swedish-speaking, 'Nylands Nation',[1] whereas his brother Christian broke with tradition by enrolling himself in the Häme division which was overwhelmingly Finnish in outlook. But still Sibelius took virtually no part in its life and did not even attend the party given for freshmen in the autumn of 1885. He studiously avoided being drawn into the language war which raged in student circles; he spoke Swedish with his friends and his neutrality in the language question was in practice coloured more by having Swedish as his mother tongue than having acquired his formal education in a Finnish-speaking school. But towards the end of his student days Sibelius was drawn into closer contact with Finnish-speaking circles and the young Finnish liberals. At this time the inflexible line taken on the language issue began to soften a little as both the Finnish and Swedish liberals made common cause in the face of the increasingly menacing tone of the St. Petersburg press.

His first contact with the Finnish camp in Helsinki was Armas Järnefelt, brother of the writer, Arvid. Armas had studied the piano and the theory of music at the Institute from the autumn of 1887, though like Sibelius he had prefaced his musical studies with a half-hearted excursion into Law. Armas introduced Sibelius into the Järnefelt family, one of the most lively and stimulating in Finland; aristocratic in origins yet democratic in outlook; at one and the same time ardent Finnish sympathizers yet thoroughly international. The head of the family, Lieutenant-General Alexander Järnefelt was one of the first prominent figures in public life to take up the cause of the Finnish language. After serving in the Russian–Turkish war, he was appointed Governor first of Mikkeli and then of Kuopio. His untiring advocacy of the Finnish language earned him the detestation of the Swedish-speaking upper classes into whose higher echelons he had been born. Among the Finnish-speaking community with whose problems he sympathized, he was not entirely at home on account of his aristocratic bearing; as a conservative he felt out of tune with the developments of his time and with the liberal ideas of his sons. Of their friends Sibelius was one of the very few whom he liked unreservedly, though being a man of few words and reticent in feeling, he did not always show it.

The general's wife Elizabeth came from another aristocratic family from the other side of the Baltic; her maiden name was Clodt von Jürgensburg and the family had strong artistic leanings. Her uncle was the famous Peter Clodt, the sculptor whose horse statues adorn the Anichkoff Bridge at St. Petersburg while her brother and cousin taught at the Petersburg Academy of Art. She had a highly developed moral and religious sense and in the 1890s fell under the sway of Tolstoy's theories. Elisabeth Järnefelt learned Finnish but not Swedish and went so far in her Fennomania that she did not mix with a single Swedish-

---

1. Members of the university normally belong to a 'student corporation'. These are recruited on a regional basis. *Tr*

peaking family. But the general had not bargained on Elisabeth making friends with her sons' friends, and keeping open house for the liberal young Finns. Elisabeth became in fact the centre of a literary and musical salon with distinct nationalist-liberal party colours. Her most successful protégé was Juhani Aho who drew much of his literary inspiration from her company. Aho had first looked up to her as a higher being and subsequently fell in love with her, only to transfer his affections to her daugther, Aino. In the way his path and that of Sibelius, unexpectedly became entangled.

The general's hopes were centred on his son, Arvid, who read law at the university. His ambition was to see him enter public life and espouse the cause of the Finnish language; but Arvid became neither a senator in Helsinki nor the Finnish Envoy at St. Petersburg. He chose to follow in the footsteps of Tolstoy with self-imposed hardships and a spell in a prison cell, and at the end of it all an honoured place in Finnish letters. The third brother, Eero (Erik) had inherited the mantle of the Clodts; he studied first in St. Petersburg and then Paris before returning to Helsinki in the summer of 1888 to paint land-scapes in the French manner from Savolax which he exhibited in the following autumn. Of his future brothers-in-law it was to Eero that Sibelius formed the closest attachment.

In the same autumn, 1888, the General was transferred from Kuopio to Vaasa (Vasa) and while waiting for the new governor's residence to be pre-pared, Elisabeth Järnefelt rented a flat in Helsinki in the house of a business-man, Reswoy, and here she stayed with Armas and two of her daughters, Elli and Aino. The Sibelius brothers soon became frequent visitors to the flat and in later years Jean spoke affectionately of this time as their 'Reswoy period'. In the following spring Elisabeth wrote, 'Armas has had his Sibeliuses here: one of them plays the violin rather well and it was a real pleasure to hear him and Armas improvise together.' Sibelius's first meeting with the seventeen-year-old Aino has suitably romantic overtones. Aino came into the drawing-room to take part in a pantomime which Armas was accompanying when she sud-denly became aware of the intense gaze to which the newcomer was subjecting her. Sibelius's eyes, according to a later description, had a distinctive light-blue colour which was both intense and penetrating: his gaze seemed to bore into and through the person he was looking at and exercised a quite hypnotic fascination over people. Aino was so disturbed that she was unable to complete the mime.

Aino's delicacy of profile and her appearance is graphically portrayed in Juhani Aho's novel *Yksin* (*Alone*) while Eero Järnefelt captured some of the poetic almost ethereal quality of his sister in an early sketch. Martin Wegelius thought her the 'prettiest girl in all Finland'. Together with the sense of duty and uncompromising beliefs she had inherited from her father, Aino had a certain stoicism in her make-up. 'Don't for one moment imagine that I am not sensible of the colossal reserves of iron and strength that you possess!' Sibelius once wrote her. He appreciated her honesty of mind and simplicity of character, which reminded him of his mother: 'I hope you will always stay like that,' he wrote, 'equally open and true, equally loving and responsive. . . . It is your simplicity that I value most. It is this same simplicity that is the most important thing in art too!' In the beginning of the 1890s Aino became interested in Tolstoy's teachings though not to the same extent as her mother or Arvid.

Each of the three brothers, Arvid, Eero and Armas reflected some facet of the family's artistic inheritance. Aino's artistic talents though real were not so pronounced. She translated some Maupassant into Finnish and wrote some short stories which were published in *Päivälehti* at the time of her engagement, but above all she was musical and played the piano. 'You are much more of an artist than you think,' Sibelius told her. 'Your feeling for music is impressive though your taste is almost too fastidious.'

In one letter Sibelius reminded Aino of an occasion when she was still living at Reswoy's. 'You came from Arvid's and we met on the stairs. You stopped for a moment. I thought of kissing you but I was afraid that it would be the last time I should be allowed to visit you. My eyes never left you, as you remember, and Arvid always said, "Don't look at my sister like that!" I hoped I would find something I didn't care for in your appearance and character but never found anything. I was already your captive then, however much I struggled!' There seems no reason to doubt the truth of Sibelius's assertion that he was Aino's 'captive' as early as their time at Reswoy's. In a letter to General Järnefelt in the autumn of 1891 he wrote that he had fallen in love with Aino at first sight but that this feeling went so deep that his 'pride and self-sworn allegiance to art' inhibited him from admitting it even for himself.

During the last year he spent at the Institute Sibelius paid court to another young lady from Helsinki society, Betsy Lerché, the twenty-year-old daughter of a Finnish senator to whom he had been introduced by Walter von Konow. Betsy Lerché had many features that reminded him of Aino: she was slim; she came from an aristocratic family with a foreign background—her mother was the daughter of a British diplomat at the court of St. Petersburg—and she had studied the piano there. She was like a breath of fresh air from the outside world and in Sibelius's company her ready laugh was often heard. In later years after her marriage with a university professor, her laughter was rare. Sibelius composed a salon-like waltz for her and even marked a few excited bars *à la Betsy*. She replied with some charming lines in French.

In spite of his interest in Betsy Lerché, Sibelius continued to visit the Järnefelt salon where the great issues of the day, artistic, social and religious were ventilated. Victorian hypocrisy was discussed in the Järnefelt family circle and when Sibelius touched upon the subject in a letter a couple of years later, one can almost detect an echo from these discussions.

It was inevitable that in a small town such as Helsinki that Sibelius would sooner or later meet the Järnefelts. His meeting with Busoni on the other hand, trikes one as one of the most unlikely encounters one could have imagined.

Showered with success, intent on an international career, Busoni stepped ashore at Helsinki one September evening in 1881 closely followed by his dog Lesko. On the quayside he saw the jovial, Silenus-like Wegelius waiting to welcome him. The standard at the Institute however came as something of a shock; his piano pupils were for the most part sheltered young ladies struggling their way through the studies of Cramer and Clementi and all of them looking as if they had a blood transfusion from the Gulf of Finland's fish. The fact that the Institute was not even in a position to put its own string quartet on to a professional footing amazed him. So did the absence of a student orchestra at the Institute: there were no classes in wind playing in Wegelius's time.

There was hardly one concert at the Institute in which Busoni did not take part. He gave five recitals during the academic year 1888-9 which offered a survey of piano literature from Bach to Schumann and Chopin. With the Institute's quartet in which Sibelius still played second violin, Busoni played the Schumann Quintet at a concert given at the University on 14 February 1889 and according to all accounts he dominated the proceedings. It was, incidentally, the first and only time that the two composers took part in the same piece together on the same concert platform. Right from the beginning Busoni determined to make his stay in Helsinki as short as possible. His success with the public was of benefit neither to his career nor his development, as he saw it.

But there was one bright spot in his life here: the circle of friends that he gathered round him, his pupils, Armas Järnefelt and Adolf Paul, their friend Sibelius, and Armas's brother, Eero. Sibelius wrote later, 'From the very first moment we struck up an intimate friendship and, in spite of the fact that Busoni was a teacher and I a pupil, we met every day.' The five friends usually met at Ericsson's café or, when Busoni felt so disposed, at Kämp's restaurant and these were occasions that Busoni clearly recalled later in life. 'We, "pupil Sibelius", the Järnefelt brothers and Adolf Paul formed an inspiring cabal and called ourselves "Leskovites" after my Newfoundland dog, Lesko.' Busoni dedicated to each of the five one movement in his *Geharnischte Suite* which he conducted in its first version in Helsinki in 1890. As yet Liszt had not assumed the central position in his musical world that he was to do in later years; in fact it was Wegelius who urged him to explore Liszt more fully. Busoni's attitude to Wagner was at this time obscure, but afterwards he became known as an anti-Wagnerian. In Helsinki however he did play at his very first concert at the Institute, Tausig's transcription of *The Ride of the Valkyries*.

For Sibelius the time he spent with Busoni was of enormous value and stimulus; their interchange of ideas in no small measure contributed to his development and in all probability to his artistic breakthrough in the spring of 1889. Sibelius's conversation, to quote Flodin's memoirs', 'delighted in paradoxes and similes; one was never absolutely certain what was intended seriously and what was only an effervescence, a bizarre whimsy playing in his rapidly working mind. His light hair would fall untidily over his forehead, the eyes were penetrating as if he were looking into a faint mist, but when his imagination was at work, his gaze deepened and his eyes shone with a blue intensity.' Eero was the man who, in a few well-chosen words, could puncture Sibelius's wilder flights of rhetoric and fancy. Armas brought to the group different qualities, an exuberance and a highly-strung temperament; Busoni had discovered his gifts as a Mozart interpreter and Sibelius, too, was often to stress his Mozartian temperament in later years.

According to Sibelius, Busoni played a good deal at the gatherings of the Leskovites, either pieces by his favourite composer or his own works and he 'encouraged us in our turn to improvise, and I made frequent demands on his indulgence in respect of my pianistic inadequacies'. This opportunity of being able to study Busoni's playing at close quarters and seeing his transcendental technique, flawless memory and inexhaustible repertoire should have left Sibelius in no doubt that he had no possibility of attaining any remotely comparable level of mastery as a violinist. If he had not abandoned his virtuoso dreams already, he did so now. When he sat on the platform playing the Schumann quintet with Busoni at the keyboard, he must have felt himself a very secondary figure. But when he developed his own musical ideas at the piano, frightful though he was as a pianist, he emerged as the equal of Busoni in inventive capacity. This insight surely spurred him in his creative work and the friendship with Busoni served to bring him a new perspective.

In some ways Busoni and Sibelius were drawn together because they were so unalike. Busoni was an intellectual with a distinct philosophical turn of mind; Sibelius lived in a private world and was largely dominated by instinct. In 1890 he wrote, 'I am no philosopher and never will be; this kind of thinking is the most difficult thing in the world for me and something I will probably never attain.'

Their attitude to nature was different. Busoni was a sensitive observer of natural beauty: he wrote after his arrival in Helsinki, 'Here the countryside is a paradise, a picture, indescribably beautiful and I find enormous satisfaction in looking at it.' But Sibelius did not 'look at nature' in the ordinary way; he lived in it and through it. Arvid Järnefelt describes him as 'a creature of nature. If you see him out in the countryside, even if it is only in a field, he seemed in an exalted state, he seemed to live life to the full. A bird has only to twitter and he responds immediately; a shepherd girl has only to sing a snatch of melody and it is indelibly registered in his mind. Everything that he drank in, that he heard, saw, or smelt, became 'wholly Sibelius'; he lived each moment so intensely when in the country that he reminded one at times of an animal.' The sound of the cranes was something that was to haunt him through his life; the scent of the earth on a spring day inspired him to explore new worlds of sound, while in an enraptured moment he wrote: 'It is strange that there is nothing else in the whole world either in art, literature or music that has an effect on me comparable with that of the sight and sound of swans in flight. For me this is a haunting sight and gives life its lustre.'

However unreserved his admiration of Busoni the pianist, Busoni the composer, remained a mystery to him and he failed to appreciate his real worth.
Busoni isn't really a very good composer', he wrote in 1890 at a time when he
knew only the first Violin Sonata and the Prelude and Fugue. At the Institute's
final concert of the spring term in 1889, Busoni played two of his own works,
the Variations on a Theme of Chopin, the C minor Prelude—presumably in
its first version—and, together with a colleague, his *Finnlandische Volksweissen*
for piano, four hands. This latter work is based on folk tunes, more recent and
lyrical in character than the ancient runic melodies which attracted Sibelius
and he presumably found Busoni's stylistic excursion horrifying.

Busoni, on the other hand, realized Sibelius's worth as a composer from the
very first and gave him every encouragement during his early years, both in
words and deeds, and in the first quarter of the present century championed his
symphonies. Sibelius once said half-jokingly, 'Everybody's life has its great
tragedy and mine was that I wanted to be a great violinist whatever the cost.'
He never became this and in time gave up playing altogether, thus avoiding a
cleavage in his activities that might in time have wrought real tragedy to him.
It is here that a shadow crossed their otherwise harmonious relationship.
Busoni would have gladly exchanged all the eulogies Sibelius lavished on his
piano playing for a single word of *genuine* praise of his music. But for that, sad
to say, he waited in vain all his life.

On a couple of occasions during his student life, Sibelius paid his respects to
the venerable Pacius, who lived in retirement in Helsinki. Of course, he was
fully aware that 'the Father of Finnish Music', as he was known, had not
in fact founded a national style, and after his death, he contested some of the
obituaries that had appeared in the Swedish press, 'With respect, I fail to discern
anything other in Pacius's music than reminiscences of Italian and German
opera.'

At the end of 1889 Sibelius was admitted to hospital for a short time. When
Aino Järnefelt met him in the street a little later that spring, she was horrified
by his pale and worn appearance. He visited the Järnefelts and Elisabeth wrote
to her eldest son in Kuopio, 'He is very intelligent, very pleasant and very
fond of us. When he came out of the clinic he came straight here and was so
pleased to be with us. He seems terribly nervous and is so completely a musician.'
Creative activity had overshadowed his interpretative activities more and more
during this term.

Looking over his work from the last year as a student of Wegelius, there is
a fugue that has a certain documentary interest. In all probability it dates from
the autumn of 1888 and is not complete, a page is missing from the manuscript.
The theme is not a conventional academic fugue subject and serves to modify
the picture of Wegelius as a strict academician:

Ex. 19

The leap of a ninth in the initial bar, the syncopation in the next, and the gradually increasing density of activity until we get the final onrush of semiquavers, gives the subject an individual character. Certain features of the piece prompt one to think of the *Voces Intimae* Quartet of twenty years later where one encounters the same semiquavers in an inverted form. Even the closing bars of the stretto suggest the Quartet:

Ex. 20

The fugue is representative of the officially approved studies Sibelius pursued, and it seems a good deal more forward looking than the free composition he was doing with the strong links with Tchaikovsky and Grieg.

His first work to appear in print was a song, 'Serenade' to words by Runeberg, published in an anthology of Finnish song. The earliest work to which he eventually assigned opus numbers, however, are the two pieces for violin and piano, the Romance in B minor and an Epilogue, which in its first version was called *Perpetuum mobile*. The Romance begins with an expressive theme over a chord of B minor, an added sixth providing the effect of a strong dissonance. This chord recurs in the slow movement of the *Kullervo* Symphony:

Ex. 21

The *Perpetuum mobile* is surely one of the most curious of Sibelius's student pieces. The solo part swirls over a pedal point on G: the key-centre hovers between D minor and E minor before the pedal point finally reveals itself to be

Jean Sibelius's parents, Maria and Christian Gustaf Sibelius

Maria, Linda and Jean Sibelius

the dominant of C. The most original feature however, is an idea in which the tritone figures prominently:

Ex. 22

The theme foreshadows the Fourth Symphony and oddly enough in the September of 1911, four months or so after the completion of the symphony, Sibelius noted in his diary: 'Working as if I were a youngster with a future. But these youthful pieces ought to be worked over again. There are some good things in them that ought to be rescued.' At the end of the month, Sibelius reworked both the Romance and the *Perpetuum mobile* renaming it at the same time. Maybe there is an inner relationship between the symphony and the earlier piece which would explain his sudden renewal of interest in it. The change between the *Perpetuum mobile* and the Epilogue is really more than a re-working; it is in fact a fresh composition based on the old material. The tritone motive acquires a rhythmic shape that comes much closer to the symphony. In the Romance, Sibelius undertook only minor technical improvements, such as the more idiomatic re-casting of the piano part.

Among Christian Sibelius's surviving papers there were some solo pieces for violin and for cello that clearly originate from these study years. There is a four movement Suite for violin and piano, inspired by the virtuoso style of Vieuxtemps and Wieniawski and presumably composed as a bravura piece to show off his own technique. As in the Vieuxtemps *Ballade et polonaise*, the first movement opens with a lyrical idea, suitable for warming up one's fingers and getting stage fright under control.

A brilliant cadenza leads into an allegro movement which in its turn is followed by a waltz. The Polonaise at the end is in a typical virtuoso style:

Ex. 23

These leaps and octave passages are a preparation for the violin writing that Sibelius was to cultivate in the concerto. There are one or two pieces written for Christian; an *Andante molto* which shows his Tchaikovskian melancholic style, and the cello parts alone survive from a Fantasy and Waltz, presumably the same as the so-called 'Lulu' Waltz for cello and piano.

A new work of Sibelius, the Suite in five movements for string trio was given at one of the Institute's concerts on 13 April 1889. 'When this work began, we were immediately aware that this was something that was far more than a student work,' wrote Busoni in an article presenting Sibelius to the Zurich public in 1916. Only the first three movements, Prelude, Andante con moto and Menuetto have been preserved complete; the violin part of the last two movements is missing. In the Prelude the parts blend to form a chord to which the viola trill lends an almost impressionist air. Afterwards the viola takes up the melody:

Ex. 24

For the first time a progression that is to be one of Sibelius's most characteristic fingerprints makes its appearance. The specifically Sibelian touch comes in bars 3 and 4 where, over a pedal point on the tonic A, a dominant minor ninth (E sharp, G sharp, B and D, omitting its root C sharp) of the relative minor key (F sharp) resolves on to the triad of F sharp minor which, because of the pedal appears to be in its first inversion. Long-sustained pedal points on the tonic in the major key which become mediant in the related minor, are to be found throughout Sibelius's output from the early works down to *Tapiola*. This last chord, the first inversion of the minor triad, has a particularly melancholy colouring.

One is tempted to ask where Sibelius acquired this particular harmonic sleight-of-hand. It is worth noting that similar progressions are to be found in the Russian composers at about the same time, particularly when their oriental mood takes them; the D major episode from Balakirev's *Islamey* or the Polovtsian Dances from *Prince Igor* are two cases in point. It is highly improbable that Sibelius would have known much of this repertoire as early as 1889 with the possible exception of *Islamey* which Busoni may well have played him before including it in one of his Helsinki recitals in 1890. In any event this is a progression that was, as it were, 'in the air' at this time. In the hands of Borodin and Balakirev it acquires colourful oriental sensual overtones; in Sibelius's it has the scent of Nordic lyricism.

The A major Suite's first (and presumably last) performance gave rise to some controversy in the press. 'To be perfectly frank, I was impressed by this début,' wrote Flodin, who then went on to say in the very same breath, 'but one thing gave me cause for concern; that was the total absence of melodic invention'. Later in his diary Strauss was to call Sibelius's melodic invention 'almost inexhaustible' and Busoni referred to him as 'ein finnischer Schubert'. Flodin was so obviously wide of the mark in this instance that Csillag who had taken part in the first performance was roused to protest: 'We have here a richly endowed melodist; a young nightingale was making its first attempts at song and the discerning listener could tell at once from its quality that the bird is genuine!'

Before the end of the season Sibelius was able to present yet another new work, a four-movement string quartet in A minor. When he finished it, he showed the work to Busoni who 'sat down at the piano at once, played through the quartet from beginning to end without for a moment having had the chance of looking at it beforehand. And *how* he played it!' The work had its première at a student concert on 29 May. Unfortunately the complete score has been lost although the first violin part survives; so, too, does a fragment of the scherzo (the second trio section in F minor, though the first six bars of this are missing, and the final reprise of the scherzo in F) which turned up in Christian Sibelius's music library in 1964. The main idea of the trio is given to the cello:

Ex. 25

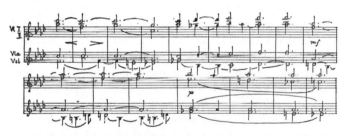

The modulations are more complex than in any of Sibelius's earlier work. The main section begins thus with the viola's pianissimo figure being answered fortissimo very much in the style of Beethoven:

Ex. 26

Unfortunately the reviews give no indication of the work's style as a whole. When in the following autumn two of its movements were played in Helsinki the critic of the Swedish-language daily, *Hufvudstadsbladet* praised the Adagio for its felicitous handling of polyphony and the finale for its splendid climax.

Robert Kajanus was present at the concert in which the quartet was first given and, like Flodin, he realized that Sibelius, who was nine years his junior had leapt to the forefront of Finnish music. He remarked to Wegelius at the end of the concert that there was scarcely much point in others, such as he himself, bothering to compose any more, a remark that seems to have irritated the latter. Perhaps Sibelius himself was present at this exhange; in any event he appears to have been introduced to Kajanus some time on that evening. Kajanus's remark reveals something of his basic attitude to Sibelius: a compound of admiration mingled with an undertone of bitterness. From the very beginning he appreciated and admired his art but none the less he felt somewhat pained to think that he could no longer regard himself as the most gifted composer in the country.

Wegelius was satisfied with the quartet but later the following year was to describe the first movement as 'far from good'. He obviously gave his pupil complete freedom now and made no attempts to impose a classical academic style or the Liszt–Wagnerian school on him. Both in the A major Suite and the A minor Quartet Sibelius revealed his own style for the first time to the public gaze. As early as February 1889, that is to say before these two compositions saw the light of day, Wegelius recommended Sibelius for a state scholarship:

'Herr Sibelius has mastered fugue with ease. With the help of his academic proficiency he has made rapid strides in his composition, having attempted to write for all the important instrumental forms and in particular one of the most difficult media, the string quartet, with rare instinct and talent. His formal skill is matched by a genuine musical impulse, a lively inventive capacity together with a rich and distinguished fund of inspiration, and thus as a composer his future gives rise to the most promising hopes.' Wegelius exaggerated the extent of Sibelius's technical skill. A composition pupil who had as yet not tried his hand at writing a symphony or a work for soloist and orchestra can hardly be described as having 'attempted all the important instrumental forms', but the testimonial had the desired effect, and the Finnish Senate granted Sibelius a travelling scholarship of 2,000 marks for further studies in composition and the violin.

On 31 May 1889 Sibelius left the Institute at the end of his four-year period of study. Considering that he had started virtually from scratch, his course had not been a long one. But his musical education was by no means complete; Wegelius felt that his pupil had made sufficient progress in mastering chamber and instrumental music and that he himself was not the right person to guide his studies in orchestration. In his recommendation Wegelius had undertaken to give Sibelius 'requisite advice and information . . . concerning studies and teachers abroad'. In actual fact he treated his twenty-three-year-old pupil as if he were a good deal younger and the terms of his recommendation left Sibelius relatively little freedom of manœuvre. Albert Becker, a sound but dull Berliner was to be his teacher. One wonders what would have been the consequences had Sibelius been allowed to proceed to St. Petersburg to study with Rimsky-Korsakov. How would that have influenced his development as a symphonist and his relationship both to opera and to folk music? Above all how would it have affected his orchestration? At this time Sibelius could have studied in Russia without feeling any political or psychological inhibitions. Eero Järnefelt had spent a couple of years at the St. Petersburg Academy of Art where his uncle, Michael, and cousin, Nikolai, were teachers, and he suggested that Sibelius should enroll at the St. Petersburg Conservatoire. But for Wegelius, the very thought of sending his pupils to Rimsky-Korsakov and to Russia, which he loathed, was preposterous.

In the testimonial Wegelius wrote on Sibelius's departure from the Institute, and oddly enough dated March 1890, one can detect a slight note of reservation about his future prospects. In the finished testimonial he writes, 'We are convinced that Herr Sibelius . . . will one day assume a prominent place in the musical life of the country', whereas in his first draft he had written, 'one of the most prominent places'. It seems as if in spite of everything Wegelius was not wholly satisfied with Sibelius's development. It only needed an incautious comment on Sibelius's part about his new teacher, in the autumn of 1889, for Wegelius to lay down the law as if he were an impudent schoolboy. 'No person with any common sense is going to endorse all your musical ideas; there lies your Achilles heel, my boy, that you haven't yet learned to distinguish the wheat from the chaff, the gold from the dross, which can also glisten in the sunshine. You are in need of a good spring-clean in this respect and when you have had it you will feel the benefit. After that you can write again anything that you want to, but you will no longer want to write the first thing that comes into your head.'

The three leading figures at the Institute reacted in different ways when confronted with Sibelius's talent. In Wegelius he seemed to arouse a paternal affection, a despotic protective instinct and an element of irritation perhaps even jealousy; in Kajanus, admiration mixed with a trace of envy. Only in Busoni did Sibelius's genius evoke a pure Apollonian *joie de vivre*.

CHAPTER FOUR

Berlin: 1889–90

IN the summer of 1889 Sibelius began work on a new quartet in B flat major though he did not finish it before his departure for Berlin. Wegelius appears to have liked what he saw of the sketches for in the following spring he wrote to Sibelius: 'A benevolent genius must have been at your side when you composed the B flat Quartet—was it wise of you to allow him to stretch his wings in flight—an escape?' The same summer Jean and Christian gave concerts at the casino in Lovisa; Jean's *pièce de resistance* was his violin sonata while Christian played the Cello Fantasy and the 'Lulu' Waltz. Christian, writing to Axel von Bornsdorff, said: 'I think the fantasy is among the most beautiful and magnificent cello pieces I have ever heard. . . .The audience went wild with enthusiasm.'

Alma Söderhjelm, the historian and novelist, has described how Sibelius would wander among the crowds that thronged the resort, slim and with an alert, springy gait, at times so deeply engrossed in his own thoughts that he was totally unaware of any passers-by, at other times outgoing and delighted to come upon friends and acquaintances. Sibelius used to play for Alma Söderhjelm and her friends and at one time confided to them his plan to compose a work based on Shakespeare's *Macbeth* and described in detail some of his intentions. But Sibelius was as yet ill-equipped to give orchestral substance to his Shakespearean vision.

In the autumn Sibelius set out for Berlin. He embarked at Helsinki on 7 September 1889 on the steamer *Storfursten* (*The Grand Duke*), and among his travelling companions were Eero Järnefelt and Juhani Aho, both on their way to Paris, and two new acquaintances, Werner Söderhjelm, a philologist and historian, and Ilmari Krohn, the musicologist-to-be and composer. Söderhjelm, *un homme du monde*, was also travelling to Berlin and had been asked by Wegelius to keep a watchful eye on Sibelius.

Many tears were shed at their departure. Aino Järnefelt had come to the quayside, presumably to bid her brother farewell, but Sibelius did not see her, or affected not to see her. Perhaps he felt that were he to take farewell of her in public he might appear to be committing himself to her in some way. At

:ast this is how Aino justified his behaviour to herself. In fact relations between
1em were under some strain. He had not visited the Järnefelts during the
1mmer in spite of a letter from Eero enclosing a drawing of Aino that he had
1ade and ceremoniously cursing him for neglecting them. He had however
ound the time to stay with the von Konows where he had met Betsy Lerché.
When Aino Järnefelt made her way home from the quayside she wept copiously.
And so, too, did Hanna Wegelius, though less copiously and much to the dis-
leasure of her husband. Once Sibelius had gone, it felt as if half the Institute
1ad left.

The very first evening they arrived in Berlin, Söderhjelm took Sibelius to
he Kroll Opera where *Don Giovanni* was being given with Francesco
l'Andrade in the title-role. This was the first Mozart opera that Sibelius had
:ver heard. At first Janne did not feel at home in the atmosphere of a big city:
Up to the present it has been impossible for me to compose here as the Berlin
treetboys appear to be virtuoso whistlers and it is impossible to escape the
ncessant noise they make; now I am becoming a little more accustomed to it
ɔut I have not managed to do much work up to now. Everything is very new
:o me and I only stare and gape at things; it certainly takes time before one
gets used to it.' Streetboys whistling can hardly have been the reason for
Sibelius's inactivity. After the relative quiet of Helsinki the atmosphere of
Berlin made him restless; his health, too, gave grounds for anxiety and he had
to spend a few days in hospital. Above all his first encounter with his new
composition teacher depressed him. At the end of September he had his first
lesson after which he reported to Wegelius that, 'Becker is a stuffed shirt from
top to toe. When he saw my quartet he nearly had a heart attack (in particular
he could hardly get over the fact that I had used the minor and major form of
the same triad in immediate alternation). He looked through the music and also
sang the second theme in the finale (I should add that he can't play) and argued
that I couldn't possibly have felt that, and that it could only have been written
as a result of calculation. He was particularly worried by the false relation here.

Ex. 27

He should of course, hear how the phrase sounds an octave lower. Naturally I
had the effect of its overall sonority in my mind. He has begun to give me a
thorough grounding in the strict style; there's nothing wrong with this, I
suppose, except that it is pretty tiresome. Incidentally I have begun to feel my
way a little more in city life though up to now I have made very few friends
among musicians here and so have little to report on that score. Becker is still
a bit haughty in his attitude but I daresay he will thaw out in time.'
Wegelius was somewhat annoyed that Sibelius should think fit to criticize
Becker and answered at once: '*Mon cher Jean*, The composer of the B flat
minor Mass and *Die Wallfahrt nach Keevlaer* is no "stuffed shirt from top to toe"

—You can put such ideas out of your mind.' However Sibelius had been tactful enough to refrain from saying that nothing Wegelius had taught him was any good in Becker's eyes. At the age of twenty-four he was faced with the bitter fact that in the opinion of a famous German teacher his craftsmanship as a composer was inadequate. But this is often the fate of young musicians who, coming from the periphery of Europe, continue their studies in a great continental centre. Sibelius's aunt consoled him with the thought that 'a change of school always means that one has to start all over again'.

Sibelius presumably exaggerated Becker's pompous academicism. If his teacher did really give himself airs and behave loftily, he soon relaxed and later in the autumn wrote to Wegelius to thank him for sending 'den lieben jungen Mann' and added: 'Er interessiert mich sehr und ist entschieden begabt' (I am very interested in him and find him exceptionally gifted).

But Sibelius was not far from the truth in writing of Becker as a 'stuffed shirt'. After his ponderous B flat minor Mass of 1878, each successive work betrayed an increasing pedantry and he became the archetype of the conservative composer. His style appealed in particular to Kaiser Wilhelm II, who loathed the untuneful modernists, and Becker was loaded with honours and high office. He directed the Cathedral Choir and sat on the governing board of the Royal Academy of the Arts. It was from Becker that Sibelius acquired his taste for 'the company of princes and counts', a taste which he was to have occasion to cultivate a year later in Vienna.

Becker did however enjoy an impressive reputation as a teacher of counterpoint. 'Lieber langweilig aber im Stil' was his motto. Sibelius wanted to compose in a much freer style and wished he could have written a piece for Wegelius's birthday in November, but as he wrote at the same time: 'Becker will not hear of anything except his fugues. It is insufferably tedious to do nothing but write like that; I know the German Psalmsbook back to front by now. You asked me to tell you what I am working at and wanted to see my finished exercises. I can't imagine that the latter have much interest; since everything is forbidden, what can one write? I have analysed several of Bach's fugues (and even some of Becker's own) as well as some Bach motets. Now I am to go on to writing instrumental fugues. . . . I have learned never to argue with Becker or betray my feelings by so much as a gesture, nor do I defend my stupidities.'

A four-part setting of the words *Mein Gott, mein Heiland, ich schreie Tag und Nacht vor Dir* with Becker's corrections bears witness to Sibelius's contrapuntal struggles, but apart from these he appears to have written nothing during the autumn. Possibly he submitted a work for a competition run by a Finnish educational organization designed to enrich the repertoire for chorus and horns. Christian had sent him some of the latest Finnish poetry at the same time pointing out that the expiry date for entries was not far off so that Jean would not be able to compose a choral piece on a text from the *Kalevala*. A piano sonata for Becker was sketched but never completed.

There is no doubt that Sibelius learned a great deal from Becker's strict schooling and that it was an admirable preparation before beginning to write freely for orchestra. Even if he felt its constraints oppressive, he did at least learn to master counterpoint thoroughly. But Sibelius was doubtless in need of more encouragement than he received from Becker. His composition was in a period of crisis whose primary cause, he told his brother, was his inability to work with the same spontaneity as before and his growing doubts as to his talent. Plunged into the midst of Berlin's musical life, he was forced to scrutinize his first musical impulses more critically and look at the ideas in a new light. In Helsinki he had been the white hope of Finnish music; in Berlin he was just one music student among many. Sibelius's feelings are reflected in a few words that he jotted on the back of a receipt from Becker, dated 14 October 1889, in which he tries to resist his depression: 'Try to be a man and remember always your own responsibility. Don't give in to passion but develop what gifts you have harmoniously. Don't imagine that you are anything other than you are. Don't think of becoming a great man. Work intelligently. *Si male nunc et* (!) *olim sic erit.*'

Recalling his Berlin period Sibelius told Ekman, 'There was nothing more sterile than the transition from the 80s to the 90s as far as music was concerned. Nothing new appeared.' Here Sibelius allowed his judgment to be swayed by purely subjective considerations. It is hardly necessary to point out that a very great deal that was new was appearing elsewhere in Europe; in Budapest Mahler had just conducted the first performance of his First Symphony in the autumn of 1889, Strauss's *Don Juan* had scored a great success at its first performance in Weimar and a few days later the young composer was able to play another new work through to Hans von Bülow, namely *Tod und Verklärung*. The following spring Tchaikovsky's *Sleeping Beauty* made its first appearance at St. Petersburg, Bruckner was working on the second version of his Eighth Symphony, Brahms on his last chamber works and Debussy was on the threshold of a richly productive decade that was to see *Prélude à l'après-midi d'un faune* and the bulk of *Pelléas et Mélisande*.

In Berlin, however, very little of this could be discerned. The most prominent figure was Bungert, an imitator of Wagner, as pretentious and empty as the statues adorning the Sieges Allée and totally devoid of any genuine creative impulse. Not even the Brahms–Wagner controversy was conducted with the same intensity as it was in Vienna, and as a forum of modern music, Berlin was in no sense comparable with what it was to become ten years later when Richard Strauss, Nikisch, Weingartner and Busoni were all active. The main attractions at the beginning of the 1890s were the Philharmonic concerts under von Bülow where soloists such as d'Albert, Stavenhagen and Teresa Carreño made their appearance. But compared with, say, the Dresden Opera, the Royal Opera in Berlin was to use Nielsen's words, 'rather crude and military'; Berlin could not as yet match the great European musical centres.

Sibelius had no better luck where visiting composers were concerned; he

missed Tchaikovsky who had conducted a concert the year before, and Bruckner who was to come the following year to attend the German première of his
Te Deum. The only exception was Strauss whose visit firmly imprinted itself
on Sibelius's memory. Von Bülow conducted the Berlin première of *Don Juan*
and afterwards, in Sibelius's words, 'a shy young man with a large shock of
hair' came on to the platform to acknowledge the applause. *Don Juan* doubtless
gave him some food for thought: while he was spending his time churning out
fugues for Becker, here was a composer only one year older, who had to his
credit an orchestral work of astonishing maturity and technical virtuosity.
Sibelius must have had many occasions during these years abroad on which he
had to fall back on his reserves of 'unblushing self-confidence', as he put it in a
letter to Aino.

Wagner appears to have aroused conflicting emotions in him. After having
heard *Tannhäuser* and *Die Meistersinger* at the Royal Berlin Opera, he wrote
of his impressions to Wegelius: 'This is certainly strong stuff. When we meet
I shall give you my reactions in greater detail and let you know how I felt.
The music roused me to a mixture of surprise, disappointment, joy and so on.
On both evenings I was ill but you can depend on it that I shall never forget
them.' Sibelius was careful not to hurt his friend's Wagnerian susceptibilities
and hence postponed a more detailed description of his reactions as was his
wont when embarrassing or sensitive subjects came up. He had written off
the overture to *Die Feen* as an imitation of Weber and the only positive quality
he could find in it was Wagner's insistence on the main idea which is rarely
absent from the texture. On the other hand, he wrote to his Aunt Evelina that
he was bowled over by Wagner and it is surprising therefore that he makes
no reference in his correspondence to *The Ring* which was given at the Royal
Opera that autumn. Nor does he make any mention of the Berlin première of
Verdi's *Otello* in the following spring. It seems likely that his operatic appetite
was satiated at the beginning of his time in Berlin and that he concentrated on
orchestral and chamber music concerts towards the end of his stay there. In
the same concert as the *Die Feen* Overture, he heard two 'wonderful pieces' by
Berlioz, two scenes in fact from *Lélio* including the famous tempest, Liszt's
Psalm and the D minor Symphony (No. 7) of Dvořák.

In February 1890 Robert Kajanus came to Berlin to conduct a performance
of his *Aino* Symphony at one of the Philarmonic Society's popular concerts.
Sibelius seems to have been impressed more by the potential power of the text,
taken from the *Kalevala*, than by the work itself. As he later told Ekman, 'The
Aino Symphony opened my eyes to the rich possibilities that the *Kalevala*
offered for musical setting.' However it was Beethoven rather than contemporary music that was Sibelius's central musical experience in Berlin. Hans von
Bülow opened the autumn season with the *Eroica* and finished it with the Ninth;
he opened the spring season with the Fifth. Sibelius copiously annotated his
miniature scores. In addition he heard von Bülow's piano recitals which included
the late piano sonatas, Opp. 101, 106, 109-111. Sibelius had always admired

von Bülow's editorial comments to the Beethoven sonatas and studied them closely.

Nor did Sibelius neglect to attend the chamber music concerts given by the Joachim Quartet whose programmes included the late Beethoven quartets, then rarities in the concert hall.

Sibelius also went to many of Joachim's sonata recitals and ought in all probability to have heard the first performance in Berlin of Brahms's D minor Sonata, Op. 108, though Brahms was not one of his favourite composers and never became one. Presumably he went to hear his childhood idol, August Wilhelmj and admired his superb tone; he must have also heard the French virtuoso Sauret, for in general Berlin offered splendid opportunities for the instrumentalist. Violinists could study with Joachim and pianists with Heinrich Barth; Sibelius contented himself with Fritz Struss, a pupil of Joachim and a close friend of Becker. The choice of a relatively obscure violinist puzzled Wegelius and Sibelius himself did not think him a master-violinist but none the less decided to continue with him so as not to offend Becker. However later in the spring he did leave him for another teacher, though not Professor Wirth whom Wegelius had suggested. Sibelius no longer regarded the violin as his chief subject of study and during the spring took lessons primarily so as to have something to show his scholarship board.

Berlin swarmed with foreign music students: Scandinavians, Russians, Hungarians, Rumanians and Anglo-Saxons. Sibelius was drawn into a circle that was predominantly Scandinavian though it included a couple of Americans and a German. Among his best friends were Fini Henriques, the Danish composer and violinist, who was studying with Joachim, and the American cellist, Paul Morgan. Henriques was something of a bohemian even among bohemians, a much-sought-after chamber player even if he forgot to turn up to rehearsals; Morgan, more introspective by nature, took a great deal of interest in the various bargains Sibelius found in the Berlin second-hand music shops and eagerly discussed the great Brahms–Wagner controversy. The group also included two other Joachim pupils: Schnedler-Petersen, a Danish violinist (not the equal of his countryman, Henriques) who later came to Turku to conduct there, and Theodore Spiering, an American violinist and conductor, who led the New York Orchestra during Mahler's guest appearances. There were two Norwegians, the author Gabriel Finne and the pianist Alf Klingenberg who confessed that he preferred to flirt rather than practise scales. A kind of honorary president in this little coterie was Christian Sinding who was the senior of them all by a few years. He and Ottakar Nováček used to make frequent visits from Leipzig where Nováček was a member of the Brodsky Quartet. Adolf Paul came from Weimar, penniless and dissatisfied with the world; the circle was completed by some young ladies who studied musicians rather more closely than music.

The Scandinavian colony had a somewhat precarious economy; and so as to spread their expenditure more evenly over the month they all entrusted their funds to their 'treasurer' Schnedler-Petersen, who was briefed not to hand out more than 10 marks at a time. Immediately after this arrangement had been set in hand Sibelius asked for 100 marks. This he did not get; he did succeed however in raising 200 marks from a Finnish music-lover. On Sunday afternoons they all foregathered at a Berlin *pension* where Sinding, Sibelius or one of the others played a piano, which Grieg had at one time used, to accompany the others who danced with chairs in their arms. Then they went in procession doing the goose-step and stamping a special rhythm down Berlinerstrasse to their local hostelry, Augerstinerbräu. The local residents had accustomed themselves to this spectacle and used to shout to each other, 'Die Schweden kommen'.

Relations between Sibelius and Adolf Paul were friendly but stormy interludes developed. Paul's allowance from home had been cut off, he lived in penury and continually borrowed money from his friends who began to avoid him. If one is to believe his autobiographical novel, *A Book About a Man*, Sibelius had realized that Paul as a musician was following the wrong course and encouraged him to give up music in favour of writing. Sibelius was often at the home of Werner Söderhjelm and spent Christmas Eve with him and his wife, and on this occasion played the Vieuxtemps *Ballade et Polonaise* for them. Writing to his sister Alma, Söderhjelm reported that 'Sibelius is working very diligently. We are extremely attached to him, he is richly endowed in talent, full of originality and imagination though somewhat lacking in restraint both in his thinking and in everyday life.' Undoubtedly his propensity to pay 10 marks for a theatre ticket appeared wildly extravagant to Söderhjelm who reprimanded his younger friend in no uncertain terms: 'You are too old now for your way of life to be excused as "impractical"; with your present attitude you will get nowhere.'

Sibelius's extravagance got him into trouble with Wegelius. On one occasion he asked him to see whether the Governor-General of Finland would use his good offices to secure complimentary tickets for the Royal Opera in Berlin as he was a state scholarship holder. Wegelius's reply shows some indignation: 'There is no reason why you should not content yourself with the seats that every other musician of your age is happy with; for 1.50 you should be able to get a seat where you can both see and hear.' This admonition however fell on deaf ears: it would never occur to Sibelius to get anything other than the best. Money was always to remain a vague and unreal concept for him. He had never had to earn his living in his youth although the bankruptcy that followed his father's death must have cast some shadows over life. He despised money but at the same time stood in some awe of it. 'Money is mere trash', he once informed a wealthy music-lover at the dinner table, having cheerfully accepted a donation from the same lady earlier in the day!

It was in Berlin that for the first time in his life he had relatively large sums at his disposal and it was his incapacity to handle them that threatened him with constant disaster. After being there for less than a month, he wrote to Wegelius: 'If I continue spending at my present rate I shall need an annual budget of 12,000 Reichsmark. Yesterday I went through my accounts and you can well imagine the shock it gave me.' Wegelius urged him to cut this figure down to 2,000, full knowing that he would not. Even allowing for the fact that his lessons with Becker cost 80 Reichsmark a month, he ought to have been able to live on half the amount he was spending. At least this was his brother's view, reasonable enough in all conscience, as he watched Jean's bills for restaurants, refreshments and the like, grow in alarming fashion. The first telegram appealing for funds arrived as early as the beginning of November and was followed by others that gave his mother and Aunt Evelina more than one sleepless night. Christian's studies also suffered. Between November and March, Jean's relatives borrowed from various sources more than 2,000 Finnmarks but when the time came to send the money to Berlin they realized that Sibelius had forgotten to give them his latest address. No wonder, then, that Christian should accuse him of an 'extraordinary lack of foresight' and sent him detailed suggestions as to how to manage his budget. He pointed out that many Finnish students who had gone to Berlin managed to live more cheaply there than in Helsinki! Christian entertained all sorts of anxieties as to his brother's way of life though the only thing he knew for certain was his bad financial straits. By March all sources of help were exhausted and even Christian's trousers had been sold!

Christian was constantly worried by the thought that his brother would lose further scholarships by sheer absent-mindedness; he wired Berlin asking him to fill in application forms. Becker wrote a supporting testimonial praising his pupil's 'diligence and progress', but Wegelius did not think it strong enough and Becker wrote another in which he testified that 'Herr J. Sibelius who has regularly attended all his lessons, has completed his studies in counterpoint and fugue with success and diligence and has begun the study of the other musical forms'.

In April Sibelius was awarded a further scholarship of 1,200 marks from Nylands Student Corporation, and their decision shows considerable liberality of outlook when one bears in mind the fact that Sibelius had never taken any academic qualification at the university. But even so, this did not solve Sibelius's financial troubles and in the following month even the long-suffering Christian grumbled, 'If you think about it, you have not written during the past two months about anything other than money; we know nothing of what you are doing and hearing or how you are enjoying life.' Sibelius had even entertained the notion of writing to Wegelius and explaining in detail his financial problems but thought better of it.

However money was not his only problem. At the beginning of November he told Wegelius: 'According to the doctor my health is "precarious" but I feel perfectly all right in myself. I am quite happy as long as that is the case. At times I become extremely melancholy.' Some days later he had to go into hospital but was soon on his feet again.

Sibelius had no reason to feel that his friends had forgotten him while he was in Berlin. In October Wegelius put two movements from his A minor Quartet into the Institute's hundredth concert, while in the following month *The Water-sprite* was given once again to mark Wegelius's birthday. Halvorsen, who was now teaching the violin at the Institute, spoke highly of the violin obligato in the Sibelius song. Busoni told Christian to say that he always thought of him and often spoke of him while Christian himself could report that he enjoyed much reflected glory. When he was invited to the Lerchés, Christian wrote, 'When one is *your* brother, one is treated royally.'

At the end of November Wegelius went abroad and in the course of his travels made a detour to Berlin for the express purpose of seeing Sibelius. He reported afterwards that his pupil had 'successfully mastered vocal polyphony and was conscientiously and energetically pursuing his broader musical and artistic studies.' In March he asked him to send in a choral piece for performance at one of the Institute's concerts. If, as it seems, Wegelius had little understanding of Sibelius's problems at this time, Busoni on the other hand, realized that Berlin was not the right place for him. In November, we learn from a letter that Aunt Evelina wrote to Sibelius, that Busoni was planning a visit to Berlin at Christmas, but he can hardly have been pleased, when he came, with his friend's development. Sibelius had no new work of any size to show him and the Bohemian way of life so energetically pursued by the Scandinavian circle as well as their pub-crawling could not have escaped his notice.

Busoni acted quickly: he insisted on Sibelius going with him to Leipzig where he was to play the Sinding Piano Quintet in E minor with the Brodsky Quartet. The whole incident must have reminded Sibelius, Strindbergian as he was, of Falck in *The Red Room* saved by Dr. Borg from the clutches of the newspaper hacks. Adolf Paul also went with them and neither he nor Sibelius had as much as a pfennig to their names at the time. Sibelius had spent his last coppers on a new top hat which he had bought in Sinding's honour and he wore it all the time in spite of the fact that it rained continuously throughout the eight days they were in Leipzig. Sinding's quintet was received with a mixture of cheers and boos but all were agreed on one thing: the Brodsky Quartet and Busoni had played magnificently. The concert gave Sibelius an incentive to write a piano quintet of his own; according to Paul he had toyed with the idea before his Leipzig trip and Busoni probably promised him to play the piano at its first performance. When they all returned to Berlin, Sibelius rather grandly made a present of his rain-soaked top hat to their taxi-driver and with this splendid gesture, the autumn's fallow period came to an end.

Busoni had other long-term plans for his friend and on his return to Helsinki suggested to his colleagues at the Institute that Sibelius should either study with Draeseke in Dresden or Bruckner in Vienna, and it was obviously on Busoni's advice that he abandoned Berlin in favour of Vienna in the following autumn.

In March Christian wrote to him suggesting that it would be 'a very good thing if you could write a splendid new work and have it performed here; there would be something in the newspapers about it and that would make a salutary impression on the authorities'. Wegelius intimated that he would be delighted to have a new quartet from him though if he had to write a quintet he should by all means do so. Needless to say Sibelius was anxious to show that he could write other things as well as string quartets and occupied himself for the best part of the spring term on the Piano Quintet.

After their trip to Leipzig Sibelius and Paul did not meet for a couple of months, doubtless to their mutual benefit. Paul was in the process of completing his metamorphosis from pianist to author and found his friend's absorption in his own world and reluctance to extend more than a certain measure of sympathy a source of irritation. Sibelius's refusal to be drawn into the problems of others was a necessary protective mechanism even though it was at times regarded as aloofness. Even in the most trying circumstances Sibelius would smile his most enigmatic smile, which infuriated his friends, and would seem to be transported into another world. But Paul was curious to know how the quintet was progressing and eventually made an effort to see him. He describes their reunion in his somewhat fustian way: 'I found him at the corner of the Potsdamerstrasse where he was standing by the bill-boards studying concert posters. He stood out from the rest of the crowd with his chequered suit and was good enough to recognize me, adding in all seriousness that it was generally thought that I had perished of starvation. He had searched the neighbouring lakes and waters for my body but in vain. As soon as he overcame his initial disappointment that there was no corpse and that I was still alive, he invited me to celebrate the great event; the great event being, not my return to the fold, but his new piano quintet. (There was never any question of his asking about my book!) Sibelius bought a bottle of wine which they took up to his room where he sat down at the piano without further ado and began improvising a slow, dream-like prelude from whose depths a pregnant musical idea gradually emerged. This dominated the proceedings, everything growing organically from it, while Sibelius fell into transports of inspiration. The piano almost literally trembled as the music swept over me; I had never heard him improvise so eloquently. This was his piano quintet in embryo whose birth-pangs I was witnessing. Suddenly he got up and began to pace the room shaking the ash from his half-smoked cigar so that it glowed, "I'll never finish it," he said with agitation, "I only squander my time at parties or idle the days away in complete inactivity," and then began to bewail his wasted life at great length so that the exalted mood which had given birth to this splendid music was swept aside in a wave of self-recrimination, certainly unjustified in one who loved his work so much.'

He finished the quintet in April and instead of sending each movement as and when it was ready, as Wegelius had suggested, he sent the whole work. But up until the very last minute he did not believe that it would be played. In a letter to Werner Söderhjelm who was on a visit to Italy, he wrote: 'You can well believe how I have felt since the realization struck me that my quintet is absolute rubbish. It remains to be seen whether it will be performed, at present it does not look as if it will, as Martin (Wegelius) said that rehearsal time was short, even though I sent it quite a long time ago. I think the work has disappointed them for their expectations were too great. I cannot compose anything decent at present though I am sure that I have something to say. Compose I must. I have a lot of new ideas about music which really does seem to be going downhill. I am sure you have the same feeling.'

Sibelius's misgivings were at least partly unfounded. There was not enough time to prepare a five-movement work but then it was by no means certain that Wegelius ever planned to put on the work in its entirety. Busoni was not particularly happy with the second movement, the intermezzo, and the fourth movement, the one in waltz rhythm, was run through in Wegelius's presence and the latter mentioned to Sibelius in his letter 'We did not care for it.' They do not appear to have looked at the finale at all.

Busoni and the Institute's Quartet played the first and third movements at a concert on 5 May and they scored a distinct success. Busoni himself described the first movement as 'wunderschön', and his only criticism concerned some passages where the keyboard layout was ineffective. Halvorsen was impressed by the brilliant violin writing and asked Christian whether his brother had written a violin concerto. Wegelius had mixed feelings: on the surface he appeared highly satisfied and even summoned all the Institute's pupils to an extra rehearsal of the two movements, but in a letter to Sibelius he did not spare him his tongue: 'The first movement is admittedly impressive in its structure, but not in other respects. Don't misunderstand me: there are passages that have both imagination and technique, but looking at it as a whole, the movement is clumsy. First and foremost, it is badly laid out for the instruments and does not come off: because (1) the piano writing is bad, (2) you use the upper register of the cello—one misses bass support in the texture throughout the movement; even when the four strings are on their own it does not sound as it should. There are too many awkwardly written passages—above all at the very end. Furthermore: there is no flow—just one section tacked on to another. Finally, one is not sure for a large part of the time whether the character of the movement is an allegro or a grave; the tempo is not sufficiently defined in character. I ought in fairness to say that the first movement has *interested* a lot of people—it has also interested me. Hanna says that she thinks it may be a little autobiographical; *à la bonheur*—but that sort of autobiography has no appeal for me: a composer ought to keep his gropings to himself; only when he has succeeded in finding something in his search worthy of the name of Art.'

Wegelius's critique was anything but constructive. In any case Sibelius had not groped in the dark but had found something of substance. Even Karl Flodin who once again wrote of Sibelius's 'thematic sterility', was impressed by the work's seriousness and ardour. But Wegelius was doubtless soured by

Jean, Christian and Linda Sibelius in 1877

Jean Sibelius in 1888

the fact that Sibelius had chosen to ignore his advice: 'I told you at the very beginning that I had my doubts about the quintet—and with good reason. . . . That the quintet was a hazardous experiment for so poor a pianist as you, was something that you refused to believe.'

But Wegelius went still further: 'Originality does not consist of all our curious whims and fancies; on the contrary the real self emerges only when one is free of them.' Wegelius seems to have discerned something of Sibelius's 'real self' in the third movement of the quintet which is more Viennese classical than the first. It did not occur to him that an essential part of Sibelius's individuality would have disappeared with the 'curious whims and fancies'. But Sibelius was quite capable of taking care of himself in his dealings with Wegelius.

The G minor Quintet explores much the same area of feeling as the unfinished G minor String Trio. In that respect the choice of the same key is significant even though the outer movements of the quintet have greater astringency and a more Nordic character than anything in the somewhat Tchaikovskian trio. There are, too, parallels with the Sinding Quintet in E minor: both works make use of the Aeolian mode in their introductory bars and the main idea in the Sibelius is closely related in rhythm with the second subject of the Sinding. Both works have a waltz-like scherzo and the idea of calling his second movement, Intermezzo, was obviously suggested by Sinding's example. Sibelius's piano writing with its thick chords, tremolo, chromatic scales and accompanying figures also reminds one of Sinding, though it is by no means as successful in its layout. Finally, both composers follow the cyclic principle by returning in the finale to the motive from the first movement. However, for all the similarities, the Sibelius has much greater character of style.

The first movement begins with a highly charged introduction: over bare fifths in the piano the strings outline an idea whose rhythm anticipates that of the clarinet introduction of the First Symphony. The pregnant, detached phrases separated by rests, even momentarily suggest a much later work, namely the opening pages of *Tapiola*. The main theme grows organically out of the introduction and is first heard in the piano part while the strings have a pizzicato countersubject:

Ex. 28

The rhythmic pattern of the main theme recurs in some form or other through-out the movement and the counter-subject is to play an important part par-ticularly in the final climax. Sibelius tends to think in terms of germinal seeds rather than finished themes.

The second subject is introduced on the viola by a short chromatic descent:

Ex. 29

The right-hand line in the piano gives the impression of being at one and the same time Sibelian and national. Without ever being directly influenced by folk music, a composer can absorb the varying shifting moods of the landscape, its intangible atmosphere, the intonation of his countrymen's language as well as their temperament, and in so doing succeed in creating a style that never directly has recourse to folk melody. It is in this sense that one can speak of this passage having a certain national colour. Of course, it is not always easy to draw the dividing line between the personal and the national elements in a composer's style, for by soaking himself in the atmosphere of a country, the composer can develop a personal style which afterwards serves as a model for a national music. To a large extent this was the case with Sibelius and Finland.

In the development Sibelius combines the rhythm of the first subject with the chromatic contour that introduced the second:

Ex. 30

He builds up new melodic ideas in much the same way in, for example, the development section of the Second Symphony.

Of the other movements it is the Andante that probably best rewards attention: it has two contrasting themes, the first of which has a hymn-like character (evocative of Schubert's *Der Tod und das Mädchen*):

Ex. 31

The second is in a march rhythm:

Ex. 32

At the end of the movement the two themes are combined. The finale is not without merit and has a certain fire, but the seams in its structure are all too visible. In the coda a variant of the original idea turns up in E minor but we are plunged directly into G minor with the theme in its original form:

Ex. 33

The tension between minor keys a third apart, which is incidentally also characteristic of Strauss, builds up a powerful climax.

The first and third movements of the quintet are in my view the most convincing expressions of *Sturm und Drang* in his early work and Wegelius was not far off the mark when he detected an autobiographical element in the first. The rest of the quintet does not really live up to these, though it cannot be denied that it has in places a certain rough-hewn monumental quality to commend it.

In May Sibelius applied for another State Scholarship and Becker wrote yet a third testimonial, at least four times the length of the one before. From this document it transpires that Sibelius had written fugues for chorus and orchesrta and that in connection with this he had studied a certain amount of orchestration. But Becker emphasized that Sibelius had not been able to develop his individuality or his national style in this form but that the time would soon be ripe for him to abandon this strict discipline in favour of free forms. 'It is a pleasure to record that Herr Sibelius who, up to now has been only able to show his diligence as a pupil, has an original talent which, when it has matured as the result of further studies, excites high expectations.' The good relationship that Sibelius had eventually established with Becker had continued. During the spring, Becker had composed an oratorio in honour of the memory of Kaiser Wilhelm I which according to one critic was 'a hotchpotch of watered-down Mendelssohn, undigested Brahms and misunderstood Wagner'. Evidently

Sibelius had helped correct the proofs and possibly helped also with the actual composition. But one can well question his suitability as Sibelius's teacher and doubtless the pupil parted from him in the firm conviction that he would never return.

In June Sibelius once again alarmed his relatives with news of a relapse in his health. His mother and Aunt Evelina wept, Christian telegraphed his brother, without being sure of the address, and sent him money. At the same time he could give Jean the good news that he had been awarded a further scholarship of 2,000 Finnmarks for the next academic year. After his uncle Pehr's death in January 1890, Aunt Evelina who had herself undergone an operation for cancer, moved back to Lovisa where, in preparation for Jean's return, everything in the old house was made tidy and comfortable. Christian urged his brother to come home as soon as the doctor allowed him to travel: 'Here in Lovisa everything is as it was, the grass slopes are as green and rich in foliage as they ever were, everything is as peaceful and everyone has become so old.' And so in the early summer Sibelius returned from Berlin to his childhood paradise.

CHAPTER FIVE

Vienna: 1890–1

O N HIS return from Berlin Sibelius convalesced for a while at Lovisa before going on, a little later in the summer, to spend some time with Wegelius at Granholmen. Thence he made his way to Ätsäri where the Järnefelts were staying and to Aino who impatiently counted the days to his arrival. But alas, Sibelius was held up by a severe August storm and only arrived on the very same day she was due to leave for Vasa. She had already taken her place on the train when she saw him get out of his compartment on the opposite platform. But they later met at Vasa itself in the Governor's residence to which the Järnefelt brothers invited their friend. After the affair with Betsy Lerché, relations between Sibelius and Aino were a little delicate. During the summer they made music together, he playing the violin and she the piano, but her brothers were a little worried that old wounds might be reopened. Some six months later Sibelius wrote to her about this visit, 'When I left Vasa and you were all assembled on the station platform I whispered something to Armas, as perhaps you will remember. But he did not pass on my message which was to thank you for our musical evenings together. Armas told me that he did not want you to think about me. This was the first time I had understood that you had never really forgotten me. I left Vasa in a strange, half-demented mood . . . when I came down and saw you in the hall that last afternoon, I saw you had tears in your eyes. I loved you already at that time, in a strange sort of way, but I would not have been able to say so for a million marks.'

Only a month later he plucked up courage and did so. He had met Aino at one of the Institute's musical evenings in Helsinki and after the concert he escorted her back home. At the door Sibelius proposed to her and she accepted him. 'When afterwards I had you in my arms, I thought that you were the ideal that I would myself like to attain.'

The following night Aino read the manuscript of Juhani Aho's short story 'Yksin' ('Alone') in which Aho writes of his unrequited love for her. If it was intended to influence her in his favour it came too late, for when she returned to Vasa, Sibelius had her train compartment bestrewn with flowers.

*   *   *

Sibelius himself returned to Lovisa for a few days in September where he completed his String Quartet in B flat. This first saw the light of day at a concert the following month in Helsinki, on 13 October 1890 when it was given by the Institute's Quartet led by Johan Halvorsen. In his review Karl Flodin spoke of the new work showing the stamp of its young composer's personality in every bar. It is closer in spirit to the F major Violin Sonata than to the more sombre G minor Trio or the Piano Quintet. While in the quintet, Sibelius works with a small germinal cell that provides the basis for subsequent growth, the string quartet unfolds in long-spun lyrical shapes. The main theme has a classical triadic shape with a pentatonic touch in its very first bar:

Ex. 34

By way of contrast the second subject is more chromatic and craggy:

Ex. 35

A dotted rhythm is taken up in the development with an insistence that recalls late Beethoven or Schumann and there is a short passage in F sharp minor, *più lento*, which shows that Sibelius had not forgotten his love of Tchaikovsky. The development builds up to a climax which signals the reprise and at this point the writing is more orchestral in character. The Andante movement opens in lyrical fashion rather like a Finnish folk melody though perhaps more sophisticated in character:

Ex. 36

The long-sustained note with which the waltz-theme of the scherzo opens is characteristic of Sibelius's melodic style:

Ex. 37

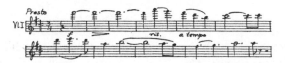

The layout of the texture is again reminiscent of orchestral rather than chamber music:

Ex. 38

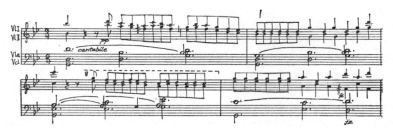

Over the cello support, the viola has a broad cantilena line while first and second violins move in parallel thirds, much in the same way as do the woodwind in the symphonies. The main theme of the rondo calls for uninhibited playing; its rhythm:

Ex. 39

anticipates the finale of the Violin Concerto where it is of course far more effectively developed; another similarity is the idea of repeating the phrase in a higher octave.

The B flat Quartet is undoubtedly a more consummate work than the G minor Piano Quintet even if one misses some of the bolder touches of the first movement of the latter.

Perhaps Sibelius may have been influenced by Wegelius's somewhat harsh criticism of the quintet and it was more than just politeness that prompted Sibelius to tell him that he had played a greater part in the genesis of the quartet than the composer himself. Even if the quartet does not in any sense anticipate the orchestral music of the 1890s inspired by the *Kalevala* or the First Symphony, its light texture and classical proportions gives a foretaste of subsequent stylistic developments. In any event it is the only chamber work from these student years that Sibelius eventually dignified with an opus number.

One October morning in 1890 he set out for Vienna and was seen off at the station by Martin and Hanna Wegelius, Arvid Järnefelt's wife Emmy, and a host of other friends. The fact that he was travelling 'third class so as to economize' did not fail to make its effect on them for his extravagance was by now known to be prodigious. He had told only a few close friends of his secret engagement, though most of his circle found in him a greater maturity and assurance. While he was waiting at Hangö for the ferry to Lübeck, he sat down and wrote his first letter to Aino as a fiancée: 'Your father evidently sensed that there was something between us as his attitude was chilly when we said good-bye. Do you think that he knows we are in love? Not that it concerns anyone apart from you and me.' As had at first been the case with Becker, Sibelius was quick to misinterpret other people's manner. Järnefelt was ageing and was uncommunicative and reserved on this occasion: there is no reason to imagine that he was unduly chilly or distant. Like all the other letters written before their marriage, this was in Swedish 'as it does not take five minutes to write out each word' but none the less he asked his fiancée to reply in Finnish. Evidently his school Finnish was getting rusty since he also wrote in Swedish to Armas Järnefelt although he knew the family only spoke Finnish at home.

On his way to Vienna Sibelius dropped off in Berlin for a few days to see his old set of friends who had now added to their numbers two newcomers, Carl Nielsen and Aino's brother, Armas. The two great Northern composers probably met at a dinner given by Adolf Paul's patron, Dahlberg, but Sibelius was not in good form on this occasion and struck his companions as far too earnest to be good company! As far as Sibelius was concerned, Berlin had lost what little lustre it had: 'I could not work here,' he wrote to Aino, 'the place seems worse than ever.' His first impression of Vienna however augured well for the coming year; 'This is a place after my own heart; it has gaiety and light . . . the air intoxicates me and my head echoes with the sound of waltz tunes all of them like Schubert's.' If the atmosphere of the city banished any lingering melancholy, its air was not the only thing that intoxicated him. He visited the Esterházy cellars and explored their delights with enthusiasm.

But as far as his studies were concerned Sibelius's arrival had not been properly prepared. Recalling his own bitter experiences of the Austro-Hungarian capital, Busoni had written a letter of recommendation to Brahms but had some difficulty in explaining why its bearer had not more to show for his age, '*Seiner nordischen Herkunft gemäss ist er später entwickelt als wir.*' It was hardly wise to write to Brahms in these terms for by the time he was twenty-one he had three piano sonatas, the D minor Piano Concerto, and much else besides, to his credit. In any event Brahms did not bother with pupils at this stage in his life and Sibelius would have had no chance of acceptance. Bruckner had just been granted an honorary pension and withdrew more and more from the world. Sibelius wrote home to Aino that he was 'mortally ill'. Eventually Hans Richter agreed to see him and was very friendly but referred him to Robert Fuchs, who taught composition at the Conservatoire where he was professor. Sibelius wired home to Wegelius for advice and his reply was a letter of introduction to Karl Goldmark, who after the success of his opera, *The Queen of Sheba*, was an international celebrity. Sibelius laid siege to Goldmark's house for several days without gaining admittance though on one occasion he thought he heard the great man 'screaming and carrying on in an inner room'. Eventually on 12 November, he was admitted to the Presence: Goldmark received him in his dressing-gown and stockinged feet. Presumably Sibelius's demeanour and bearing had as much effect as Wegelius's letter of introduction since the great man agreed to go through his compositions and give him advice even though, as he did not fail to point out, he had not taken any pupils for many years. Sibelius had with him the B flat Quartet but Goldmark did not so much as glance at it.

His first piece of advice to his young Finnish pupil was to go through some orchestral scores of Mozart studying in particular his clarinet writing and the relation it bore with the rest of the orchestra. He himself had apparently been given this advice earlier in his career by Anton Rubinstein. Otherwise he was far too eclectic himself to want to influence Sibelius in any special stylistic direction.

One of the first things Sibelius did in Vienna was to go to *Don Giovanni* at the Opera which he enjoyed so much that he could not sleep and sat up the whole night sketching out a violin concerto. He wrote a couple of songs, 'Hjärtats morgon' ('The Heart's Morning') and 'Likhet' ('Resemblance'), both of them settings of Runeberg 'in whose poetry' he wrote, 'I find a greater sense of reality and truth than in the work of any other poet I have read up to the present.' He wrote an orchestral overture for Goldmark consisting of some thirty-eight pages of score in the course of a week and showed it to his teacher on 19 November. He describes the lesson in a letter to Wegelius the self-same day: 'I have just come back from Goldmark. Had written an overture. It was '*manches Schlechte und manches Gute, als Anfang ganz gut*'. My handling of the orchestra was quite correct apart from one place when the flutes were a little too wild. After this he criticized the piece itself in more detail. I was there half-an-hour in all. He wrote a note testifying that I had begun my studies. I say, he has a damned good reputation here in Vienna and as his pupil I enjoy great prestige everywhere. This is the kind of education after my own heart.'

Sibelius was as much impressed by his teacher's shrewd Jewish intellect as by his agreeable manner. He was very much an *homme du monde*, though capable of uncompromising frankness, but he was not a teacher in the real meaning of the word. He showed the general direction in which he wanted his pupil to work and evidently did not worry too much about details of craftsmanship. Therefore Sibelius followed Richter's advice and enrolled at the Conservatoire as a pupil of Robert Fuchs. He explained in a rather apologetic letter to Wegelius why he had decided to go to two masters: 'I came to realize that I need a more thorough kind of teaching than Goldmark gives. Fuchs is a highly skilled orchestrator, a professional to his finger tips, and is also a successful composer. But above all, he can easily get works performed because of his influence with Jakob Grün who is quite a power in the *Tonkünstlerverein*.' It seems from this as if Sibelius was trying to disarm possible criticism by holding out the prospect of a performance of the B flat major Quartet in Vienna. Fuchs himself was a modest and unassuming person of great integrity whose orchestral serenades had earned him an international reputation at that time. Before Sibelius, his pupils had included Wolf and Mahler and afterwards were to number not only Schoenberg's teacher Zemlinsky, but Franz Schreker and Franz Schmidt. Sibelius did not record in any detail the course of his lessons with Fuchs and his comments were merely confined to saying whether his work had met with approval or not. Everything suggests that he was more conservative in outlook and more subtle in his tastes than was Goldmark and he was undoubtedly a skilful contrapuntist and a fine craftsman with great feeling for detail.

Sibelius took up the violin once again even if he does not appear to have taken any formal lessons: 'I have begun to play the violin again even if I am too nervous to be a really good player; besides my gifts in that direction are limited but it might be a useful accomplishment in the future.' Undoubtedly he hoped that should the need arise, he would be able to earn his living as a violin teacher or an orchestral player. Conducting was another possibility that crossed his mind and as a long-term objective the possibility of succeeding Faltin in charge of musical activities at the university was a distant but attractive prospect. In any event the violin seemed to him the best solution to his immediate and short-term problems. 'I practise every day,' he told Aino, 'If only I could pluck up enough courage to play in Helsinki in a year or so.' All this planning was to one end and one end only; to make a good enough living to set up house with Aino. Sibelius doubtless recalled, perhaps with a touch of bitterness, a toast that Armas Järnefelt had proposed when they were at a party together in Berlin in which he had said, 'I hope that in three years or so Sibelius will be worthy of my sister.'

In Vienna he joined the Conservatoire Orchestra which Robert Fuchs conducted and returned from its rehearsals with a headache and the out-of-tune chords he had heard ringing in his head. Working in Fuchs's orchestra gave him a healthy foretaste of what life would be like were he ever to be an orchestral player. He met many new people, 'for the most part conservatoire students, self-important and conceited, with long hair and shabby trousers'. Among others he met Carl Frühling, later to become well-known as an accompanist in Vienna, the violinist Christoph, the Hungarian pianist Arpád László, who insisted on playing him his very Hungarian compositions which bored Sibelius to tears, and the Rumanian cellist, Dinicu who subsequently made a name for himself in his home country. Sibelius seems to have enjoyed their company for Aino seems to have received many cards with chivalrous greetings scrawled on the back from the various wine parlours they conscientiously explored. He broadened his knowledge of the orchestra by making friends among other musicians than string players and asking them to demonstrate their instruments. 'Yesterday', he wrote to Wegelius on 11 January 1891, 'I was at Heber's—he is an oboist—and he played to me for about three hours on his cor anglais so that I now feel I know the instrument's potentialities inside out.' The benefit he derived from this can be seen as early as the same spring in his *Ballet Scene* and, of course, a few years later in 'The Swan of Tuonela'.

Even if Sibelius's first weeks in Vienna were not wholly untroubled, for Goldmark had been elusive, his spirits were high. Hence the gloomy tone of his letter of 21 November comes as a surprise: he writes to Wegelius: 'It is as if I have lost my sense of direction. What is happening to me? I have the feeling that there is someone standing behind me all the time. Perhaps it is Death calling? More likely it is only a reaction after the intoxicating first encounter with Vienna. But take no notice, I am only talking rubbish.' A clue to the reason why Sibelius should find himself off balance comes at the end of the same letter when he writes '*Tristan und Isolde* was mounted here at the Opera in so brilliant a fashion that I would not have conceived it possible.' He was undoubtedly disturbed by *Tristan* even if its impact was not as strong on this occasion as it was to be in Munich three years later when he was in the middle of his own *Kalevala* music drama. For music students in the 1880s and 1890s *Tristan* was as much of a shock as, say, Stravinsky's *Le Sacre du Printemps* for the generation between the two world wars. Sibelius now wrestled with his 'extremly difficult' composition exercises. 'I've now composed three, yes *three* full scores and torn them all up,' he told Wegelius, 'but still I shall get it right in the end; perhaps the tenth or the thirteenth attempt will be successful. I often tear up my musical ideas though not without tears.' Goldmark himself was far too absorbed in his own work to see Sibelius who had to content himself with a few words with the great man now and again. In January Sibelius wrote home to Wegelius full of indignation: 'The only thing he had to say about a movement of a symphony that I showed him was "die Themen kommen nicht zur Geltung". Nothing else whatever. You can see that now while I am at the beginner's level in orchestration, I need a teacher who is less of a genius. Three weeks ago he took it into his head to re-work a Cello Sonata and said, "My dear boy, please don't come near me for another month" and added "bringen Sir mir dann etwas fertiges und tüchtiges." And of course I will.'

In his letters to Aino written in the autumn of 1890 one can detect a steady growing interest in everything Finnish, not only the *Kalevala* and other aspects of Finnish culture, but the language itself. He asks her to write in Finnish whose musical qualities appealed strongly to him. He writes to her of his plans for future compositions: 'I have in my mind two contrasting moods which I want to develop naturally and logically as well as to make them more intense and highly defined. I am going to use a large orchestra and am trying to aim for greater realism than I have ever done before. In the world around us there is also music: it must be hewn from its source and put to use. I am glad that you like Finnish and all things Finnish: this I well understand.'

Two days later on Boxing Day, he wrote: 'I am reading the *Kalevala* a lot and am already beginning to understand much more Finnish. The *Kalevala* strikes me as extraordinarily modern and to my ears is pure music, themes and variations; its story is far less important than the moods and atmosphere conveyed: the gods are human beings, Väinämöinen is a musician, and so on.'

Sibelius, it would seem, associates the Finnish language and folk music, and his own melodic style has some affinities with the speech rhythms and intonation of the language. Among them is the absence of an upbeat, the generally frequent appearance of spondaic and dactylic rhythms, the descending fifths that occur at the end of a phrase and the habit of beginning an idea on a long sustained note and ending with a descending suffix. The parallels are obvious: in Finnish the accent is on the first syllable of a word, the intonation tends to fall and in a sentence of normal length it first rises always to fall at the end. The way words are built, too, offers an analogy: one long single syllable is the basic word to which a variety of modifying syllables (case-endings and suffixes) are added.

However this is not an analogy that should be pressed too far. To begin with, it is difficult to discern whether Sibelius's melodies can have been inspired by the language or by folk music. Moreover, one must remember that Sibelius's imaginative world and his whole outlook was to a great extent moulded by his Swedish mother-tongue. When he is setting a Swedish text, one encounters the same melodic characteristics that are attributed to the influence of Finnish, though yet another qualifying factor is that the Swedish, as spoken in Finland, is influenced in its pronunciation by Finnish. At all events the whole question of Sibelius's melodic style and its relationship to language is complex.

Sibelius's description of the *Kalevala* as 'theme and variations' refers to the poetic form of the runes, and possibly to the way in which the runic incantation was endlessly repeated and varied. Sibelius was clearly fascinated by the supernatural element in the poem, which is not a narrative epic in the same sense as the *Iliad*, the *Odyssey* or the *Nibelungenlied*. When he speaks of the

tory being less important than the mood and that the narrative plays a subservient role to the evocation of atmosphere, he might be speaking of his own
composing methods at this time. In November 1890 he wrote to Aino: 'I am
in the middle of a new orchestral piece. I have several ideas but am not satisfied
with any of them. I have the general mood and atmosphere very clearly in
my head but its expression is not yet properly defined.' The atmosphere he
found in the *Kalevala* was gradually to assume a defined musical expression
and with it a national music style was slowly to form.

Vienna, the hub of the Austro-Hungarian Empire, was the meeting place of
many different nationalities; Austrians, Bohemians, Hungarians, Italians, Croats
etc. The atmosphere was conducive as much to a synthesis of these diverse
cultural elements as it was, paradoxically enough, to a refinement of national
self-consciousness.

In Goldmark Sibelius saw the synthesis of various stylistic elements, while in
Fuchs he had the Viennese classical tradition with a strong emphasis on the
Austrian folk element and a touch of Schumann's dreaminess. Among Sibelius's
friends Dinicu represented a country with yet untapped riches of folk music,
and the day before Christmas Eve, he visited him and wrote down several
Finnish folk tunes or melodies of his own based on folk models which made
a great impression on the Rumanian. Presumably Dinicu played some of his
home country's folk music on the cello and this contact may well have served
to stimulate further his awareness of the national in music.

Sibelius regularly attended the Vienna Philharmonic Subscription concerts
which were conducted by Hans Richter. The first concert of the autumn
season took place in November when Grieg's Piano Concerto was given.
Rather late in the day, Grieg had just become fashionable in Vienna and
Sibelius had a chance to hear the most Scandinavian of composers in the most
Viennese of all settings. But a concert on 21 December offered a contemporary
work which was to fire his enthusiasm: the Symphony No. 3, in D minor
of Bruckner which was given in the presence of the composer and in its revised
form. Sibelius wrote to his fiancée immediately after the concert: 'Today I went
to a concert. There, a composer Bruckner was booed. To my mind he is
the greatest of all living composers; perhaps you remember Martin W. speaking about it. After the concert was over, his admirers carried him to his coach
and there was much cheering and general commotion. It was his D minor
Symphony (No. 3) that was played and you cannot imagine the enormous
impression it has made on me. It has its shortcomings like anything else but
above all it has a youthful quality even though its composer is an old man.
From the point of view of form it is [?] ridiculous.'

The struggle between the Wagnerians and the supporters of Brahms still
raged though after the death of Wagner, it was Bruckner who bore the brunt
of Hanslick's attacks. At this particular concert Bruckner's admirers were so
numerous that he was called on to the platform to acknowledge applause

between movements! Sibelius was incautious enough to declare his hand i
front of a group of Brahmsians. 'After the concert we were together with som
other musicians and you can't imagine how heated our exchange became. A
the height of the argument there was a scuffle in which my foot was hurt, an
now I limp a little. Musicians are really a dreadful lot.'

Three days before this concert Sibelius wrote to Wegelius, 'It is as if th
Devil has got into me. I cannot find what I am looking for and everything
that I have written up to now and all my other efforts strike me as puerile. . .
I could cheerfully burn up everything I have done with the exception of the
quartet, which I have no right to do since you had a hand in it, perhaps a
greater part of it than I. Just at the moment I feel like setting about Brahms
I am clenching my fists in my pocket.' A few weeks later he got to know
the F major String Quintet of Brahms and Busoni's violin sonata and though
them both beneath criticism. 'I do not understand how they manage to get
these and works like them published.' During the spring the Opera gave
Siegfried and the work made a powerful impression on him and prompted
him to enroll in the Wagner Society.

After some months in Vienna, Sibelius began to find his feet and gained
some self-confidence. Already in the autumn he had sent his quartet to the
Leipzig publisher, Kistner, but it had been rejected. His friend, Christoph
brought him and the other members of his quartet together; he was the second
violin, and the leader, Alois Rosenberg became a staunch friend. With the
other members of the group Sibelius had the opportunity of showing his
prowess as a chamber music player and was evidently highly thought of. He
now set about trying to get his quartet performed first in the Conservatoire
and then in the *Tonkünstlerverein*. He knew full well that a composer as young
as he, and from so remote and unknown a country, would be looked at with
some suspicion and that his style was in any event too advanced for conservative
Viennese taste. But his determination emerges in his letter to Wegelius of
18 December: 'One gets nowhere in this city unless one engages in intrigue.
I have already started and have sought out the friendship of Frühling, among
others, and he knows everyone there is to know. Next spring I shall get myself
into the Vienna Artists' Club and then I shall start to intrigue, to lie and to
make myself affable. I have had practice at this before.'

His intrigues were confined however, to asking Fuchs to recommend him
for membership of the *Tonkünstlerverein*. In addition to this he had hopes of
joining the Vienna Philharmonic and at the turn of the year practised much
more than usual. On 8 January he called on Professor Grün and they agreed
that he should be auditioned on the following day. He found Grün very stiff
and formal, and so froze himself. Both men were obviously on their guard
to be polite and correct. The day after, Sibelius made his entry on to the stage
of the Vienna Opera, walked towards the footlights and began to play, first
for Grün alone, and then for his colleagues on the Opera Board. After that he
took part in an orchestral rehearsal.

The very fact that Grün did not send him packing at once shows that his
application was taken seriously, but it was more than two years since he had
played in public and gradually he began to lose his nerve. After about an hour
he began to feel sick and his body started to tremble, the metallic taste in his
mouth returned and he felt as if he would faint at any moment. Grün's verdict
was that he had played 'gar nicht schlecht' but he tried to dissuade him from
becoming a violinist on account of his nerves. His advice was to concentrate
on the piano as he was, after all, a composer. It is not clear whether Sibelius
had wanted to join the Philharmonic only for the spring term as a means of
supplementing his scholarship and of gaining both experience and prestige or
whether he really entertained the idea of becoming a permanent member of
the orchestra. In any case he had seen enough of the constant grind of rehearsals and performances to judge how his composing would have fared, so
that the outcome of his audition was a cause for congratulations. But when
he got back to his room Sibelius broke down and wept. Afterwards he sat
at the piano and began to practise his scales.

Even so far as the B flat Quartet was concerned, Grün proved to be a stum-
bling block; Sibelius had naïvely interpreted some polite phrases of interest
as binding promises and was bitterly disappointed when no performance
transpired. To Aino he quoted liberally from K. A. Tavaststjerna's poem
'Reserve': 'I have forged a heart of Reason and it cannot weep', adding that
he himself has no more tears, and could weep on that very count. Suddenly he
was overwhelmed by a sense of isolation and the heaviness of spirit to which
the Scandinavian sensibility is prone and which is so striking a contrast with the
Viennese *Gemütligkeit*. 'The Germans say that pessimism comes from Russia and
the Scandinavian countries, and just now I am inclined to agree with them.'

The North was a vague geographical concept in the eyes of his student companions. They took him to be a countryman of Grieg's and when Svendsen's
singularly feeble Octet was given in Vienna during the spring he was at the
receiving end of one or two derisive gibes. The only person to side with him
was Alois Rosenberg, but in a way Sibelius was quite happy to find himself
pitted against the pack, and to feel 'alone against them all'. Rosenberg's quartet
rehearsed Sibelius's quartet on two occasions; on the first they sight-read it.
'They were so pleased with it that they were quite taken aback. I was thrilled
to the depths of my being. They were quite exhausted afterwards, though
naturally they had some savage criticisms to make.' At the second rehearsal
Sibelius himself played the second violin part, and afterwards the ensemble
gave a party in his honour. Sibelius fell into a strange mood that night and
was overcome by a feeling almost of solemnity: 'It was as if someone had
rewarded me for all the suffering I had undergone in life.'

The day after New Year's Day he wrote to his fiancée but without developing his ideas on music and speaking of his work only in passing. There is

nothing special about the letter; he speaks of this and that, and nothing in particular, but we quote the letter complete as it gives us a good picture of his day-to-day life at this time.

My own Aino darling,

Thank you for your letter and your Christmas cards. Your relatives have all been very kind to me. Please give them my respects and thank them most warmly, won't you. But it is you, who love me more than anyone else has done, and I want you to be sure that I love you and belong to you with all my heart. Every time you write to me I discover some new aspect of your personality. It makes me feel as if you are a store of treasures to which only I have the key, and you can imagine how proud I am to own it. You are so natural and sincere, which I like. When in the future we have a home of our own and are together alone we must never be anything other than wholly ourselves, natural, tender towards each other, and devoted. I think and hope that you will be content with me in this respect. It is perhaps unmanly to say so but, you know, Aino, that I have always wanted to be caressed and have always missed its absence. At home I was the only one who was demonstrative and this in spite of the fact that I was basically very shy. But up to now only you have caressed me and perhaps you have thought it tiresome of me to ask you often to do this, my darling. This could well have remained unwritten but as I am writing as quickly as I am thinking (hence my superb handwriting!) and this came into my head, it can just as well go into the letter. I sometimes cannot believe that a person like you loves me, for you are a wonderful woman.

You must always be quite open and candid. You can never be too open for you never need to blush even for your most inward thoughts. When your heart is overflowing and there is no one to whom you can speak openly, write to me for you will never find me lacking in understanding. I understand you very well.

At the moment I am working out some first-class ideas and I think the results will turn out well. I work more slowly than I used to with the result that I think over what I do more carefully. A friend of mine called a moment ago and gave me a ticket for tonight's concert: he is my best friend here and his name is Alois Rosenberg. He leads a quartet—you remember him. My room is rather large and has two windows and a high ceiling. In the middle of the room there is a grand piano on which all my music is piled in a mountainous heap. The furniture consists of two easy-chairs and a sofa that has seen better days. Between the windows there is a small mirror which together with the washstand is the most handsome thing in the room. Besides this there are two cupboards, three tables and a wicker chair, which I have bought to harden myself to discomfort. On the fireplace there is a clay picture of a saint. The room faces on to an inner courtyard and the house has five storeys. My first meal of the day is at 12 noon and I take my evening meal at seven. It is cold here and I use up a lot of fuel. One can go to a coffee house and sit there over a cup of coffee reading the papers for about two hours without having to feel in the least obliged to have anything else. You cannot get Finnish newspapers here but I see some news from Finland in the Swedish press. You must not die as long as I live and nor will you. For you cannot possibly believe that having learnt to know you I would ever be happy with anybody else. I cannot resist the temptation of sending you my mother's letter and excerpts from my sister's. They got your cards yesterday as we thought they would. Do not think for a moment that my mother would be offended by my sending you her letter; so that you can make sense of the first sentence I had better explain that my letters home have often only been about three lines long. You know what mothers are like. I enclose all my sister's letter. Do you think she has been in love with the lieutenant whose marriage she mentions? Please do not ever discuss the subject with her.

I am feeling very well at the moment. On New Year's Eve I went on the razzle with some friends and had, of course, a 'divine' time. We toasted you often, perhaps too much, as you can imagine. Congratulate Arvid from me on his becoming a judge and give my respects to your lovable mother. Your Christmas cards are very handsome and I am ashamed that I didn't send any myself but I hope, my own darling, that my letter to you arrived in good time. My summer plans are not yet decided but you are marvellous people to have invited me to come to you. Look after your health and be of good cheer. Dreams often mean their opposite. Don't forget your own

Janne

Please give my love to Emmy (Arvid Järnefelt's wife) and thank her for her greetings.

Sibelius often assumed different roles in his dealings with different people, even roles that were out of character, but in this letter he was his true self even at the risk of seeming unmanly. His craving for tenderness and some demonstration of affection had never met with much response from his mother who recoiled into her shell at any show of feeling. Aino on the other hand met this need and in her he sought a sanctuary from his inner doubts and the nervous tensions of his daily struggles. He wrote to her earlier in the autumn, 'You are already closer to me, my darling one, than either my mother or sister.' Sibelius's vulnerability and insecurity may partly be due to the absence of a father figure in childhood. Even as a student in Helsinki he had lived with his mother and family and it was only in Berlin that he had to stand on his own two feet and try and make his own way in the world. His engagement to Aino gave him a certain stability. In his letter he touches briefly on his sister's lot: Linda was a considerate and motherly person and ner highly nervous disposition does not appear to have been attracted to the opposite sex, for she was to remain a lonely figure throughout her life.

In time Sibelius began to live like a genuine Viennese. Along with all the other music students he frequented the gallery at the Opera where standing room cost only 40 kreuzer. He was sent into transports by the playing of the Helmersberger Quartet and delighted by Patti's brilliant coloratura singing though he was put off by her poor taste and artificial appearance. He saw Goethe's *Egmont* given with Beethoven's incidental music which he liked, even though he could not bring himself to admire the German style of acting: 'They have to put so much intensity into everything, even into something quite insignificant', he wrote to Aino. But the opening words of Klärchen's monologue, *freudvoll und leidvoll*, imprinted themselves on his memory. On another evening he had gone to a French operetta with some young first-year art students and their models. 'One of them had with him a large bottle of wine which he passed round to everyone. The opera began seriously enough but by the end everyone was dancing the can-can. I enjoyed myself hugely.' He heard Johann Strauss conducting his own waltzes and on one occasion had dinner with Berté, the composer of *Das Dreimäderlhaus*, whom he found more lively and less 'puffed up' than most of his other Viennese acquaintances. He held a group of Hungarian officers, who had just returned from riding on the great Hungarian plains, spellbound by his description of his volatile changes of mood. They drank many toasts in Tokay and ended up by inviting him to their home town, Szeged. He later told Ekman that he was introduced to Brahms at the fashionable Café Leidinger, though he makes no mention of this at the time in his letters which seems surprising.

From the less fashionable Ronacher he wrote to Aino, 'Half the *demi-monde* is here and they are all enjoying themselves drinking wine, looking at the show and talking. I am thinking of you far too much to take pleasure in watching the girls even if some of them are quite attractive.'

In his letters to Aino, Sibelius often dwells on the contrast between them; he, experienced in the ways of the world and disillusioned; she, 'a pure and chaste being'. Like the heroes of Tolstoy and Pushkin he has a 'past' which he makes no attempt to hide. 'I am not an innocent, though this is the result of circumstances rather than wantonness. But whatever my feelings may be, I have always had a strong sense of propriety of what is *comme il faut*. But perhaps I have been altogether too frank.' One can almost hear Eugene Onegin talking to Tatiana, or Konstantin Levin addressing Katya. Sibelius had read *Eugene Onegin* in Vienna and thought so highly of it that he sent it to Aino.

Tolstoy's *Kreutzer Sonata* with its condemnation of the sensual was a work that he loathed even though he admitted that it was a masterpiece. At this time Zola greatly appealed to him and, having read *Thérèse Raquin*, he wrote

Aino, 'I have all the propensities towards vice that most men have and perhaps more than most. But this must not alarm you for, having concerned myself so much with art, I could never be unfeeling.' He tells her not to read *Nana* in which, he says, 'Zola has written many things you don't need to bother your head with. Do not misunderstand me and think that I am trying to play the role of a Victorian father.'

Sibelius doubtless wanted to protect her from Zola's realism; hence it seems particularly ironic that she should have served Juhano Aho as the model for his character Anna in 'Alone', the first Finnish short story to have any semblance of Zola's boldness. Aino gave Sibelius a copy of it for Christmas and he read it on Christmas night itself. The story begins with the narrator—the book is written in the first person—making his farewells to Anna in whose features it is not difficult to recognize Aino, and setting out for Paris. Reading it Sibelius had no difficulty in placing the occasion; he and Aho had been fellow travellers on the Grand Duke in the autumn of 1889. Possibly Sibelius even caught a shadowy glimpse of himself in the book when the narrator and Anna are together in an out-of-doors restaurant in Helsinki but she has no eyes nor ears for him but keeps her gaze steadily on a fountain and eventually goes to talk to a tall, handsome student there. The story ends with the narrator having a fleeting affair with a Parisian *coquette* on Christmas Eve in whom he seems to discern the features of his beloved Anna, for whom he still longs hopelessly. The whole story has a stale atmosphere but the erotic scenes are described with a realism that was entirely new at the time in Finnish literature. 'Alone' scandalized Finland at the time and was even attacked in the Finnish parliament. Reading the book that Christmas night must have been a disturbing experience for Sibelius, whose immediate reaction was to pour out his feelings in a letter to Aino.

'I devoured the book greedily when I started it: I felt I saw you everywhere, so sensitively has he captured you. Poor man! When I finished I was close to tears; I hardly thought that I had any right to you but then immediately felt ashamed of thinking such things. In him I have a dangerous rival and indeed it still feels strange to me that you should have preferred me. Afterwards I must confess that I had quite made up my mind to go and see Aho with a brace of pistols and let them decide our fate. You think perhaps that I am off my head, a Don Quixote, but in my earliest childhood I often recall having heard the expression that only a duel to the death can settle such matters. As you read this I am sure that you are thinking that nothing will come of these threats; isn't that so? But it certainly will if I see him going under. If you could see me now you would think me very calm and I should be calm when the shot was fired. I would surely hit him since he was far from calm when he heard that you loved me. If he were a plump and prosperous business man it would not matter but Finland needs people like him.'

Sibelius presumably got the idea of the duel from the book itself since its central figure tells his French mistress that he had caught Anna with another lover. When his mistress asks him whether they fought a duel, he answers, 'Yes, we did and I hurt him in the hand.' Sibelius waited some twelve days before sending off the letter and subsequently regretted writing it. He had behaved selfishly and had thought only of Aho's feelings and his own, not those of Aino. He subsequently assured his fiancée that there was no question of a duel since he no longer had only himself to think of.

In his relationship with the Järnefelts Sibelius showed signs of a distinct inferiority complex. 'Tell me everything that your father says about me whether it is good or bad', he once asked Aino, and when her letter was late in reaching him on one occasion his imagination ran riot: he thought the General had discovered their secret and forbidden her to write to him and that her brother Eero had advised her against marrying him. Aino put an end to the charade of secrecy by telling her father of their engagement. General Järnefelt, in actual fact, was much taken by Sibelius's impulsive, considerate nature and had complete confidence in his future as a composer. Moreover as Sibelius had been educated in a Finnish-speaking school and in many other respects measured up to his aristocratic ideals Jarnefelt was only too delighted to think of him as his future son-in-law. Sibelius put off writing to him for several weeks but finally sent him a 'formal' letter whose beginning read: 'The reason, Sir, why I did not tell you that I loved your daughter before this, was my conviction that you, as her father, could only view with misgiving a man of such modest expectations as my own. As I feel confident that my future prospects will be much more favourable, I will naturally wait until the time is ripe.'

'I would like to have seen his face, when your father read my letter,' he wrote to Aino a few days later. Somewhat surprisingly he had written to the General in Swedish, partly no doubt because he felt at greater ease in expressing himself and partly as a means of asserting his own independence. The previous November he had discussed with Aino the whole language question in an easy-going fashion 'Naturally you will remain a Fennoman: it would not be like Aino Järnefelt to change her colours, and it will be interesting to see if this ever occasions any friction between us.' As was the case in Berlin, Sibelius mismanaged his budget in a tragi-comic fashion and confessed that he was 'entirely helpless in everyday practical matters'. 'It is all right while I still have money to throw about and fritter away as I do for I have a number of guardian angels who safeguard my interests, but this really can't go on indefinitely.' He gave parties for his friends which seemed to him to cost twice as much as they should. Among his first purchases in Vienna was a new top hat and his linen was always spotlessly white and newly pressed. 'It is one of the ironies of fate that I who have all the tastes of the rich, should be as poor as I am.' His extravagance earned him the title 'le comte' among his circle of friends.

Sibelius was armed with letters of introduction that opened the doors to the Viennese nobility. After Christmas when they returned from their country estates and the season was about to begin, he prepared his entry into what he called 'high life'. 'I shall soon start doing the rounds with all my letters of recommendation. The upper ten have all come home and Vienna resounds to their waltzing and laughter.'

One of the people who introduced him into Viennese society was the Finnish baritone, Filip Forstén who had once given a recital in Hämeenlinna. Forstén had made his name as Pauline Lucca's partner and had appeared on the operatic stages of Stockholm, Vienna and London and had even on one occasion in St. Petersburg been accompanied by Tchaikovsky in some of his songs. Lucca was married to Baron Wallhofen who was enormously wealthy and she installed Forstén in one of the apartments of the baronial palace nick-naming him 'Mopserl'. Wegelius had asked Forstén to keep a protective watch on Sibelius and see to it that the newly betrothed student behaved himself, a by-no-means simple task. Sibelius described him 'as a good person though not over-endowed with intellect'. He borrowed money from him, which Forstén borrowed in his turn from Lucca.

The way having been carefully prepared by both Wegelius and Forstén, Lucca received the young student with great amiability and Sibelius undoubtedly felt a little abashed in her presence, though he wrote: 'Lucca wants of course to treat me like a protégé but I regard myself as quite as good as she and her baron.' With the latter he discussed the finer points of cigars and of hunting. In Lucca's salon he experienced 'the eleventh hour of a culture that sprang from the home and probably ends there', to quote Schnabel on the Vienna of the 1890s. He came into contact with the Viennese nobility who exercised their traditional functions and served as patrons of the Arts. 'They do absolutely nothing', said Sibelius after having played billiards with one of his newly discovered aristocratic friends. But he saw the dangers both to his purse and his time were he to cultivate their uninterrupted company. Even so their way of dedicating themselves wholeheartedly to the pursuit of pleasure and their streak of *fin de siècle* resignation appealed to him. 'Last night I was with the "high life" here and got through 20 florins. But I have won a lot in another way; I learn so much from these people for even if they are dissipated, they are very intelligent and refined. I enjoy their company whereas on the other hand I cannot abide the musicians here; they are so dull and sober. There is an aristocracy, and by that I don't mean people of high birth, but a natural aristocracy who have sensibility and a view of life that the ordinary masses don't understand. These people are the ones with whom I feel most at home.'

Sibelius met many people of high birth at a brilliant party given by Pauline Lucca one evening. He could not wholly shed his artistic pride and his inbred responses when Lucca came towards him and asked why he was standing there on his own. He replied rather tartly, to Forstén's horror, that nobody had bothered to introduce him to the ladies. He was, of course, introduced both to the Princess of Reuss and other women of rank but noted with displeasure that the artists who had performed at the soirée did not eat with the other guests. 'Had I been one of them I would certainly not have put up with it. Anyway I noticed that I made a sympathetic impression on many people there and received many invitations from other guests. You may think that I behaved rather like an upstart but, you know, my father had a similar spirit.' The high spot of the evening came when Lucca sang the Habanera from *Carmen* 'for the very last time'. 'I was absolutely mad about her,' he confessed to Wegelius, 'and cold shivers went up and down my spine.' Lucca invited him to her summer residence at Gmunden where Goldmark was also a frequent visitor but Sibelius declined the offer; he did not want to become another 'Mopserl'.

Sibelius also spent a lot of time with another aristocratic family, the Amadeis who were friends of Wegelius. 'It's good for me to spend my time with them —and it also stops me from turning into a restaurant *habitué*. At the Count's we talk about hunting, horses, dogs, and music—music seems to be counted as a sport here.' Countess Amadei, however, took this particular sport quite seriously and had made a sizable donation to the Philharmonic the previous year. Her son even tried his hand at composing and at one of their musical evenings some of his songs were performed. Sibelius found them somewhat sickly but was tactful enough to compliment him on them and in return was praised for his Romance for violin. 'We liked each other about equally,' Sibelius wrote somewhat ambiguously. When the time came for his return home, the Count put his carriage at his disposal and he was driven in state the length and breadth of Vienna to his modest room at the corner of Waaggasse and Wiedner Haupstrasse. Maria Sibelius who was not exactly overwhelmed by letters from her son, sent him a form to fill up. One of her questions read, 'Do you spend all your time with the high and mighty?' to which he answered truthfully enough, 'Yes, more's the pity.' To the question 'What sort of food do you get?' he merely answered, 'I eat with the lower orders!'

In a letter to Aino shortly before Christmas, Sibelius touched on a number of issues related to composition. 'I think I know what you need to be a composer at the present time. It is not the capacity to turn out three hundred works or so: far from it! The majority of people cannot distinguish between a time-beater and a conductor and likewise between a note-spinner and a real composer. It is my conviction that only a thoroughly normal person (never mind what peculiarities he may have) can compose a modern work. You must not think that it is easy for us, conscious as we are of the weight of tradition and prejudice; it is only people of great inner strength who can stand the test. Don't think I am trying to be philosophical; I am no philosopher and never will be; nor need I be. The only thing I must have is criticism, self-criticism. The greatest composer of all, Beethoven, did not have the greatest *natural* talent but he subjected everything he did to the most searching self-criticism and by doing so achieved greatness.'

Sibelius's standards were high: he felt the weight of the Viennese classical tradition and sought strength in Beethoven's example. Here was proof that one did not necessarily have to possess a musical talent of such natural and overwhelming superiority as Mozart's to be a great artist. The down-to-earth talent that Beethoven possessed attained genius as a result of self-criticism and that was something that he felt by implication that he could do. In spite of the fact that he felt at times 'close to decadence', as he put it to Aino, he always had a strange conviction that he would achieve something of moment. 'There are times when I think that I have had a marvellous idea and my pace quickens and my pulse throbs. I feel like this at the moment and the question that storms in my head is Why? The only thing that can restore me to an even keel is a feeling of resignation or indifference. But that is not something that comes to order. If I felt like that, then I would be old; and old I will never be.'

On 7 January, Sibelius set Runeberg's poem 'The Dream' and subjected it to his growing powers of self-criticism. It struck him that it had the same shortcomings as his earlier Runeberg setting, namely, its sense of logic and sequence was weak. 'But it is new and also Finnish. I believe in the future of a national Finnish music, however much the knowalls may turn up their noses. The deep melancholy and insistence on one mood or phrase which is at the heart of so many Finnish folk songs, though it can be a shortcoming, is none the less a characteristic.'

Sibelius was at this time at odds with the world. The immediate reason for this was that Fuchs had called his latest piece, possibly a new overture, 'crude and barbaric'. This occasioned an outburst about Germans in general and Austrians included, 'The Germans are far too conventional and do not respond in the least to new movements either in art or literature. They loathe both the French and the Russians, and one cannot talk about anything Scandinavian without their trotting out the conventional nonsense about "barbarians". One cannot escape the conclusion that as far as art is concerned the Germans are finished. They could not produce an Ibsen, a Zola or a Tchaikovsky; they see everything through blinkers—and bad ones at that!'

Even the fiasco at his audition for the Philharmonic served as a spur to further efforts. He went through his new overture mercilessly with a comb and cut out the offending passages. He made a setting of Tavaststjerna's *Fågellek* ('Birds at play') admitting that he may 'have misunderstood the poet a little, but that does not matter: one should try and convey the impression the poem makes on you rather than be too literal.' He was reluctant to try his hand at settings of Finnish texts since he still felt uncertain about matters of intonation.

But he was on better terms with Fuchs, who was pleased with the progress of his 'Finnish barbarian'. So much so that when he applied for a scholarship to 'Nylands Nation' for a second year, Fuchs wrote a glowing testimonial. Sibelius liked Fuchs whom he found more open to reason than Goldmark. The

latter was at the height of his career and fame, and Sibelius was scrupulously careful not to show him anything unless he was reasonably satisfied with it himself.
He burnt one of the orchestral exercises he had written the previous autumn.
In general Sibelius was in a highly nervous state at this time; he could not
work well and to steady his nerves he played baccarat, drank profusely, lived
the life of a playboy and was taken for a rich man from the North, with his
evening dress and high hat. Afterwards he felt pretty ashamed of himself and
became prey to morbid thoughts, even imagining his own funeral. 'Someone
with a more practical turn of mind could go far with my gifts: I am to a
certain extent nationalist but . . .' He didn't pursue this particular line of thought,
but it is clear that he began to see a national Finnish art as the best means
of finding his own musical identity. Now, for the first time, he started planning
a large-scale work in several movements. He told Aino of his plans: 'I have
looked at my earlier sketches and found that the weakness lies more in the
working-out than in the ideas themselves. My aim is to create something new,
a kind of suite or rather symphony. I shall begin with an overture that will
immediately establish the mood of the work. The other movements have the
character of episodes although they will be independent and "abgeschlossene".
I am working very hard but when things are going well, then I enjoy working.
I already have the overture in my head: it has an atmosphere of spring and
of love. The second theme represents you, melancholy, feminine and yet
passionate. You know, I really am cut out to be a composer; I can see that
now.' He then adds prophetically, 'My work will be denigrated in the beginning and then in later years, it will be overrated: life is like that.'

On 12 February, Sibelius showed his new overture to Goldmark who com-
plimented him on the progress he had made. But then Sibelius took his hand
and looked him straight in the eye and said, 'Tell me what you really think.'
Goldmark looked somewhat taken aback and after a while began to criticize
the piece more thoroughly. He felt that too much of it was merely manufactured and then added something that was to make a deep impression on
the young composer, 'Your themes haven't enough real character though the
second subject is *quite* good.' With his feeling for colour Goldmark immediately
sensed the national flavour of the second theme though he confessed to no
great enthusiasm for it. 'Because you are a Finn your music has a national
character that has greater meaning for your countrymen than it has for me.'
Goldmark also gave him some general advice. He thought it unwise for a
young composer to take Berlioz and Wagner as models; Sibelius should content himself with less ambitious canvases for a while, study Haydn, Mozart
and Beethoven and aim for greater simplicity of style. 'Work over your ideas
more thoroughly so that they have greater inner character. Beethoven recast
his some fifty times.' These words went home; Goldmark's criticisms coincided
very much with his own. 'My powers of self-criticism are the equal of his.
I want to achieve real artistry, not something half-way or merely respectable.
My overture, for example, is better than Busoni's *Concertstück* for orchestra but

not as good as his Toccata and Fugue.' For all his criticism, though, Goldmark
seems to have been quietly impressed by the overture and suggested to Sibelius
that he show him his new works every three months. This was not, as one
might imagine, a polite way of getting rid of him; on the contrary, Goldmark
asked him to make an arrangement of the Overture in E for piano and spoke
vaguely about getting a run-through of the work with the Philharmonic or
the Conservatoire orchestras. Two months later he spoke in flattering terms
about him to Filip Forstén and in subsequent years appears to have been
particularly proud of his pupil. However this seems to have been the last
occasion on which he gave the young Finn a lesson.

In spite of all this, Sibelius had parted from Goldmark with some measure
of hurt pride, though he did not let it affect him. His reputation at home and
pressure from his creditors called for a new work for the Helsinki season.
'It is a pity that people insist on my turning in a new piece every year. My
work becomes laboured: I really need to devote a year to intensive study and
not to try and compose like one of the old masters. But then what is studying
if it isn't composing!' Adolf Paul wrote from Berlin to say that some friends
had played through the B flat Quartet to an invited audience. Christian Sinding
had been there and had been highly enthusiastic: 'What a tremendous talent
. . . and what an imagination! And excellent ideas. But one expects only the
very best from a talent of that order—and he could have made more of his
ideas. Of course, it is important to be able to write quickly but it never hurts
to prune a work.' Paul had great plans afoot for Sibelius and promised to
manage his affairs much better than he could imagine himself—on condition
of course that he had the exclusive right to do so.

The B flat Quartet was also played at one of the Institute's concerts in
Helsinki but without the success that had marked its première. Flodin had
second thoughts and took back a lot of his earlier praise; the piece now struck
him as 'formless'. Ilmari Krohn thought him still at the *Sturm und Drang* phase
of his development and waxed eloquent: 'Let us hope to God that his inner
struggle meets with victory; then the Finnish people will find their most
sacred and inspired ideals enshrined in his noble harmonies. It is he who has
given voice to the Finnish people's struggles', and so on. Sibelius was displeased: a piece of absolute music was made the vehicle of national struggles,
'Krohn's review, to put it frankly, makes me sick. Why write such rubbish?
It is neither true nor does it make a decent impression on anyone.'

Sibelius's symphonic plans began to take shape towards the end of February;
he wrote to Aino that the symphony was to be in three movements or four,
contrasting in character but with the same basic source of inspiration and
something along these lines:

Ex. 40

The idea he quoted in his letter is a well-known Finnish folk tune, in the melodic minor and with a characteristic descending contour. A month later we find him writing about it in greater detail: 'It is in E major; the first part is, as you know, an overture; the second is an idealized Ball scene although there are some realistic touches. The third begins with a recitative which in actual fact paves the way for the last a set of very free variations on a Finnish theme. The whole atmosphere of the work is permeated with the vitality and intensity of spring, a time which as you know, has a tremendous effect on me. Strange that one should be so much at the mercy of one's senses; it holds one back somehow.' With a view to getting a performance Sibelius wrote to Kajanus. His tone is a good deal more direct than in his letters to either Aino or Wegelius; he obviously wants to make an impression on his older friend but at the same time stands in some awe of him. Their relationship was in many ways a complex one: 'Forgive a somewhat uninspired letter. The reason why I haven't sent you anything before this, is that everything I have written before, strikes me as rubbish. I am now working on something which Goldmark has called "damnably good" . . . but now I have the ideas for a symphony in my head which I shall put down on paper as soon as I can. Will you, my friend, play it? You know that my many creditors are expecting a success; otherwise I shan't be able to pay them off. Please forget your past feelings of antipathy for me; I am truly your friend and want you to be mine. The best regards from your unfortunate Jean Sibelius.' To this he adds a footnote, 'I am not going to live much longer so you can take the risk!'

Sibelius felt ashamed of this letter after he had sent it and apologized saying that he had been recovering from a party.

At the beginning of April Sibelius suddenly interrupted work on the symphony, giving as his reason that he had not learnt to handle symphonic form with the requisite assurance. He wrote out what were to have been the first two movements with the aid of a copyist calling them Overture and Ballet Scene. He then sent the two pieces, his 'envois de Vienne', to Kajanus but a couple of days later was overcome by doubts and wired to Helsinski asking Kajanus not to perform them. But the latter ignored his telegram and included the overture in a concert on 23 April. The following day he sent a congratulatory telegram to Sibelius. The critics, however, were as reserved as the public: Flodin thought the piece bordered on the grotesque. On 28 April, Kajanus repeated the overture and on this occasion added the Ballet Scene which if anything caused greater bewilderment than the overture. 'It was as if the closing bars cocked a snook at the public', wrote the anonymous reviewer— probably Oskar Merikanto—in *Päivälehti*.

A few days later after this, his début as an orchestral composer, Sibelius wrote to Wegelius asking whether he too had found his new pieces formless and drew a parallel between his own technique and that of Zola. 'In Zola there is too much development as indeed there is in my overture. It is not a good work though it does have a certain technical accomplishment in its favour. To my shame I must admit that my heart was in it when I composed it, the usual excuse when something turns out to have no heart at all! The Ballet Scene is an altogether different matter; this springs from a bitter experience. . . . If I were to describe it in detail you would agree that I have taken it to its logical conclusion. I have never wept as profusely as I did while writing this.' In the self-same letter he had just complained that Zola and company had not taken 'realism' in their novels to its logical conclusion!

The overture is in sonata form and the main theme rises in arch-like phrases over an ostinato figure in the bass, the middle register being filled in by wood-wind chords and tremolo violas and cellos.

Ex. 41

The third and fourth bars briefly remind one of the kind of line to be encountered in Finnish music. The second group is more sombre in mood and colouring and comprises two main ideas. A feature of the first is its repeated notes:

Ex. 42

The second only appears in its complete form in the development:

Ex. 43

The last theme in particular has something of the flavour of a stylized runic melody. This latter idea has something of the flavour of a runic melody, albeit a stylized one: the first phrase is in the minor and moves within the compass of a fifth; the theme ends, characteristically enough, with a descending fifth broken by the supertonic, E, while the tonic itself is repeated.

The Ballet Scene is a vision of a dance which whirls hectically past the bystander, in much the same way as Ravel's *La Valse*. It is in the form of a free rondo and like Ravel's masterly score lacks the real gaiety and high spirits of the Viennese waltz proper. They both have a dream-like, almost daemonic quality. The main theme is announced on the oboe and accompanied only by pizzicato strings:

Ex. 44

The first four notes are the minor form of a familiar enough figure and it is not impossible that Sibelius wanted to pay an oblique tribute to Mozart by this allusion to the finale of the 'Jupiter'. It assumes the role of a unifying thematic factor in the various waltz episodes that follow each other in rapid succession. After this there is a largamente section, introduced by the first three notes and a contrasting fugato section marked molto vivace where the violins are divided in five. The divided strings with their accompanying castanets and cymbals acquire a transparent almost impressionist sonority:

Ex. 45

The score calls for relatively large forces; in addition to the normal classic-romantic orchestra Sibelius uses cor anglais, bass clarinet, tuba, castanets and cymbals. None the less his handling of the orchestra is highly restrained.

There are two occasional pieces from this spring whose origins are somewhat unusual. At his brother's suggestion he wrote a march for the students in 'Asis' (the Anatomy Department of the University). This begins with a slow, grotesque idea which gradually turns into a wild czardas. He was thanked by telegram for '*la pompeuse marche d'Asis*', which strange to say, was originally written for string quartet! The second was an entry in a competition organized by the well-known Viennese fencing master, Hartl, for music to accompany his demonstrations. Some forty or so composers took part and the first prize went to a conductor who concocted a potpourri of well-known Viennese tunes. Sibelius's entry was thought to be far too serious and not Viennese enough but as the most accomplished of the competitors he was given the job of scoring the prize-winning piece for a fee of 10 Gulden. His own contribution does not survive; nor does another work begun in Vienna, an octet for strings, flute and clarinet, which according to the composer 'contained the seed of nothing less than *En Saga*'. The octet is something of a mystery; strange to say, Sibelius did not mention it at all in his letters to Aino, in whom he otherwise confided all his musical plans. There is of course the possibility that some of the themes of *En Saga* may even have their origins in the competition piece as an accompaniment for various fencing positions! Another piece, a quartet for two violins, cello and piano comes from this period and was written for the Euterpe Society of Helsinki: earlier in the spring he had sent Aino some music, a theme and seven variations for piano, which he arranged for piano quartet in April, adding a short adagio introduction. This shows that his instrumental writing was already impregnated by orchestral habits of mind.

Even while he was making a fair copy of his overture and Ballet Scene, Sibelius had already begun to plan a new symphony, the *Kullervo*. On 12 April he attended a performance of Beethoven's Ninth Symphony under Richter, an experience that may well have fired his ambitions to think once again in symphonic terms. He wrote Wegelius the following day, 'You know, I was so overwhelmed by it that I wept. I felt so small, so small. Richter was splendid! Wagner's remarks about the Ninth really hit the nail on the head.'

Once again he wrote to Aino: 'I have a clear idea of the general atmosphere

of the symphony but I have not as yet a single musical idea properly formu-
lated. I have already torn up at least fifty ideas so far. I stay in bed in the mornings until about 9 or 10 but work out musical ideas in my head for as much
as four hours. That is now my main work apart from this unbearable violin
playing and the actual job of writing my music out. I always have the complete
piece in my head before I write it down though it may not be complete in
every detail.' It would seem that he had taken Goldmark's words to heart and
was becoming more selective in his choice of musical ideas.

To try and recapture something of the atmosphere of Finland, Sibelius took
walks in the forests on the outskirts of Vienna. 'It was just like home, birches
and spruce trees. Here and there are violets and cowslips. All my moods derive
from the *Kalevala*—I am now getting a clearer idea of my symphony. It is
completely unlike anything else I have written up to now. The basic idea
goes like this:

Ex. 46

When Sibelius showed the beginning of the new symphony to Fuchs he
received so much praise that he blushed. 'Everyone thinks I am so strange and
original, unnatural and highly strung.' His work on *Kullervo* progressed satisfactorily and he planned journeys to Italy and to Bayreuth when all his plans
were upset: he was admitted to hospital for the third spring in succession.

In his letters home from Vienna Sibelius emphasizes that he is well with
such frequency that it would seem that he is secretly worried by his health.
He was certainly in better shape than he had been in Berlin: both the autumn
and the winter had elapsed without any hospital visits but at the beginning
of April he suddenly told Wegelius that all his money went on doctors' bills
and that his plans to go to Italy had fallen through. His letters to Aino during
the following month of May became shorter and less communicative. She
noticed, too, that they came from Josefstadt and not from Wieden where
he had always sent them before, although he had not told her of any change
of address.

He told Kajanus what was really happening: 'I am going to have an operation
for the first time in my life. The doctors go their rounds looking important.'
Only when the operation was successfully over did he write to Aino putting
his cards on the table. He admitted that all his recent letters had been artificial
since he had not wanted to tell her that he had spent the last three weeks in
hospital. 'The truth is that I have had to undergo a painful operation. I had
the beginnings of a stone. Professor Neumann thinks I may have had it for
several years. It seems to have been the cause of many of my troubles, among

94

other things the shaking I get when I have stood too long and which I have
difficulty in disguising. Such things strengthen one's character and rouse the
defiance that everyone has who has to fight against his lot in life. But one can
forge one's own happiness. I have learned a great deal in recent times as you
know, and I think that people nowadays brood far too much and fall prey
to melancholy far too easily, myself no exception. One must not expect too
much of life. No, one must face it boldly and look it straight in the eye.'

In the hospital, an exclusive private nursing home, he read Wagner's prose
writings and Keller's *Der grüne Heinrich* which Wegelius had recommended.
Keller's idealism appealed to him but he found the book rather pale: he was
beginning to tire of Zola though. He did not do any composition during this
period as experience had taught him that the outcome was poor when 'one
cannot go out and be together with people and with animals'. June found
Vienna in the grip of a heat wave and Sibelius felt a great longing for the
northern summer. But the clinic would not discharge him until his bill was
settled. At home in Finland Christian Sibelius had great difficulty in raising
a loan but on 3 June he was at last able to telegraph his brother that a relative
had placed 1,000 francs at his disposal. Encouraged by this news Sibelius
started work again. He planned to rework his B flat String Quartet and submit
it to a competition announced by the St. Petersburg Chamber Music Society.
But nothing came of it. Sibelius's style had developed too much for him to
be able to revise the piece successfully. On 8 June, Sibelius left Vienna for
Berlin where Adolf Paul and other friends received him with open arms.
They drank Aino Järnefelt's health in champagne with such enthusiasm and
ardour that Sibelius's funds were exhausted and he had to wire home for more
money. He was even forced to sell some of his clothes. So he made his return
incongruously attired in evening dress, a white scarf and a light overcoat, like
a latter-day Lemminkäinen, from Lübeck homewards via Hangö and Reval
(Tallinn) to Helsinki.

CHAPTER SIX

Kullervo

A FTER his return from Vienna Sibelius had some difficulty in settling down to work again. His creditors had reminded him of their existence and back in Lovisa he felt that the winds of misfortune were beginning to blow. So that it was with something approaching relief that he repaired to the Järnefelt's summer house, Tottesund near Vasa where Aino's enthusiasm for *Kullervo* served to deepen the bonds between them. From these idyllic surroundings Sibelius took a week off to attend a song competition at Ekenäs where he was to be one of the judges; the others included Wegelius, Faltin and Flodin. At the competition a horn septet from Lovisa played an Andantino that Sibelius had composed especially for them.[1]

In August Sibelius spent some time at Wegelius's while in the neighbourhood of Ekenäs and it was here that the sole fruit of the summer's labours, the song 'Jägargossen' ('The young huntsman') to words of Runeberg, came into being. Wegelius lost no time in filling in the background to the latest Helsinki gossip, though by the side of Viennese musical life, the intrigues in the Finnish capital must have seemed pretty small beer. On the way back to Lovisa Sibelius spent some time in Helsinki where he met Busoni's successor at the Music Institute, William Dayas who had been a pupil of Liszt. He spent the early autumn partly in Lovisa and partly in Helsinki where he was joined by Aino Järnefelt. Money soon ran out but Sibelius succeeded in borrowing 150 marks to keep himself in cigars and to pay off some small debts.

In a letter of 12 October 1891, he tells Aino from his retreat in Lovisa, 'I spend my time eating apples, smoking, longing for Europe, and composing.' He advertised in the local paper, *Östra Nyland* for pupils in violin and musical theory and had soon collected some nine pupils and in addition to this he took charge of an amateur orchestra. Mornings and nights were set aside for composition. 'You know, it doesn't worry me any more when I have to destroy what I have been writing over the past two or three days,' he told

1. In a letter to Axel von Bonsdorff, Sibelius's brother wrote (22 August 1889), 'Besides this Janne has also written some pieces for a horn septet here', but judging from the parts the Andantino dates from 1890-1.

Aino; 'I have such marvellous ideas (marvellous in my view anyway) but most of them turn out to be impossible to realize or at any rate very difficult in practice. But no doubt that is as it should be. Now when one has written a little, one begins to reconcile oneself to that fate. But still there is no other way of hastening our wedding than having a new composition ready.' At times he rebelled against his solitude but on the whole he was pleased that he had gone to the country in search of peace and quiet. And in search of his inner self!

Armas Järnefelt's and Adolf Paul's letters were a breath of fresh air from the outside world. Becker had asked through Järnefelt to see a copy of Sibelius's Suite in A and besides this had told him that he thought the young man 'damnably talented' though he needed to conquer his nerves. A reminder of Sibelius's stage-fright came that very autumn: a concert in which he was due to take part was advertised in *Östra Nyland*, but on 1 December the paper reported that when the time came for him to appear 'Mr. Sibelius for some obscure reason went on strike'. Earlier in the autumn (19 October) Abraham Ojanperä gave three of the Runeberg songs composed in Vienna at a concert of the Music Institute and these met with general approval. Flodin wrote that Sibelius had more successfully captured the national flavour of his country than any other living native-born composer.

Sibelius was by now wholly absorbed in his work on the *Kullervo* Symphony. 'My work progresses, albeit very slowly', he told Aino. 'I do not want to strike a false or artificial note in art and hence I write and then tear up what I have written and think a great deal about what I am trying to do. I believe none the less that I am now on the right lines. I see the pure Finnish elements in music less realistically than before but I think more truthfully.'

Obviously this less realistic picture sprang from his ability to put a greater distance between himself and his material. He strove to get away from the kind of nationalism that relies on more or less direct borrowings of folkloric material. Instead he was bent on transforming certain national elements and infusing them into his own personal style: in so doing he would create a musical atmosphere that is strongly national in implication rather than overtly nationalist. To further these purposes he had of course to immerse himself in genuine runic song and at the end of October he wrote to Aino of his intention to go to Borgå shortly. A new edition of the *Kalevala* was due to be published. Moreover, Larin Paraske, a runic singer from the territory south of the Karelian isthmus, was brought to Borgå in 1891 and had a vast repertoire at her command. Sibelius met Larin Paraske presumably some time in November, for in the following month he sent a picture of her to Aino with a caption to the effect that they became good friends. According to Yrjö Hirn, however, they had already met earlier that summer. In an essay on Paraske, Hirn wrote: 'I found myself with Jean Sibelius on a journey from Lovisa. He was five years my senior and at the time his head was full of the ideas that were to culminate the following year in *Kullervo* and was anxious to hear what the

Karelian runic melodies were like when they were sung in an authentic way. I was naturally glad to be present when they met. Exactly how much this meant for Sibelius's works inspired by the *Kalevala* I would not like to say. I do remember this much however: that he listened to her with great attention and made notes on her inflections and rhythm.'

Paraske's incantations obviously made a deep impression on them both: she sang such runes as had been preserved orally, as well as others of her own composition, among them a lament on the death of her husband. One can with some certainty form a picture of the kind of runic song that Sibelius heard Paraske perform. In general, runic singers confined themselves to a handful of melodies—and in some cases to a single basic melody. The same basic pattern can be discerned in the following variants that were noted down from her performances.

Ex. 47

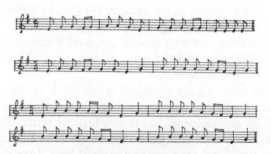

Presumably it was these or similar variants of a basic melodic formula that Sibelius heard and he could reaffirm the truth of his definition of the *Kalevala* as 'theme and variations' both from a literary and a musical point of view.

In November Sibelius was troubled by a rushing noise in his ears and went to Helsinki to consult a specialist who told him frankly that his ears were so defective in structure that his hearing would gradually decline. He forbade him to smoke, drink or bathe in cold water and even prescribed leeches. Ominously he told him to take great care of his ears. 'Now above all', Sibelius wrote to Aino, 'I listen to orchestral music intensively while I can still hear so that when my hearing goes altogether I can imagine the actual sound more clearly! These are not hypochondriac fantasies but something that is happening in deadly earnest though I can scarce believe it myself. What a fate! Were it not for you I could not survive the prospect of deafness. But now my first impulse is that we immediately (we? turn ourselves into peasants?) get ourselves a cottage and settle there. Surely Aino loves the deaf Janne every bit as much as the one who could hear. I think I could compose even though I were deaf. Beethoven was the only one ever to have done so. Don't breathe a word of this to a soul: I simply could not bear them saying that "it sounds like that simply because he can't hear what he's writing".'

Even in later life Sibelius had some trouble with his ears. However when he was sixty he still conducted and never became deaf. Accordingly one wonders how accurate the diagnosis was? We are tempted to the view that his specialist deliberately exaggerated his condition so as to reinforce his injunction to the composer to give up drinking and smoking. Sibelius's notion of going off to live in the country no doubt reflects the Järnefelts' current craze for Tolstoy. Arvid had succumbed to the new wave of enthusiasm that invaded the family, abandoning his law studies to embrace the simple life and take up the career of a shoemaker.

On 24 November, Sibelius made his début as a conductor at a popular concert given by Kajanus's orchestra when the programme included his Overture and the Ballet Scene. On another occasion he played in the orchestra returning afterwards to Lovisa to continue wrestling with *Kullervo* whose first movement was giving him great difficulty.

To tell the truth, Sibelius was displeased with himself and we find him writing one December evening to Aino while a storm raged outside the house: Now I really must take myself by the scruff of the neck and get down to it if I am ever going to make anything of myself. I am too readily prone to allow the mood of the moment to take possession of me: I would not call myself slothful, for I can work hard when I want to. But I mean for instance that if I have written something that is rubbish and that I *know* to be rubbish, then I begin to make excuses for it and justify it to myself. It always hurts when you have to cut out something you have written, particularly if you have put your heart and soul into it up to that point. But you know that well enough my dear. Today I have managed to get several pages nearer the end.' This night marked the beginning of a period of intensive work which culminated in the first performance of *Kullervo* some four months later. On 17 December he wrote to Aino suggesting that they together should choose the words he was to set in his new work. 'When I get the whole picture into focus I shall tell you what I propose. You can then give me your views, for you have a greater feeling for literary matters than I have. There are many things in the introduction to *Kullervo* into which I have put my whole heart and soul but there are others that aren't so good. The climax tells how Kullervo journeys by sledge and meets his sister to whom he makes love: I thought of portraying this by a broad melody, some hundred bars or so, on the violins, violas and cellos in unison with some rhythmic byplay in the lower brass. The whole climax is more powerful than anything I have ever done before. I have it already. . . . The whole introductory movement is in strict sonata form.'

Three days later he wrote: 'I am still undecided as to whether to have a narrator or not and turn it into a *mélodrame* (in which case the wonderful scene between Kullervo and his sister would lose its force) or to have two singers to portray the characters (Ojanperä and Mme. Achté) and describe everything else in purely musical terms. As far as the opening is concerned I don't want to go into too many descriptive details but rather concentrate or one or at the most two episodes or tableaux (I mean Kullervo's Childhood and his time as a herdsman working for Ilmarinen). After the first allegro I think one wants a pastoral mood by way of contrast. It would be a more musical solution after the initial allegro which is in the minor, than to have a lullaby immediately after, which also has something melancholy about it. I am thinking in practical terms of the public.' In the end Sibelius did not let these concerns worry him unduly: in the end he followed the dramatic introduction with a movement called 'Kullervo's Youth', albeit with a lullaby-like main theme.

Kullervo made rapid strides. 'The more I immerse myself in Kullervo's fate the more I feel it somewhat foolhardy to tackle such themes, and feel small by their side. I am going to have two singers and begin with his childhood. I have already written a lullaby and this theme will grow in intensity on each return. A few days later Aino received a message, 'Today, just now in fact, I have finished the first movement. I have drunk your health in my imagination and in reality drunk toasts with Aunt Evelina. Tomorrow I shall work out the lullaby in more detail.' The same letter quotes the main theme of the fourth movement.

In Helsinki Sibelius was becoming a name to be seriously reckoned with. When the Liberal paper *Päivälehti* put on a charity concert to raise funds his Ballet Scene and two of his Runeberg settings were included; although he now had mixed feelings about having the Ballet Scene performed (he had come to dislike it), as a liberal he was pleased to see his name appearing in the company of Kajanus, Merikanto, Aho and other members of the circle associated with *Päivälehti*. His *Perpetuum mobile* for violin and piano was included in the Christmas album published by Nuori Suomi (*Young Finland*).

The *Päivälehti* circle was made up of writers and artists of liberal outlook who also wanted to see national feeling strengthened against the Russian occupying power. Up to this time Alexander III's good will had offered a certain guarantee against the attempts currently being made by the pan-Slav group of extreme Russian nationalists to tighten Tsarist grip over the autonomous Grand Duchy. But the threat of increasing Russianization was real and was increased by the so-called postal decrees of 1890. In this situation Finnish cultural figures did all they could to counterbalance Russian pressure and focus foreign attention on Finland's predicament. In the autumn of 1891 Sibelius was drawn into this struggle and his name also became prominent in another (and in the view of many, less flattering) respect. Adolf Paul's autobiographical novel *En bok om en människa* (*A Book About a Man*) was published and bore a dedication to Sibelius. In it Paul describes his youth and his life as a student both in Helsinki and Berlin: Sibelius appears in it as the author's best friend, the composer Sillén. The previous Christmas Sibelius had read with some displeasure a portrait of Aino in Aho's book and now it was Aino's turn to read with similar lack of enthusiasm of the boy-genius Sillén and all his goings-on in Berlin. She read of how Hans (Paul's alias in the book) at the height of a fever made a physical attack on Sillén. Even Sibelius himself complained to Paul the following spring that his portrayal of him had spoilt his credit. The picture of Sillén spending half his time lazing in bed, going on lonely pub-crawls, and drinking so as to get the feel of the underworld, pawning his watch to buy cigars, finding it quite impossible to pass an oyster restaurant, regarding women as easily seen through as a cheap novel is quickly read; none of this enhanced his standing at home particularly among his creditors and backers. But to later readers, some of the remarks Paul attributes to Sillén have an up-to-date ring about them, though of course, it would be improper to attribute all of them to Sibelius himself.

'It is a sign of intellectual poverty to speak of art for art's sake. It's there for everyone: it is the last thing in the world that should appear peculiar. Everyone has a right to it, the tramp as well as the over-refined, highly educated bourgeois. One should not try to pose complex mathematical problems for the benefit of posterity. The street-loafer ought to have his life, his passions every bit as well described, as the lives of the rich.'

The round of Christmas and New Year parties at Lovisa bored him. He took refuge in Rydberg's novel *Vapensmeden* (*The Armourer*) and Dostoievsky's *Crime and Punishment*. 'I think he stands head and shoulders above Turgenev, this Dostoievsky', he wrote to Aino on New Year's day. In his present state of mind he was more impressed by fanatics like Lars Gudmundi in the Rydberg novel or Raskolnikoff in the Dostoievsky than the indecisive heroes of Turgenev. He composed energetically and cut ruthlessly: he got stuck at times and at the end of January left Lovisa for good and settled in Helsinki 'for the sake of my hearing and inspiration'. The day before his departure he wrote to Aino. 'It is impossible to work here any more since I have come to know everyone. It's nice to come here sometimes for peace and quiet. But peace and quiet don't suit me: I always think they will but am always disappointed.'

Sibelius's friends in Helsinki did all they could to find him a suitable post in the musical world. Werner Söderhjelm overwhelmed him with advice: that he ought to join Kajanus's orchestra; that he give violin lessons; that he take over from the retiring *Kapellmeister* at the Swedish Theatre; and perhaps that he take charge of the so-called Symphony Chorus that Kajanus had long intended to set on a permanent footing. Fortunately for his composing, Sibelius did not fall in with any of these plans save for rare occasions when he took part in Kajanus's rehearsals. Instead he retired to Brunnsparken where he had lived during his student years and installed himself in a room in the bathing establishment far out by the sea.

Although Sibelius had made up his mind not to lead an active social life, he saw a good deal of his friends and the bond between him and Kajanus was further strengthened. Only a year had elapsed since he had written from Vienna that Kajanus and he were not on particularly good terms: now he was singing a very different tune. Presumably he felt some remorse for his earlier remark when he discovered the extent of Kajanus's loyalty. The latter had performed his works and gave him the opportunity of conducting them himself. During the spring of 1892 they met almost every day and Kajanus planned to make his young friend his successor as teacher of theory at the orchestral school. He learned, too, that Kajanus had made a highly flattering speech about him while he had been at Lovisa to members of the *Päivälehti* circle. One of their conversations, by all accounts a somewhat precious exchange, centred on the subject of artistic envy. Sibelius recounted the occasion to Aino in a letter dated 5 February. 'One thing that pleases me is that through Arvid's beliefs and enthusiasm for Tolstoy, I have succeeded in ridding myself of envy of others' artistic achievements. (Kajanus admitted that he plagued himself a great deal on that score.) . . . it is hell to spend sleepless nights tormented by such feelings. But now I am altogether free from this. One wants to escape this kind of feeling and think only about the work one has in hand.'

Whatever his feelings may have been, the achievements of others spurred him to more strenuous activity. Time and again in reading his notes and letters, one comes across this kind of sentiment: 'all my colleagues are forging ahead while I remain at a standstill.' But intrigue at the expense of others was foreign to his nature.

At one of their meetings at the famous Kämp restaurant, Kajanus's first wife charged Sibelius with keeping his infidelities from Aino. In this she was less than fair, for Sibelius in his letters had never tried to disguise the truth. On the contrary, he admitted that he readily succumbed to passion and told Aino that he had been unfaithful to her during their engagement, and that he was both sensual and jealous by nature. He wrote, too, that he regarded marriage with her as the only way of saving himself and attaining his true goal.

As his friendship with Kajanus deepened, the more delicate his relations with Wegelius became. Some time earlier Werner Söderhjelm had warned him not to spoil his relationship with Wegelius by too open an association with Kajanus. Sibelius himself continued to adopt an attitude of strict neutrality in the conflict between his two friends. On the 29 February he wrote to Aino, 'Kajanus and his wife paid me a visit here today and tonight I went to dinner with Martin. You see that I have no part in their quarrels. But Hanna (Wegelius) no longer speaks disapprovingly of Kajanus in my presence. If only one could put a stop to this nonsense between them.' But in spite of all good intentions small rifts began to appear between the two men. Wegelius probably understood and accepted the fact that the young composer had to make contact with the country's leading conductor. But it naturally irked him that his favourite pupil had become a friend of his arch-enemy.

In addition to this there were political complications: Wegelius became with the years a more and more staunch supporter of the Swedish faction and watched with concern how Sibelius became more and more drawn into the

ennoman circles and embraced their ideals. Probably he attributed this to
the subversive influence of Kajanus and the Järnefelts and when Sibelius spoke
to him of his plans for *Kullervo* there was some tension between them. He
mentions this in a letter to Aino dated 5 February 1892: 'I am extremely fit
and my head is full of plans for the future. It is a pity that I haven't anyone
here with whom I can share them so it only remains to go one's own way.
I am sorry to say so but I shall have to break with Martin. He cannot bear
seeing any of his pupils standing on their own feet. Kajanus was forced to do
the same thing and also the organist Sjöblom. It is easier for them than it is
for me since I am so much in his debt. One still doesn't have to repudiate
one's debt of gratitude on that account, but he behaves so strangely. Can you
believe it but when I told him I was composing to a text drawn from the
Kalevala, he went completely red in the face and said, "Ugh!"' No doubt
with the thought of Aino in mind, Sibelius added, 'I can't swallow that sort
of thing! That goes for the whole of the Swedish Theatre faction, all those
imported Stockholmers; I loathe them. One of these days I shall show them
what I think of them.'

However matters never came to a head between them and no break occurred.
Some days later he told Wegelius of his plans to marry and the latter promised
to do all in his power to find him a post in the Music Institute. At the beginning
of March Sibelius played over the most recently composed parts of *Kullervo* to
him and as he happened to be in a receptive frame of mind, he showed interest
in the work. Sibelius assured Aino that Wegelius was his old self but none the
less their relationship was not the same as it had been during the previous years.

Sibelius's outburst against the 'Swedish Theatre faction' can have also been
prompted by his sympathy with Karl August Tavaststjerna, whose poems he
had set in Vienna. Tavaststjerna had earlier come into conflict with the manage-
ment of the Swedish Theatre and in the spring of 1892 he was hounded by
the Swedish-language press for his unflattering picture—in the novel, *Hard Times*
—of the behaviour of the Swedish upper classes and the poverty and deprivation
suffered by the Finns during the years of hunger in the late 1860s.

Now he planned a dramatization of the book, in Finnish, a gesture that
was to be regarded as a further betrayal of the Swedish-speaking community
But behind his cynicism and pessimism Sibelius discerned a likeable, sensitive
person: already the previous autumn he had paid a visit to the poet at his
home in Malm just outside Helsinki and he recounted with evident delight
the latter's attitude to marriage in a letter to Aino: 'Do you know that
Tavaststjerna asks nothing else of his wife other than that she spares him the
task of bringing up other people's children. That is real marriage and love!'
Presumably this same autumn Sibelius made the acquaintance of the painter
Axel Gallén (later known as Gallen-Kallela) who was Tavaststjerna's neighbour
at Malm. Gallén had just completed his triptych, *Aino*, again inspired by the
Kalevala but their friendship did not fully ripen at this time as Gallén went to
Paris in March.

Tolstoyan notions rear their head again in his exchanges with the Järnefelt
Writing to Aino he reflects some of her brother, Arvid's enthusiasms: 'In m
new sheepskin coat I look like a veritable peasant. It feels so nice: it woul
be good if one did not have to pretend to be upper class in other circumstanc
as well.' After he had read Aino's short story, 'Kirjansitojan leski' ('The book
binder's widow'), also much influenced by Tolstoy's teachings, Sibelius wrot
cautiously, 'My dear Aino, you can well imagine that I am too subjectiv
and set afire by anything of yours. When we meet I shall tell you in detail (
the impressions it has made on me.' Of course, he did nothing of the kind.

At this time her brother Armas was still in Berlin but two of his piece:
a Romance for violin and a Lyric Overture for orchestra were performe
in Helsinki. Sibelius told Aino what he thought of the Romance and at th
same time gave vent to his feelings about Wagnerism. 'I think that Armas i
too good to indulge in this kind of thing, you know the kind of melodi
sequence that Sinding and others have got from Wagner. This sort of thin
has no effect in the long run. It works well enough for a short time but i
large-scale pieces it is, as far as I am concerned at least, extremely irksome.
The Romance prompted some general reflections on the Järnefelt family, thei
attachment to tradition and their slowness in shaking off its mantle. Yet Sibeliu
concludes by prophesying that Eero will one day be recognized as Finland'
greatest painter and Armas as her greatest musician!

Sibelius's letters to Aino give us a unique opportunity of following th
Kullervo Symphony's birthpangs in detail and almost constitute a working
diary.

(*Letter postmarked 31.1.92*) My work will go quickly now that I have
everything sorted out. Both the larger sections of the *Kullervo and his sister*
are as good as finished. But you know the scene where he actually takes
her which I had first thought of in terms of song and declamation: this
I cannot get right. It would be difficult, this third movement.

(*Letter dated 16.2.92*) I am worried that my symphony won't be ready
in time for the spring. The more I get into it, the larger the subject looms.
I have decided against having the words declaimed but the narrative will
be taken over by the choir. Today I have departed considerably from
my original plan: I shall end the piece with the chorus telling of Kullervo's
death, the orchestra give them full support. My first idea of doing this
entirely orchestrally strikes me now as banal and theatrical. I must also
reduce the number of movements for purely practical reasons.

(*Letter dated 4.3.92*) I've got a good idea for the fourth movement. The
section (*läksi ilotellen* (!) *sotaan* (went to battle with mighty warcries) I am
treating quite literally. There are some march-like ideas that build up to
a climax. Yesterday I was at my wits end because I thought they were so
dreadful, went out for a walk and met Martin W. to whom I played

them. He happened to be in the mood for music and was wholly enthusiastic, really enthusiastic. He has seen the third movement, the one for two soloists and chorus and orchestra; he thinks the women will be embarrassed and won't sing. You, darling, would understand! There is a passage perhaps which could be less vividly portrayed in the orchestra after the words *verat veivät neion mielen* ('clothes now checked the young girl's temper') and where the orchestra goes on. In case the ladies are troubled by this I shall give it to the male choir. Martin said that I have caught the epic character of the poem superbly: that's going too far! He also took me to task for certain crude touches that were in his opinion unjustified: that's also idiotic! I'm optimistic about the fourth movement. If I get this right, there's only the finale to do and this has the great advantage of being with choir. It's in this movement that the choir tells of Kullervo's death. After that I have nothing else, no apotheosis or the like.

(*Letter dated 7.3.92*) I'm writing day and night now; otherwise I won't have the work ready in time for May. I've been so full of life and energy the whole morning that I have felt that nothing was beyond my powers. I must have the piece ready in time even though everyone seems doubtful that I will, Kajanus, Martin and others. Just now your terribly depressing letter came. It affected me physically—it is making me have doubts myself when you, angel, add your voice to the others.

(*Letter dated 12.3.92*) How nice it would be to be left in peace in one's room but today a debt of 500 marks is due and I must naturally try and repay it. Strange, all these money troubles; they depress me most of all. But never mind about them; it's seven in the morning. I shall now begin work: everything I wrote yesterday has to be scrapped.

(*Letter dated 14.3.92*) Yesterday at Erik's I saw a wonderful portrait, more impressive than anything else I have set eyes on. Its whole effect is overwhelming altogether. The movement I am working on, *Kullervo goes to battle* was finished but it doesn't really make its effect, even though the ideas seem to have worked out naturally. After I had seen this portrait at Erik's, I felt that the movement lacked something that his picture had, namely a sense of unity. The movement was strung together, it was in segments. Besides this the second idea was dull. I think it will be better now.

(*Letter dated 23.3.92*) During the last few days I have been at my wits end over my work—have entertained suicidal thoughts and such like. We'll see now whether we can get it ready for the spring.

(*Letter dated 27.3.92*) In the last four days I haven't slept for more than a couple of hours and that was this morning. At the moment I'm very pleased with my work and think it splendid. Not that it is finished yet. But everything is wonderfully clear in my head. O, how I long to get on to the podium and show everybody what I have done.

(*Letter dated 4.4.92*) I am still having terrible trouble with copying and with the scoring. Last night was the tenth in a row that I have been up all night till eight in the morning. Another five days work and I hope it will be finished. Then, of course, it has to be rehearsed.

(*Letter dated 6.4.92*) Both the last days have been spent on rehearsal and getting miserable. I envy all those people who soon reach their goal, people like Kajanus and Armas, who develop rapidly. The time is now half-past nine and I ought to work but can't. My thoughts are with you and have been so all day. Love is a strange thing. I can give myself so wholeheartedly to you, and to my art. I think that fundamentally you are both one and the same thing.

Sibelius conducted *Kullervo* himself. In so far as it called for large resources, soloists, chorus and orchestra, it was a bold venture. At the rehearsals it was vital for him to counter a number of psychological disadvantages. The orchestra regarded him as a composer-conductor without the requisite technique. The majority of them were German who knew nothing of the mythological inspiration of the work. When they first saw their parts they were altogether confounded: some of them laughed to themselves, others laughed openly doubling up over their instruments. The choir was composed of several disparate elements: city gentlemen who got themselves up in evening dress on the night of the première, and as a welcome stiffening, youths from the Church music school in much simpler attire.

Gradually Sibelius won over his players and singers. He spoke German with the former, Swedish with the city gentlemen and Finnish with the boys whom he placed in suitable strategic positions. What he lacked in conducting technique and experience, he made up for by the sheer power of his personality.

When the day of the première came, the Ceremonial Hall of the University was completely sold out. Besides the ordinary concert-going public there were others attending out of patriotic zeal. Sibelius made his entry, looking very pale and his first downbeat was particularly tremulous. Later on he appears to have mastered his nerves but it is clear that the performance was by no means without hazard. The orchestra apparently swamped the soloists, Abraham Ojanperä and Emmy Achté: Achté's daughter, incidentally, for whom Sibelius was later to write *Luonnotar*, was among the audience. Sibelius kept the choral and orchestral forces under his command firmly together: it was a formidable initiation and was greeted by a prolonged ovation.

The fact that *Kullervo* met with an almost unprecedented success has been attributed by some commentators to its patriotic character rather than its musical content. True, the appeal to national sentiment that *Kullervo* makes did not fall on unreceptive ears but that alone would never have led to the work's *succès d'estime* had its musical content not been compelling. Indeed musically the work was regarded as revolutionary in its nationalism by the side of Pacius, von Schantz and even Kajanus who himself had written a

ymphony based on the *Kalevala*. Generally speaking *Kullervo* was well abreast
f its time and as far as Finland was concerned it was progressive without
eing radical. For those among the Helsinki public who knew their Berlioz,
iszt's *Faust Symphony*, or *Die Walküre* and *Parsifal*, *Kullervo* would have
resented relatively few problems even if they did not fully understand it.

Sibelius also fascinated the public as a conductor. Olin Downes who was
resent more than twenty years later when he conducted the première of
The Oceanides wrote that alone among living composer-conductors with the
ossible exception of Rachmaninoff, Sibelius had the power to bring to life
he innermost soul of the music. One can of course, say that the Sibelius of
914 was a very different proposition from the young man who stood before
he Helsinki public in 1892 but the fascination he exercised did not rest on
his expertise with the baton. From the very beginning of his career he had a
personal magnetism and a compelling grip that no course of conducting studies
or even practical experience on the podium could bring.

In his review of the concert, Flodin wrote that Sibelius had now ranged
himself unreservedly among the protagonists of nationalism as many Scandinavians and Russians had already done. 'When Sibelius writes for the chorus
who narrate the tragic events in the drama of Kullervo, he does so in the
simplest monotones and in $\frac{5}{4}$ time; and in so doing follows the ancient runic
pattern.' But Flodin, for all the telling points that he made, did not sufficiently
stress the symphonic elements in the music. Sibelius was as much concerned
with the symphonic implications of his ideas as with their nationalist overtones. Flodin's review prompted a long letter from Adolf Paul, then living
in Berlin, refuting this view of Sibelius as primarily a nationalist, and arguing
that in his individuality he transcended the nationalism current in his day. All
this, however, oversimplifies Flodin's review which had gone on to say,
'Sibelius has established his own voice . . . and with it creates *his* own music
in *our* own music.'

The programme note called *Kullervo*, a 'symphonic poem for chorus,
soloists and orchestra', and the autograph score bears this title too. But in his
letters to his fiancée he had spoken of the work as a symphony and he even
did so in later life. The three purely orchestral movements, the first, second
and fourth, follow traditional patterns: sonata-form, rondo and scherzo, while
in the two choral movements the third and the fifth, Sibelius writes freely in
a *durchkomponiert* manner as did, say, Liszt in the *Dante Symphony*. The co-
existence of these two formal structures serves to give the work some of its
inner tension and its contrast. None the less Sibelius succeeds in holding these
diverse elements together remarkably well: in the finale he recalls themes from
earlier movements and so effectively completes the symphonic circle. Another
source of strength is the unity of the thematic substance itself: the main ideas
seem to belong to one another. Already many of the individual traits of

Sibelius's mature style can be discerned: ostinato figures, long-sustained peda
points, the modal flavouring of much of his thematic invention, the darl
colouring of his sonorities and the epic character of the climaxes. These are
of course, surface characteristics which give a very incomplete idea of th
nature of the music, its architecture and logic.

The *Kullervo* Symphony has no real precedent in Finnish music: the neares
approach to a precursor is perhaps Kajanus's *Aino* Symphony but that is heavily
endowed with Wagnerian chromaticism and the final chorus with its overtone
of *Lohengrin*, and the *Kullervo* Symphony are worlds apart in atmosphere and
quality. Needless to say the fact that Kajanus had drawn on the *Kalevala* for
a big choral and orchestral work must have spurred Sibelius to follow suit
but the musical inspiration for the work comes from the mainstream European
masters, the symphonies of Beethoven, Bruckner, Berlioz and Liszt and perhaps
to a lesser extent, Wagner.

How is it that after a number of respectable student pieces Sibelius was
suddenly capable of composing a work of such ambitious dimensions and
such conviction? Obviously some catalyst had released him from the bonds of
eclecticism and academicism. Perhaps the reading of the *Kalevala* in Vienna
had paved the way and certainly the impact of the primitive folk music that
he had encountered in hearing Larin Paraske served as a powerful generating
agent. Although the comparison should not be pressed too far, it is arguable
that the runes of the *Kalevala* provided Sibelius with an experience not unre-
lated to Bartók's first encounter with ancient Hungarian peasant tunes. Sibelius,
of course, never became a folk music expert and in his total output the folk
element plays a relatively insignificant role in comparison with Bartók.

The melodies written down from Larin Paraske[1] give an idea of the runes
Sibelius would have heard. Generally speaking, a runic melody usually consists of two rhythmically more or less symmetrical five- or four-beat phrases
built up on the first five notes of the minor or major scale. The choice of notes,
sometimes extended, corresponds with that of the five-stringed kantele.[2]

Spondees, dactyls and inverted dactyls are a distinctive feature of the rhythm
of these runic melodies. Repeated notes are common and, as in plainsong,
reciting notes appear. At the end of a phrase the tonic is usually repeated,
often on a full-length beat, a kind of 'Finnish ending' that crops up in more
recent folk melodies too. A runic singer did not usually command a large
repertoire of melodies, and a canto was usually intoned—by one or two singers
—on one and the same melody, which was repeated either unchanged or
slightly varied. The technique of variation concerned rhythmic details, intervals and ornaments, glissandi or tremolandi.

Unlike many more recent folk-songs influenced by classical and romantic
music, runic melodies do not necessarily give rise to the kind of schematic

1. See p. 98.
2. Some experts incline to the view that the kantele's third was so vague that its major
or minor character is unclear.

harmony one finds in most popular music: tonic-dominant-(sub-dominant)-tonic progression. Sibelius does not directly borrow runic melodies in *Kullervo* but rather uses them as stylistic models, as a kind of reservoir of ideas from which he incorporated elements into his own musical language. In the harmonization of motives influenced by folk music Sibelius obviously followed the principle he was later to express in these terms: the harmonies should 'create . . . the climate in which one could imagine folk-song having come into being'. As a result he gives various modal interpretations of the thematic material.[1]

As far as form is concerned, the runic themes led him away from classical period formations. As far as the orchestration is concerned he undoubtedly remoulded certain things in Bruckner, whose Third Symphony he had heard in Vienna. The main theme of the first movement is presented in different sound constellations that one associates with Bruckner. First, in clarinets and horns against a string background. Then, in the woodwind texture over a sustained horn note which has the colour effect of organ registration:

48

A reader for whom the *Kalevala* is unfamiliar may need some guidance at this point. Much of its power resides in its poetic rather than its narrative qualities and in the feeling one senses of the supernatural. As far as the *Kullervo* legend is concerned this is possibly the strongest narrative in terms of action of any in the epic. The pattern of the drama has some points of contact both with Greek tragedy and the Volsung myth as used by Wagner. The protagonist:

> Kullervo, Kalervo's offspring, the old man's son in light-blue hose,
> Glorious golden hair had he, shoes with ribs of leather on them

has traits both of Oedipus and Siegmund. The background is an internecine

---

1. Sibelius's ideas at this stage correspond with the principle Bartók was to formulate some thirty years later: the more primitive a theme, the greater the harmonic freedom it gives the composer.

feud: Kullervo is brought up by his uncle, whose warriors have killed his father and all his retinue. As a little boy Kullervo swears vengeance

> Shall I avenge my father's foul wound,
> Seek retribution for my mother's tears?

He is sold as a serf to Ilmarinen, the mastersmith, rebels against his yoke and takes a terrible revenge for an injury, returns to his family, who in the epic have suddenly been reincarnated. He seduces his own sister without knowing it, takes up arms against his uncle and subsequently vanquishes him only to throw himself on his own sword, consumed by pangs of conscience for his crime of incest.

Kullervo himself then, is a figure of tragic dimensions predestined by fate to misery and disaster. In the first movement, Sibelius as he himself described it, paints a general picture of him in broad brushstrokes without dwelling on any dramatic details. The main theme is in E minor with an Aeolian inflection and which establishes the basic mood of the work:

Ex. 49

The theme has a powerful Brucknerian sweep to commend it; even its colouring has something Brucknerian about it. The theme emerges on the woodwind from a groundswell of strings over a tonic pedal point, and its rising figure of tonic, fifth, octave must surely have been conceived under the influence of Bruckner's Third Symphony. Equally its inspiration can be thought of as Finnish since many folk-songs and particularly those of the lyrical genre such as 'Niin minä, neitonen, sinulle laulan' were well known in Sibelius's youth, and the latter was sung in a choral arrangement by Kajanus:

Ex. 50

Niin mi-nä, nei-to-nen, si-nul-le lau-lan kuin o- malle kul-lal- -le- -ni!

The folk-song begins triadically while Sibelius eschews the minor third and instead gives the line greater character by using the supertonic and in so doing lends it a certain buoyancy and dash.

The second group is composed of two ideas: the first is a horn call, rising from *f* sharp over an augmented fourth, with a (mixolydian) seventh in the accompanying tremolando. It almost foreshadows Bartók's modal practice. It seems to symbolize the forces of fate, an assumption which is confirmed in the finale by the sung text.

Ex. 51

The second appears in the exposition in this form:

Ex. 52

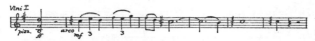

But in the reprise it assumes a simpler, more majestic form strongly reminiscent of runic melodies:

Ex. 53

The key is E minor but the centre of gravity in the last example sinks a major second on to D; in a similar way the final note of a runic melody can come as a surprise.

In the development section Sibelius treats the opening idea though without the second, in canonic imitation, in much the same way as did Bruckner in his Third Symphony:

Ex. 54

The Kullevo theme appears in various guises and keys which reflect different aspects of the hero's psyche: E flat minor represents the mystic, while C minor portrays the hero and seer.

Gradually the atmosphere lightens as the predominantly minor key-colouring
is eroded. The woodwind enter with a variant of the main theme in C major
and the darker features of Kullervo's musical portrait are for a moment
banished. There is a surprising modulation to E major where the woodwind
again present the main theme which apart from a rhythmic modification is
in its major form, identical with that sketched by Sibelius in his letter from
Vienna (18.4.91) when the first ideas for the work came to him. The music
modulates to the tonic E minor and the recapitulation is launched. At the
end of the movement the main theme recurs in a fanfare-like manner on the
woodwind and brass as if to say, the introduction is over and the action can
begin.

The second movement, 'Kullervo's Youth', is in the form ABA1B1A2.
Sibelius himself described it as a lullaby with variations which increase in emotional intensity. The main idea sombre in tone and relentless in its onward tread
has an air of foreboding that through its dark colouring and dissonant harmonies
senses both Kullervo's tragic fate and his heroic stature:

Ex. 55

The theme outlines all the notes in the Dorian sixth (between B and G sharp)
with the exception of the second, C sharp. The insistent hovering around the
dominant, its modal character, and the rhythmic pattern which is characteristic
for many runic songs, gives the idea a certain antiquated flavouring. The
continuation reflects the impulsive and expressive side of Kullervo's character:

Ex. 56

The descending figure is distinctly reminiscent of Tchaikovsky. The first
group also includes a figure that leads to a modulation:

Ex. 57

This idea moves within the narrow confines of a fourth and bears further witness in its effectiveness and insistency to the composer's feeling for the primitive. Some of Paraske's runic intonations provide an interesting point for comparative study.

The contrasting section is of a lighter, pastoral colouring:

Ex. 58

Possibly this survives from the movement that Sibelius had projected in the autumn of 1891 on 'Kullervo as herdsman' and which he subsequently abandoned. The solo clarinet and the cor anglais and the sustained chords in the strings give a quasi-impressionistic effect while the woodwind writing later on shimmers like light over the surface of a lake and foreshadows an element in his stylistic personality that was to emerge at its most eloquent in *The Oceanides*. Like the great runic singers Sibelius varies his main theme on each occasion it recurs but none of these transformations is far reaching although they signalize the technique of metamorphosis that he achieved in his maturity. A certain monotony prevails but is broken by the varied modes and instrumental combinations. When the brass declaim the fate-like rhythm of the opening bars the idea is transformed from a lullaby to a cry of protest and revolt. Kullervo shakes his clenched fists after having broken his beloved knife, and the only relic of his childhood, on the stone which had maliciously been baked into his bread by the wife of Ilmarinen, to whom he had been sold as a slave.

The third movement is arranged like a symphonic act of an opera in two scenes, separated by an orchestral interlude. The distribution of roles is like that of Greek drama: the chorus plays the part of objective narrator, while the soloists—Kullervo and his sister—express the fluctuating emotions.

The lay-out and the most important keys are as follows:

Orchestral introduction (Lydian F major)
Scene One
(chorus, Kullervo and his sister)

1. First meeting (Dorian D minor). After paying his tithes, Kullervo flings himself on to his sleigh and starts his homeward journey. A maiden comes towards him, and Kullervo wants to entice her to him, but she mockingly replies: 'Death perhaps sits in the sleigh!'

2. Second meeting (Dorian E minor). Kullervo is rejected by another maiden who encounters him on his journey:

3. Third meeting (Dorian C sharp minor). A third maiden, the unknown sister, comes towards him on the path leading 'Over Pohja's murky pine heaths, over Lapland's savage country'.
(In the symphony the sister sings the parts of the other two girls as well.) Kullervo drags the unknown girl on to the sleigh despite her resistance.

4. Kullervo tempts the young maiden with white silver and costly clothes (E major). Chorus:
Clothes now checked the young girl's temper, silver likely pleased the maiden,
Kullervo, Kalervo's offspring, the old man's son with blue socks on him
Flattered and then stroked the young girl, smiled, enticed and gently dallied—

Orchestral interlude (Dorian C sharp minor).

Scene Two
(Kullervo and his sister)

5. Dialogue between Kullervo and his sister (A flat major—A flat minor). When 'God's blessed day dawns' after the seduction, the girl asks Kullervo about his family and learns that he is Kalervo's 'poor son'. She then reveals that she is Kalervo's 'poor daughter'. They both realize they have committed incest.

6. The sister's song (Dorian C sharp minor). She describes how she got lost in the forest and laments that she was not killed instantly then:

Should my life have early ended,
In my second year have perished, would I then the following summer
In the pasture grass have glistened, would have carried pretty flowers,
Without need to hear such evil, without need to know perdition.

The sister then throws herself into the whirling rapids.

7. Finale. Kullervo's lament (Dorian, then natural F minor):

Wretched is my life and hapless, and a worthless villain am I
Who seduced my own dear sister, who has known my mother's offspring!
Death fulfilled his task but badly, failed to find his proper victim
When to take me he neglected when I was but two nights old.

The central key relationship, F—C sharp—F, a major third, provides a strong form-building factor. In many later symphonies similar relationships play a decisive role.

KULLERVO

The brilliant orchestral introduction, allegro vivace, begins with a motive that recalls the Karelian dances of a trepak-like character which Sibelius treats freely in $\frac{5}{4}$ time:

Ex. 59

$\frac{5}{4}$ rhythms do appear in certain kinds of Karelian trepak variants such as the trepatchka or the ribatska where they alternate with the normal $\frac{4}{4}$ of the genre. After this introduction Kullervo's three meetings are depicted. Each of these episodes begins with the chorus describing the scene, in the Dorian mode and in $\frac{5}{4}$ time, and the resulting music has a stylized runic quality about it:

Ex. 60

By contrast with these epic elements come the dramatic exchanges between the two protagonists. At the end of the third meeting the sister gives vent to her bewilderment in an explosive outburst:

Ex. 61

Even as late as his year in Vienna, Sibelius maintained that he was uncertai
about certain stresses in Finnish but in this movement he composes (for th
first time in the history of Finnish music) a recitative of great skill that
completely secure in its treatment of the spoken language. When the siste
is tempted with 'the white silver and costly clothes' the music displays a
almost Rimsky-Korsakovian sensuousness, although Sibelius would not hav
heard much of his music at this date.

The next passage describes the seduction in an orchestral interlude (the on
to which Sibelius made reference in his letter of 17 December 1891), and thi
can be regarded as the centre of gravity of the movement. The violins hav
an impassioned figure punctuated by a rhythmic accompaniment from the res
of the orchestra:

Ex. 62

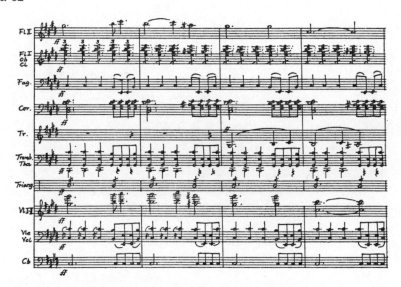

This is no Tristan-like meeting in the grounds of a castle nor the gentle
erotic fancies of a faun in the impressionistic landscape. It is an encounter
between two primitives who experience all-powerful sensations and feelings
on their eventful journey over snow-covered wastes. Sibelius's orchestral
writing here is sparer and his sonorities more granite-like than those of *Lemminkäinen and the Maidens of the Island* which treats a similarly erotic theme
and on which he was to embark only a few years later. Only in the closing
bars of this episode do we encounter any hint of Tristan-like sensibility.

After this there follows a short passage in A flat major which conveys something of the lovers' ecstasy before they make their discovery that they are
brother and sister. In the sister's lament we hear her vain cries echoed from the
forest:

Ex. 63

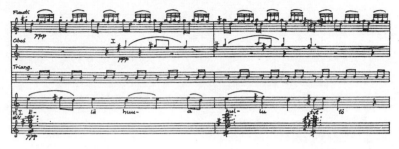

Again the melodic line moves within a narrow compass and foreshadows the recitative style which Sibelius was to employ in some of his later songs. The sister's monologue of lament ends with a chord of C sharp minor sustained on the woodwind: and without any attempt at transition, Sibelius plunges us immediately into F minor and Kullervo's song of woe. This particular relationship between minor tonalities a third apart (in this case C sharp minor can equally well be regarded as D flat) seems to be a favourite one of the young Sibelius.

Kullervo's Lament is accompanied by convulsive chords on the orchestra and in it Kullervo longs for death but before this swears vengeance on those who have crushed his family and sold him into slavery:

Ex. 64

The next movement depicts Kullervo going forth to battle and gives us a picture, both colourful and vivid, of his proud and arrogant bearing. There are piccolo trills, timpani rolls, cellos pizzicato, while in the theme itself, the flattened leading note and the minor sixth cast a shadow on the air of optimism:

Ex. 65

Another theme suggests Karelian and Russian influences as far as rhythm is concerned:

Ex. 66

To what extent Sibelius was influenced in this passage by the music of the Karelian folk instrumentalists must remain a matter for conjecture. There is a faint reminder of the Russian Dance from *Petrushka* both in its rhythmic ebullience and in its harmonization all on the white notes. Another passage in the middle section is surprisingly enough redolent of the Glinka–Borodin tradition with which Sibelius was in all probability unfamiliar:

Ex. 67

The opening of the finale is mysterious and dream-like: motives from earlier movements appear and recede like remembrances of the past. Kullervo's sword has been given him by the god, Ukko, just as Siegmund's sword was a gift

om Wotan—granted to him to defeat his enemies. Here the difference be-
ween the *Kalevala* and the Volsung myth as used by Wagner can be seen.
Wotan is compelled to let Siegmund fall in the fight with Hunding as a punishment for the crime of incest. But the god of the *Kalevala* is not a god who exacts
unishment. Kullervo's success in arms could be taken as a sign that Ukko is
favourably disposed towards him. Kullervo is driven towards death by his own
conscience. His gentle mother speaks to him from the grave:

> Take thy faithful dog as comrade, and depart into the wasteland,
> High thee to some forest corner, there to meet with forest maidens!

Kullervo's repentance—evidence perhaps of the Christian influence at work
in the *Kalevala*—is the central theme of the introductory scene of the Finale.
Kullervo wanders like a sleep-walker back to the place where he had 'embraced
his mother's offspring'. The feeling of a dream is underlined by the almost
cluster-like tremolo in the violins accompanying the narrative of the chorus:

Ex. 68

The choral part is a recitative variant of the horn signal in the first movement.
Its symbolic function as an element of fate is clearly apparent here: it drives
him back to the scene of his crime and towards his expiatory death.

Other reminders of the first movement also appear. The runic subsidiary
theme sounds like a lacrimosa in the strings and woodwind, while the chorus
laments in harmonies reminiscent of the Orthodox funeral service:

Ah, there the grass so green does weep, there laments the lovely lime-tree. . . .

In the following scene the tritone interval presages death, the piccolo and
flute cry like birds of ill-omen, the recitation of the chorus returns to the
incantation motive of the second movement, the invocation of the shamanistic
youthful years:

> Kullervo, Kalervo's offspring drew his sharp sword from its scabbard,
> Turned it this way turned it that, thought awhile and listened carefully,
> Goads it to its fatal purpose. . . .

The solo parts should refer the music back to the more operatic level of the
third movement. These are not supplied by the text. The only directly quoted

lines are in the answer of the sword to Kullervo's fateful question, and the
are repeated by the chorus:

. . . Why should I not with willing heart
This guilt-infected flesh consume, now drain the blood by crime besmirched

The coiling arpeggios in the strings might symbolize his tormented conscience
When Kullervo throws himself on the point of his sword, the trumpets blaze
forth in a strident minor second, while the seduction-lament motif is heard in
the string figuration.

The orchestra engraves Kullervo's epitaph in a formal lament. The runic
subsidiary theme sings its elegy, but here, as at the end of the first movement
it runs into a conciliatory major episode with touches of the horn signal, the
theme of fate. When the lament fades away in a pianissimo the memory of
everything evil is expunged, and one feels that one is looking at the true face
of the tragic hero. In the coda the Kullervo theme appears in a monumental
tutti in which the chorus interposes:

His own life so took he swiftly, and by death he was subjected.

Even here Sibelius gives proof of his ability to endow a symphonic theme
with definitive significance.

The symphony was repeated at a matinée concert the day after its première
and the fourth movement alone was included in a popular concert, the last
of the season, on the day after that (30 April 1892). In the following March
Sibelius conducted three further performances of Kullervo before withdrawing
it: he permitted no other complete performance of it during the rest of his
lifetime. Not until 1935 did he consent to a performance of the third movement at the Kalevala centenary, and twenty-two years later, some months
before his death, Kullervo's lament was included in the programme of the
Sibelius Festival in Helsinki.

What was the reason for this ban? He told Cecil Gray in 1930, that he was
not satisfied with Kullervo in its existing form. But he did not want to undertake only a touching-up of the more obvious shortcomings for fear of upsetting
the work as a whole. Gray agreed by saying that a partial revision would
almost inevitably have resulted in failure. 'The only really satisfactory method
of rewriting a work is to revise it from beginning to end, and without doubt
Sibelius feels that it is more rewarding to compose new works than to revise
old ones.'

True—but Sibelius had never before shrunk from radical revisions, for
example En Saga (1892, 1902), Tulen Synty (The Origin of Fire, 1902, 1910),
The Fifth Symphony (1915, 1916, 1919). He obviously did not want to touch
Kullervo because in his heart of hearts he knew that it was a successful if not
fully mature work.

Sibelius's unwillingness to have it performed sprang from psychological origins. He was at pains to appear as a unique and independent phenomenon, uninfluenced by other composers or by folk music. He emphasized to his first Finnish biographer, Erik Furuhjelm, in 1915, that he had first learnt to know runic song in the autumn of 1892, *after* having completed *Kullervo*. He wanted to forget—and succeeded in doing so—that *before* writing *Kullervo* he had gone to Borgå expressly to listen to Larin Paraske. But *Kullervo* remained as a monument to the inspiration he derived from folk music, and everything it had meant for his artistic liberation. But there was another reason too. *Kullervo* might well have signified the start of a Mahlerian line of development which would have resulted in another Eighth Symphony. Instead, Sibelius chose a symphonic line which led further and further away from *Kullervo* towards works which were classical and concentrated. The more time passed the greater would be the contrast between *Kullervo* and his ideal. Besides, symphonies with many long movements for chorus, soloists and orchestra were not in fashion in London and Paris in the 1920s and 1930s.

In old age his attitude to the ban on the performance of the work seems to have relaxed. In 1955, when considering allowing Eugene Ormandy to conduct the second and fourth movements, he said to his daughter Eva: 'They are quite different from *Lemminkäinen*, which blazes with vitality and youth. *Kullervo* has power, too, but of a different kind.' He began to be reconciled to the idea that the symphony in its entirety might be taken up after his death, and finally accepted it as something quite natural.

The complete performance which took place in Helsinki in 1958 under his son-in-law Jussi Jalas was certainly not in conflict with his last wishes.

Maria Sibelius had worried that her son would be unable to support a wife in any reasonable degree of comfort, but after the success of the *Kullervo* Symphony Sibelius's prospects looked a good deal brighter, as he had himself predicted in his letter to General Järnefelt. The date of the wedding was fixed in early June. In February Sibelius had written to Aino suggesting that were they to marry in the spring they should spend the summer in Karelia but when spring came, he hardly had funds enough to meet his simplest daily needs and was compelled to live on borrowed money. In order to finance their honeymoon, Sibelius hit on the idea of combining it with collecting folk-songs and to this end the university gave him a grant of 400 marks and offered a further 200 should the venture yield fruit. Kaarle Krohn, the chairman of the Finnish Literary Society furnished him with a list of all the runic singers that he should visit.

The marriage ceremony took place in the Järnefelt family home at Tottesund. Sibelius's side of the family was represented by his sister Linda and brother Christian, his mother having succumbed a few weeks before to a nervous condition which incapacitated her. The bridal couple set off on their honeymoon spending twenty-four hours at Imatra[1] before continuing north-wards into the Karelian interior. At Joensuu they hired a square piano and embarked with it on one of the inland steamers arriving at Lieksa, on the east coast of Pielisjärvi early one morning. The somewhat haphazard and im-provised nature of their journey was typical of Sibelius: he still had no idea where they were going to stay. By a stroke of good fortune they secured quarters at Monola to the north-west; their piano was unloaded on to two rowing boats and borne to Monola.

Monola itself proved to be idyllic with birch trees adorning the water's edge while on the opposite side of the lake stretched the forests covering the hills of Koli. Perhaps it was this sight that prompted him to set Runeberg's 'Under strandens granar' ('Beneath the Fir Trees') with its atmosphere of trolls and water-sprites at play. This piece, incidentally, was originally conceived as an orchestral tone poem before it turned into a song. It was at Monola at any rate that Sibelius made two other Runeberg settings; 'Kyssens hopp' ('The Kiss's Hope') and 'Till Frigga' ('To Frigga').

Having established his headquarters in Karelia Sibelius had originally planned to make small expeditions in search of runic song taking Aino with him. But in the event he was unwilling to expose her to the hardships of travel in this part of the country. She made her way back to Kuopio while he went on alone eastwards to the remoter parts of Korpiselkä. Some folk melodies that survive among his papers probably come from this Karelian journey: there are some four runic melodies, two wedding songs and a dance-like song of less greater antiquity than the others. One of the former is from the *Kalevala* ('Kullervo, Kalervo's son') while the notation of one of the wedding songs appears to have given him a headache since he tried writing it in both $\frac{3}{4}$ and $\frac{5}{2}$.

For all its paucity the material must have given Sibelius some insight into folklore and showed him, if nothing else, that runic melodies did not neces-sarily have to be slow and mournful. However it would be idle to pretend that Sibelius achieved any spectacular results in his expedition: he showed relatively little scientific interest in folk-song collecting, even if he was later to do some editing of folk tunes for the supplementary volume published by the Finnish Literary Society for the *Kalevala* (1895) and also arranged six folk-songs for piano.

His journey should be judged against the general background of interest that ran through Finnish artistic circles at this particular time. More than half a century had elapsed since the *Kalevala* had been published and by now the time was ripe for artists, poets and musicians to create something original but in its spirit. Sibelius was not alone in his expedition into inner Karelia. Gallén had set the pace by spending his honeymoon on the eastern side of the border and while Sibelius went off to Korpiselkä, Gallén made a further pilgrimage to Kuusamo; they were not alone. Louis Sparre and the sculptor Wikström made their travels here and so did Eero Järnefelt and Juhani Aho. The spirit

1. Incidentally, Stravinsky was to spend a few days here during his honeymoon.

of the *Kalevala* epic and the upsurge of interest in Karelia were two dominant features of the Finnish cultural scene in the nineties but they were by no means isolated phenomena but rather a parallel to the preoccupation with symbolism and primitivism and the development of *l'art nouveau* on the continent.

Sibelius returned from Korpiselkä towards the end of July. He and his wife stayed awhile at Kuopio where they saw a lot of Minna Canth, the dramatist, and the literary circle that she gathered around her. Among her summer guests were Tavaststjerna and Aho: the good lady herself was in the throes of an enthusiasm for Theosophy and Buddhism, and in addition arranged séances in her home. In Tavaststjerna she found a ready and sympathetic listener to her theosophical speculations: both of them were keenly interested in Tolstoy. But Sibelius was sceptical about the spiritualist table rappings and did not hesitate to tease his hostess about them: nor did he ever come to share the common interest in theosophy, as Scriabin was to do. He surely breathed a sigh of relief when the nocturnal conversation with the spirits was interrupted by the return of Tavaststjerna's wife, Gabrielle from a party who brought them down to earth with her disarming coquetry.

CHAPTER SEVEN

En Saga

IN THE autumn of 1892 the newly-weds set up home in a wooden house in Wladimirinkatu (now called Kalevankatu). Their new flat had plenty of room but was sparsely furnished. Christian lived with them as a tenant and, of course, Janne gaily threw himself into the part of the jealous husband. Some months before their marriage Sibelius had written to his fiancée arguing that the only way to ensure that an artist does not go downhill on marrying is for his wife to be understanding and not to try and force him into middle-class domesticity. 'The last thing he must become is the kindly, drowsy, pipe-smoking head of the house: he must be free to continue his imaginative life undisturbed as before, that's absolutely essential! The sort of marriage that centres solely on rearing children is anathema to me—there are other things to think about if you are an artist.' He was fortunate himself in that respect: Aino was disinclined to put him on the social treadmill or turn him into a respectable, middle-class worthy. She was a person of great character to the extent that even in times of hardship when he was writing potboilers to make ends meet, she would tell him not to waste his time but to write symphonies. At nights she would lie awake waiting for the sound she liked above all others: the rasp of his pen preparing the manuscript paper ready for writing out the music he had just conceived. She was at times the victim of depression and took a blacker view of life: then she would retire and immure herself within a wall of silence, but it was the compound of the poetic and the stern unbending integrity that was her strength and that fascinated him. She had the quiet unassuming qualities of the true aristocrat and providing that her station in life was maintained, demanded nothing for herself. Sibelius had asked her when he was living in Vienna whether she thought she could tolerate his bohemian way of life; marriage with her struck him as the only realistic solution to his problems. 'People always say that it is the end of an artist when he marries, but with me the opposite is the case.'

He estimated that on his own he could manage on 3,000 marks a year if he really tried and with 500 less if he were living with Aino. These somewhat bewildering sums were based on the sure belief in Aino's powers to stabilize him and his housekeeping and his way of life. But things did not work out quite as planned. As the years wore on he became more and more extravagant: Aino never attempted to keep too watchful an eye on his outgoing expenditure; nor did she indulge in recrimination on his other outgoings! She was too wise for that and too proud.

But Sibelius had to prove himself now as a breadwinner. The idea of joining Kajanus's orchestra did not appeal to him; playing under Fuchs in Vienna had given him quite enough headaches to put paid to that notion. Nor did the idea of becoming a professional chorus master make much appeal to him with all the inevitable chores of preparing other people's music. Only teaching was left. Wegelius offered him some work at the Music Institute and Kajanus did the same: he took both chances. At Wegelius's institute he had a theory class and took some violin pupils. The job was no sinecure: the most interesting pupils naturally went to Wegelius himself. At Kajanus's Orchestra School Sibelius gradually took over from Kajanus's own theory classes and again had some violin teaching. At times he had as much as thirty hours' teaching a week and even though he was free for long periods during the summer, Adolf Paul wrote to him that he was exploited and was in any event unfitted to be a school teacher! Eventually at the turn of the century Sibelius gave up teaching and received only a few select pupils, among them Leevi Madetoja and Bengt von Törne.

In the autumn he also returned to his old place at the second desk of the Institute's string quartet and during their 1892–3 season took part in about ten public concerts. But he began to realize that he could no longer live the double life of composer, teacher and executant and decided not to go on with his violin playing and left the quartet at the end of the season.

Undoubtedly Paul was right: Sibelius was not a born teacher and lacked the urge to pass on his learning to others. For him teaching was not a stimulus but merely a hindrance to composition. Nor did he feel the impulse to publish his thoughts on composition and teaching, or a treatise on instrumentation, as did Schoenberg and Rimsky-Korsakov. And unlike Stravinsky, he kept his aesthetic theorizing to himself. Nevertheless he was not wholly without merits as a teacher. Otto Kotilainen, a song composer who attended his classes in the 1890s, described how this 'tall, slender figure with bright sparkling eyes and a bushy shock of hair' would burst into the room, politely send off the girls to go for a long healthy walk, give him some work to do, and then promptly disappear. But unlike Wegelius he was no stickler for the rules. 'If the melody and the harmonies sounded all right and the piece as a whole made a good impression on him, he would content himself with a bare mention of any of the rules involved, and would go on to praise the student's individuality.' When Madetoja went to him for a couple of years in 1908, Sibelius greeted him with the words, 'I'm a poor teacher.' Madetoja himself wrote in later years: 'It wasn't teaching in the normal sense of the word. Rather short, searching comments. He didn't waste much time on the fugue that I had taken along with me to show him but talked about more general aesthetic problems. "No dead, unnecessary notes. Every note must live." When he was dealing with a pupil of Madetoja's talent, he concentrated on central issues in much the same way as had Goldmark. Any mediocrity can teach himself the necessary craftsmanship but for a genuinely creative talent he would say, "What is the study of composition if it is not the act of composing?" '

As early as September 1892 the press had carried reports that Sibelius was to publish a collection of Runeberg settings before Christmas. Abraham Opanjerä sang two of them in public, 'Under strandens granar' and 'Till Frigga' on 16 December roughly at the same time that the Finnish publisher Otava brought them out. This was the first volume of his to appear in print that bore his name on the title page and it was engraved in Leipzig by Breitkopf and Härtel. The Finnish public inured to the watery Leipzig romanticism of Pacius, von Schantz, Faltin, Ehrström and their like, found these pieces new and disturbing. Oskar Merikanto's review of them in *Päivälehti* echoes this: 'Though the songs bear the imprint of the composer of *Kullervo*, the original use of rhythm and the bizarre harmonies make a confusing and even tiring impression on the uninitiated ear.' The first of the Seven Songs is 'Under strandens granar' which Sibelius had composed on his honeymoon at Monola by Lake Pielsjärvi. Inspired by a Serbian folk-song, Runeberg gave his poem the character of a folk ballad. The words tell how a water-sprite seduces a handsome youth whom he lures into his power. Sibelius's setting is in a free, recitative-like style. In part he keeps to the pentameter rhythm in the solo line; elsewhere he draws out the line of the verse to six- or seven-beat phrase lengths. The rhythm and the uneven phrase repetitions as well as the introduction of the Dorian and Phrygian modes serve to lend it an archaic flavour. The piano part sounds like a straightforward transcription of a long string tremolando passage broken only by the fanfares suggesting the ride, and a seductive flute solo.

Even if one didn't know, one would guess that the song was originally thought of in terms of a symphonic poem:

Sibelius does not allow himself to be worried by the thought of parallel fifths. This passage, for example, sounds for all the world like a harbinger of Debussy's 'Canope' (*Préludes*—II):

Ex. 70

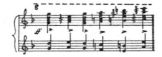

Stylistically 'Under strandens granar' differs as much on the one hand from say, Wolf's densely packed miniatures or Strauss's opulent *lieder*, as it does on the other from the complex psychological portraits of Mussorgsky. Sibelius's central concern in this song is with nature and its pantheistic feeling is dominant. In this song he can be said to have created a new kind of song type: an incantation to nature, and in that sense 'Under strandens granar' presages his most remarkable contributions to the literature of song, 'Höstkväll', 'På verandan vid havet', and 'Luonnotar'.

'Till Frigga' is also ambitious in scope. Runeberg's poem has a majestic tread:

> Mig ej lockar din skatt, Afrikas gyllne flod!
> Ej din perla jag sökt, strålande ocean!
> Friggas hjerta mig lockar, röjdt i tårade ögats dagg.

> Your treasure does not allure me, Africa's golden river!
> I have not sought you jewels, bright ocean!
> Fricka's heart draws me, betrayed in the dew of tears.
>
> (*literal translation*)

Sibelius sets this in a spacious $\frac{9}{4}$; the rests on the strong beats in the accompaniment as well as the slowly rising vocal line suggest a solemn almost evocative atmosphere:

Ex. 71

Motives with a similar rhythm are a feature of Sibelius's later melodic style, as for example, the first movement of the Second Symphony, and are often attributed to the influence of Finnish speech rhythms. Here, however it springs from a Swedish context. This passage later in the song:

Ex. 72

clearly anticipates the slow movement of the Second Symphony.

'Våren flyktar hastigt' ('Spring is flying') is much closer to the conventional *lied*. Both in its outline and the treatment of its melodic ideas, the song reflects the transition from despondency to hope that occurs in Runeberg's poem. The girl's lament that her beauty will fade as quickly as the spring passes, is in E flat minor:

Ex. 73

When the boy answers in the tonic major, the contrast is not only one of tonality but a psychological transformation. This was the only one of the songs that Sibelius later scored.

'Drömmen' ('The Dream') had been written in Vienna the previous year and
bore witness to Sibelius's awakening interest in the *Kalevala* and runic melody:

Ex. 74

The five-beat phrase lengths of the line are written down in $\frac{3}{4}$, the upbeat
in the second is a concession to the rhythm of spoken Swedish. [After the
evocative main section in F minor, there is a static middle section. Sibelius
contents himself with merely hinting at a reprise and the song ends abruptly.]

Both the melodic line and the semiquaver accompaniment in the piano part
of the next song, 'Jägargossen' ('The Young Hunstman') makes one think of
Schubert. The tension between the two minor tonalities, in this case G minor
and E flat minor, a third apart, is characteristic, and the song explores a darker
world and broader human dimensions than its title would lead one to
expect.

'Hjärtats morgon' ('The Heart's Morning') has a dark pathos that is underlined
by the low-lying alternating chords in the accompaniment. The song, like its
companion, 'Kyssens hopp' ('The Kiss's Hope') belongs to the Scandinavian
romans tradition. The latter with its fanciful story of the dialogue between two
as yet unborn kisses has strong Griegian affinities.

There is a further Runeberg setting from this period, a melodrama written
for performance at a ceremony at the Music Institute in honour of the poet's
birthday on 5 February 1893. This draws on verses from the cycle of poems
called 'Svartsjukans nätter' ('Nights of Jealousy'), in themselves so lyrical that
they are an incitement to a composer. Sibelius's setting is for voice, violin,
cello and piano and the composer himself described it in later years as 'belonging
wholeheartedly to his romantic period and having little to do with Runeberg'.

Up to this point Sibelius had still not written a purely orchestral piece that
had established a place in the repertory and after the success of *Kullervo*,
Kajanus had urged him to do so. During the summer and autumn of 1892
Sibelius worked on *En Saga* the first performance of which he conducted at a
Helsinki concert on 16 February 1893. Though it lasted twenty minutes instead
of the seventy-five minutes of *Kullervo*, it was not quite the straightforward

repertory piece Kajanus had had in mind. Indeed after its première Karl Flodin had written that it "posed the listener a series of puzzles", but after having heard it for the third time—the piece was performed on no fewer than five occasions during the year—he wrote of "its incomparable beauty". Merikanto, too, hailed it as Sibelius's finest work to date though he thought that it could be cut with advantage. The piece inspired Axel Gallén to do an aquarelle in the form of a diptych: on the left there was a fantastic landscape and to the right a portrait of the composer in half profile. A small thin part of the canvas remained blank, the idea being that Sibelius himself would fill this in with a quotation from *En Saga*. But he never did so, presumably because he found no connection between Gallén's painting with its trees and knotted roots, apples, castle, river and snowflakes all somewhat suggestive of Japanese paintings, and his own tone poem. The Japanese element may well have been inspired by contact with Gauguin's Bretagne painting. But whatever the merits of the landscape, the portrait of Sibelius is I think the best that has ever been made. No other artist has so successfully captured the visionary quality and the contemplative side of his nature.

Nearly ten years later, in the summer of 1902, Busoni invited Sibelius to give the work in Berlin that autumn and before doing so, the latter submitted it to a thoroughgoing revision, conducting it for the first time in its new definitive form in Helsinki on 2 November 1902 with great success. Flodin wrote that the work had gained both as a whole and in many points of detail from the revisions and that it was now more cogently argued while 'the aural effects are no less individual or striking in character'.

Some people have sought for the background of *En Saga* in the primitive mythological world of Ossian or the *Kalevala*: others have seen it as an epic folk tale in romantic dress 'with the simplicity of a folk-song, the gloom of the wilderness and the splendour of the princess and all her riches' as Elmer Diktonius put it. Flodin felt the raging tempests of Francesca and Paole in the *Inferno* of Dante while Olin Downes was gripped by an irresistible impulse to abandon civilization and set out to hunt the polar bear. However it was Walter Nieman who came nearest the mark when he wrote: 'It is rather a question of a state of mind, the musical atmosphere a saga engenders in the listener, irrespective of whether it is Icelandic, Swedish or Finnish.' In the 1940s Sibelius told his secretary much the same thing: '*En Saga* is the expression of a state of mind. I had undergone a number of painful experiences at the time and in no other work have I revealed myself so completely. It is for this reason that I find all literary explanations quite alien.'

As an old man Sibelius answered a foreign inquiry by saying that if one has to find a literary and folkloristic source for *En Saga*, the atmosphere of the piece was far closer to the *Eddas* than to the *Kalevala*.

En Saga opens with a rising and falling second on horn and bassoon over arpeggio strings which shimmer like a seascape:

Ex. 75

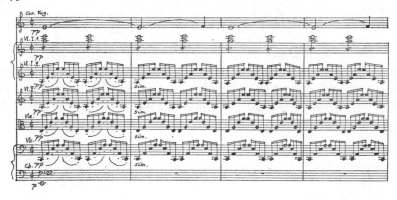

This sheen of light is suddenly extinguished and the woodwind intone a new idea, an archaic sounding motive that keeps within the compass of a fourth:

Ex. 76

With its stepwise motion and its tendency to hover around the same note this idea has much of the character of primitive folk melody. From it comes one of the basic motives of the whole work.

The strings resume their arpeggio pattern in which they are joined by flutes, while on the horn there is a rising fifth, a premonitary sign of the epic main theme. The rising second returns and the horn makes a further effort to adumbrate the theme. The woodwind figure reappears only to be swept away by a string arpeggio pattern from which the epic main theme appears on the bassoon:

Ex. 77

As the key rises stepwise, so the theme itself assumes a slightly modified contour:

Ex. 78

The whole of the introduction, which is dominated by the divisi string
arpeggio writing, is impregnated with a kind of fairy-tale atmosphere; only
now, when the tempo changes to allegro does the real musical action begin:

Ex. 79

The idea of transforming an idea from the slow introduction to serve as the
main subject of the Allegro has its roots as far back as the French overture but
it found particular favour towards the end of the nineteenth century. The
Allegro begins in D minor though it is strongly Dorian in flavour, but soon
modulates to the predominant key centre of the work, C minor. There is a
small development section within the framework of the first group itself and
as Nils-Eric Ringbom has pointed out, it is the second clause of the main theme
that assumes the leading role in the drama and eventually gives birth to the
following viola theme with the subsequent violin comment:

Ex. 80

This viola theme has, of course, already been prepared by the woodwind in
the introduction. It is a more concentrated form of the second clause of the
main theme, as is the violin comment too! Thus, the basic ideas of the tone
poem are polarized: one is an epic theme, narrative in character, (Ex. 77), the
other a theme of action, with a more highly defined rhythmic shape.

For about the next 120 bars the musical argument takes place over a typically Sibelian pedal point on the mediant (E flat in C minor): only once does it rise stepwise to G, before returning after a few bars to its original E flat. Further on in the work long sustained pedal points, mostly on the mediant or dominant, serve to underline the epic, brooding atmosphere of the piece.

The second subject sounds a note of insistence and menace:

Ex. 81

With the sole exception of an octave leap, this moves entirely within the compass of a fifth and in the minor form of the scale. Because of this it has some of the primitive, archaic flavour that Sibelius was striving for.

The final element in the second group is a dance-like figure on the woodwind with the falling minor second of the opening now on the strings:

Ex. 82

The latter is repeated to almost hypnotic effect and leads directly into a kind of modified counter-exposition where the main themes appear in various guises and combinations. The triplet figure in the viola theme (bar 19 of Ex. 80) gives rise to a mysterious forward-moving episode on the strings *sul ponticello* and with this passage we cross into the development section. From the dance-like theme a sequential wave-like motion is generated and over this the second subject makes some dramatic entries:

Ex. 83

This kind of momentum which gathers when cumulative energy is built up may well be what Schoenberg meant when he spoke of both Sibelius and Shostakovich having 'the breath of symphonists'. The rhythm of the viola theme gradually emerges and reduces the temperature while its violin pendant appears on various solo instruments. When all this activity subsides and only a pedal point is left, four solo violins and a viola recall the opening minor second which they harmonize in a subtle and poignant way:

Ex. 84

A fragment of the second subject restores the music to new life and woodwind fanfares herald a veritable orchestral stampede:

Ex. 85

Against the rhythm of the viola theme, the fanfares and the insistent rhythm the main idea grinds to a sudden halt. Various themes then reappear only to vanish like visions and memories from the past: finally comes the epilogue in E flat minor. There are poignantly accentuated string chords *ppp* over which the solo clarinet plays the main epic theme *dolcissimo* as the saga draws to an end and then the cellos whisper the other leading motive (Ex. 180) until it, too, fades into the darkness and only the rhythm remains.

En Saga belongs formally to the freer sonata pattern evolved by Liszt in his symphonic poems and the sonata and other works. Even in the various sub-sections of the work, there is a tendency for the material to be subdivided into a miniature exposition, development and reprise, so that the form of the whole isreflected in the structure of the parts. After the introduction, *En Saga* retains its same basic tempo and in this respect differs from the one-movement structures of Liszt and Strauss; the B minor Sonata on the one hand and *Don Juan* on the other, both have built-in sections of an adagio or scherzo-like character. In its definitive form *En Saga* has no such interlude but in its original form there was. This occurred in the development section where there was an extended interlude with entirely new thematic material:

Ex. 86

Here we see the origins of the fanfare-like figure in the reprise. In the first version the lyrical idea was developed and the tempo gradually slackened. There was a Wagnerian sounding chromatic series of modulations after which the string theme was built into an expressive cantilena. In revising the work, Sibelius cut out this lyric episode replacing it with the *sul ponticello* passage and with the second subject counterpoint and it is this that Ringbom rightly calls 'the greatest and most important gain in the revision'.

The first version of *En Saga* betrays its close proximity with *Kullervo* in several ways. It shows much the same unevenness: the orchestration is rough-and-ready, formally it is less expert with some of the transitions appearing a bit abrupt. There are even some thematic connections between *Kullervo* and the revised *En Saga*. The opening of *Kullervo* with its rise first of a fifth and then a fourth recurs in the fanfare-like motive (ten bars before letter Q) of *En Saga*, while the rising and falling minor second at the beginning of the tone poem recalls the second group of the first movement of the *Kullervo* Symphony. There is even a rhythmic correspondence between the epic mean idea (Ex. 77) in *En Saga* and the motive from the second movement of the *Kullervo* Symphony circumscribed by the fourth (Ex. 57). But the typically national features of *Kullervo*, such as $\frac{5}{4}$ phrases, runelike melodies and so on, are not present in *En Saga*. In his revision Sibelius did not merely content himself with improving on details but re-structured the piece from new artistic premises. He consciously strove to insist on a mood or rhythm: the new version reveals fewer tempo changes, a lower rate of key change and longer sustained pedal points. By eliminating the middle section and instead working over the themes of the exposition more thoroughly Sibelius achieved a tauter more concentrated whole. The orchestral sonority is better balanced and more richly differentiated but although he refined the texture he did not take advantage of the revision to introduce timpani but retained his bass drum, cymbals and triangle as in the original. If the final version stands head and shoulders above its predecessor, it is because it reflects Sibelius's technical assurance and artistic maturity after the Second Symphony. The material of the work itself, however, remains part and parcel of the world of the 1890s and belongs in the company of *Kullervo*.

In 1893 Sibelius composed his first *a cappella* male choir song, 'Venematka' ('The Boat Journey') to a text from the *Kalevala* (Rune XL, lines 1–16). Already in the first bar the abrasive effect of the ninth marks a break with the polite tradition of domestic song writing. 'The Boat Journey' also serves to show that the *Kalevala* did not always inspire gloom and brooding but could also give rise to quite cheerful music:

Ex. 87

Cheerfully Väinämöinen and his herdsmen pilot their small craft among the inlets and islands under the watchful eyes of the feminine inhabitants! Towards the close the major key is suddenly darkened by the flattened sixth and seventh and the piece is enveloped in a mist of sound. A student group, Ylioppilaskunnan Laulajat, sang it for the first time at their spring concert in 1893. On the same scrap of paper as 'Venematka' Sibelius began to sketch another song for male choir, 'Heitä, koski, kuohuminen' ('Rapids, cease your foaming') which continues the narrative where 'Venematka' left off. Väinämöinen, Ilmarinen and Lemminkäinen and their followers have stopped to pause by the rapids and so as to appease the daughter of the rivers, Lemminkäinen sings a magic tune. The chorus begins serenely enough with some $\frac{5}{4}$ phrases and the two-part setting is pregnant with atmosphere; the music culminates in an ecstatic outburst before breaking off. Sibelius never completed the piece.

Among the first of their friends to visit the Sibeliuses in their new home was the poet Tavaststjerna. On a drawing-room table he found a copy of some of his poems and was flattered to see that it had been much thumbed. It was one of their last meetings for Tavaststjerna went abroad after the autumn of 1892. Although *Hard Times* had enjoyed a great success, he became increasingly unhappy with the way in which things were moving in Finland, and went into self-imposed exile. He regarded himself as a Finn, a Lapp, a man of the forest and detested Helsinki. Sibelius, too, regarded himself in later years as a man of the forests but where urban life pained and demoralized the poet, it acted as something of a stimulus on the composer. But as Tavaststjerna disappeared from Sibelius's circle, Axel Gallén re-entered. In the spring he returned from

Paris and soon he, Kajanus and Sibelius were at the centre of a constellation that brightened the artistic horizon in the Helsinki of the 90s. When they were home, Adolf Paul and Armas Järnefelt joined the gathering which was to become known as the 'Symposium'. While Tavaststjerna was gentle by nature and closer to Sibelius in temperament and sympathies, Gallén was made of sterner stuff and his magnetism both fascinated—and at times repelled—the composer.

Gallén had the liveliness of mind and breadth of vision of a man of the Renaissance and at the same time was touched by the decadence of the 1890s. His obsession with death puts one in mind of the Spanish Renaissance painters. When one of the nationalist leaders, Lauri Kivekäs, died in 1893 he rushed off to the mortuary to paint him, briefly exhibited the work and then after a few days sent it off to his widow. Another of his works, which reflects something of the aura surrounding the 'Symposium', shows a typical diner fresh from the Kämp, top hat in hand, walking stick under his arm, puffing his cigar in his mouth, having himself driven to the edge of the ice from whose depths the figure of death leers at him. In the snow by his side lies the inevitable bottle of benedictine, the indispensable requisite of a gentleman of the 1890s. The *Kalevala* exercised a powerful fascination over him, too, but at this point he had yet to embark on his finest *Kalevala* pictures which date from the second half of the decade. Again, like Sibelius, Gallén was a nature worshipper. In his landscapes and portraits of Finnish peasant life, he captures some of the desolation and melancholy that one encounters in Sibelius's portrayals of nature in the *Four Legends*.

As the most senior of the three and as a leader of Finnish musical life, Kajanus played a dominant role in the circle. His talk is said to have been of a philosophical turn of mind and Gallén who painted two portraits of him admired both his manly bearing and the spiritual qualities he felt him to possess. It was this aura of leadership and a taste for the grandiose that drew Kajanus and Gallén to one another. One wonders whether Sibelius felt slightly excluded from this relationship though some years later after their friendship had undergone some strain, Kajanus wrote to him 'Gallén's presence draws us nearer one another' (20 June 1899). Naturally Gallén's and Kajanus's relationship was less highly charged than that of the two musicians whose bond was in part professional. In one sense the latter drew them closer: the Philharmonic was placed at Sibelius's disposal whenever he wanted it. It was his laboratory, as it were, where he could try out various instrumental effects and see how his new scores really sounded in practice. On these occasions Kajanus gave him many helpful words of advice in matters of conducting and possibly gave his reactions in matters of scoring.

But when in 1952 a biography of Kajanus appeared in which it was suggested that theirs was a continuing artistic interaction and that Sibelius consulted Kajanus right up until the time of the Fifth Symphony in matters of scoring, Sibelius was stung to indignant protest.

Adolf Paul's role in the 'Symposium' evening was to stimulate ideas in others. Seen from the vantage point of the 1890s he would have seemed a man of the future. In Berlin he maintained a lively contact with artists like Edvard Munch, the Danish poet Holger Drachman and the Polish art critic and theorist, Stanislaw Przybyszewski as well as Strindberg whom he met almost daily during the autumn of 1892. On one occasion when Paul, broke as usual, wanted to send a letter to Sibelius, it was Strindberg who bought the stamp for him! Paul wanted Sibelius to collaborate with him on either a fantastic pantomime or a Finnish opera based on some folk subject. 'That's what we still badly need in Finland. Besides both of us need money and writing for the theatre is a good way of making it.' Sibelius thought Paul's books ten years behind the times, which infuriated him: 'My books have not appeared ten years too late. You have learnt that from people who could have written books like mine but didn't dare to. Do you really believe that people will admit to themselves the plain sexual implications of mother-love that I (first of all) emphasize in Oedipus? And do you think people like to be confronted by a crime, so psychologically motivated and presented that it loses the very character of a crime? Do you think they are willing to confront the possibility that madness is not madness? Or are prepared to hear that religion is only an extension of sexual instinct?' Paul's outburst reflects the psychological ideas then fashionable in Berlin and through him Sibelius came into contact with psychoanalytical ideas as early as 1892.

Occasional guests of the Symposium were the violinist, Willy Burmester, the leader of Kajanus's orchestra, and Alfred Reisenauer, a pupil of Liszt, who during his short career paid frequent visits to Helsinki. Burmester relates how they met and philosophized and bandied theories about that made him smile later in life, but the discussions were still of no mean value in bringing together minds of different character in useful intellectual exercise. After an exhausting concert they might be stimulated to talk by glasses of benedictine and cigars: at others they were spurred to musical activity. On one occasion Burmester and Reisenauer played all night from eight in the evening until five in the morning traversing the complete violin sonatas of Beethoven and Brahms with a couple of Grieg's thrown in for good measure.

The 'Symposium' evenings reached their high-water mark when in the autumn of 1894, Gallén exhibited a painting inspired by them; thus the nocturnal festivities of the trio became public knowledge. The picture shows Sibelius, Kajanus and Gallén himself in a haze of 'inspiration', their thoughts floating far away. The fourth of the drinking companions, unable to follow their fantasies, sits slumped over the table. The moon—or Jupiter—and blood-red clouds in the background might well serve as a back cloth for Wilde's *Salome* while an artificial light gives the faces an unnatural pallor. Paul relates how the idea of the picture originated one evening at the Kämp and how the first version clearly shows Gallén's theosophic leanings and their interest in Assyrian and Egyptian notions of life and death. The original canvas showed he planet Jupiter against which several astral bodies were outlined, while on he left Gallén had painted a flayed female sphinx as a symbol of passive matter! n the finished work of art Gallén does succeed in capturing a note of ecstasy in Sibelius's gaze and affords us some clue of the composer at a relatively little-known period of his life. Speculations on life and death, mysticism, theories of love, symbolism in the *Kalevala*, all surely occupied him, but even if he was carried away by the mood of the moment, his thoughts always returned to an open-minded scepticism. He certainly did not follow Gallén's enthusiasm for the *Kalevala*'s symbolism though their discussions were not without consequence for his creative work: his next project after *En Saga* was destined to be, not a *verismo* opera, but a symbolistic drama based on the *Kalevala* with no lack of magic rites and astral figures.

Sibelius lived a very busy life during this period: composing, teaching, conducting, playing chamber music as well as 'dining, holding forth and playing the dilettante in the evenings'. His wife was not able to look after him as much as she would have liked—he was so rarely at home. Indeed during the first years of their marriage she returned on a number of occasions to her parents' home at Vasa, and this in spite of the far-from harmonious relationship her parents enjoyed. The Sibeliuses had difficulties in making ends meet. His income from the Music Institute and the Orchestral School did not go very far. In one letter written in early December probably to the industrialist Borgström, he went so far as to describe his financial situation as 'more than serious' and asked his support in seeking a loan of some 3,500 Finnish marks, no small sum in those days. At the same time he sounded out the possibilities of credit at Lovisa. No definite answer could be secured before the new year and Aunt Evelina was afraid, that this uncertainty might cast a shadow over their first Christmas of married life. At the new year Sibelius went to Lovisa to try his personal powers of persuasion on the bankers. Evelina described his visit in a letter to Maria and the rest of the family (3 January 1893): 'Janne came on New Year's Day at the height of the storm and cold, so freezing that he needed to be bedded down with three blankets during the night. The next day with its waiting and uncertainty was a long one for him: only today was he able to get out and make his pleas to the Board. All went well and a short while ago he came home with his three thousand, quite convinced that had he not come in person he would never have got the money. He was the only one of the many who sought loans, to get one. He has just gone out now to get some fresh air and returns tomorrow at ten o'clock in Hirn's company. It was so good to have him here. He played beautifully for me. When I asked him if he had the money for his return journey without breaking into his three thousand, he answered: 'Yes.'

This was to be the last occasion on which Sibelius was to visit Lovisa while his aunt was alive—and possibly the last altogether. In March Aino gave birth

to a daughter who was christened Eva in her honour. One can assume that sh
was well enough to take pleasure in this token of devotion; but in June she die
She had once declared that at her death her nephew should inherit the hous
and land at Lovisa where he had composed her favourite piece, the slow move
ment of the B flat String Quartet. But this was not to be: the heirs sold th
property as had happened three years earlier at Turku when his uncle Peh
died. In neither case did the property remain within the Sibelius family, fo
property, like money, ran through their fingers.

CHAPTER EIGHT

The Boat that Foundered

E VER since he had come into contact with Wagner's music dramas and prose writings, Sibelius had cherished the ambition of creating a *Gesamtkunstwerk*. The *Kullervo* Symphony was not the synthesis of words and music he wanted since poetic considerations were subservient to symphonic needs. But surely, he may have told himself, the *Kalevala* could form the basis for music drama every bit as well as the Nibelung legend had done for Wagner's tetralogy, and Väinämöinen could be as viable an operatic character as was Siegfried. And so, in the summer of 1893 he decided to compose an opera, *Veneen luominen* (*The Building of the Boat*) to a libretto that he himself fashioned from the *Kalevala*. The extent to which he had swallowed Wagner's doctrines emerges in a letter written early in July to the poet Erkko:

I believe that music alone, that is to say absolute music, is in itself not enough. It arouses feelings and induces certain states of mind but it always leaves some part of one unsatisfied: one always asks questions, why just this? Music is like a woman, it is only through man that she can give birth and that man is poetry. Music attains its fullest power only when it is motivated by poetic impulse. In other words when words and music blend. Then the vague atmosphere that music engenders becomes more defined and things can be said that not even the most powerful language can formulate. You have given such positive witness of friendship,—could you not help me? The content of the words is drawn from Runes 8 and 16 of the *Kalevala*.

Väinö, who is as young as he can be without offending a Finn's susceptibilities, rests by the shore on his journey away from the gloomy land of Pohja. Dusk approaches and the sky reddens. Kuutar, the daughter of the Moon, is discovered on a bank of clouds, singing as she weaves. Väinö falls hopelessly in love with her and pleads for her hand. She promises to be his if he can turn the splinters from her spindle into a boat by his song.

Scene 2. Clear Daylight. Väinö builds his vessel with song while

Sampsa Pellervoinen (not a singing role) passes the wood to him. Three words are missing: the three words of magic that Väinö needs to complete his task.

The third scene comes directly from the sixteenth Rune of the *Kalevela*, verses 148–370. Väinö goes down to Tuonela, the kingdom of the dead, to discover what the secret words he needs are. I have altered the ending so that Tuonetar (the goddess of Death) pronounces the three magic words while Väinö lies steeped in half-slumber.

Scene 4. The action takes place on a large lake under a dark sky. Väinö ferries his new boat and sings of his burning passion. The sky reddens and the daughter of the moon reveals herself on a cloudbank weaving and singing, and gradually comes nearer so that Väinö who stands in the prow can embrace her. On that scene the curtain goes down.

I am so taken with the whole idea that it gives me no peace.

The ideas in the letter are, of course, not Sibelius's own but merely a Wagner *réchauffée*. 'Every musical organism is in its essence feminine. It can give birth but not conceive . . .' is a theme which Wagner develops at some length in *Oper und Drama*[1] and which Sibelius merely paraphrases. He appears to give wholehearted allegiance to the Wagnerian concept of the *Gesamtkunstwerk* but there is something about the enthusiasm he generates for this project that does not quite ring true. Admittedly the choice of a mythological subject prompts some Wagnerian parallels: the building of the boat by Väinö and Sampsa Pellervoinen almost recalls the forge scene in *Siegfried* while Väinö's journey prompts reminders of Siegfried's Journey down the Rhine. Nor is it too fanciful to connect Väinö's journey to the realm of the dead with Tristan's vision:

Dem Land, das Tristan meint, der Sonne Licht nicht scheint.

Sibelius's choice fell on a part of the *Kalevala* that offered ample opportunity for colour. The daughter of the moon is

> shining brilliantly on the rainbow
> arrayed in robes of dazzling lustre
> clad in raiment white and shining
> where she wove a cloth of gold
> interwoven through the silver,

Väinömöinen

> decks out his red ship with gold and silver
> one sail red, the other pale blue,

and Sibelius was undoubtedly attracted by the possibility of orchestral colour that this afforded him. It is no accident that the *Four Legends* Op. 22 (the *Lemminkäinen Suite*) which emanated from the opera project is far richer in colour than either the *Kullervo* Symphony or *En Saga*.

1. Vol. 1 *Gesammelte Schriften und Dichtungen*, vierte Auflage, Leipzig, 1907, III, pp. 314–16.

THE BOAT THAT FOUNDERED

The libretto Sibelius outlined undoubtedly lacks the essential ingredient of opera: dramatic tension and tragic conflict. Erkko was probably not the right man to refashion the text, for his own dramatic output is singularly lacking in intensity but he was doubtless *faute de mieux*, the best to hand. Besides he belonged to the *Päivälehti* circle and had hailed the appearance of *Kullervo* with a poem celebrating its success. The initial impulse for these operatic plans came from an opera competition promoted by the Finnish Society of Letters as early as 1891. The subject was to be drawn from Finnish history or mythology, the works were to be completed by 1896, and a first prize of 2,000 Finnish marks was offered.

Later in the summer of 1893 Sibelius went to Kuopio to meet Erkko and together they worked on the libretto. It was incidentally during this time that the overture, which was subsequently to become 'The Swan of Tuonela' was composed. A little later, in September, Erkko wrote to Sibelius inquiring about his progress on the score and suggesting further changes in the libretto. But when Sibelius subsequently showed the libretto to Kaarlo Bergbom the director of the Finnish Theatre, his verdict was unfavourable, and Sibelius, his enthusiasm dampened, put the project aside for the time being.

While he was at Kuopio Sibelius was also visited by Richard Faltin whose presence he signalled with a new three-movement piano sonata written earlier in the summer at Ruovesi. The sonata contains many worthwhile ideas but is flawed by its unpianistic layout. Sibelius thinks in terms of the orchestra and the piano writing has the fatal touch of *Klavierauzug* about it. The opening idea is fluent and has a certain Nordic charm even if the left-hand becomes locked in a slow tremolo of a fifth, Sibelius's meagre equivalent of an orchestral pedal:

Ex. 88

Generally speaking the listener cannot fail to be reminded of Grieg's early sonata in this work. In contrast to the first movement and the pale Scandinavian flavouring of the finale, the andante in ABA1B1A2 form has a genuinely national feeling. The main idea is in B flat minor with a Dorian inflection (a G natural and an A flat) and comes from the unfinished choral piece based on the *Kalevala* called *Heitä koski kuohuminen*. But Sibelius had modified the five-beat phrases and changing rhythms to the more conventional four in a bar in the piano version:

Ex. 89

The contrasting idea in a Phrygian C sharp minor sounds like a stylized kantele figure (the Phrygian D appears in the bars following Ex. 90):

Ex. 90

The main idea is then worked up to a climax over powerful arpeggio figures before it dies away to the simplest possible harmonies. The last movement sustains an almost unbroken tremolo and works up to a somewhat feeble climax. Sibelius told Bengt von Törne in later years that he composed piano music only when he was at a loose end and had some free time on his hands. But the Sonata in F major Op. 6 was certainly not conceived as a trifle 'in free moments' but rather more ambitiously as a repertoire piece in the grand manner.

From a pianistic point of view the Six Impromptus, Op. 5, written in 1893, are the more attractive proposition. The last two draw on material from the *mélodrame, Svarts jukans nätter* (*Nights of Jealousy*) though in No. 6 the transplantation is not a happy one. No. 5 frankly imitates the lute in the layout of the texture and apart from some bars where the figuration outstays its welcome, the piece is pianistically more successful than the sonata:

Ex. 91

The same idea, incidentally, though in march rhythm is used in No. 3. One passage leaves no doubt as to the extent to which Sibelius's thinking was dominated by *En Saga*:

Ex. 92

No. 2 takes the form of a Karelian trepak and its main idea seems to resound to the stamping of feet and the swirl of bodies, two elements well depicted in the main idea:

Aino Järnefelt in 1890

Jean Sibelius in about 1890

Ex. 93

In No. 4 one encounters yet again the influence of runic melody. The motive is confined within the compass of a fourth; it is insistently repeated with slight variation both rhythmically and melodically:

Ex. 94

As in the fourth movement of the *Kullervo* Symphony one can discern folk influences from Russian Karelia. No. 1 is closely related to the coda of the Piano Quintet; its dark colouring and the ambivalence between the Dorian and minor sixth serve to generate a feeling of melancholy.

After the success of the *Kullervo* Symphony and the announcement that he was embarking on an opera based on national mythology, Sibelius was the student idol and when during the spring of 1893, the students of Viipuri Student Corporation at Helsinki University were planning a series of historical tableaux drawing on episodes from Karelia's past. Sibelius seemed the obvious composer to approach for incidental music. The tableaux were to be performed during the autumn and the proceeds were to go towards projects that would strengthen Karelia's cultural ties with the rest of Finland. This, it was thought, was the most effective way of meeting Russian cultural penetration, and as such it clearly engaged Sibelius's sympathies. During the time he had spent in Korpiselkä Sibelius had learnt to admire the people as well as their folk art and was attracted by their poetic and half mystical view of life as much as he was concerned by their poverty. The tableaux too appealed to him: they offered opportunities to combine and interweave Finnish and Swedish elements since Viipuri Castle, in which many of the tableaux were set was the eastern bulwark of Finland during the Swedish period.

He continued working on the *Karelia* music when he returned to Helsinki in the early autumn where incidentally he found a new flat. Right up until 1904 when they moved to Järvenpää, the Sibelius family led a somewhat peripatetic existence. So as to save money they often gave up their town flat at the end of the term in May and rented a simple country house for the summer. When the new term came in September they took their furniture out of storage and moved into a new flat. He also fitted in concert tours to the provincial towns of Finland as well as foreign travel; and so as to help him work more intensively he lived part of the year away from his family or from either his own or his wife's relatives.

The Viipuri Students' Gala took place on 13 November 1893, and Sibelius conducted the orchestra though, as he complained in a letter to his brother, not much of it was audible as everyone was either applauding or shouting. Although present-day taste regards the penchant of the 1890s for pageants and the like with superior disdain, they did afford an excellent means of circumventing the Tsarist censorship. Things that could not be put directly into words either on the stage or in the press could be hinted at in a stage spectacle of this kind.

The Overture is a frankly patriotic piece offering a synoptic view of Karelian history: its opening idea suggested to most of Sibelius's compatriots a picture of Viipuri Castle:

Ex. 95

The second subject 'in the Finnish style' might be thought of as interpreting the fate of the Karelian people:

Ex. 96

Sibelius did not hesitate to include a fanfare and from this grew the famous March theme that appears in the third tableau. This piece could so easily have degenerated into a commonplace potpourri and it is a tribute to Sibelius's growing powers that by some miracle he succeeded in welding such disparate elements into a whole. Although the Overture does depict historical events it is possible that the composer first thought of it in different terms. On the same sheaf of manuscript on which he sketched the first subject he notes in red pencil, 'A soul who seeks happiness' (instead of 'happiness' he first wrote 'Karelia'

ut erased it). 'Seeks but does not find. He gets anxious. He goes away and
ries to destroy happiness. Bacchanal. He goes in search of solitude by the side
of a distant forest lake. It is evening. A lonely water bird sings its sad song.'
Perhaps the *Karelia Overture* sprang from an entirely different imaginative
world than the purely historical context in which it now fits.

The first tableau takes us to the thirteenth century: there is an exchange
between two runic bards:

Ex. 97

Viipuri Castle itself is depicted in a fugato section:

Ex. 98

The repeated notes give the theme a faintly Gregorian flavour, clearly
inspired by the stage directions: 'The peasants put down a huge block of stone;
Bishop Peter holds the golden cross over it in blessing while the monks pray
and the choir boys swing their censers.'

An intermezzo begins with a string *tremolando* and the fanfare on the horns
first broached in the Overture and then the famous march with its colourful
chivalry is announced. The tune is too well known to need quotation.

To the sounds of this processional come the Karelian hunters bearing their
tribute in the form of furskin to the Lithuanian prince. The fourth tableau
takes us to the fifteenth century and shows us Karl Knutsson, who was elected
King of Sweden and Finland in 1448 twice deposed and subsequently reinstated.
We see him pictured at Viipuri Castle where he listens to a minstrel singing.
The music has the unmistakable flavour of the Scandinavian ballad:

Ex. 99

Knutsson's turbulent story unfolds and after a climax the music dies away over
a dramatic tremolo only to then turn into C major where it seems to recall

past glory and power. In the original a singer is then introduced who is given the words from the ballad, *Dansen i rosenlund* of Arvidsson, about a swain who rode in rose-laden groves where he came upon a vision of maidens and virgins dancing. In the revised version however Sibelius replaced the tenor with cor anglais:

Ex. 100

The next tableau portrays the siege of Käkisalmi (Kexholm) Castle by Pontus de la Gardie to a great clatter of weapons and the sound of battle music. The battle signals are taken up in the *Alla marcia* (*Marsch nach einem alten Motif* was the original title but Sibelius rubbed it out in the manuscript):

Ex. 101

Like some other similar ideas in Sibelius's early work, the contrasting idea is pentatonic in character. At the climax towards the end of the piece the main theme is heard in close imitation and thicker orchestral garb. Next, the siege of Viborg and its fall is illustrated by a fast-moving fugue while the seventh tableau shows how the city was reunited with the Duchy of Finland in 1811. A report in the *Nya Pressen* (14 November 1893) described it thus: 'The curtain rises showing Finland, a virgin who holds the shield with the lion in one arm while the other is draped round a young Karelian woman who stands close to her as if inviting protection.' The music ends with a brilliant setting of *Vårt Land*, Pacius's hymn, which had become the national anthem. At the first performance the public rose to its feet and joined in.

Six days later Sibelius conducted a concert version of the *Karelia* music (in eight movements) in a programme that also included *En Saga*, the three Impromptus for piano and some songs. Later on, as is well known, he made three numbers into the *Karelia Suite* ('Intermezzo', 'Ballad', and 'Alla marcia') Op. 11, publishing the Overture separately. The Suite became a popular repertory piece first in Finland and then abroad. Along with *Valse triste*, *Finlandia* and the *King Christian II* music it served to lay the foundations of his reputation as a composer in the lighter genres. This popularity was in later years to become something of a handicap to him in more sophisticated musical circles. For his part Sibelius seems already at the first performance to have entertained some doubts about this piece. Perhaps he felt that the only novelty of his at this new concert would hardly sustain comparison with the Strauss of the symphonic poems. His artistic pride was also involved: the popularity of the complete *Karelia* music might in some measure be due simply to the patriotic fervour its quotation of *Vårt Land* kindled. This was not a wholly pleasing thought. He wrote to his brother from Helsinki on 21 November: 'Now the concerts and everything are over. It all went splendidly and (save for a few of course) everybody was delighted. You will hear the new suite for yourself in due course though a good deal of it will get cut out for practical reasons (including for example, the ending with *Vårt Land*). It is very fresh. The new impromptus also went down well. We made about 400 marks. I have a lot to tell you but— oh, well I am in such a state that I can hardly collect my thoughts. Helsinki is its usual self. There are lots of concerts and the usual public. Dayas (the professor of piano at the Music Institute) is presumably going to play my Sonata soon. Sometimes I am depressed and at others in good spirits but I am like that. I envy you living in the country. You wrote so beautifully about the heaths and moorlands. Now it must be in the grip of winter. Are you going to St. Petersburg? I am often afraid of dying.'

It is difficult to trace any coherent development in Sibelius's output during the working year of 1893–4. His operatic plans lay dormant while he concentrated—or dissipated—his energies on giving lessons and composing various short pieces. Among the most substantial of these is the three-movement choral suite, *Rakastava* (*The Beloved*) based on texts taken from the *Kanteletar*, a collection of lyrical folk poetry, that he sent in to a competition sponsored by a student choir. *Rakastava* was even further removed from the typical repertory piece of Finnish student choirs than *Venematka* had been. The jury was put off by the at times complex choral style and Sibelius had to content himself with second prize, the first going to Emil Genetz, his former teacher at Hämeenlinna, who submitted a patriotic song of traditional stamp. But the jury's decision was not endorsed by the critics when the two works came to be performed at the students' spring concert.

Rakastava breathes much the same earthy and erotic atmosphere as do the poems. The elegiac first movement has something of the overtones of a stylized folk-song:

Ex. 102

The choral layout of the second movement is surprisingly modern. Against a swirling background sung on the syllables *ei–laa*, an evocative atmosphere, the singers have the text *quasi parlando* ('here went the path of my beloved'):

Ex. 103

The whole piece, only fifty-six bars long, is built in this way and communicates a restrained yet intense joy. The third movement ('Good night—Farewell') has a thematic reference to the first, and is madrigalian in feeling and Dorian in its harmonic colouring. A solo tenor sings of the sorrows of parting and in setting the text Sibelius does not hesitate to follow its rhythm and to alternate seven- and five-beat phrases:

Ex. 104

The coda is an apotheosis of love; the two lovers are engulfed by the sad harmonies of the still summer night:

Ex. 105

A little later there is an interesting progression; were one to insert an A flat major triad between the two following chords thus:

Ex. 106

the first is perhaps best thought of as the chord on the flattened sub-mediant (the dominant of A flat which stands in a Neapolitan relation to G minor) and the resulting progression is a foretaste of the two famous examples in *Valse triste* and at the end of the Seventh Symphony:

Ex. 107

Rakastava also exists in a hastily written arrangement for male choir and strings as well as in a more effective version for mixed choir *a cappella*, both of them dating from the 1890s. The work is best known from the revision Sibelius made in 1911 when he transcribed it for strings, triangle and timpani.

The winter of 1893–4 turned out to be quite lively. Adolf Paul returned from Berlin and his visit was the cause of unending celebration and on New Year's Eve at one of the gatherings attended by Sibelius, Gallén and Dahlberg, they all sent off a telegram to Strindberg in Brno telling him they were drinking Pommery![1] The spring was however relatively unproductive. Sibelius composed a cantata for the graduation ceremonies at the university in May to a text by one of the *Päivälehti* clique, Kasimir Leino. The work was the outcome of a commission secured for him by Faltin who also engaged him to lecture at the university for a month. Doubtless he was grooming him as his successor and did all in his power to advance his career. Judging from a rather unsavoury exchange of letters between Sibelius and Leino published in *Päivälehti*, it seems that the Academic Cantata was thrown together at the last moment. Instead of drawing on such contrapuntal expertise as he had acquired from Becker, Sibelius turned in a banal, homophonic choral piece. It still remains in manuscript though the composer did publish the *alla marcia* section under the title *Juhlamaarssi*.

The Academic Cantata held up work on another commission. The city of Vasa held a choral festival during the summer and asked Sibelius for a new work. Again inspiration was slow to take fire and according to one newspaper report he virtually finished it while the festival was in progress; appropriately enough he called it *Improvisation for orchestra*. Thanks to the enterprise of its conductor, Axel Stenius, the Vasa Festival was ambitious: its prospectus included Haydn's *Creation*, a Cherubini Requiem, Schumann's *Paradise and the Peri* and Mendelssohn's incidental music to Racine's *Athalie*. Most of the leading Finnish composers of the day were invited to the final concert: both Faltin and Wegelius conducted their own choral pieces, Kajanus conducted his *Aino Symphony*, while Sibelius and Järnefelt represented the younger generation. Järnefelt composed a tone poem whose programme celebrated the medieval castle of Korsholm near Vasa.

Sibelius's piece was awkwardly placed between the heavyweight cantatas and Järnefelt's patriotic work and in any event was ill-suited to outdoor performance.

1. Strindberg's reactions are quoted in Paul's *Min Strindbergsbok*, Stockholm 1930, p. 149. 'I received a drunken cable signed by Messrs Dahlberg, Sibelius and Gallén, in which I was addressed with familiarity and informed that they were consuming Pommery. The wire cost me 1 gulden 50 kreutzer in cab fare. Life must be very boring in Finland!'

Its reception seemed to him lukewarm by the side of the ovation which greeted Järnefelt's piece, and to make matters worse, the General himself was there to witness his son's triumph and his son-in-law's setback—at least, that is how Sibelius evidently saw it. Of course, his recollections of the event may well have been coloured by his youthful 'Järnefelt complex', for other more objective observers recalled that the Improvisation was well received. In the first version of the piece, the climax led to a final section in a Spanish dance rhythm complete with tambourines. This was omitted when it was given its Helsinki première in the spring of 1895 under the title *Vårsång* (*La Tristesse du printemps*). Its opening idea is one of the longest themes in Sibelius's entire output and runs to 32 bars:

Ex. 108

Something of the 'tristesse' of the sub-title is to be found in the second subject. However *Vårsång* is primarily a work apostrophizing the qualities of the Nordic spring and in particular its quality of light. In the final climax the light breaks through on the brass and the bells in an outburst in G flat major. In its original form the work was in D major but Sibelius subsequently transposed it to his favourite 'Nordic' key, F major. It contains little that is genuinely Finnish but leans on the wider Scandinavian tradition of Grieg, Svendsen and Sinding. Though it hardly ranks among his most individual compositions it still enjoys a popularity among student orchestras. Looking back on the year's work Sibelius had no reason for undue satisfaction. He had admittedly won some success with his *Karelia* music but as an artist he had not fulfilled any of the promise of *Kullervo* or *En Saga*. Doubtless the struggle with *The Building of the Boat* dampened his enthusiasm and stemmed the flow of inspiration. To evade its problems he allowed himself to drift: he taught during the daytime, caroused during the evenings and took on commissions in which he had little or no interest. Not until the summer of 1894 did he once again turn to the sketches for the opera; they proved to be a Pandora's box.

After spending the early part of the summer at Orismala he set off at the beginning of July on a visit to Bayreuth. On his way however he made a short visit to the poet. Paavo Cajander, the translator of Shakespeare, who lived not far from Hämeenlinna. Presumably the subject of an opera was mooted since Sibelius mentions the possibility of a libretto in his letter to Aino (on 9 July 1894), one of the first he wrote her in Finnish: 'Our discussion about the text yesterday evening was profitable. He made me a definite promise and seemed enthusiastic. He also made very detailed notes as well so that the project seems to have got off to a good start. I did not go to see von Konow as I plan to begin my Wagner studies in earnest. I have bought vocal scores of *Tannhäuser* and *Lohengrin*. I am studying *Lohengrin* as best I can. It's a blessing that Achté has the score of *Walküre*; I can take it with me to Bayreuth. What luck! Otherwise it would cost 200 marks. I shall copy out bits of it.'

A great deal of Sibelius's pregnant, slightly Strindbergian prose style, is lost when he writes in Finnish. It is clear notwithstanding that he still thinks in Swedish and even reverts to it in the middle of a clause. But on the other hand the ungainliness and the residual Swedish habits of expression have a certain charm that naturally does not survive translation. Even when he writes to Aino to tell her how much he misses her he is a little handicapped by his Finnish: 'I shut my eyes and see you, my darling, so clearly before me. Yes, I do love you dearly. When we are parted one realizes how much we mean to each other. Don't we? Write to me of your love. I dream but even more make fantasies around you. The last thing you gave me will never leave my soul, my wonderful Aino.' He suggests that they should send each other *billets d'amour* in especially small envelopes, enclosed in larger ones, and then burn them up after reading them. At their parting Aino had been the bravest: 'First, I must praise you darling for being so strong and manly in not weeping when I left. Our parting was so difficult for me.'

Wegelius thought that every Wagnerian should, like Siegfried, make a journey down the Rhine and to meet this particular requirement Sibelius took the river boat down from Hamburg. Surrounded by chattering tourists he watched the castles and vineyards glide by before disembarking at Mainz. When he arrived at Bayreuth he went off the very same day to hear *Parsifal* and left the performance feeling a full-blooded Wagnerian: 'Heard *Parsifal*. Nothing in the world has ever made so overwhelming an impression on me. All my innermost heartstrings throbbed. I was beginning to think of myself as a dry old stick but it is not the case. You say in your letter that you hope that a guardian angel will protect me. Look, we must each commend our children to the holy spirit's protection. I can even feel my child gradually coming to life. I felt it only today. . . . I can't begin to tell you how *Parsifal* has transported me. Everything I do seems so cold and feeble by its side. *That* is really something.' That letter to Aino was written on 19 July 1894; *Parsifal* was the overwhelming experience of his stay at Bayreuth though his enchantment with Wagner was not long lived. The day after, he went to *Lohengrin* and wrote immediately to tell Aino, 'It did not have the impact on me that I had expected. I can't help finding it old-fashioned and full of theatrical effects. In my opinion *Parsifal* stands head and shoulders above everything else. You can judge the effect *Lohengrin* had on me when I say that when the performance was over I thought of my own opera and went around humming bits of it. I am the only one who believes in this opera of mine.' Whether his belief was as strong as all that is another matter.

His next letter home (21 July 1894) finds him in a less happy frame of mind: 'I picked up a copy of the *Allgemeine Muzikzeitung* this morning to find a very fulsome review of Fini Henriques among other things. All my friends seem to be making headway while I am at a standstill if not in reverse. This is not so much said in "jealousy" but springs from deeper roots if you understand me. It is a good thing that he is enjoying success; he deserves to. Now this evening I am sitting at the Café Reichsadler and from where I am seated, I can see Leoncavallo who is all the rage here. He is thirty-five, much fatter than Ojanperä, and consorts quite openly with his mistresses. Two of them are sitting beside him now and fawning on him. His airs of superiority and self-assurance annoy me, you know. He is just starting to smoke; everything he does seems so carefully calculated for its effect on others. But perhaps you are laughing at me and perhaps rightly so.'

This letter shows quite clearly that he was not in a creative frame of mind. Had he been working satisfactorily on *The Building of the Boat*, this kind of trivia would not have engaged his mind. The atmosphere of Wagner worship was also proving tiresome. 'Every hansom cab that Wagner has been in is "historisch"; everything in this town is like that!' He was put out of humour by a couple who munched salami during a performance; the Kaiser's sister, he thought looked like a scullery maid, but in spite of all his irritation he cannot but admire the general high awareness of culture. 'Underneath the plebeian surface one is aware of a fine, 1,000-year-old cultural tradition. My landlord, for example, though he is working-class is a well-read man and gives the impression of being highly sensitive.' He is still hopeful about his own operatic plans too: 'I have been tremendously happy, you understand; full of fire and energy. While I have heard *Tannhäuser* and *Lohengrin* I have thought only of my own opera. What is still lacking are strong musical ideas, ideas that have a real character and identity of their own. It is a matter of inspiration. Now, so as not to waste time while I am here, I have decided to do some counterpoint studies. I shall buy Richter's book and try to work out some system to use in teaching. When I get to Munich I intend to go and see some leading musician there and find out what his methods are. I shall also occupy myself with scoring and go to the opera a lot. Then things can look after themselves.' Bayreuth was plagued by a heatwave; men went about in their shirt sleeves and women's dresses clung to their bodies. The aesthete in him began to react against perspiration and also against the heavy German cuisine. A few days later on 23 July he took the train to Munich.

Sibelius stayed just outside the town on the Schwabinger Landstrasse and two days later on the evening of 25 July he sat at a table in the Hofbräuhaus and wrote to Aino of his plans for Munich: 'Tomorrow I shall get hold of a piano and set down to work. I have a number of new ideas. The opera season begins on 8 August: I shall buy the vocal score of *Walküre* and compare it with the

full score. Then I can see what Wagner's intentions are, then study the
actual means he uses to realize them. Don't you think that this is a good idea?
I think I shall learn a lot from it.' But once he settled down to work on his
own opera his mood vacillated from optimism to gloom. At times things
seemed to go well; at others badly. His music seemed to him terribly behind
the times.

On 28 July he writes at length about his struggles with his new music
drama:

I have been thinking about the opera. The first act is flawed by Luonnotar's
motive which is in the minor and is rhythmically weak. It does not offer
sufficient contrast with the first recitative. It is strange that I have not
noticed this before now. The theme ought to be at the same time both
dreamlike and poetic. I shall let the sound of the wind dominate the whole
of the first act. Kuutar's motive will fit into the scene in the underworld which will be full of atmosphere. I am trying to give the whole
opera a strong folk character, that's to say, I am trying to make it easily
grasped.

There are large collections here. The other arts fascinate me more than
do other people's music. I have been studying Wagner; everything seems
familiar and clear (in the passages I have studied). Wagner's music does not
have an overwhelming effect on me in every respect. In my view it is
altogether too well calculated. I do not like it when a piece of music is so
carefully worked out. Besides his musical ideas themselves strike me as
manufactured (not fresh); one notices it immediately and it robs the music
of some of its impact. One can't hammer out themes by force but one must
accept or reject them when they come. I have been in good spirits and think
I have come a long way in my work. It will be a great thing if I succeed
in bringing it off.

I have become clearer in my mind about one or two things concerning
myself. If I lose my self-confidence, even if only for a short while, I get very
unhappy. It always leads to attacks of jealousy and one meanly clings to one's
own pride. The fact of the matter is that I am far too much the victim of
my own moods. Take, for example, this opera. The opening idea is superb,
one of my best. Its argument is that something worthwhile is attained only
through some act of self-sacrifice. But if I am not in the right frame of
mind I immediately react against this and want to put it aside for an
ordinary *verismo* opera. I have already worked out a plot for it: it is set
in the seventeenth century. A young student is engaged to a peasant girl.
He takes himself off abroad and there sees a dancer with whom he falls in
love; he is unfaithful. On his return he describes the dance and the dancer
so vividly that his fiancée suspects what has happened and is overcome by
sorrow. However they meet later on in the forest. In the last act he meets a
funeral procession and learns that it is his fiancée who is being buried. And

her father turns on him and says: you are to blame! something in that style. At times I am more interested in this libretto; at times the other. But Munich has so heady an artistic atmosphere that I have my original libretto more in my thoughts and think it the most important of the two. But I am like that. Still both operas are progressing and that is really something.

One wonders whether in this libretto he mentions Sibelius reveals more than he intended to. His student's adventure with a ballet dancer sounds an autobiographical echo of his own escapades in Berlin and Vienna; possibly it is the 'very sad episode' that lies at the heart of the *Ballet Scene*; the funeral procession sounds like a recollection of *Tannhäuser*. To be frank I am inclined to think that Sibelius no longer really believed in his operatic plans and that his new libretto is a smokescreen to disguise the truth that the first was no longer working out and that he was torn between it and a new project.

At this juncture Armas Järnefelt, a fanatical Wagnerian turned up in Munich together with his wife, a singer, Maikki, full of promise and thoroughly temperamental, and they dragged Sibelius back to Bayreuth for another *Parsifal*. Sibelius was as impressed as he had been before. His doubts about *The Building of the Boat* came to a head on 10 August:

> I am now racked by doubt and brooding. I feel as if I have no talent whatsoever. So much is lacking; yet I cannot renounce music and give in to self-doubt particularly when I have prided myself on my refusal to be second-rate. But every time when I work on a scene for any length of time there comes a point where I realize that perhaps I ought to give it up altogether. But I have become very fond of a lot of it and the beginning has real worth. So I can neither bring myself to give it up nor can I go on. There it is, Aino. If only one could give reality to everything one sees or hears inside one. But always when one gets it down on paper one does it so clumsily that the effect is lost. I have made some slight progress in orchestration. If you Aino, my dearest, could read a full score I would send you a page or two so that you could see for yourself. I have done a piece in the style of a march (quite new and short even though I don't know what it will be like seen in its proper context.) There you have a piece which in its way is good (I like it anyway). I am gifted enough to try my hand at bigger works and perhaps it is because of this that I am getting further and further from my real self. Perhaps I have the sort of talent that is best at home in smaller forms.
>
> One thing I have decided and want your advice about. I want to settle down somewhere and get an ordinary manual job. I have thought of Axel Grönberg's factory if there is a job to be had there. For preference I want to be in the country (now that I see this on paper it feels as if I am running away from something though I can't quite grasp in what way).

We should try to make enough money for me to go abroad and hear some major works on the continent.

This seems a little more serious than the usual ebb in his spirits. He seems to have been caught off balance; something has given him the feeling that his talent is second-rate. The explanation comes a little further on in the same letter: 'I went to hear *Tristan und Isolde* the day before yesterday; nothing not even *Parsifal* made as overwhelming an impression. It leaves one feeling that everything else is pale and feeble by comparison.'

Earlier on when he was living in Vienna, Sibelius had been overwhelmed by *Tristan* and now coming to it when he himself in the throes of his own opera, its mastery served to dispirit him. Needless to say he was far from being the only composer to be bowled over by *Tristan* but its effect on him was not limited to being aesthetic; it drove home the realization that his gifts were not such that he could devote his life to music drama and carry on where Wagner left off. At the same time he was sensible of the fact that he did possess a certain operatic talent and had succeeded in *Kullervo* in drawing a musical portrait with great assurance while the *Karelia* music showed his skill in setting a dramatic scene. Later on this talent was to flower in his incidental music to *Pelléas et Mélisande* and *The Tempest*. Strauss is supposed to have urged Mahler to write an opera and might well have done the same to Sibelius; both of them had the requisite dramatic sense and feeling for contrast. Mahler's imagination was more directly fired by words and he responded to the relationship between words and music in a wholly different way from Sibelius; indeed in this respect his art reveals a directness that has no immediate parallel with Sibelius. One might well say that the epic and dramatic vision in Sibelius had a longer and more arduous journey to its goal of musical fulfilment than was the case with Mahler. In the same way Wagner's smoothly functioning thematic metamorphoses and the subtle psychological shifts in the motivic representation of character seemed almost too obvious to Sibelius.

Sibelius's idea of getting a job at Axel Grönberg's factory was little more than a gesture of despair. He wanted to eliminate at all costs any obstacle that stood between him and his composing. 'The main thing', he went on in the same letter, 'is to get away from teaching theory at least for a few years and do something else. I possess enough general practical ability to make myself useful in other ways.' Here is a relic of his Tolstoyan notion of the desirability of earning one's living by the sweat of one's brow. Sibelius had tried his hand in an iron foundry; he tried to forge a simple nail but with somewhat lamentable results. Feeling depressed in Munich, Sibelius obviously remembered Axel Grönberg who had wined and dined him so well and this notion of working for him was no doubt coloured by rosy memories of cigars and champagne and good company. This same letter, incidentally, also touches on his impulsiveness. 'You wrote in your last letter', he tells Aino, 'that you find my changeability, my surrender to the impulse of the moment, difficult to bear.

Of course, you are right and it is not a good thing and I shall try to free myself from it but this is more easily said than done. It is something that is part of you for ever.'

Tristan ultimately dealt the death blow to Sibelius's opera even though he made a further attempt to work on it some days later. He wrote to Aino on 12 August: 'I am just off to see *Walküre* now. I have much greater assurance. I have been able to excise a lot of music that I felt did not ring true, or was artificial. Do you know what I mean? It should be in this style or that or one should enjoy this or that so as to make the right effect.' The last remark is doubtless directed against Wagnerians in general and Wegelius and Armas Järnefelt in particular. Sibelius was becoming consciously aware of the need for him to shake off the hypnotic influence of Wagner.

A few days later he wrote (on 17 August):

I have got caught in a labyrinth and must use all my ingenuity to find the way out. Everybody goes through this kind of experience at one time or another during life. As long as one can emerge with one's hide intact. Yesterday I went to see *Götterdämmerung* [he had seen *Siegfried* a few days earlier]. It is marvellous but only in places. I am not so confirmed a Wagnerite as the others. And I will say what I think to anybody. I have been feeble and cowardly and tried to model myself on other's ideals. This isn't right. If I had as much money as I have ideas, I would be a millionaire.

In another letter[1] he says: 'I sometimes think my idea of giving up teaching and settling in the country and working in a foundry is a bit too utopian. In the long run I would not be able to stand it. But I have determined never to write a single note for the sake of writing but only if I have something to say. And I shall only write music that will always mean something to me.'

Although he still struggled with *The Building of the Boat* for another fortnight or so his attention was beginning to turn to the symphonic poem. On 19 August he writes to Aino:

I have found my old self again, musically speaking. Many things are now clear to me: really I am a tone painter and poet. Liszt's view of music is the one to which I am closest. Hence my interest in the symphonic poem. I'm working on a theme that I'm very pleased with. You'll hear it when I get home; that's if I have got so far with it and don't begin to have too many doubts.

This, the first mention of a symphonic poem, could well be one of the *Four Legends* (the *Lemminkäinen Suite*), for Sibelius had the ability not only to take reverses in his stride but to turn them to positive account. His operatic Boat may have foundered but the wreckage served him in building a new work.

1. A second letter written on 12 August but not posted until two days later.

This is not to deny that he still found difficulty in leaving the sinking ship and was still clinging to his operatic illusions. The same letter (19 August) goes on: 'As far as my opera is concerned I believe it will be my most important work in the sense that all of me will go into it not just my musical personality.' The other operas he heard in Munich made precious little impact on him. He writes of Leoncavallo as 'a dreadful primitive' having heard him conduct excerpts from *Pagliacci* and *I Medici* and his letter, heavily laced with irony, draws parallels between the love duets from *Pagliacci* and Gounod's *Faust*. He was even more scathing about the *Kunihild Overture* of Kistner, an imitator of Wagner. 'And such people get to the top while Busoni and others like him don't get a hearing. The papers say that Leoncavallo is an "elegante Erscheinung". He certainly looks pretty stupid but apart from that I daresay he is quite harmless.' The Wagner season in Munich ended with *Die Meistersinger*, Sibelius's favourite Wagner work, '*Meistersinger* surpassed all my expectations," he wrote on 21 August, 'and completely bowled me over.'

It is clear from all this that Sibelius's relationship with Wagner was a love-hate affair; he was never indifferent. It is all the more curious that in later years he insisted in conversations with his biographers that the Bayreuth Festival didn't interest him very much, and that he only heard *Lohengrin* and *Tannhäuser*. He completely suppressed the fact that he had seen *Parsifal* twice as well as *Tristan*, *Walküre*, *Siegfried*, and *Götterdämmerung*. Nor did he breathe a word about his intensive studies of Wagner scores at this time. What may have turned Sibelius from Wagner was not so much the *leimotiv* technique but his musical personality. In later years he told his pupil Bengt von Törne, 'Wagner is gross, brutal, vulgar and totally lacking in the finer feelings. For example he will shout, "I love you, I love you, etc. . . ." In my view this is something that should be whispered.'[1]

This was the obverse side of the coin for Sibelius but there was also another side. He was obviously attracted by Wagner's sense of mystery and his orchestral palette. Wagner provides a model for many of the colouristic devices in the *Four Legends*, more particularly 'Lemminkäinen and the Maidens of the Island', the sequential climaxes of which have their ultimate origins in *Tristan*. Writing in 1930 Cecil Gray summed up the then current view of Sibelius's relationship to the Master of Bayreuth.

Sibelius would seem to be practically the only modern composer—certainly the only one of his generation—who has neither been influenced by Wagner nor, what amounts to very much the same thing, reacted violently against him. The ferocious anti-Wagnerism of Debussy, for example, is in itself highly suspicious, and a most eloquent tribute to the potent wizardry of the master of Bayreuth; one does not need to be told by his biographers that at heart Debussy had always a secret admiration and affection for the music of Wagner—the fact is clearly written in every bar

1. Von Törne: *Sibelius—A Close-Up* (Faber).

of his music, and much the same may be said of those who fulminate so violently against it. They detest it because they cannot get away from it, in fact. Sibelius, on the other hand, does not detest Wagner for the good reason that he never loved him. Not even when, as a young man, he visited Bayreuth during the height of the Wagnerian cult in the early 1890s did Wagner mean anything to him at all one way or the other; and the proof of this is to be found in the fact that it is impossible to lay one's finger on a single phrase in his entire work which one could attribute to the influence of Wagner, or which would not have been exactly the same even if Wagner had never lived.[1]

As we have seen Sibelius's attitude was by no means as straightforward as Gray maintains or rather as Sibelius himself maintained in his conversations with the English critic. Indeed this very hostility to Wagner as expressed to von Törne was as suspect as Debussy's and his debt as great. For both of them Wagner was a landmark by whose position they charted their course. Sibelius's conscious (or unconscious) suppression of his experiences at Bayreuth may of course be prompted by an anxiety to forget the failure of his own operatic project. It may spring from his general tendency to deny the effect of other influences on his style for undeniably there *is* an influence. It is significant that in later life Sibelius made no favourable reference to Wagner in any context whatever, nor for that matter did he go on record in praise of Liszt, the example of whose tone poems stood him in good stead in dealing with the crisis Wagner's impact had occasioned. His last letter from Munich (22 August) told Aino, 'I was very taken with *Meistersinger* but, strange to say, I am no longer a Wagnerite. I can't do anything about that. I must be led by my inner voices.'

After Munich Sibelius shook off the Wagnerian dust and drowned his own operatic sorrows by making a trip south to Venice. Here he bathed in the Adriatic and gloried in the relaxed Mediterranean atmosphere. He felt far more at home in Italy and on 23 August wrote to Aino, 'Germany has lost its hold over me; Italy is in many ways like Finland, it is complete in itself; both countries are so Shakespearean.' His Venetian trip was short-lived. A south wind brought in its train a tremendous heatwave and Sibelius soon went north in search of cooler air. A stomach complaint forced him to break his journey at Innsbruck where he immersed himself once again in the atmosphere of the Austrian Alps. 'Yesterday when the train left Italy the sun was just on the point of setting and the mountains were bathed in golden, farewell colouring. I always seem to come to life again when I am abroad. My stay in Berlin and Vienna was another matter. I dislike living according to some prearranged pattern. In Berlin, without noticing it myself, I was becoming the person that everybody wanted me to become. Not a person in my own right, even if I was in my music.'

1. Cecil Gray, *Sibelius*, pp. 202–3.

Kullervo

'The River of the Dead' (1893) by Axel Gallén-Kallela. The face
of Robert Kajanus is depicted in the top left corner

A few days later he arrived in Berlin whose musical life had a stronger impact on him than ever after the balm of Venice. He wrote to Aino on 30 August. 'I am now with Busoni, Nováček and Paul. It is good to see them though it is not like the old times. We have all changed in the meantime. Everybody is now concerned with realizing his own ambitions; it is sad to see that we are all concentrating on this. Now I have decided to jump in the deep end and try to swim and trust my own resources. I am planning to go to Leipzig, to Breitkopf and Härtel with my (*Karelia*) Suite, which I am thinking of re-orchestrating. I can't stand living cut off from everything.' His visit to Breitkopf however did not take place until four years later.

Sibelius's friends had their own problems to cope with. Busoni was preparing for the coming season and practised five hours a day as well as doing some work on a new Bach edition. For the moment Sibelius felt cut off from him: 'I think Busoni has become cold of late. Of course, he is a master and he has made great strides, but he lacks soul to quite an extent. That's my opinion anyway. Otherwise he should make a great name for himself this coming winter and thinks only of his career.' (2 September). But the disenchantment soon passed and we find Sibelius remaining in Berlin solely to show Busoni the score of *En Saga* and the *Karelia* music, which he afterwards sent him from Helsinki.

While he was in Munich Sibelius and his brother-in-law Armas had been to several exhibitions where he had seen work by the newer German painters, Stuck, Klinger and above all, Böcklin. After this, Berlin's art galleries struck him as of slender interest and he expressed a preference for sculpture rather than the endless battle pictures exhibited there. Presumably he did have the opportunity of seeing some more of Böcklin including *Gefilde der Seligen* in which swans are pictured gliding on a black expanse of water. It is undoubtedly a contributory source of inspiration to the world of symbolism that forms the background for the *Lemminkäinen* pieces. Sibelius also carried out his plan to study Liszt's tone poems and spent the first few days of September eagerly studying the score of the *Faust Symphony* in a music library. 'It is a marvellous piece and I am learning a lot from it,' he told Aino (7 September). From other letters we learn of his opera-going; he was enthusiastic about *Carmen*, *The Bartered Bride*; he went to see *Falstaff*, then only a year old, on the express instructions of Busoni. 'I feel I am much more independent in outlook', he told Aino (2 September) 'than when I left Finland. It had been a hard schooling. If only I could now develop all my ideas in music. I am always so full of false pride. Busoni will doubtless deal with all that and do me good.' Full of creative fire Sibelius wrote off to Wegelius to ask him for leave of absence from the Music Institute. This was granted and much relieved he wrote to Aino, 'The next thing is to get rid of my orchestral classes.' In mid-September he returned home.

CHAPTER NINE

Lemminkäinen

BACK in Helsinki, Sibelius once again repaired to his old haunts. Symbolism was all the rage in the Finnish capital and one October day Sibelius went to see his friend, the painter Magnus Enckell and enthused about the Böcklin pictures he had seen in Germany. Some weeks later Enckell was to see them for himself and wrote from Berlin to Yrjö Hirn, 'Böcklin really surpassed my expectations and *Vita somnium breve* looks exactly like Sibelius described it. There is a sense of delight but it verges close on melancholy.' In Helsinki the artistic world resounded to the scandal caused by Gallén's latest exhibition and in particular his picture, *The Problem*, which showed the Symposium brethren, Paul, Sibelius and Kajanus in their cups. In allowing himself to appear in this painting Sibelius placed himself in the eyes of many people among the decadent and it was not only the more hidebound, respectable bourgeois who were shocked. Earlier in the year the painter, Edelfeldt had voiced some of these reservations, 'I do not understand all this symbolism; no doubt the fault is mine. The strangest thing, it seems to me, is that Paul, Sibelius and company all find it so epoch-making!' Such was the stir caused by *The Problem* that Gallén went so far as to get both Kajanus and Sibelius to signify publicly in writing that they had agreed to the picture being exhibited. When Gallén left Helsinki that autumn, the famous 'Symposium' began to break up; Gallén returned to Ruovesi, joining Paul in Berlin in 1895, and with that, this particular epoch in Sibelius's life came to a close.

Sibelius's musical reputation was very much centred on Helsinki; during the 1894–5 season no fewer than sixteen concerts included pieces by him among which were *En Saga*, the *Karelia* music, *Vårsång* and the Impromptus. Apart from this there were other concerts including some in Turku. His name was also beginning to appear in the other Scandinavian countries. In October the Danish singer, Sigrid Wolff gave three of the Runeberg songs at a Copenhagen symphony concert where they were not a success. Writing in *Politiken*, Christian Kjerulf was quite savage about the first two songs and in particular 'Under strandens granar'. He found them altogether unusually thinly constructed, their declamation extraordinarily clumsy, awkward, tasteless and altogether devoid of distinction. All the more surprising then, to find himself admiring 'Jägargossen' ('The young huntsman') which he found well drawn and distinguished, indeed, the last two verses he thought extraordinarly beautiful and evocative. In the end his reaction was a positive one; 'an obvious talent which can easily be frittered away'.

In fact this was moderately encouraging but Sibelius none the less had diffi- culties in getting down to composition that autumn. Whether he made any progress on the tone poems that he had begun in Munich is not known. He had rented a separate room so that he could work undisturbed away from the house in Brunnsparken in which he had installed his family earlier that autumn. In November the couple celebrated the birth of their second daughter and in the same month, Aino's parents moved to Helsinki as the General had been appointed Secretary of State for Defence. Sibelius continued his support of patriotic causes and charitable concerns. He wrote a melodrama for speaker, strings, horn and piano, a setting of Rydberg's poem, *Skogsrået* to be performed in aid of a lottery to support the Finnish Theatre, and shortly afterwards reworked the piece turning it into an orchestral tone poem. In this form it was played at an all-Sibelius concert on 17 April 1895 together with another novelty, the Serenade for baritone and orchestra, to words of Stagne- lius, some of the movements from *Karelia*, the piano sonata, and *Vårsång*. The whole concert was repeated two days later.

Skogsrået (*The Wood-Nymph*) can best be thought of as an experiment. After his Wagnerian summer Sibelius was still trying to find his feet as a tone-poet using Liszt's example as a starting point. In *Skogsrået* he strictly follows the narrative and allows it to determine the musical shape of the work. The melodrama itself concentrates on four episodes from Rydberg's poem: the hero, Björn's travels or wanderings, the evil machination of the dwarfs, the love scene with the wood-nymph and the hero's *Weltschmerz*. The tone-poem works more thoroughly over the material and welds the different sections together into a more coherent unity. Yet Sibelius does not wholly escape from the episodic origins of the piece. There are some splendid melodic ideas and the scoring is luxuriant and effective: Björn is portrayed in chivalrous style in C major (on trombones), the cunning of the dwarfs by a sly, insidious A minor figure, and the love scene by a long, flowing solo cello cantilena. Shades of *Lohengrin* can be discerned towards the end:

Ex. 109

None the less *Skogsrået* has some fine music in it and could have been one of Sibelius's most characteristic essays in this form had he perhaps waited a little longer before reworking the material of the melodrama.

Sibelius's admiration for Stagnelius had already found expression as early as the summer of 1887 when he had composed the suite, *Trånaden* inspired by Stagnelius's poem 'Suckarnas mystär' ('The Mystery of the Sighs'), during his stay at Korpo. Now he returned to the great Swedish romantic and in his setting of *Serenad*, we have further testimony of his Wagnerian encounter. Several years later he used a motive from *Serenad* in the song, 'Långsamt som Kvällskyn' ('Slowly as the evening sun') (1910).

Most of Sibelius's creative energies were consumed during the years 1893–5 by his opera and in its shadows—or its immediate wake—he produced nothing of importance. It needs no great insight to see that his preoccupation with *The Building of the Boat* had an injurious effect on his other output; he squandered his time and energies on small commissions and other potboilers. *Karelia* and *Vårsång* come at one end of the period and the orchestral version of *Skogsrået* comes at the other. The whole period may be said to find him in a fallow trough; the first summit of his creativity is represented by *Kullervo* and *En Saga* after which the curve begins its descent. Its nadir was the summer of 1894 at Bayreuth and Munich after which his creative powers gradually gathered strength and he overcame his depressed condition. Naturally there were daily changes of mood just as there were ebbs and flows in his inspiration but this does not affect the overall creative pattern.

The summer of 1895 found him on the threshold of a new creative ascent. He spent the summer in the peace and tranquillity of Vaania near Lahtis in Vesijärvi living simply on a farming estate where he had no access to his usual piano. He passed the time of day with his host and in the evenings he and Aino went rowing on the lakes where they fished for perch. The idyll was interrupted by business trips to Helsinki to raise credit.

While in Vaania he composed the part-song 'Työnsä kumpasellaki' for male voices *a cappella*, also known under the title 'Saarella palaa' ('Fire on the Island')[1] which was performed for the first time during the autumn. He also worked on a collection of runic melodies for the Finnish Society of Letters, most of which derived from the collection by A. A. Borenius-Lähteenkorvas, well known as a specialist in this field.

After his Karelian expedition a few summers earlier Sibelius had evidently come to be thought of as an expert on folk music and he was sent the work of other folklorists, often amateurs in musical notation, for his revision. The edition he compiled together with Borenius-Lähteenkorva is not our concern here, but it is obvious that the work he did had immediate effects on his own creative career. For this contact with the legacy of runic melody renewed his passion for the world of the *Kalevala* which had ceased to sway his imagination for a while when he had himself abandoned his *Kalevala* opera. This confrontation with the runic tradition may have prompted him to turn to the *Four Legends*.

1. Published in the *Nine Part-Songs*, Op. 18. Tr

The autumn of 1895 found the Helsinki art world at the height of its enthusiasm for symbolist painting. Magnus Enckell was among the artist-friends of Sibelius who exhibited that autumn, influenced by his encounter with Böcklin the previous year. His *Fantasia* portrayed a smiling, faun-like Apollo surrounded by white and black swans, while a painting that made a special impression on Sibelius was Enckell's *Melancolia*. This shows a naked youth, kneeling and hiding his head in a woman's embrace, while in the background a sea opens out on which there is a lone rower. The whole picture is conceived in desolate, mysterious and unearthly colouring. Writing of this exhibition of Enckell's, the art critic, Johannes Öhquist had this to say—and his comments are worth quoting as they illustrate something of the background against which the *Four Legends* were conceived.

He writes of the reaction against the positivist view of life:

The artist seeks an expressive outlet for his inner vision in the most diverse spheres; his art is steeped in the poetry of the sagas; it is seized by religious ecstasy or by mystical self-communion. The old legends and the myth-ology offer visions of worlds yet unglimpsed and the mysteries of the Ancient East enchances his receptivity to the supernatural. The occult, the out-of-the-ordinary cast an irresistible spell. And like everything sub-merged in his inner life, the hidden forces of nature exert an equally powerful fascination. The artist searches for the most delicate and translu-cent colourings and nuances to do justice to evening, mist, dusk and night.[1]

Such was the climate that pervaded the artistic world of Helsinki and it was against this background that Sibelius worked during the autumn of 1895 and the spring of 1896 on the *Four Legends*. The opera was quietly forgotten about and he ignored the newspaper reminder that the date of expiry for the opera competition was the end of 1896.

Sibelius was evidently feeling the need to stretch his wings however. When Busoni had visited Helsinki in May[2] 1895 the two composers saw a lot of each other and Busoni, too, felt that Sibelius needed to escape from the provincial atmosphere of the Finnish capital and get a foothold on the continent. When later the same year Busoni met Glazunov in Berlin it occurred to him that he should try to get his work published in Russia. The Russians, he wrote, 'have a publisher[3] that I have always envied them. All his fortune goes in disbursing royalties, publishing lavish editions, promoting the music and advancing the careers of his protégés, all without the slightest thought of his own profits. I particularly envy them this publisher as he makes it a strict rule to see that his bounty is confined exclusively to Russian composers. One day the thought

1. In *Nya Pressen*, 6 November 1895. Öhquist and Sibelius moved in the same artistic circles.
2. Busoni visited Helsinki in May 1895 and not in February as erroneously stated in Dent's admirable biography. His Helsinki concerts took place on 12, 19 and 25 May.
3. Belaiev.

occurred to me that when it comes to something like this, the Finns should surely be counted as Russians and I raised the matter with Glazunov who visited me here and if Rimsky is his right hand, then Glazunov is his left. The latter promised to raise the subject with Belaiev and has kept his word. He writes to the effect that the question has been resolved in your favour and suggests that you send some of your work to Belaiev. The outcome will be decided by a committee of three distinguished and fair-minded artists so that I don't doubt that it will be satisfactory. I should advise you to send Belaiev *En Saga*, *Vårsång*, *Skogsrået* and to send them straight away.'

Sibelius had nothing whatever against the idea of being published by the same house as Rimsky-Korsakov and Glazunov. He sent Belaiev three scores— presumably the three Busoni suggested—together with a polite letter. But Belaiev may have been less than enthusiastic at the idea of regarding Finns and Russians as cousins or may not have liked the music: in any event they were not published. Busoni was not the only champion of Sibelius's cause; Paul was no less zealous though hardly as effective. As early as 1892 he had tried to interest Weingartner in *Kullervo* but the latter procrastinated and Paul eventually returned the score to Sibelius with a somewhat gloomy explana- tion of his attempts. Later in 1895, Paul obtained the ear of the director of Ries and Erler and played him a piece by Sibelius written for Gallén though he did not say which. Kajanus and the artist, Sattler also spoke to the same publisher who caught fire and became enthusiastic and said, 'Den Mann wollen wir lanciren!'; however nothing came of it.

As yet the time was not ripe for Sibelius to be launched abroad. *Kullervo* was too large-scale; *En Saga* too immature. As if to make up for his failure to win any success on the continent, he worked harder than ever. In April 1896 the *Four Legends* were performed with the Philharmonic Orchestra. His nervousness during rehearsal created certain tensions between him and some of the orchestra and Kajanus was forced to mediate. The first performance of the *Four Legends* or the *Lemminkäinen Suite* took place on 13 April under Sibelius's baton and they were played in the following order: 'Lemminkäinen and the Maidens of the Island'; 'Leimminkäinen in Tuonela'; 'The Swan of Tuonela'; and 'Lemminkäinen's Homeward Journey'. If anything they scored a greater public success than *Kullervo*. Critical opinion was divided on its 'Finnish' feeling; Merikanto felt 'that Finnish quality we all recognize in our hearts and which is part of ourselves'.

Flodin on the other hand took a somewhat different view: 'The specifically Finnish element . . . is by no means as marked in this, the composer's most recent work. And this we find to be an undisputed gain, for it shows that Sibelius has escaped the misfortune of mere self-repetition. In the first of the Lemminkäinen tone-poems the composer builds entirely on modern, cosmo- politan groundwork. His thematic structures are more closely related to the Lisztian style while the influence both of Wagner and Tchaikovsky can be discerned.' Flodin did not hesitate in hailing this as the peak of Sibelius's achievement up to that time but the remaining movements did not succeed in engaging his sympathies at all. 'One is finally driven to the conclusion that it is the composer's intention *per fas et nefas* to invoke in his listeners by means of atmosphere or modulation, a hypnotic power to which they must submit or exercise their own free will and flee from the concert hall.' The finale, 'Lemminkäinen's Homeward Journey' reminded him of *Kullervo*. Four years before he had written, 'Were Sibelius to compose a new tone-poem, for instance, a Lemminkäinen poem, he would be forced to fashion an entirely new vision of the Finnish milieu if he is not to repeat what he has said already for all time in *Kullervo*.'

If Flodin's review sounded a somewhat strident note, it is in its own way a tribute to the composer. All critical evaluations are relative and a critic, particularly an important critic, can write harshly of a composer of stature making it obvious that his genius is not in question, only to write perhaps the following day far more tolerantly of a mediocrity. Sibelius was big enough to be worth criticizing just as Liszt or Tchaikovsky were. The hypnotic power of his musical language contained an element that repelled Flodin just as it did Martin Wegelius. In fact his first review of the Lemminkäinen tone-poems was a mere shot across the bows to prepare for the full broadside that was to come a year later when the suite was given in its revised form.

'The Swan of Tuonela' and 'Lemminkäinen's Homeward Journey' underwent a further revision before they appeared in print in 1900. The other two, 'Lemminkäinen and the Maidens of the Island' and 'Lemminkäinen in Tuonela', were withheld for several decades and were next performed to commemorate the centenary of the publication of the *Kalevala* in 1935. After this Sibelius made a number of minor orchestral alterations before they appeared in print, their publication being held up on account of the Second World War until 1954. In the final version of the suite, the order of the two inner movements is reversed.

The day after the first performance, when the press resounded to its success, Sibelius's father-in-law died. The General kept his fighting spirit intact as well as his stoicism and his sense of humour right to the bitter end. Even during his death throes he remarked with a gleam in his eye, 'This will bring joy to the heart of the *Nya Pressen*!' (At the height of the language controversy the *Nya Pressen* had been particularly vehement in its denunciation of the General. When the Estate was divided among the Järnefelt family, the fact that Aino, unlike her three brothers, did not study at her father's expense was taken into account and a sum was set aside by way of compensation. These funds enabled Aino and Jean to go to Berlin in the spring of 1896 where they visited Busoni.[1]

Many questions about the genesis of the *Lemminkäinen Suite* remain unanswered. According to Sibelius himself 'The Swan of Tuonela' originally

1. I have not succeeded in uncovering any details about their journey apart from the

served as the overture to *The Building of the Boat* though it presumably under-went pretty drastic revision. One wonders just how much of the music Sibelius wrote for Väinämöinen was transferred to the younger hero, for even while Sibelius was working on the libretto of the opera he wanted to portray him as young and virile rather than the wise sage of the legend. Hence the younger Lemminkäinen was the more congenial subject and no doubt his escapades with the virgins of the island prompted parallels in his mind with Strauss's *Don Juan*. The hero's journey homeward after his numerous adventures is obviously a grateful subject and gave the composer the opportunity of writing music of compelling momentum. But the closest parallel between opera and tone-poem is to be found in the Tuonela episode in *The Building of the Boat* and 'Lemmin-käinen in Tuonela'. Here we find Lemminkäinen descending to the kingdom of death (Tuoni), one of the tasks set him by Pohjola's daughter whose hand he aspires to, with the intention of killing the Swan who floats on the dark, black waters of Tuonela. But he is tricked and speared through heart and liver. The son of Death dismembers the body and cuts it into small pieces which he strews in the river. Lemminkäinen's mother comes in search of her son, combs the lake with a rake and by dint of magic sews the bits together! Gallén had done a painting inspired by this legend and it is possible that during their many convivial encounters he had tried to interest Sibelius in this particular myth. Though the Swan motive was in all conscience hardly uncommon at this time; one has only to think of *Lohengrin* and *Parsifal*, Böcklin, Enckell and even W. B. Yeats who was studying the *Kalevala* at this time.

But 'The Swan of Tuonela' is not the only link between the opera and the tone-poems. Among the sketches from this period we find this motive used in 'Lemminkäinen in Tuonela':

Ex. 110

Alongside this Sibelius has scribbled 'Tuonen tytti' (the Maiden of Death). This figure from the *Kalevala* comes in the opera where she rows Väinämöinen over the river to Tuonela, but she is not found in the scenario of the tone-poem where the theme serves, paradoxically enough, to characterize the life-giving love of his mother. The extent to which Sibelius made use of other material from the opera will presumably remain unknown.

The First Legend, 'Lemminkäinen and the Maidens of the Island', draws for its literary inspiration on the events outlined in Runo 29 of the *Kalevala*. Here, as in the three remaining tone-poems, Sibelius does not follow an exact literary programme but chooses rather to evoke the general atmosphere of the poem.

certain fact, as evidenced from a letter to Busoni now preserved in the Staatsbibliotek, Berlin, of their meeting with him.

The latter serves as a starting point from which this free sonata-form piece gathers strength. The introduction in E flat major, the tonic, has something of the atmosphere of a dream landscape, the kind of world in which many artists of the period sought refuge. The subdominant triad with an added sixth, a chord that greatly attracted the young Sibelius, has an added elegiac flavour when scored only for horns:

Ex. 111

There is an air of expectancy and mystery and, as if tentatively, a short thematic fragment emerges. It appears on the oboe and is a highly characteristic figure beginning with a rising fourth and ending a little uncertainly with a triplet:

Ex. 112

The cellos reply with a subdued yet pregnant motive:

Ex. 113

and the passage ends with some rising chords that have the air of a fanfare and that resolve on to the chord that opened the work and which is thus invested with a new significance:

Ex. 114

The main theme is heard in the tonic and is a dance-like idea on the woodwind over a pastoral string accompaniment slightly folkish in character:

Ex. 115

Note that Sibelius ends the phrase with an ascending fifth and not a descending interval. He darkens the colouring by hinting at E flat minor and a little later on by introducing a major second under the tonic pedal note. The introductory motive leads into a second group where the strings adumbrate a dark expressive line:

Ex. 116

The intensity increases and the music approaches the heights of sensuousness. Lemminkäinen continues his wild pursuits until the beginning of the development section. The dance-like main theme (Ex. 115) makes a poignant appearance in E minor while Lemminkäinen can be glimpsed in the far distance. There are some passages of uncertain tonality and almost a suggestion at times of bitonality

Ex. 117

before E flat reasserts itself. What follows once the tonic is re-established is a gradual but continuous build-up which only reaches its climax at the end of the movement. Sibelius expands the reprise—or rather the combined development and reprise—by dwelling on further thematic development, by enriching the orchestral texture and thus intensifying the emotional impact. Instead of merely recapitulating what he has said earlier on, he shows new aspects of its character. The main idea which in the exposition was a kind of dance of homage to Lemminkäinen acquires a Dionysian perspective in the restatement where it is caught up in a more frenzied and furious pace, the second group is laden with chromatic passing notes and the tension is increased until it reaches bursting point and the horn fanfare of the opening enters fortissimo. Sibelius succeeds in bringing off a really sustained and controlled crescendo over a long time-span; something that he had tried to do four years earlier in the *Kullervo* Symphony but whose success was limited by his orchestral inexperience. His Wagnerian studies in the intervening four years had been invaluable and there is little doubt of his command of the orchestral apparatus.

The atmosphere of the work and its material does not inhabit the world of Finnish nationalism. Though it is highly personal, its feeling could be more readily described as Scandinavian with some Russian element. While there is no evidence that he had heard any Balakirev, apart from the fact that Busoni may have played *Islamey*, an affinity, albeit fortuitous does make itself felt. The sonata-form structures of Sibelius's early music—*Kullervo*, the present work, and though to a much lesser extent, the First Symphony—exhibit a tendency towards prolix development and reprise having a high degree of emotional tension. His Wagnerian studies had doubtless stood him in good stead for there is now no question of his command of the orchestra. The coda may well have been inspired by the lines about Lemminkäinen's farewell that were printed in the programme-note at the first performance.

> Wherefore goest thou, Lemminkäinen
> Why depart, O handsome hero.

Accompanied by a string motive drawn from the main theme, the flutes and clarinets call with a phrase based on its opening:

Ex. 118

There is an almost impressionistic feeling about this coda; the E flat major scale with its flattened sixth and seventh acquires a quasi whole-tone flavouring (from C flat to G at least) and the glitter from the woodwind cries serves to underline this atmosphere.

'The Swan of Tuonela' with its death and water symbolism does not lack precedent or parallel in the music of its time. Apart from the obvious Wagnerian examples, these themes occur in *Sadko* as well as in Liadov's *Enchanted Lake* and later on in Rachmaninov's *Isle of the Dead* inspired by Böcklin's picture. It occupies a special place in the Finnish and Scandinavian context. Gallén and Enckell, we have mentioned, but beside Böcklin we have Puvis de Chavannes on the continent and Edvard Munch in Norway.

Sibelius allows the flowing water, the darkness surrounding Tuonela, the swan's cantilena to capture something of his feeling for death. By leaving out flutes, clarinets, trumpets and including parts for cor anglais, of course, as well as bass clarinet and bass drum he darkens the palette. In the opening bars the chord of A minor is gradually (and most magically) moved through the whole strings, *divisi con sordini*, giving a continuous but ever-changing sonority:

Ex. 119

It is, of course, possible that Sibelius had the example of the *Lohengrin* prelude in his mind but the refinement with which he spaces the chord creates a wholly individual sonority. The cor anglais solo begins in a highly characteristic fashion with a sustained note followed by a triplet ornament and a descending fifth, the whole phrase being in B flat minor and beginning with a Dorian sixth. The cellos, and then violas, answer with an ascending phrase in which A, previously the tonic and now the leading-note of B flat minor, is strongly emphasized:

Ex. 120

If Sibelius had not heard the shepherd's 'alte Weise' in the third act of *Tristan* I doubt whether he would have conceived the work throughout in terms of a cor anglais solo. In both recitative-like melodies the sonority of the instrument underlines its association with death, but whereas Wagner's shepherd's song is distinguished by frequent points of melodic climax, Sibelius's line is a gently flowing one, unbroken, predominantly diatonic with the Dorian sixth, without the chromaticism of the Wagner. When the tritone does appear it is to striking effect:

Ex. 121

Harmonically Sibelius achieves striking effects with the simplest of means. By employing triads in bold succession and changing their function tonally he succeeds in modulating no less than three times in the course of the first fifteen bars, from the opening A minor to B flat minor, and thence to B minor and C minor. If one regards the modulatory changes in *Tristan* as sensual and ardent, modern by the side of the majority of works written at the time, those in 'The Swan of Tuonela' could be thought of as cold, icy, frigid and tinged with an almost Palestrina-like archaism. Only at one point in this desolate, deathlike landscape do we find any sign of human life. A pizzicato on the strings engenders an atmosphere of uncertainty and anticipation, the Swan's lament rises and suddenly becomes a cry of longing. Then, there is a magical modulation from A major to C that seems like a momentary lifting of the mists that enables us to catch a glimpse of the shores from which a horn fanfare is heard. The harp glistens like a flicker of light in the distance but the vision fades and the horn

ry is repeated *con sordino*. And then the brass and timpani intone a deathlike
rhythm over which the strings pour out the swan's lament cantabile (*con gran
uono*) in the main key, A minor. It is echoed by the cor anglais, *dolcissimo*, over
a muted string tremolando, *col legno*, bass drum, while the harp and the timpani
uned in minor thirds toll out the fateful rhythm:

Ex. 122

And then all movement comes to an end, the swan disappears and dusk gives
way to darkness. As in the introduction the flow of the waters is depicted in
the rising A minor chords, the strings recall their theme and finally the solo
affirms the majesty of death. No doubt the attempt could be made to analyse
'The Swan' formally and contrive some textbook formula but it would not
do it justice. The overall impression it leaves is of an organic entity within
which the musical line flows freely and rhapsodically but is subjected to a strong
inner discipline.

In 'Lemminkäinen in Tuonela', the world of the dead seems peopled and
one seems to discern their cries. In this respect Sibelius's tone-poem might be
compared with *Francesca da Rimini* or the Liszt *Faust Symphony*. Even if the
concept of retribution after death is not commonly encountered in the *Kalevala*,
Lemminkäinen is pursued by avenging furies for his attempt to commit sacrilege
within the kingdom of Death itself. If Parsifal was forgiven his crime against
the hallowed swan on account of his purity, Lemminkäinen is not: it was for
worldly motives that he tried to kill the Swan of Tuonela. Only the power of
his mother's love is strong enough to save him. And so in this movement
Sibelius conceives the kingdom of death as an inferno rather than a land of
shadows, dark and unpeopled; from the very outset the double basses and
cellos set the mood of menace:

Ex. 123

The tempestuous string writing mounts in intensity and over it there are angry cries from the woodwind:

Ex. 124

The above idea bears a strong relationship with the driving motive that opens the last of the four legends, 'Lemminkäinen's Homeward Journey'. The expressive intensity of the tone-poem is screwed up until it culminates in a powerful outburst. The following woodwind theme:

Ex. 125

could well show Lemminkäinen's last conscious thoughts of his mother as he sinks towards death. The theme is a good example of Sibelius's use of the tritone and the acoustic scale within the framework of major–minor tonality; he obtains similarly a variety of modal effects later on in his life, in the Fourth Symphony to name only one example.

At this point the mother enters the picture and the middle section for strings has something of the melancholy of a lullaby:

Ex. 126

By dint of repeating motives and by the use of the Dorian mode Sibelius induces the atmosphere of monotony that he associated with the Finnish runic melodies. The inferno quickens to life once again as if the furies were battling with the mother for her son's life, and the coda portrays the triumph of her healing powers; the solo cello's insistence on G sharp, the lydian fourth, in the context of a D major chord, makes a most telling poetic effect. Compared with the freely constructed framework of 'The Swan of Tuonela' with its sense of n onward-flowing recitative, the ternary structure of 'Lemminkäinen in uonela' is relatively straightforward. Certainly with its successive climaxes ased on tremolandi as well as the excessive reliance on sequential progressions, reminds one more of Liszt than any other Sibelius work.

In the final movement, 'Lemminkäinen's Homeward Journey' Sibelius builds series of crescendi from an opening motivic cell. 'He takes the tiniest drop of ound and from it draws a veritable ocean', as Oskar Merikanto wrote in *äivälehti* (14 April 1896). In an interview[1] Sibelius spoke of this movement vith some autobiographical overtones: 'I think we Finns ought not to be shamed to show more pride in ourselves. Let us wear our caps at an angle! Vhy should we be ashamed of ourselves? That is the underlying sentiment hroughout "Lemminkäinen's Homeward Journey"; Lemminkäinen is just as ;ood as the noblest of earls. He is an aristocrat, without question an aristocrat!'

A three-note motive serves as the motivic germ of the piece:

Ex. 127

This germinal cell opens out and acquires a pendant:

Ex. 128

Shortly afterwards Sibelius adds yet another motive:

Ex. 129

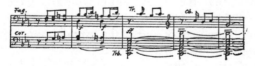

And later on the descending fourth is further transformed:

Ex. 130

1. With A. O. Väisänen: *Kalevalaseuran vuosikirja I*, 1921.

This descending fourth plays a vital structural role in the work. In the nex example, for instance, it appears with the intervening steps filled in:

Ex. 131

A descending fourth in longer note values is later on combined with inde-pendent semiquaver figuration in which a fourth also plays an important part

Ex. 132

The main idea returns in E flat minor and builds up a motoric ostinato while the pendant also contributes to the sense of frenzy; the brass weigh in with combative fanfares. The movement gathers in speed until a quasi presto at which Lemminkäinen's mount thrusts ahead in a wild and furious gallop. Sibelius skilfully reserves his orchestral forces and only in the closing pages is there a complete tutti.

The use of a germinal cell throughout 'Lemminkäinen's Homeward Journey' adds another dimension to the rondo form in which the piece is cast. Instead of the classical rondo pattern with its clear demarcations each section grows organically out of its predecessor and so the overall impression it leaves is of a continuing and tightly knit variation form.

The relationship between the two motives built on a descending fourth in the last two Legends could suggest that Sibelius had toyed with the idea of a *leitmotiv* but the composer categorically denied this and was not even aware of the relationship.[1] Taken as a whole, the *Four Legends* or the *Lemminkäinen Suite*, is symphonic. 'Lemminkäinen and the Maidens of the Island' constitutes a sonata-allegro preceded by a slow introduction, 'The Swan of Tuonela' per-forms the function of a slow movement, 'Lemminkäinen in Tuonela' can be thought of as a kind of 'scherzo macabre', and 'Lemminkäinen's Homeward

1. See Nils-Erik Ringbom, p. 58.

ourney' forms a characteristic rondo finale, allegro con fuoco. Sibelius could, of course, have called the work, *Sinfonia quasi una fantasia* or *Legend Symphony* or some such title. In spite of the wealth of musical pictorialism that we have found in the *Four Legends* the structure of the four pieces leans more towards the 'absolute' symphony than one would have expected. Indeed in his old age Sibelius was prepared to regard both *Kullervo* and the *Four Legends* as symphonies.[1]

After the Impromptus and the Sonata, Sibelius tried his hand at another pianistic genre, the salon piece which had not at the end of the century acquired the unfortunate overtones of the present century. Indeed the designation was a simple and practical means of indicating to the player that a 'morceau de salon' made less demands on his technique than the 'morceau de concert'. The latter, of course, was not a genre to which Sibelius had turned his talents for he had never really learnt to think in pianistic terms. His fingers were naturally attuned to the virtuoso technique of a Vieuxtemps or Mendelssohn but had never developed any feeling for Chopin or Liszt. It never occurred to him that the pianistic layout of a Chopin could give way to a new kind of keyboard sonority such as that evoked by Debussy or that one could carry the pianistic difficulties of Balakirev's *Islamey* one stage further as did Ravel in *Gaspard de la nuit*. Accordingly his mistake was to use as a model of keyboard writing something that was already at the time of its composition pretty undistinguished: the keyboard miniatures of Tchaikovsky. Poetic feeling is powerfully distilled in the smaller pieces of Schumann, Chopin and Mendelssohn but in Tchaikovksy's waltzes, mazurkas, polkas, nocturnes and songs without words it is for the most part less deeply characteristic.

Other forces also served to shape the character of his piano pieces. There was simply no market in Finland for piano pieces that were too demanding technically: Sibelius's Finnish publishers looked askance at difficult figuration and advised him to confine himself to simple accompanimental figures, ta-ta-ta-ta or simple syncopations, boom-taa-ta! A short cadenza at the end did not matter: amateurs could always leave that bit out. It is hardly surprising that Sibelius given his own disinclination as well as market pressures did not enjoy writing for the instrument. When in later years his children asked him why he nevertheless composed these salon pieces he replied, 'So that you should have your bread-and-butter!'[2] But in the long run he undoubtedly damaged his reputation by publishing a large number of piano pieces that are grossly inferior in quality to his orchestral output.

In his collection of ten piano pieces, Op. 24, Sibelius gathered together pieces from the years 1894 or possibly 1895 to 1903 and ranged them in chronological order. Many of them contain first-rate melodic invention which more often

1. See Levas I, p. 165.
2. Mrs. Katarina Ilves to the author.

than not is obscured by clumsy writing. In the A major Romance (1895) we find an excellent theme emerging from the darker register of the keyboard

Ex. 133

At the turn of the century Alexander Siloti used to include this together with the Ballade from the *Karelia Suite* in his recital programmes and in a letter to the composer (14 March 1900) wrote of his delight with the Romance and spoke of his intention to play it and the *Karelia* movement in Russia, Germany and England. He included it in a Helsinki recital in April the following year. The less successful middle section of the Romance is probably the reason for its disappearance from the repertoire. The main idea of the D minor Romance (1896)[2] breathes the air of Slav melancholy and Tchaikovsky's influence looms large particularly in the coda of the piece:

Ex. 134

The most accomplished piece in the Op. 24 collection is the well-known D flat major Romance whose theme begins like a cello cantilena:

Ex. 135

The thematic development is interrupted by a cadenza with alternating octaves, passage work of various kinds, and one of the few examples of pianistic virtuosity, albeit modest, in Sibelius. It was much praised and played during its day and Elmer Diktonius wrote after having heard Nicolai Orloff play it, 'Sibelius had never written so effective a piano movement.'

1. Ekman dates both the Impromptu and the Romance in A major as 1894 written in Vaania in the summer of that year on the strength of Sibelius's own information. This must however be inaccurate as the composer did not spend the summer at Vaania that year but in 1895 and 1896. The two pieces were published in December 1895. If Sibelius recalls the place of composition correctly—which seems more probable— they were written in the summer of 1895.
2. Ekman lists this as 1895 but the earliest sketch of it derives from 1896.

The main idea in the Barcarolle (1903) has none of the Venetian overtones
or sonority of Chopin's or Liszt's studies and none of the gentle melancholy of
Tchaikovsky's Barcarolle, 'June', in *The Seasons* but is rather a boat journey
across dark, desolate waters. But when the composer goes on to develop the
piece he drifts helplessly into musical commonplaces.

Caprice (189) could well be a piano transcription of a violin piece that
Sibelius had never got round to composing. By writing it in one voice laid out
for two hands he imitates violinistic effects such as saltando, pizzicato, spiccato:

Ex. 136

Similar influences are to be discerned in the Idyll (1898). It begins with a
somewhat Chopinesque idea but when the melody subsequently turns up in the
left hand the right assumes something of the nature of a violin obligato:

Ex. 137

It all sounds like an anticipation of an episode from the adagio of the Violin
Concerto where the main theme is heard on the orchestra against solo flourishes.

The Impromptu (1895) seems to look forward to *Valse triste*:

Ex. 138

However Sibelius was not at home in the medium of the piano miniature but
on the other hand he had a much stronger feeling for the solo song. He had
already made a promising start with the seven Runeberg songs and now his
style began to be more sharply defined.

Arioso (The Maiden's seasons) Op. 3, to a poem of Runeberg is, as its title implies, more naturally vocal in character and less inclined towards recitative than, for example 'Under strandens granar'. The song is said to have been written in 1893 but Sibelius revised it in 1911 writing the accompaniment for strings and then arranging that for the keyboard. The maiden, in Runeberg's poem, laments the fate of the roses that the frost has taken and at the same time reflects on her own misfortune. In much the same way that Runeberg sets lyrical detail against the perspective of a larger framework, so Sibelius dwells on the whole rather than the incidental poetic detail. The solo line has an imposing breadth and flow with a subtle interplay between $\frac{6}{4}$ and $\frac{3}{2}$:

Ex. 139

The subtle interplay between $\frac{6}{4}$ and $\frac{3}{2}$ is characteristic of Sibelius's cantabile style. Later evidence infers that an early version of *Arioso* never existed; the song was *composed*, not revised, in 1911 (see Vol. II).

Op. 17 consists of seven songs which according to the list of works published by Ekman, Solanterä and others, come from the years 1891–8. However certain references in letters and the dates of premières suggest that some of them were not composed until the beginning of the present century. Among the first to be written was 'Se'n har jag ej frågat mera ('Since then I have questioned no further'), another Runeberg setting, which is strongly Dorian in inflection. Sibelius shows himself here in his most compelling melodic vein. The whole song consists of some simple, yet significant phrases which are however more than adequate in conveying a human situation. It was this song that made a strong impression on Brahms when the young Finnish singer, Ida Morduch, a pupil of Lucca and later on the mother of Sibelius's biographer, Ekman, sang it with Hanslick accompanying at the piano. Brahms asked to hear the song again and sat down at the piano himself. After having heard it once more and complimenting the singer he said of Sibelius 'Aus dem wird wat'.[1] Brahms incidentally knew Runeberg's poems in German translation and had called him 'einer von den granz grossen'.[2]

1. Ida Ekman retails the incident in a letter to Sibelius (9 November 1942).
2. Wolrad Eigenbrodt: *Runeberg in Deutschland* in *Johan Ludvig Runebergs hundraårsminne: Essays published on the Poet's Centenary* by Svenska Literatursällskapet i Finland LXII, Helsinki, 1904, p. 119.

'Fågellek' ('Play of the birds') (Tavaststjerna) was written during his year in Vienna and offers an almost pre-impressionist and transparent keyboard texture. The other two Tavaststjerna settings in his collection, 'Sov in' (1894) ('Sleep on') and 'Vilse' ('Astray') (1894? 1902),[1] bear the imprint of a typical Nordic romance style.

'En slända' ('A dragonfly') (Oscar Levertin) (1898? first performed on 10 January 1904)[2] differs from the other songs in the collection in its expressionistic texture and Lisztian harmonies. The recitative-like solo line interspersed with the aphoristic piano comments, wanders from key to key. The trills in the closing phrases vibrate like the dragonfly's wings while the melismata sketches its flight:

Ex. 140

All of these are settings of Swedish-language poems. The two Finnish settings, 'Illalle' ('To the evening') and 'I lastu lainehilla' ('Driftwood') have a folk-like character. 'Illalle' prompts one's thoughts to turn to the variation technique employed in Finnish runic songs. The whole song, a setting of a sonnet by Forsman-Koskinies, arises from this phrase:

Ex. 141

which is varied melodically:

Ex. 142

and rhythmically:

Ex. 143

1. In a letter to his wife dated 11 July 1902, Sibelius speaks of 'Vilse' as being in a new revision *ny bearbetning*. Its first performance took place on 17 September 1903 at a recital given by Aino Ackté.
2. Its more advanced style and the date of its première (10 November 1904) suggest a later date than that cited in Ekman's list of works.

By repeating this phrase fourteen times, as many times as the sonnet has lines, the composer builds up a tension that is also reflected in the harmony. The vocal line breaks off abruptly at the end of the song and Sibelius, as so often is the case in some of his finest songs, refrains from completing the piece with a piano postlude, thus departing from the traditional convention of lieder composition.

'I lastu lainehilla' (1898? 1902?)[1] to words of I. Calamnius-Kianto has a folk-like charm of melodic line but this is not enhanced by its accompaniment which has a certain rhythmic monotony.

Sibelius is no *lieder* composer in the ordinary sense of the word. When he does succeed in this small form, it is when he is suggesting a larger canvas. Just as some quite small buildings can often give an impression of being much larger than in fact they are, so some of Sibelius's songs give a much more spacious impression than that of mere miniatures.' *Arioso* and 'Se'n har jag ej frågat mera' certainly fall into this category.

1. In a letter to his wife dated 11 July 1902 Sibelius writes, 'I have already set Ilmari C's poem', and as Sibelius had never set any other poem of his, his reference is presumably to 'Lastu lainehilla' which is thus of later date than has hitherto been supposed.

   Both Forsman and Calamnius are Swedish names which the poets subsequently abandoned for the Finnish forms of the name. Ilmari Calamnius thus became Ilmari Kianto though so as to avoid confusion both forms are occasionally encountered hyphenated. *Tr*

CHAPTER TEN

The Maiden in the Tower and Academic Rivalries

I N ONE of his notebooks in which he sketched some of his thematic ideas
Sibelius also made sporadic diary entries. Most of these are from the
autumn of 1896 and the remainder come from the following year. These
short exclamatory phrases are less concerned with the day-to-day events
of his life than with his moods at the time of writing. They show that he has
not as yet overcome his youthful oversensitiveness and propensity to depression.
If anything it had become worse. At the end of August 1896 he was in a state of
considerable apprehension and tension: the coming season was fast approaching
and he had taken on far too much. He had promised to write a one-act opera
to raise funds for the Philharmonic Orchestra; he had teaching commitments at
the university now that Faltin had retired and it fell to him to compose a
cantata in honour of the coronation of Tsar Nicholas II. Moreover to enhance
his candidature now that Faltin's chair was vacant, he had to prepare an important lecture. His anxiety in the face of these forthcoming trials can be
discerned in the sketchbook:

> 22 August 1896: O ye Godfathers! It is strange how empty life often seems.
> This is because I am not clear inside my own mind: I hardly know what it is
> I really want. And yet it could and indeed ought to be totally different—
> my art and Aino! I am not a powerful enough support for Aino. How I
> really fear other people—in particular their jealousy and prejudice. And
> yet I understand it so well. What have I done today—hm! I have read
> Fredrik(a) Bremer. Tried to compose but it has not been with *schwung*.
> Why does it come so rarely these days? Perhaps my excesses *in Venere* or
> *in Baccho* have produced a spiritual paralysis. I won't find my form for the
> Coronation March. My energies are sapped—my mental vitality. By the
> evenings I am often tired. It seems as if all I want to do is to sleep away my
> life—and it was not like that in my childhood.

The next day life seemed a good deal brighter:

> 23 Aug. Most of what I wrote yesterday is quite wrong. Life seems

so rich again. *Nox sine excessu.* Last night I read *Bullarsjön* and saw myself mirrored in it. What vitality, vitality, ἐνεϱιά *cum excessu.*

In the next few entries he becomes increasingly conscious of his changes of mood:

24 Aug. Life is like the ocean waves, sometimes one is at the top—at others at the bottom. Ebb and flow. Full and empty.

25 Aug. The air is cool. There is a mist hovering over the lake, almost dreamlike. Life is full of poetry. Have worked well.

Sibelius was staying in the country at Vaania. September 1st was approaching, the day on which people traditionally moved back from their summer houses to the capital, and he felt the inner pressures grow:

29 Aug. Keen atmosphere. Worked la-la. *Pression.* . . .

30 Aug. (Worked) Done a little composing.

31 Aug.–1 Sept. Two days on the spree. *Infelix.*

4 Sept. (Am not so quickly crushed). Passing. (Fear, Weakness.)

5 Sept. 'Have no fear, my son'. Loneliness. (your finances will sort themselves out). Economic disorder. Economy οεκονομια.

After the relatively quiet summer Sibelius had got himself into economic difficulties by the beginning of the autumn. On 10 September, after he had been on another spree, the situation brightened momentarily when 'a man of honour' agreed to act as a guarantor for his debts. But this arrangement only led to new excesses:

11 Sept. Work. Enjoyed myself in the evening.

12 Sept. Work, sleep.

13 Sept. Relapse. Pull yourself together. What the devil do you think will become of you if you carry on like this. Frightful after-effects. Hypochondria etc.—My God!

His teaching began in mid-September and was an additional source of strain!

14 Sept. My first day, when I have to get through both my own work and this slavery. Try thinking of the lesson as an exercise in reasoning. At the bottom of it all is my disputation. Went to a meeting with Kajanus.

After the lesson. You are dissatisfied but what grounds have you? Schnéevoigt was ironical (rhetorical?)[1] Why should it worry you? Talk to Kajus. Or better still: keep it to yourself.

One cannot help noticing Sibelius's difficulties in being at ease in his dealings with other people. Georg Schnéevoigt, a teaching colleague and leader of the cellos in the Philharmonic Orchestra, caused him irritation. Even later when he was famous as a conductor, he had a reputation for mischief and Sibelius

1. The autograph is not clear.

can have found him stuck-up and self-assertive. He wants to talk openly to the proud, if unbending Kajanus but something tells him not to do so. In general he was found kindly and considerate by both his friends and colleagues but his inclination to keep things to himself may have resulted in him being un-approachable even haughty at times.

Sibelius set great store by friendship. At the end of a September week full of hard work alternating with 'relapses' Kajanus was a great source of strength: 'Cajus is a friend and a noble personality.' But Sibelius's sensitiveness often bordered on mistrust and he easily interpreted indifference as enmity.

> 23 Sept. Went out in the evening. I seemed to see hatred in everyone's face—well, what if there is—what do these worthless expressions stand for. Are you really such a wretch that if Tom, Dick and Harry take no notice of you, you are finished. Ugh. . . . The more one is noticed the more one is hated. That is an almost certain sign of greatness. Perhaps you want everyone to smile amiably at you. God help us! Syrup. Marzipan.
>
> Now you have to finish the following jobs: Compose the opera by the First. Then make a piano reduction. Get a meeting of the ladies (Phil-harmonic Orchestra Committee). Afterwards the Coronation thing.

On 24 September Sibelius had a meeting with his librettist, Rafael Hertzberg, known for his naïve historical novels, his prose reworkings of the *Kalevala* and his translations into Swedish of Finnish folklore. Even if Hertzberg did not rise to the mediocre heights of Erkko as an author, he still had a certain sense of what worked on the stage. The story of the steadfast maiden accosted by the lecherous castle bailiff, imprisoned in a tower in the castle, abandoned by her father but saved by her lover and finally united with him through the timely intervention of the mistress of the castle is not wholly without point dramatically but Hertzberg's style is embarrassingly awful:

> *The maiden:* You vile wretch, you would use violence against a woman.
> *The bailiff:* However much you may resist, in my arms I will take you.
> *The maiden:* Vile wretch, coward! Oh, I am undone. (*She falls helplessly into the arms of the bailiff who carries her slowly into the castle.*)
> *The bailiff:* Now you are mine.

This was the operatic albatross that he had chosen to wear round his neck. The simple plot falls into much the same category as the romantic libretto he had himself sketched out in Munich. He no longer aspired to write a kind of music drama in Wagnerian fashion on the *Kalevala* mythology but contented himself with a one-acter roughly along the lines of *Cavalleria Rusticana*. The modest forces required in the orchestra, the brass comprised only two horns, trumpet and trombone, indicates its chamber dimensions.

The overture begins with a ballad-like theme, the presence of an added sixth creates an atmosphere of anticipation reminiscent of the *Karelia Suite's* Intermezzo:

Ex. 144

This gives way in turn to the maiden's poetic idea in E major which ends on a characteristically Sibelian minor sixth chord:

Ex. 145

The bailiff's lust and aggressiveness is portrayed in a chromatic figure:

Ex. 146

The overture comes to a rapid climax and its folkloric atmosphere gives way to the *verismo* character of the opening scene. The curtain rises to discover the heroine picking flowers along the shore while the oboe outlines a love motive over the accompaniment of a whole-tone trill in the strings and thirds in the clarinets:

Ex. 147

Then follows a dramatic scene between the maiden and the bailiff distinguished by writing that is vocally grateful in bel canto style with some ringing top notes approached by effective leaps:

Ex. 148

As in the symphonies Sibelius shows his command of musical movement and his capacity to build up a convincingly realized climax:

Ex. 149

An orchestral interlude leads into the second scene where the maiden imprisoned in the tower laments her fate:

Ex. 150

Her lament is suddenly interrupted by a chorus of peasants singing in praise of spring:

Ex. 151

This choral episode is one of the key moments in the opera: the maiden recognizes her father's voice and the contour of the vocal line reflects both her sense of relief and a note of anxiety. But her father rejects her and the theme associated with this has something of the Finnish character one encounters in *Kullervo*:

Ex. 152

The next scene forms something of a contrast: the maiden's lover appears on the scene and the love motive is heard in conventional Nordic harmonies. The maiden's entry during the love duet that follows suggests that Sibelius had just a little of Puccini in him. The maid sings of her 'burning agony' like some Nordic Mimi or Madam Butterfly:

Ex. 153

La Bohème had had its première earlier in the year but it is more than likely that Sibelius did not know the work. A little later on in the duet the bel canto assumes overtones of sanctimony:

Ex. 154

The last two scenes—the bailiff's abortive attempt to separate the lovers together with his subsequent undoing and the jubilant final chorus—are less than impressive.

Sibelius does not work with *leitmotivs* in the accepted sense: neither the maiden's nor the baron's theme is developed after the opening scene even though one figure associated with the bailiff's menaces does turn up in the seventh scene. The love motive is the sole exception: it crops up in a number of contexts but is not developed either musically or in its range of psychological association. From the structural point of view the opera falls into the usual conventions, arias, duets and so on, linked into a continuous whole by interludes while it would seem that Sibelius quite consciously avoids Wagnerian speech melody.

Considering that it is a first attempt. *The Maiden in the Tower* has moments of unmistakable effectiveness and met with great success at its first performance on 9 November and at a subsequent benefit performance given for the composer. Indeed the box office was besieged by the public. One critic in *Nya Pressen* discerned the influence of Gounod in its erotic lyricism but thought it a pity that the composer 'had thrown away so much good music on so simple a yarn'. Sibelius, of course, had hardly been spoilt by good librettists; but it is interesting to note that there may have been some question of a collaboration with no less an artist than Strindberg some two years earlier. Adolf Paul had tried to persuade the great Swedish dramatist to write an opera and had offered his own services in working on the libretto, suggesting Busoni—and in all probability, Sibelius[1]—as the composer. Strindberg was enthusiastic about the idea but the sudden breach that developed between the two authors put an end to the project. Sibelius's and Strindberg's paths were to cross some years later when the incidental music to *Swanwhite* was composed.

Emmy Achté planned to revive *The Maiden in the Tower* the following year but Sibelius refused to give permission for the performance, giving the excuse that he wished to revise it.[2] But the revision never took place and, as he put it in later years, the Maid was allowed to remain in the Tower. His attitude towards opera took some years to clarify and even as late as 1910 he asked in his diary, 'Have I abandoned opera because of laziness?'

A few days before the first performance of the opera, Sibelius conducted another new work, *Cantata for the Coronation of Nicholas II* for soloists, chorus and orchestra which the university had commissioned in honour of its former Chancellor. The ceremony at which the cantata was first performed took place on 2 November and the Tsar and his consort were depicted in plaster reliefs. Unlike his predecessor, Alexander III, Nicholas II was no great friend of Finland and did little to curb the ambitions of those in St. Petersburg who sought to erode the Grand Duchy's autonomy. Something of the anxiety in Finnish circles was expressed in the address given by C. G. Estlander at the ceremony and it could have given Sibelius scant pleasure to set the official banalities of Paavo Cajander's text.

> Hail to thee, young Prince,
> hail to the new dawning day!
> . . . with Hope's joy in their hearts,
> the Finnish people greet thee!

1. Dr. Stellan Ahlström has told me that there was a proposal that Sibelius was to be the composer and that the libretto was to be based on one of Strindberg's works. I have not been able to trace Adolf Paul's letter but judging from Strindberg's reply dated 25 June 1894, it would seem that he had suggested Busoni. Knowing the enthusiasm with which Paul championed Sibelius, it would seem unlikely that Sibelius's name should not, as Dr. Ahlström points out, have been discussed.
2. Leppänen: *Tulesta tuhkaksi*, Helsinki, 1962, p. 236.

Ex. 155

Terre   nuori   ruhti- has   uuden   aamun   koit-   to

The cantata is a typical piece of *Gebrauchsmusik*. It would doubtless have filled the bill had it not been for a spot of trouble. According to the university records part of the trouble was attributed to the fact that at least some of the orchestral material was missing at the rehearsals. Sibelius himself gave a different explanation: the tuba player turned up at the concert itself in a highly inebriated condition and gaily improvised in the middle of a fugal section, ruining the effect of the piece! In all probability the incident hardly enhanced Sibelius's chances of a university appointment, for in the eyes of the public the responsibility for the overall effect lay with the composer-conductor!

As early as his year of study in Vienna Sibelius had had his mind on the possibility of a university post. This was relatively well paid considering its few duties though the salary was not really enough to live on with any degree of comfort: however it enjoyed a prestige in Finland comparable, say, with that of 'Master of the King's Music'. However, events took a dramatic turn when Sibelius learned of an unexpected rival—and a powerful one in the person of Robert Kajanus, whose duties at the Philharmonic Orchestra, one would have thought, took sufficient toll of his energies and time. A third candidate was the composer and musicologist, Ilmari Krohn but since greater emphasis was placed on artistic rather than scholarly attainments he was undoubtedly the least formidable of the three contenders.

At a lecture which served as evidence of his academic attainment Sibelius chose to read a paper entitled 'Some reflections on Folk music and its influence on the development of Art music'. The paper was to be read on 25 November and in Tampere his mother anxiously speculated on his performance. She wrote to her younger son, Christian: 'Otherwise my thoughts are now with Janne who, at 2 o'clock undergoes his test. I fancy I hear him stammering a little at first, but then when he stands with his lecture in his hand I feel much less anxious, for at the mere sight of it well written out, all will be well.' Doubtless her anxiety would not have been so readily dispelled had she seen the paper her son read. The first pages are neatly set out in ink but the continuation is jotted down in pencil while towards the end he has assembled bits and pieces and stuck them together from almost illegible notes. Sibelius, it need hardly be said, did not confine himself to his written text and according to the examining body his paper was 'full of original ideas of which some appeared to occur to him on the spur of the moment which was why the disposition of his argument seemed up to a point aphoristic and fragmentary'.

To judge from the surviving notes Sibelius's thesis came closer to a subjective artistic manifesto than an objective academic dissertation. He tends to project his own personal sympathies and attitudes on to an historical situation and interprets events in a way that at times casts doubt on his grasp of history. It was clear, he argued, that tonality is bending under pressure but we cannot merely destroy one system without putting a new one in its place, and he argues that one cannot artificially construct a key system but that it must already have a living existence. It is clear from what he says that the imitators of Wagner and Liszt are the composers he has in mind: for him their so-called 'interesting' modulations and harmonies represent a self-conscious and unspontaneous art. His own artistic thinking, his spontaneous thinking, is firmly anchored in classical tonality.

Talking of harmony he speaks of the indivisibility of a melodic idea and its harmonic accompaniment. Those who have any experience of composition, he maintains, know that a melody and its harmonies emerge at one and the same time.[1] He discusses the harmonization of folk melodies as well as their rhythmic complexity. Finnish folk music, he says, reveals a wide variety of rhythmic combinations. His own music employs five, seven beats in a bar while in the folk melodies he had edited for the commentary published by the Kalevala Society he had noted such original rhythms as $\frac{15}{8}$ and $\frac{17}{8}$. Such rhythmic notation was fashionable at the time; one has only to think of the $\frac{11}{4}$ passages in the first act of Rimsky-Korsakov's *Sadko*. Speaking of national elements in music as well as individual style he has this to say:

> We speak of an artist's individual personality and also of national personality. The individual style is—to express myself briefly—that stamp an artist imposes on his own work; the national style is accordingly the stamp that a people imprints on the composer. The history of music illustrates the important role played by folk music in this respect in a quite striking fashion.
>
> We see how fruitful an influence folk music is in a composer's upbringing. . . . An artist who is thoroughly steeped in his country's folk music must naturally have a different view of things, lay stress on certain points, and find his artistic fulfillment in a completely different way from others. And in this lies much of his originality. In his work, however, he must free himself particularly as far as his expressive means are concerned from any suggestion of the parochial. He will achieve that in proportion to the stature of his personality.

The Coronation Cantata, the opera and his lecture, left him with an unhappy aftertaste. On 30 November he noted in his sketchbook, 'Now all the fuss and the duty composition is over. Are you happy? No. Tired and miserable. Isn't this the result of pursuing pleasure? Surely. All our life together springs from the pursuit of pleasure.' A few days before this Sibelius had received a letter

1. We find Tchaikovsky, for example, writing to Madame von Meck (6 July 1878): 'An idea never occurs to me without its accompanying harmonies.'

from his mother who now lived at Tampere. 'Today the schools have a holiday so that the children can go skating and some of them have just gone past with their skates and their fresh and lively faces; my mind returned to the time you were their age, but have you continued to go skating since you have been grown-up; it would be nice if you could turn to such pleasures.' Maria Sibelius was suffering from ear trouble that Christian's medicines seemed powerless to assuage. Janne went and stayed with her and after his visit wrote in his sketch-book: 'At mother's, Simplicity. O *simplicitas*.'

He was left in uncertainty about the fate of his application to the university for the affair dragged on through the whole of the spring term of 1897. A special appointment committee was set up with Faltin as chairman and it finally reported back in Sibelius's favour. 'A composer of Sibelius's standing', read their findings, 'would indeed be an adornment to any university', and in the final pages of their recommendation the committee even went so far as to suggest that the composer should be relieved of economic worries and be given 'a position that would leave him sufficient time and peace of mind to devote himself to composition'. The report pronounced on Kajanus in somewhat peremptory terms suggesting that he was well placed in his present conducting post where he could make the most useful contribution to the musical life of the capital and implied that by the side of his other comprehensive activities, the university music would assume a subsidiary role.

These sentiments could perhaps have been expressed more tactfully but be this as it may, Kajanus took offence: first of all, the committee had implied that as a composer he was no longer to be reckoned with as a figure of any great importance while Sibelius's music, on the other hand, was a vital national interest! Twenty-five of the votes had been for Sibelius while three had been cast for Kajanus. Many people imagined that Kajanus would accept the verdict and gracefully withdraw from the scene. 'It would be shameful were Kajanus to contest this decision,' wrote Emmy Achté to her daughter, Aino, then staying in Paris, 'for he would lose most people's sympathy: it would seem as if he were trying to take the bread out of Sibelius's mouth.' None the less, Kajanus had no intention of meekly retiring from the ring. And so he took up the challenge and penned an appeal, pressing his claims. 'One might well imagine', he wrote, 'that the committee wished to recommend that Herr Sibelius be offered some kind of composition scholarship or bursary rather than a university teaching post.' He then turned his fire on Sibelius the conductor, albeit obliquely, by arguing that the easiest task any conductor faced was to direct his own compositions. Kajanus blamed the committee for what was, perhaps unconscious, partiality in glossing over everything that was not to Sibelius's advantage; the *longueurs* in his works, his unsuccessful direction of the Coronation Cantata as well as the weaknesses, both in logic and presentation, of his lecture.

Sibelius made no public reaction. Kajanus's pronouncement, though, came as a tremendous blow to him. Kajanus may well have imagined that his personal relations with Sibelius would remain unaffected by the polemical exchanges that were very much the order of the day in the Scandinavian countries in such circumstances. But if he did so he was a poor psychologist. For Sibelius such behaviour from a friend was quite unthinkable and his attitude was never quite the same after this episode. For all the gratitude Sibelius felt for the championship he received from Kajanus's baton the unreserved trust of their earlier friendship had been broken and there was a certain reticence between them for some time. Kajanus for his part never quite rid himself of an inferiority complex in his dealings with the composer. But it was from his lips that the charming saying about the conductor's role comes: 'I'm only the coachman. The main thing is to be sure that the fellow you're driving is a genius.'

Before the final decision was taken on the university appointment Sibelius composed another work, a new cantata for the university encaenia in the Spring when honorary degrees and the like were conferred. Although the new piece does not rise to great heights of inspiration, it is a good deal more interesting than its two predecessors and certainly more polished in craftsmanship and richer in harmonic resource. Sibelius later published an arrangement of nine of them for mixed choir *a cappella* and one of them, *Soi kiitokseksi Luojan* (Let thanks ring to the Lord) is widely sung in Finnish schools.

The Cantata for the University Encaenia was perhaps the best response Sibelius could have made to Kajanus's appeal which had cut little ice with the university consistory. But in the final analysis they could only make a recommendation: the decision itself lay in the hands of W. C. von Daehn, the Secretary of State for Finnish Affairs at St. Petersburg,[1] who was also Chancellor of the University. An astute politician he sensed that the majority feeling in the ruling party was not in Sibelius's favour. Indeed Senator Yrjö-Koskinen in a letter to von Daehn some months after the affair had blown over wrote that 'it would have been unfortunate had Sibelius received the university post'. The fiasco at the performance of the Coronation Cantata may well have influenced feeling; but more probably the argument that most strongly weighed was the feeling that the university needed a reliable, practical musician rather than a temperamental young genius! In any event von Daehn overruled both the committee and the consistory, and appointed Kajanus. The decision was undoubtedly a blow for Sibelius but it was one that was soon to be softened.

Before the decision became known Sibelius went on holiday with Walter von Konow as his companion to visit the great Italian art centres. They proceeded to Venice, via Berlin, Dresden and Vienna: from Venice he wrote home,

1. Perhaps High Commissioner in St. Petersburg would be a more up-to-date description of his functions and status. *Tr*

'I am in good spirits. Walter is travelling and eating First Class, while I g(
Third. I feel like a gentleman's gentleman!' After going by boat to Ancona th(
two friends went walking in the Italian countryside sharing the simple foo(
of the peasants, but the composer's letters in praise of their bucolic existenc(
do not quite ring true. Reading between the lines one can guess that he did no
altogether share von Konow's tastes and did not always feel entirely at hom(
in the company to which he was drawn.

After another week or so they returned north early in July and althougl
Sibelius had had mixed feelings about the holiday it did serve to take his min(
off the university. As he could not afford to spend the summer at Hangö as h(
had originally planned, he went with the rest of the family to stay with Aino':
mother at Lojo where they remained for some weeks. Later on Lojo was mad(
more congenial to him when a little shed-cum-cottage was built for him s(
that he could retire and compose in peace and quiet. On this occasion he di(
not particularly enjoy his time there: the Tolstoyan doctrines practised in the
house hold did not really appeal to him. He did not like seeing his mother-
in-law, who was of noble birth, waiting on her servants who lounged idly
on the grounds!

When the nights drew in towards the end of August and the first hints of
approaching autumn touched the capital, Sibelius returned to Helsinki while
his wife went to the von Konows. There he started work on *Koskenlaskijan
morsiamet* (*The Ferryman's Brides*)[1] a ballad for voice and orchestra to words by
Oksanen. 'Can you imagine it,' he wrote to Aino, 'The Ferryman is already
sketched. Kiss the children and try to think of me kissing you. I am starting
now on another piece. The Ferryman can tie up for a bit. It is to be given
in October. Everything is very peaceful here. I have just given the keyboard
a battering and am quite out of breath as a result.'

It was at about this time that he was beginning to conceive a new orchestral
piece based on Heine's poem about the fir tree that dreams of the palms of the
south. 'Every day I get a clearer picture of my new symphonic poem', he
writes on the 25 August.

'First of all, I had thought of it in terms of several short movements, perhaps
ten in number, but now I have given up this idea. There would be no sense of
unity. I have decided to characterize the tree with a forest song and its dreams
of the south with a countersubject. Between them there will be variations or
episodes on the forest song. All of it will be clothed in a kind of *clair-obscur*!'

Aino was at the von Konow's so that she could be near her mother-in-law
whose health may have been giving the family some anxiety. Christian went
over for a long week-end but she was still afflicted with rushing noises in her
ears. Sibelius as he said in this same letter, 'had not the conscience to take any
free time', and stayed in Helsinki. Undoubtedly he did not want to interrupt
the flow of inspiration but his absence may not have been solely due to his

1. A more literal translation is *The Rapids-Shooter's Brides* but this more accurate title
does not seem to have supplanted *The Ferryman's Brides* in general usage. *Tr*

absorption in his creative work: he had a strong aversion to the atmosphere of the sickroom and the advancing shadows of death, and above all he loathed family gatherings. His relations with his mother had undergone a brief moment of strain and she had not always been able to conceal her jealousy of her daughter-in-law. In any event Sibelius did not visit his mother at Lahis in the late summer and when she died in November, he must have reproached himself on that score.

On 2 September he went to a recital given by Aino Ackté, who at the age of twenty-one had only a month earlier been given a two-year contract with the Paris Opera. On this occasion she sang *Se'n har jag ej frågat mera* (*Since then I have questioned no further*) and later was to be associated with some of his most demanding vocal scores including *Höstkäll* and *Luonnotar*. He became caught up in the daily round of teaching commitments (he speaks of his whole day being taken up by teaching in a letter to Aino of 6 October), finishing *The Ferryman's Brides*, correcting proofs of a piano arrangement he had made of the *Karelia* music and so on.

The Ferryman's Brides was soon finished. In general Sibelius showed good judgment in his choice of verse and so it is difficult to see why he chose so conventional a poem as Oksanen's. Perhaps the story itself attracted him or perhaps he felt that he should set a Finnish rather than a Swedish-language text as the repertoire undoubtedly needed strengthening and in his search failed to uncover anything better. The opening with its four-note motive[1] over a pattern of rising and descending chromatic thirds describes the unceasing play of the rapids and the three-cornered drama is effectively portrayed but frankly the piece can hardly be described as a landmark in Sibelius's output. He abandoned, at least for the time being, his tone-poem based on Heine, though seven years later he conducted a piece inspired by the same theme at a charity concert. Teaching plainly took its toll on his energies and time: Niklas Achté described him at this time as being under great nervous pressure and seemingly at odds with everybody. Indeed it must have seemed to him that his position was becoming untenable; that it was impossible to reconcile creative work and the drudgery of earning his living. For eighteen months he had concerned himself with the trivial round of duties and composed three commissioned works of no real importance; at the same time he had tried to better his economic position —without any success. In order to compose he needed more time to himself and also the ability to put some distance between himself and his everyday environment. The Italian trip with Walter von Konow had admittedly been short but it was none the less sufficient to stimulate his imagination. But no sooner had the stimulus begun to register than he was caught up in the usual treadmill. His next major work only came after he had spent the best part of the following spring abroad (in Berlin) and had cut down on his volume of work.

But the conservatoire's mills ground on, and at a concert at the end of the

1. It resembles the four-note figure in the last two Lemminkäinen Legends as Nils-Eric Ringbom has pointed out.

month, a symphony by Ernst Mielck, a youth of twenty and a pupil of Max Bruch, was given its première. Its eclectic classicism made a considerable impression: Flodin spoke of its Beethovenian spirit. There were some barbs in his review obviously aimed in Sibelius's direction. 'We have often deplored the weakening sense of form in the young composers of our present generation. They can all turn out Rhapsodies, Symphonic Poems, Suites galore, but few dare to test their strength against the magisterial symphonic edifice: the reason for this is that so few command the art of being able to develop a musical idea to its logical conclusion, so that it has a general rather than passing significance, a spiritualized form thus giving the imagination a distinct objective towards which it can strive.' [1]

Flodin's broadsides mingled with the applause that greeted Sibelius's own concert a few days later on 1 November. Sibelius conducted the first performances of The Ferryman's Brides and of the newly revised Lemminkäinen Legends: the concert was sold-out and the programme met with thunderous applause. Nor were the critics any less enthusiastic the following morning. Oskar Merikanto writing in Päivälehti recorded that 'it seemed at long last as if our public had woken up for the very first time and shaken hands with our foremost composer', while Uusi Suometar went out of its way to score off Flodin by stressing the symphonic character of the Lemminkäinen Suite.

A day later (3 November 1897) Flodin returned to the attack in Nya Pressen. 'This kind of music' (he is referring to the Four Legends that he had earlier praised) 'sounds positively pathological: it leaves mixed feelings, painful and difficult to put into words since they have so little in common with the aesthetic feelings of pleasure that all art and above all music should prompt. I am no Hanslick. . . . But I must say quite frankly that music like the Lemminkäinen portraits depresses me, makes me miserable, exhausted and apathetic.' Whatever made Flodin perform this volte face? He obviously wanted to see Sibelius's thinking directed into other channels and a few weeks later in the January issue of the periodical Ateneum he further clarified his position. Up to now, he argues, Sibelius has not developed in any sense other than in the purely technical mastery of his craft. His tone poems engulf one in an all-consuming mood: hence the music has an opium-like effect. We could wish that he also thought in terms of absolute music rather than the pictorial and mystical visions. 'There is the difference between the great men of music, Bach, Beethoven and Wagner on the one hand, and our young Finnish master on the other.'

Less atmosphere and more substance: this, then, was the kernel of Flodin's argument. Inspired by Mielck's Symphony he did his utmost to urge Sibelius to follow his example and to abandon the fashionable symphonic poem. But his article reads as a general reaction against the artistic climate of the 1890s and the musical currents of the day. He begins by attack the symbolism of the German painter, Sascha Schneider; the morbidity, mysticism and the dreamlike states evoked by many of the artists of the decade appalled him. He liked only

1. In Nya Pressen.

one episode in *The Ferryman's Brides* together with the opening of the first of, what he called, the Lemminkäinen rhapsodies. 'Here the composer showed with what touching eloquence his lyre can speak when the gloom of Saul does not descend and his dark midnight fantasies do not consume his soul.' His sentiments echo those of Wegelius who, like Flodin, was anxious to save Sibelius from those 'dark fancies' and lead him over to the Elysian fields of classical art.

What did Sibelius himself make of all this? Certainly Flodin's words must have upset him but it seems unlikely that they would have had any direct influence on his development. Flodin had overlooked the symphonic aspect of the Lemminkäinen *Legends* and Sibelius in any event would have sooner or later embarked on a symphony without 'encouragement' of this kind. He certainly took no notice of Flodin's favourable views on the first of the *Legends*: indeed he withheld it together with the third, 'Lemminkäinen in Tuonela', until the 1930s, largely because Kajanus did not much care for them.[1]

But Sibelius had good news to offset the unpleasantness created by Flodin's attacks and the frustration of his own academic ambitions. As early as September 1897 there had been a move to secure him some kind of state support. In a letter to his friend and colleague, W. C. von Daehn, Senator Yrjö-Koskinen raised the subject:

Some time ago on my initiative the question of a pension for the composer, Herr Sibelius was ventilated. I also feel that his work, which has a thoroughly national imprint, is of sufficient quality and importance for it to be in the public interest for us to guarantee him some kind of minimum subsistance. More than is usual with artists, he seems to lack completely any feeling for practical affairs even to the extent that it would in my view be inappropriate to find some kind of appointment at the university for him. But a State Pension of 3,000 marks and some smaller marks of support from time to time should be adequate to enable him to continue his work and thus enrich our national art.[2]

Senator Yrjö-Koskinen's letter reflects the general view that Sibelius should in some way or other receive some kind of compensation at being passed over by the university the previous year. Even Kajanus's keenest advocates had suggested that an additional post should be created for him at the university but to Sibelius's delight however, opinion seemed to favour the idea of a grant. Two years earlier he had received a newly-created composition scholarship of 1,800 marks and in 1895 had shared a scholarship of some 2,500 marks with Kajanus. At the end of November the Senate formally approved a recommendation to the Tsar that Sibelius should be given an annual award. The request was agreed and for the ten years that followed Sibelius was guaranteed the sum of 3,000 marks after which it was turned into a permanent pension for life. 'So generous

1. This was verbally indicated to me by Mme. Aino Sibelius. It is also recorded by Santeri Levas: Vol. 1, p. 171.
2. The letter dated 17 October 1897 is in the Finnish State Archives.

and enlightened an act on the part of a government towards an artist is well-nigh unprecedented in our time and deserves the highest approbation': so wrote Cecil Gray in his biography of the composer.[1] However it may be worth mentioning that two other Scandinavian composers, Grieg and Svendsen, had received State grants at the same age, of about thirty, and even in Finland there had been a precedent.[2]

Sibelius's income from his various artistic activities comprised about half the salary he would have received as professor. No one with a family to support could live in any comfort on this. For Kajanus, the salary he earned at the university was only a welcome supplement to his main source of income, the Philharmonic Orchestra. Nor was Sibelius's situation particularly attractive compared with that of his foreign colleagues. Debussy, whose money troubles are well known, received during the last half of the 1890s an annual income of about 6,000 francs, twice that of Sibelius's, from his publisher. Tchaikovsky's annual income from Madame von Meck was 6,000 roubles a year, the equivalent of 24,000 marks. Thanks to his pension, Sibelius was able to cut down his teaching commitments and take longer holidays: some years later he decided to sever his connection with the Conservatoire altogether but by doing so he courted grave insolvency. Only ten years later his debts amounted to 100,000 Finnish marks or as many gold francs. Sibelius could indeed have done with a Madame von Meck!

1. *Sibelius*; London, 1931, p. 50.
2. When Runeberg had been passed over in 1833 at a university election, an attempt was made to create a special Chair in Aesthetics for him. When this in its turn did not materialize, he was given a life pension of 1,000 roubles.

CHAPTER ELEVEN

The First Symphony

S IBB!
    Come and take the first orchestral rehearsal of the Musette and
    the Minuet at the Swedish Theatre at one o'clock. Bring along
    the *lied* with you. I shall play that as an overture to the whole
performance—the song and accompaniment behind the dropped curtain.
Be sure to come! Bye!

Adolfus.

The letter is Adolf Paul's and was written in Helsinki some time during
February 1898. It is imbued with a sense of imminent success: his bitter irony,
the sense of foreboding and the artificial high spirits have all disappeared and
we feel that he is being carried along on the crest of the wave. He had been
married some years to a girl of good family from Lübeck and had now written
an effective play on the subject of King Christian II and the beautiful Dyveke
and had it accepted moreover by the Swedish Theatre in Helsinki. And at
last Sibelius had responded to his pleas for collaboration and had written the
incidental music. In later years Paul recalled that Sibelius had composed four
of these pieces during the mornings and afterwards played them over to him
in a small recess in Nymark's coffee-house. 'Here's the song about the spider.
And Dyveke's dance (the Musette) goes like this! It's supposed to be a bagpipes
and chalumeau, you understand. I am scoring it for two bassoons and clarinets.
You will hear what it sounds like. And here you have an overture into the bargain, an elegy for strings, short but just what is needed to bring down the curtain on all the worries and anxieties of people's daily lives. Tell me, do you want
any ballet music as well? I have done a Minuet for you too.'[1]
    Paul's description has often been construed as evidence of the speed with
which Sibelius could compose when it was necessary but it would seem that his
memory had failed him on at least one point. Judging from his note to Sibelius,

1. Adolf Paul: *Profiler*, (Stockholm 1937) quoted in Ekman: *Jean Sibelius och hans verk*,
   2nd edition, Helsinki, 1956, p. 175. (It does not appear I should add, in the English
   edition. *Tr*)

the Elegy did not exist when the play was first put into rehearsal and Paul thought of using the 'Fool's Song of the Spider' as a curtain raiser. It was this somewhat unappetizing prospect that spurred Sibelius into writing the Elegy. At the première on 24 February, Sibelius and his musicians filed on to the stage behind the curtain: 'I shall play to give you a success', he told Paul when he 'nervously but vigorously' raised his baton on the Elegy. His prophecy came true for the play was given twenty-four times at the Swedish Theatre in the spring of 1898, a rare if not spectacular achievement in the Finnish theatrical world. Even if Sibelius's music contributed to its success, it would be ungenerous not to acknowledge the dramatic power of the play itself. Dyveke, at one and the same time innocent and yet provocative, who was poisoned at the court of King Christian II in mysterious circumstances, offered grateful material to both writers and musicians at this period. Peter Heise composed his Dyveke songs to a text of Holger Drachman who in later years belonged to Paul's circle of acquaintances in Berlin and perhaps even gave him the idea of writing his play. Paul's play may not be a drama of any great moment but it is effective for all that and as such a welcome source of income for all theatre managements.

After the première of *King Christian II*, Sibelius and his wife went off to Berlin at the end of February and it was here that he composed *Sandels*, a piece for male chorus and orchestra. He called it 'an improvisation for male chorus and orchestra'; the words are by Runeberg and the work was intended as an entry to a competition sponsored by the M. M. Choral Society. Aino returned home in April and hastened to send her husband a telegram to which he answered in a frank outpouring of feeling: 'My heart nearly broke when we parted in the railway coach. The whole evening I was the victim of my feelings, much as I imagine you must have been. This our love, is in fact our life.'

'I went to Busoni's for dinner yesterday: he was extremely charming and inscribed a score to me with the dedication, "To the Finnish master and my dear friend." ' (11 April 1898)

His brother Christian joined him in Berlin to study pathology and Jean enjoyed showing him the city. They went to the opera together and saw *Figaro*, *Fidelio* and *Tannhäuser*, and heard the Joachim Quartet. They each bought themselves an elegant umbrella at Wertheim's and Christian was fitted out with a splendid top hat, an item that Jean considered an essential part of the belian wardrobe once they were in a great European metropolis.

Paul persuaded Sibelius to compose some new movements for the King Christian II Suite and redoubled his efforts to find him a German publisher. With a success in Finland behind him and contracts under negotiation both in Sweden and Germany, Paul rather enjoyed his role as champion of the young composer. Together they journeyed to Leipzig to see von Hase, head of the venerable Breitkopf and Härtel. Sibelius has described their visit in these words: 'We were led through one large room after another. Everything made

solemn and awe-inspiring impression. Paul seemed to feel very much at home
in these surroundings—it looked as if his hopes grew, the nearer the decisive
moment approached. Our progress through the huge rooms had just the
opposite effect on me. My confidence decreased at every step I took, and when
we came at last into the holy of holies, the manager's room, where the head of
the firm, O von Haase, sat enthroned at a monumental desk under Beethoven's
autograph portrait, I was almost ready to sell my compositions for nothing. I
was so impressed by the antiquity and traditions of the firm and the awe-
inspiring surroundings in general.'[1]

Breitkopf und Härtel acquired the German rights to the *King Christian II
Suite* and their catalogue was later to include a significant part of Sibelius's
output right up to *Tapiola* and the two *Legends* last to appear in print, 'Lemminkäinen and the Maidens of the Island' and 'Lemminkäinen in Tuonela'
which they published in the 1950s.

In April a new work began to take shape in Sibelius's mind. Judging from his
sketch book he had planned a programme symphony just before his departure
from Helsinki. 'Musical Dialogue: (I) The wind blows cold, cold weather from
the lake, motto for the first movement of the symphony. (II) Heine. (The
north's fir (!)[2] dreams of the southern palm). (III) A Winter's Tale. (IV) Jorma's
Heaven.' The tonal layout of the movement is F major, D flat major, C minor
and F again. On the same sheet of paper Sibelius had sketched out the theme
of the Idyll for piano in D flat: it was possibly his intention to make use of it
in the Heine movement. The title of the first movement originates from a
well-known Finnish folk song. 'A Winter's Tale' is probably an allusion to the
Shakespeare play while Jorma's Heaven comes in Juhani Aho's novel, *Panu*,
stories from 'the final struggle between the Christian and heathen faiths in
Finland' which came out for the Christmas of 1897. Aho's feeling for the past,
Karelian in inspiration, with a lightly concealed anticlerical bias appealed to
Sibelius; and his copy of *Panu* is well worn and on one page even bears some
musical jottings. Is it possible, I wonder, that the First Symphony had its
origins in this project? Two facts suggest that this is not the case: first, the key
system of the projected work bears no resemblance to that of the First Symphony, and secondly, in 1904 he wrote a piece with the same title as that of the
Heine movement. However, there is no doubt that at this time Sibelius was
fascinated by the programmatic symphony: he noted in his sketchbook in
Berlin on 2 March that he had just heard the *Symphonie fantastique*, 'O santa
inspirazione! O santa dea!'

Sibelius set to work on the First Symphony proper at the end of April. 'I
have now worked hard for three days. It has been wonderful. I'm working on
the new thing, *alla sinfonia*', he wrote to Aino on the 27th. On one of the
sketch pages, probably from this spring of 1898, we find a motive from the

1. Ekman p. 146–47.
2. Sibelius has pine: Heine's poem speaks of a fir.

finale with some other ideas over which he has written 'Berlioz?'. But Sibelius was in no mood for sustained concentration. Living in a big city took its toll and his ample consumption of wine and cigars presented him with constant temptation. 'From now onwards,' he told his wife on the 19th, 'I will write and tell you, Aino, just how much I drink and smoke, absolutely truthfully. Whether it be little or much. Yesterday I only drank on two occasions a glass of red wine and smoked one (!) cigar. Today I have smoked one cigar and drunk two glasses of white wine.' But on most days Sibelius preferred to maintain a discreet silence less too great a strain be placed on his veracity. As a doctor Christian saw it as a duty to dissuade his brother from his excesses and turn him to the path of plain living. And presumably reeling from the pressure of his shock tactics and constant warnings, Jean wrote to Gallén's brother-in-law, Mikko Slöör: 'I have got some news for you. I have become a teetotaller since the first of May. Don't tell this to my wife. I go to the opera and compose. I've also begun to take riding lessons (also a secret from my wife). I intend to come back home a dandy.' (7 May)

But when Gallén suddenly turned up from Italy and called his old friends of the Symposium evenings together Sibelius had an excuse to break his alcohol strike. On 25 May we find him writing to Mikko Slöör again. 'Unfortunately I have had a serious relapse (and even been in a fight). Gallén was there. He saved my life. Paul has had a baby son—and it all started as a result of that. This is presumably Heaven's last warning to give up alcohol! Oh dear! Well, say nothing about my fall from grace.' The fall from grace occurred in a Berlin restaurant. Sibelius and Gallén had promised to be godfathers to Paul's new-born baby and the event was celebrated by a full-scale party. At the end of their rowdy celebrations the Finns came to blows with a group of Polish street workers and it is difficult to gather whether burgundy or blood flowed more freely. Sibelius received a gash in the head or as he himself put it, had his lump of genius knocked off!

As spring wore on, so Sibelius's feelings of homesickness grew apace. 'I have bought some flowers (narcissus and stocks). They give atmosphere', he told Aino at the beginning of May. At the beginning of the following month he was reunited with his family at Elisabeth Järnefelt's house in Lojo and it was here that three more movements for the *Christian II Suite* saw the light of day; the Nocturne, Serenade and Ballade, all of them scored for a full orchestra. Paul was delighted with them and promised to forward them to Leipzig. What Sibelius needed, in Paul's view, was the stimulus of real success. 'You have both the power to fly and the wings to carry you: it only remains to take flight,' he wrote (11 August). Paul even arranged two such 'flights' for him. He managed to secure a Leipzig performance of the *King Christian Suite* under Hans Winderstein whose Philharmonic concerts at the Alberthalle enjoyed a considerable reputation in spite of competition from Nikisch. Sibelius had doubts about making his debut with incidental music in a lighter genre in the town in which Bach, Mendelssohn and Schumann had presented their masterpieces and wrote to Busoni to this effect the following month. 'It has embarrassed me to go and tell people that Winderstein has performed something of mine at Leipzig, since that something is some salon music—entr'actes for Paul's play. It's not intended as a piece to introduce me abroad, I have the greatest ambition to stand before you as a composer for whom you can have some regard.'

Winderstein conducted the Nocturne, Elegy, Musette and Serenade at the end of February 1899, sandwiching them in between two Beethoven works. They did not evoke a positive response in the *Leipziger Zeitung* which spoke of their 'Mascagni-like lyricism' and left no doubt as to what it thought of that, and referred to the Musette as 'pure drivel'. Winderstein gave the *King Christian II Suite* in Warsaw, too, but the idea of Sibelius conducting a concert of his own works with Winderstein's orchestra was never seriously followed up: he was made to suffer for his skill in writing popular genre music.

Paul's second contribution to Sibelius's cause came when the première of *King Christian II* was due in Stockholm on 4 February 1899 at the Royal Dramatic Theatre. Paul's idea was that Sibelius should come over from Helsinki to conduct the incidental music in its entirety but the plan fell through as the Stockholm pit was not big enough to accommodate a full orchestra. Sibelius stayed at home and Paul contented himself with the smaller numbers that had accompanied the original production. 'The applause' recorded the *Dagens Nyheter*, 'also for Mr. J. Sibelius's incidental music, was unusually vigorous.'

As a whole the *King Christian* music is no match for his best work in this genre. This may in part be due to the fact that the characterization does not offer the same imaginative possibilities as, say, Melisande or Prospero! Sibelius's role was confined to providing atmospheric entr'actes and episodes to cover court festivities and the like. The Elegy for string orchestra, however, is among Sibelius's happier inspirations:

Ex. 156

The theme dissolves into improvisatory cello passages as if recollections of the past were crowding into the memory. After the theme has reappeared for the third time Sibelius evokes a mood of great melancholy and achieves a striking eloquence in the closing bars.

The Musette is played by street musicians outside Dyveke's window, where the clarinets and bassoons imitate the sound of bagpipes.

Ex. 157

At times the sonority (in the original version quoted above) suggests something of the quality of baroque outdoor serenades but the harmonies are, of course, purely nineteenth-century. The minuet is neither better nor worse than the other pastiche-movements that Sibelius amused himself by writing at this period of his life. The *Fool's Song of the Spider* is readily memorable—perhaps a little too facile! The three interludes that Sibelius added later are more ambitious in their layout. Indeed the expressive string cantilena in the Nocturne anticipates the First Symphony though the atmosphere is altogether lighter and more festive. The musical language is far from complex and the piece radiates an altogether fresh and life-enhancing quality that comes close at times to *verismo* opera. The piece dies away in an elegiac pianissimo. The Serenade is a more distinguished piece. After a short introductory minuet, the serenade beings on the strings:

Ex. 158

The music increases in passionate intensity but when the curtain goes up the minuet is heard, as if from afar, in delicate instrumental colours. The Ballade concerns itself with the Stockholm massacre and is not perhaps the most successful movement. Only at the very end, when the strings build up a crescendo that culminates with the brass, is there any sense of real power.

Sandels, the improvisation for male chorus and orchestra, has the character of an occasional piece. By choosing Runeberg's poem Sibelius added to the patriotic repertory and furthermore paid homage to an heroic figure, but both the irony of the poem as well as the character of the dialogue sound surprisingly tame in this setting, and it is only at the change of scene from Sandels' headquarters to the outpost from which he observes the battle that the musical characterization acquires a sharper focus.

Another work from the spring that he spent in Berlin is the *Carminalia*, three old novice songs that Sibelius arranged both for three-part *a cappella* choir and for a two-part children's choir with organ or piano accompaniment. The songs had been discovered in Lovisa and sent to Sibelius by friends of the family. In the printed score they are said to date from the seventeenth century but in actual fact they are to be found in a collection of *Piae Cantiones* that appeared

early as 1582. The version with piano accompaniment in particular shows
Sibelius not wholly at ease in imitating medieval style.

'Are you all speaking Russian in Finland nowadays?' asked Adolf Paul in a
letter written during the autumn of 1898. His remark reflects some of the growing tension and delicacy of the political situation in which Sibelius's music came
to play a larger and larger role as a symbol of Finnish national self-consciousness.
The situation had been unsettled throughout the whole of the 1890s. Earlier
in the century from Alexander I onwards the Grand Duchy, for that is what
Finland was, had been governed as a state rather than a mere principality. But
now more menacing tones were to be heard and a programme of Russianization
was set in motion by the new Governor-General, Bobrikov. 'Russia's integrity
and interest demand that Finland, governed with a firm hand, should be
gradually reconstructed so that even to all outward appearances it should be
readily recognizable as Russian.' Needless to say, such utterances only fanned
the flames of Finnish nationalism. Finland was intent on maintaining its own
integrity and would never willingly abandon its autonomy and allow itself to
become a mere province of Tsarist Russia. On that issue all Finns were united:
only the choice of tactics divided the country. Admittedly one group formed
round Senator Yrjö Koskinen believed that the cycle of history would soon
turn and sooner or later Russian policy change and that any show of resistance
would delay rather than hasten the desired end. The other to which the majority
of the Swedish-speaking and the young Finnish parties subscribed took the view
that passive resistance was the most effective means of protest, Sibelius's
views were clear enough: his association with the *Päivälehti* circle, the group
formed round the liberal daily published by the young Finns, his upbringing in the shadow of Runeberg's ideas and poetry, his years of study with
Wegelius, who was strongly anti-Russian, made it inevitable that he would be
an adherent of passive resistance even though he took little active part in
political life. Indeed he never indulged in amateur politics at any time of his
life and scrupulously eschewed the intemperate language common in the
political discussions of the day. His contribution was firmly rooted in the
musical arena. Two years earlier, in 1896, he had written a folk-like choral
setting of Erkko's *Aamusumussa* (*In the morning mist*) which had distinct overtones of resistance against the Russians, and in the next few years the note of
protest in his work was to grow stronger in response to Bobrikov's repressive
measures.
    Sibelius showed relatively little interest in social issues though during the
1890s he was momentarily drawn into a movement, emanating from bourgeois
circles, that aimed at bridging the gap between the upper class and the growing
working-class movement. Admittedly he set Erkko's *Työkansan marssi* (*Workers'
march*) but it would be quite wrong to assume that he had any socialist sympathies. In any event Erkko's poem is far from socialist: work is seen as the

will of God, and when Sibelius's march was published in 1896 in a workman calendar, the Finnish working-class movement had yet to hoist the banner socialism. Arvid Järnefelt's Tolstoyan sympathies prompted Sibelius to work out his own views, and probably in 1899 he jotted down in his sketchbook 'Flirting with the workers worse than currying favour with the upper class One has to crush so much of your own potentiality. Tolstoy's views on music are not wholly sound as he does not recognize that there are differences i musicality. He is on the right lines: but he takes his argument to unreasonabl lengths.'

Should he really put into practice, he asks, what he has learnt from Tolsto and become a manual worker.[1] It would be a pity! Learn from what he h. taught, for he spoke with the authority of a great artist and a sage. 'When I'1 not creative, it seems to me self-evident that I ought to work in some other wa during those moments when life has no magic.' When he speaks of 'thes moments of no magic' he refers of course, to the times when inspiration faile to flow. The expression, incidentally, comes from Runeberg's 'Hjärtats morgon ('The heart's morning')

> These hopeless, endless hours
> this life in the realms of death
> without light and without magic.

As in his letter from Munich Sibelius considers—or rather pretends to conside —the possibility of working in some other discipline than that of composition

One can perhaps sense some nostalgia for the hours of practice he spent a the violin as a young man and that filled out the emptiness of the days. Th period of political tension during the autumn of 1898 was also a difficult on for him personally. On 9 September we find a diary entry: 'Autumn sun an bitter thoughts. . . . How willingly I would have sacrificed some of the financia support I have received if I only had some sympathy and understanding of m art—if someone loved my work. O, you slave of your moods, their play thing. . . .'

Sibelius stayed on at Lojo late into the autumn. Not even Busoni's concert at the end of September attracted him into town. He wrote a note of apology blaming his absence on his wife who was pregnant at this time. Another reaso was undoubtedly his total absorption with the First Symphony. It was with great reluctance that he moved back into Helsinki into a new flat that he ha rented in Liisankatu. Apart from him and his family, his brother Christian an his sister, Linda, also made their home there and in November, Aino gav birth to their third child, a daughter, Kirsti.

A month later the student choir YL gave a novelty of Sibelius's at one of thei concerts. The piece is a lullaby, *Sydämeni laulu* (*My heart's song*), the text o which comes from Kivi's *Seven Brothers*. The poem deals with death in child

1. Sibelius was totally unpractical and never busied himself with anything remotely concerned with manual labour.

hood and shows some of the mystic inclination of the Finnish psyche as well as some of Sibelius's own fascination for death. The Tuonela episode in the second and third of the *Four Legends* had shown the way in which his imagination was fired by death and its majesty and the song draws from his pen an austere lyricism and a gentle but shapely line. It also reflects something of his feeling for the Finnish language:

Ex. 159

The line, 'Siell' on lapsen lysti olla' (There the child is in safe-keeping), distinguished by the closed, lighter vowel sounds, e, i, y and the soft consonant l, is sung unison by the tenors while the words 'kaitsea Tuonelan karjaa' (the slopes of Tuonela's soil) with its sombre a, ai, uo and hard k, t, and r is given the darker colouring of the basses. It is strange that Sibelius was drawn to Kivi's poem at a time when his wife was expecting or had even just been delivered of another child, much in the same way that Mahler six years later made his settings of the *Kindertotenlieder* much to his wife's horror at a time when there were two small children in the house, one of them newly born.

Sibelius was slowly coming to realize that city life did not wholly suit him. Its temptations were far too numerous: the fashionable Kämp restaurant and two taverns, König and Gambrini, both of them popular among musicians, were close to Liisankatu—all too close indeed! The tune of the Musette from the *King Christian Suite* was made to fit the words 'Minä menen Kämpiin takaisin' (Now I'm going off to the Kämp again!) by some wits of the time. At the end of the year Sibelius moved out to Kerava, some miles outside Helsinki where the distractions of city life were less pressing and the following spring the whole family joined him there.

1899 opened fatefully. Nicholas II issued the so-called February Manifesto which deprived the Finnish parliament of its legislative powers in a number of important fields, thus delivering a fatal blow at Finnish autonomy. It goes without saying that this unleashed a wave of protest: over half-a-million Finns signed an appeal to the Tsar. Sibelius's brother-in-law, Arvid Järnefelt made his own private if modest contribution: he went to Moscow to see Tolstoy and canvas his support. For the great Russian author the Finnish response was far more than a matter of mere patriotic sentiment by which he would have been unmoved: it was more than just national pride and the flag, but individual freedom and liberty that was at stake. It was not merely permissible but a positive duty, he maintained, for the Finns to assert their freedom for the sake of all mankind. In Finland's self-defence, therefore, passive resistance was morally justified. This was Järnefelt's account of the meeting.

Sibelius was as incensed by all this as any Finn: four days after the publication of the February Manifesto he sent a patriotic note to Kajanus and set to work on a song of protest, the text of which was taken from Viktor Rydberg's poem, 'Dexippos' which offered a parallel to these events from the times of classical antiquity. It did not need too great a stretch of imagination to identify oneself with the Athenians and the Russians with the barbarian Goth. Sibelius intended his work as an impassioned call for resistance in a situation that was to all outward appearances hopeless. And so he chose *The Song of the Athenians* from Rydberg's poem setting it for boys' and men's voices, wind septet and percussion. After an instrumental introduction, the choir enters as follows:

Ex. 160

The music with its dactylic rhythms and heroic colours evokes something of the atmosphere of a Thermapolae. Even a modern Plato might have found room in his ideal state for music with so obvious a social purpose: Finland had in fact found a battle song comparable with the 'Va pensieri' chorus of *Nabucco*. *The Song of the Athenians* was the last work in Sibelius's concert on 26 April 1899, the centre-piece of the programme being the new First Symphony which he had just completed in Kerava. *Skogsrået* began the programme and each movement of the symphony itself was applauded. But if the symphony received an ovation, *The Song of the Athenians* was greeted with little short of rapture and had to be immediately repeated. Among the critics however, the voice of Flodin was silent: he had moved to the *Aftonposten*, the publication of which had been prohibited in April by the Russian censor. His colleague, Faltin noted in *Nya Pressen* that the symphonic form 'placed no shackles on Sibelius's imagination. On the contrary he seems to move in it with remarkable freedom, following the flight of his inspiration and permitting himself such departures from its discipline as he considers fitting. Few specifically Finnish characteristics are to be found in the symphony: the composer speaks the language of all mankind, yet a tongue that is none the less his own.' A month later Sibelius was awarded the sum of 2,500 marks from the State Fund for the encouragement of Finnish composers.

Writing in 1885 after the first performance of Brahms's Fourth Symphony, the German critic Friedrich von Hausegger said, 'The symphony is the key form around which the battle rages in our time. It is in the symphony that the composer of today reveals himself, and by so doing commit himself one way or the other.' The crucial issue was the survival of the Viennese classical tradition, the legacy of Beethoven, the traditional view of tonality and of 'absolute music'; the other path was that of Liszt and Wagner, the disintegration of tonality and the collapse of the classical ideals in the face of music-drama and the programme symphony. Hausegger's words were no less valid at the turn of the century when to compose a symphony was almost automatically to range oneself alongside the conservatives and to risk being thought of as the enemy of the new. For Debussy the symphony was a moribund form that could not be renewed either by the vivid colours of the nationalist school or brilliant scoring. If one takes the example of, say, Glazunov and puts his symphonies, admirable though they are in many respects, alongside those of Tchaikovsky or Brahms, one is inclined to concede the logic of Debussy's position. On the other hand, of course, Mahler had already shown before the turn of the century that the potentialities of the symphony were far from exhausted.

At the end of the 1890s Sibelius had arrived at the stage where he too should declare his stand on the symphonic issue. In many respects his position was not dissimilar from that of Strauss. Both composers had come near to the symphony in their tone-poems or their cycles of tone-poems and both had (at this point) experimented with opera. And although both composers had written a good deal of chamber music during their youth neither had come anywhere near writing a piece comparable in quality with, say, the Debussy quartet. Nor had either composer any pronounced feeling for the keyboard though both had shown greater assurance in their songs, Strauss cultivating his ineffable lyricism and Sibelius striving after the dramatic and atmospheric. Both composers were destined to be masters of the orchestra and with a sure sense of his own star Strauss chose the way of music drama while Sibelius chose the symphony. His musical course was already charted by a stranded operatic boat and other sunken rocks but two works, *Kullervo* and the *Four Legends* pointed clearly to symphonic waters. Now he altered course away from the Wagnerian and Lisztian sirens and towards the art of Tchaikovsky.

There is little doubt that Tchaikovsky's work, and in particular, the *Symphonie pathétique* which was performed in Helsinki in 1894 and 1897, found a powerful response in Sibelius and none of his works written before the turn of the century show this so powerfully as does the First Symphony. Sibelius was readily aware of his spiritual affinity with the Russian master and when some Swedish composers had remarked on Tchaikovsky's influence in this symphony, he wrote to Aino, 'There is much in that man that I recognize in myself.' Tchaikovksy's example is most clearly in evidence in the finale and in the use of a motto theme that appears at the opening of the work, as well as in many orchestral details. For all this the First Symphony has a strongly individual character. All four movements are coloured by harmonic touches and progressions that can be traced back to the String Trio in A major of 1889. In the minor, the chord of the dominant ninth appears often without its tonic, and poised over a mediant pedal point; this resolves usually on to a minor triad which thanks to the pedal point sounds like the tonic in 6–3 position. In the following example from the First Symphony the harmonic tension is heightened by an appoggiatura or suspension:

Ex. 161

From the main theme of the slow movement:

Ex. 162

At the beginning of the trio in the third movement the dissonance resolves on to the root position of the major triad:

Ex. 163

In the finale it resolves again in the minor and in the first inversion of the triad

Ex. 164

Simon Vestdijk has pointed out that these progressions are as characteristic of the First Symphony as the tritone is of the Fourth or the Dorian mode of the Sixth. Paradoxically enough this particularly Sibelian progression may well be the very thing that contributes the Tchaikovskian colouring to the work. There is a typical example of the kind of thing I mean in the trio section of the second movement of the *Pathétique*:

Ex. 165

Sibelius's first movement grows organically and the introduction contains the seeds that bear fruit in the exposition. It is pointless with the crude tools of analysis to try and illuminate the relationship between the various themes: at times it will be obvious and at others it will be only intuitively felt. But the total impression is one of organic continuity. The introductory melody on the solo clarinet, begins with a long-held note to which a slow chromatic turn is added after which the line slowly sings like the flight of a bird wounded in flight, making several attempts to rise again before taking flight:

Ex. 166

Apart from the chromatic ornamentation, the melodic line is strongly Dorian in feeling with a major sixth and a minor seventh. The second half of the theme (bar seventeen) describes a typically Sibelian melisma now with A as its tonal centre and dies away in the darker regions of G minor. The solo clarinet's tone quality—together with the accompaniment of a timpani roll for the first sixteen bars—as well as the contour of the melodic line suggested to Ilmari Krohn the atmosphere of an ancient threnody or a Karelian lament. When after the G, the strings enter, there is a certain tonal ambiguity: the key appears to be G major and it is only gradually that it is pulled towards E minor:

Ex. 167

The melodic shape is already anticipated in the opening clarinet line (bar eleven onwards), the variant of the theme in the violas and cellos is rhythmically related to the introductory motive. The oft-cited parallel between the Sibelius theme and the corresponding idea in Borodin's First Symphony[1] is more readily discernible on paper than in performance. The main theme is also distinguished on its repetition by an emphatic prefix which later on acquires a rhythmic significance later in the movement, and in the finale:

Ex. 168

The transition introduces another figure derived from the opening, transformed rhythmically, played by flutes in thirds and sounding for all the world like the twittering of a flock of birds. Again there is a strong Dorian feeling:

Ex. 169

A wider leap is added by way of completion on the oboes and clarinets:

Ex. 170

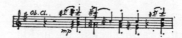

The listener is barely conscious of the derivation so totally different is the character of the idea in its new context and with its glistening harp and string accompaniment. The second group with its long sustained opening note and the characteristic Sibelian triplet is more of a complement to the first group than a contrast:

Ex. 171

That this idea, too, derives from the introductory clarinet monologue is evident when one examines the next appearance of the theme. A little later when the

1. The idea originates with Cecil Gray. Sibelius expressly denied ever having known the Borodin symphony at the time although it was played in Helsinki on 15 October 1896. *Tr*

second group is heard again the transition idea is added as a counterpoint and from its crotchet rhythm Sibelius builds up a woodwind figure of considerable momentum and an unbroken sense of movement. The music mounts to a climax broken by three repeated Bs pizzicato.

The material undergoes further transformation in the development. The strings now move in stretto and the line becomes increasingly chromatic. While the rhythm of the main theme is suggested by the brass, the second subject is heard on two solo violins while the transition theme is worked up in febrile pizzicato strings. In the end the music becomes one constantly moving polyphonic complex in which the main ideas of the movement can be discerned. But the chromatic whirlwind gradually fades when the violins and violas come to the fore with the main theme:

Ex. 172

The listener's attention is focused solely on the string melody and suddenly he finds that he is in the reprise. The effect is consistent with the telescoping process that distinguishes Sibelius's treatment of sonata form at this juncture of a movement, and the development moves seamlessly into a foreshortened reprise. There is some orchestral detail that compels admiration: when, for example, the harp just before fig. X spells out a dominant seventh chord the clarinet emerges from the texture almost unobserved and one hardly notices its presence until it continues its arabesque-like line. The scoring at the end of the movement (bassoons, lower strings and timpani) reminds one of the corresponding passage at the end of the first movement of Tchaikovsky's Fifth Symphony. Without in any way being revolutionary, the first movement foreshadows the kind of thematic thinking and the organic, metamorphosis technique that distinguish the later Sibelius symphonies.

The Andante can be described as a kind of rondo that outlines the following pattern:

A B C A1 D A2 C1 B1 A3

But this does not really do justice to the musical processes that are at work. The reprise, i.e. the section beginning after D (at A2) is to a large extent little more than an expanded and intensified version of the exposition. The thematic material of the movement is dominated by the rhythmic figure of the opening theme:

Ex. 173

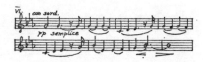

The B section, the first episode, is an ascending variant of it:

Ex. 174

A fugal interlude in the wind might well be the passage to which Sibelius referred in his sketchbooks at the time of the symphony's gestation as 'the bassoons tone-colour is so strongly Finnish in character':

Ex. 175

The C section introduces a descending variant of A's rhythm:

Ex. 176

The main theme returns on the solo cello (A1) and leads to a contrasting interlude in the sub-dominant region, A flat, *molto tranquillo*, (D):

Ex. 177

The idea derives surely from the second subject of the first movement and its pendant, a rising woodwind figure, seems an echo of the bird-like motive that immediately preceded it in the first movement. In the reprise the themes appear in darker, more subdued colourings and the tonality is predominantly minor.

The scherzo belongs firmly in the Bruckner tradition. In the more recent writings about Sibelius it is seen in terms of a sonata-design where a trio has been inserted between the development and reprise.[1] For my part, however, I feel that the movement lacks the structural complexity that one associates with sonata form. It is much closer in my view, to a kind of ternary form— or *liedform* where the main section also includes an element of thematic development. The mixolydian seventh (B flat in C) in the main theme makes a highly personal effect:

Ex. 178

In the trio he evokes a dreamlike idyll that aptly contrasts with the out-pouring of energy and the sharply defined motives of the scherzo. Sibelius so often echoes the melancholy or alternatively the demonic and terrifying side of nature that to find him in such gentle pastoral musings is rare:

Ex. 179

The reprise in so many of the scherzo movements of the latter half of the century strike an anachronistic chord as a stereotype, a tired convention, at

1. Krohn launched this particular theory and his view seems to be shared by Vestdijk and Vignal.

least when they are literal. Sibelius wisely foreshortens his reprise though by way of balance he adds a coda where the insistence on the chord of the Neapolitan key (D flat) serves to create strong dramatic tension.

The finale follows the so-called cyclic principle and opens with the clarinet melody played *forte* on the strings over a powerful brass support:

Ex. 180

But the idea does not dominate the canvas to anywhere like the same extent a did the motto themes of Tchaikovsky in the Fourth and Fifth symphonies. Even its continuation, a questioning figure from the strings, repeated sequentially, and the rough-hewn exchanges between wind and strings show that the Russian master's melodic style and orchestration still haunted his imagination:

Ex. 181

The atmosphere in the ensuing allegro molto section is more highly charged than is usual in Sibelius:

Ex. 182

The tension increases and the gestures reminiscent of the first movement become more emphatic:

Ex. 183

After the strings storm downwards the scene changes; then this *cantabile* theme makes its proud entry:

Ex. 184

The eloquent sweep of this idea on the G string is such that we feel as if Sibelius is taking farewell of the 1890s. The reprise has many exciting things but there are also times where it is evident that Sibelius's mastery of the orchestra is not yet commanding. As with the first movement, the last ends with the two famous pizzicato chords.

Sibelius's contemporaries found the work highly dramatic and, perhaps because they themselves were so steeped in programme music, they hastened to look for some literary inspiration. Furuhjelm, the author of the first monograph on the composer, saw in the first movement the stage of mythology peopled by characters in an heroic tragedy but he wisely refrained from specifying the action. A Berlin critic writing in the January 1907 number of *Allgemeine Musikzeitung*, likened it to a 'play of mourning in four acts'. Ilmari Krohn on the other hand, did not hesitate to outline a detailed programme for the symphony, as he did for that matter for its six companions which may have consciously or unconsciously inspired him. For Krohn the First Symphony evokes the Kullervo poem in the *Kalevala* and every theme performs the function of a leitmotiv. I cannot say that I find it in the least convincing; for example, he explains the absence of a final group in the first movement exposition by talking of Kullervo's failure to find any opportunity of escaping from his bondage and embarking on his heroic career! Sibelius told his secretary, Santeri Levas, with some impatience that his First Symphony had as little to do with the *Kalevala* as did any of the others. His pronouncement in an interview with Walter Legge in the 1930s[1] was no less emphatic.

1899 poses something of a problem for the chronicler of Sibelius's life; the framework is well documented, his concerts, journeys, his move to Mattila and so on, but the details of his daily life remain shadowy. We know all too little about the people he was seeing or even the works on which he was engaged. One would like to know a good deal more about his contacts with Knut Hamsun who spent the best part of a year in Helsinki from the autumn of

1. *Daily Telegraph* (30 December 1934). Quoted in Newman: *More Essays from the World of Music* 'Sibelius on Composition: the fallacy of Pure music', New York–London, 1958, p. 121.

1898 to the late summer of the following year. We learn from Tallqvist's study of Hamsun that he made a powerful impression on the composer and it is clear that they were on good terms. After leaving Finland, Hamsun went to Russia and the East and from Constantinople he sent Sibelius a line of verse in greeting.

In June Sibelius and Kajanus both went to adjudicate at a Choir Festival in Jyväskylä and afterwards went on to Axel Gallén's villa at Ruovesi to attend a christening. The scene by all accounts must have resembled one of the salon paintings of the period. On a raised platform there was a table covered with an Italian altar cloth and over it Gallén's painting, *Ad astra*, a nude with hair flaming like a halo, figured prominently. On the other walls there were his *Kalevala* paintings while a statue of the Buddha presides over the ceremony. Gallén used to do his morning exercises in front of it, a custom that encouraged the local inhabitants to think that he worshipped idols! The parish priest, albeit with some misgivings, is in attendance in this heathen stronghold while during the ceremony Sibelius sits at the piano while Kajanus and Mikko Slöör, both basses, officiate during the liturgy. Sibelius forgot where he was and began to improvise and according to one witness the theme of the coda of the finale of the Second Symphony came into being on this occasion.[1]

'Have you noticed,' wrote Kajanus shortly after this visit, 'that our friend Gallén's presence serves to draw us closer together—and the gods know the pleasure that gives me'. The tone of the letter leaves no doubt of Kajanus' anxiety to heal the breach that had arisen during the past months and he ended by inviting Sibelius to stay with him at his villa by the sea at Porkala near Helsinki. But evidently Sibelius did not accept: he stayed instead in the archipelago at Hogland, sailing and fishing with Armas Järnefelt and the author, Yrjö Veijola.[2]

At the beginning of the autumn Flodin published an article in *Aftonposten* (1 September 1899) under the title, *Génie oblige*, in which he expressed surprise that Sibelius's work had been misunderstood on its performances in Germany and Sweden (?) but admitted that he himself had needed years before he had come to terms with it and been able to appreciate 'its wild beauty'. He went on to say, 'The most national of all modern composers, Grieg, long ago received international recognition, and it is high time that this was accorded to Sibelius. But in actual fact he composes at least a generation ahead of his time.' None the less Flodin could not resist the temptation of making a personal thrust which is revealing, 'The Good Lord often allots the most beautiful of

1. Sibelius scribbled the original form of the theme on the back of a printed circular from the publishers Schuster & Loeffler, initialling it 18.6.99. Gallén's brother-in-law, Mikko Slöör added, 'S. was sitting in front of the fire at Kalela (the name of Gallén's villa at Ruovesi) and suddenly at two o'clock in the morning leapt to his feet and said, "Now, I will show you what impression this room makes on me, its basic mood." Then he sat at the piano and played the following tune.' The paper survives in the State Archives.
2. According to Sibelius's letter to Aino (26 August 1899).

melodies to the strangest of instruments and under his mask of indifference, cynicism and self-sufficiency, there could be qualities too refined and proud for their owner to be willing to display for all to see.' Was this the front which Sibelius presented to the world?

The same month, September, saw a concert given by Ida Ekman accompanied by her husband Karl, in which two new Sibelius songs were given, 'Svarta rosor' ('Black roses') and 'Men min fågel märks dock icke' ('But my bird is long in homing'): Ida Ekman was to become one of the most eloquent interpreters of Sibelius's songs.

Concert life was as flourishing as ever but the mood of the country was far from happy. Censorship tightened and in September, *Päivälehti* was banned for the best part of three months. Sibelius witnessed the growing popularity of *The Song of the Athenians* which became a symbol of freedom and was performed in every conceivable arrangement, for student choirs, the Finnish Guards, school choirs, and was given at Kajanus's popular concerts, in sports stadiums and elsewhere.

'Give me air, give me light!' Topelius's words, in *Islossningen i Uleå älv* ('The melting of the ice on the Uleå River') were also highly apposite in the climate of 1899 and Sibelius turned to the poem as a new means of protest for his next work, set for narrator, male voices and orchestra. Bobrikov and the censor had no cause for interference since the sentiments of the poem were abstract and as it had come into existence as an ode in honour of Tsar Alexander II. From the purely musical point of view *Islossningen i Uleå älv* has greater merit than the earlier cantatas and is of interest as a kind of preliminary sketch for *Finlandia*. The brass chords that punctuate the dramatic introductory strophe offer one foretaste.

> Whose slave am I that in my pride of youth
> Needs stand in bond through endless winter?
> Noble son of Finland's blue lakes
> I was born free and free I will die.

Ex. 185

The same kind of parallels can be drawn in the ensuing allegro. The text is sung by male voices, mainly in unison, while the allegro itself finishes in excited brass fanfares capped by a 'kolossales Pang' from the percussion. The adagio that follows can be seen as a kind of pendant to the hymnlike passage in *Finlandia*:

Ex. 186

The melodrama ends as it had begun with a dialogue between narrator and orchestra. The piece was first performed at a student concert in October 1899 and was followed by *The Song of the Athenians* given in classical costume.

But by far the most important contribution he made to the protest movement came in early November in connection with the 'Press Pension Celebrations'. Officially these were designed to raise money for the pension funds of newspapermen but in actual fact their object was to give both moral and material support to a free press that was battling to maintain its independence in the face of Tsarist pressure. The various activities that were planned during the three days set aside for it, culminated in a gala performance at the Swedish Theatre on 4 November. Bobrikov, who was not entirely without a certain sense of humour, proposed that the tickets for the Imperial box on that evening should be put up for auction to the highest bidder 'in the interests of so good a cause'. The main event of the evening was a set of Historical Tableaux staged by Kaarlo Bergbom, with texts by Eino Leino and Jalmari Finne with music by Sibelius.

Sibelius had, of course, tried his hand at a similar enterprise six years earlier when he had written his *Karelia* music and in the light of his experience decided to preface the tableaux with a short Prelude for wind instruments mainly as a means of first silencing and then preparing his public. In all there were six scenes, each of which he introduced with an orchestral prelude providing a suitably discreet accompaniment for the declaimed texts. The scenes were: 1. Väinämöinen's Song; 2. The Finns are baptized; 3. Duke Johan at Åbo Castle; 4. The Finns in the 30-years War; 5. The Great Unrest; 6. Finland Awakes! However, the music did not make so much of an impression on this occasion as it was to do a month later when Kajanus conducted five of the movements at one of his symphony concerts. He gave the 'Preludio, All'Overtura' (Tableau 1), 'Scena' (Tableau 4), 'Quasi Bolero' (Tableau 3) and 'Finale' (Tableau 6). Sibelius revised the 'All'Overtura', 'Scena' and 'Quasi Bolero', renaming it 'Festivo' in 1911 and published them as *Scènes historiques I*. The Prelude and the music to the second and fifth tableaux remained in manuscript, the Finale appearing separately as *Finlandia*.

The Prelude is scored for the normal complement of wind of the Romantic orchestra and is primarily a study in sonority. As in *Karelia*, Bergbom introduced his tableaux with an evocation of the heathen past. 'Väinämöinen is discovered seated on a rock playing the kantele. Not only do the inhabitants of Kaleva and Pohjola listen entranced but so do the powers of nature.'[1] The

1. The descriptions of the Tableaux come from *Hufvudstadsbladet*'s account of the occasion on the following day as reproduced in Furuhjelm, p. 185.

:ore contains no directly lyrical idea that one could identify with Väinä-
1öinen's song, rather it strikes the listener as a bustling festive piece with a
ydian fourth much in evidence that lends an archaic air to the proceedings.

The second tableau depicts the conversion of the Finns to Christianity.
3ishop Henrik baptizes a young Finnish nobleman and others await baptism.'
There are Gregorian echoes in the piece:

x. 187

The brilliant atmosphere of the Court of Duke Johan and Katarina Jagellonica
t Turku is portrayed in the third tableau, 'Festivo', which finds Sibelius in
osmopolitan mood and is among his best character-pieces in a non-Finnish
tyle. The next two tableaux explore two different aspects of war; the heat
nd excitement of battle on the one hand and the sufferings of ordinary people
n the other. Sibelius portrays a scene from the Thirty-Years War. 'From a
eight young Finnish peasants hurry to the struggle. The arbiter of battle hands
hem the key to the war, the banner of freedom.' A short melancholy intro-
luction, tempo di menuetto is interrupted by fanfares. In the battle music that
ollows the strings are heard *sul ponticello* and the muted horn cries heighten the
mpression of approaching war:

:x. 188

The mood changes and the key shifts to a gloomy A minor in the next tableau,
The Great Unrest (1700–21)': 'Mother Finland is seated among snowdrifts
urrounded by her frozen children. War, starvation, the cold, and death
:hreatens them all with disaster.' One's attention is caught by the following
dea on the strings which anticipates the music of the final tableau:

Ex. 189

With the last tableau we reach the nineteenth century. 'The powers of darkness

menacing Finland have not succeeded in their terrible threats. Finland awakes
Among the great men of the time that adorn the pages of history, one tell
the story of Alexander II, and other memories of Finland's renaissance stir
Runeberg listens to his muse, Snellman inspires his students, Lönnrot transcribe
the runes, four speakers of the first Diet, the beginnings of elementary education
and the first steam locomotive are all recorded.'

The Karelia music had ended with the national anthem and in the new se
of tableaux Sibelius was to prove himself every bit as much a patriot. The
music none the less does not specifically portray the Russian menace or the
Finnish spirit of resistance: it tries to invest the situation with a more genera
significance. While he was in Vienna eight years earlier Sibelius's enthusiasm
had been fired by Beethoven's *Egmont* music and doubtless he had its example
in mind at least when addressing himself to the same theme.

The wind and brass motive of the Andante might of course be thought to
personify an oppressor and the wind reply, having something of the tone
colour of the organ with the strings sounding a little like the *vox humana*
could be thought of as the oppressed. The hymnlike second subject has genuine
appeal: perhaps it is not too fanciful to think of Tolstoy's words to Arvid
Järnefelt as its source of inspiration. The work itself is too well known to
require detailed comment.

Sibelius was himself quite aware of *Finlandia*'s place in his output and after
a performance Nikisch had conducted in Berlin in 1911 he noted in his diary
on 31 December that year: 'Strange that all the critics who admire my music
have disapproved of *Finlandia* being performed in Berlin. But everybody else
cheers what, compared with my other work, is this relatively insignificant piece.
Yet at the same time he was not unmindful of its qualities; a few days earlier he
had noted in the same Diary, 'Why does this tone-poem catch on with the
public? I suppose because of its *plein air* style. The themes on which it is buil
came to me directly. Pure inspiration.'

In March 1900 some months before the Helsinki Philharmonic Orchestra
played at the Paris World Exhibition Sibelius received a letter from an admirer
Axel Carpelan, who chose at this point to remain anonymous, asking whether
he had considered writing an overture for the opening concert. 'You should
put something really devilish in that overture. Rubinstein wrote a Fantasy
completely based on Russian motives for the Paris Exhibition of 1889 and
called it "Russia". Surely your new overture must be called "Finlandia".
Sibelius did not write a new piece for the occasion but instead used the title
for this final tableau which served the same purpose. Something of his mood
at the time can be seen in his letter to Aino written on New Year's Day 1900
'Well, we shall see now what the new century brings with it for Finland and
us Finns. The judgment of history is not against us and the knowledge that
our cause is right lends us dignity and peace of mind.'

CHAPTER TWELVE

Paris, Rome and Heidelberg

THE artistic renaissance in Finland that Gallén had called for in the 1890s had become a reality by the beginning of the new century. Finnish artists had succeeded in assimilating the new European currents and at the same time giving them a personal and national inflection. Finland found a focus for her identity in the arts at a time when her national identity was being eroded politically. After the appearance of the February Manifesto, a formidable number of distinguished European intellectuals signed a *démarche* to the Tsar petitioning him to restore its autonomy. Partly in response to this gesture which caused a considerable stir, the Finns decided to mount an exhibition of their own in Paris and build a Finnish Pavilion to house it. In addition to this, Finnish and Polish painters, it was decided, would share a platform for their work in another Exhibition Hall since, in the words of the Finnish representative in charge of the project, Albert Edelfelt 'the pavilion is so completely different from the Russian'. The Pavilion was designed by a triumvirate of Finnish architects, Gesellius, Lindgren and Saarinen who drew on medieval Finnish castles and stone churches for their inspiration. Gallén was commissioned to do the frescoes for the vaults and the building with its mixture of the ecclesiastical and less ornate *art nouveau* stood out from the majority of the other pavilions which looked for all the world like banking houses. Indeed Anatole France, writing in *Le Figaro*, found it 'étrange et charmant'.

It was at a relatively late stage in the preparations that the idea of presenting Finnish music at the Exhibition was mooted. The suggestion was to send Kajanus and the Philharmonic Orchestra on tour through the other Scandinavian countries, Germany, Holland and Belgium, with Paris as their ultimate goal. A petition asking for State support for the venture was submitted to the Senate at the end of January—Sibelius's name was among the signatories —but it was at first turned down and the tour had therefore to be financed by private means. Edefelt, Kajanus and Westerlund, the co-director of a music-publishing house, formed a committee to set about raising funds.

But while all these plans were afoot Sibelius suffered a personal tragedy.

Early in February a typhus epidemic broke out in Kerava and Kirsti contracted the fever. She was his youngest daughter, a very lively child of much grace and Sibelius was deeply attached to her. Only a few weeks before he had written to Aino that Kirsti is 'radiant' and her death was a terrible blow to him. Indeed his grief was so marked that he never spoke of her again, throughout the rest of his life. Aino took Eva and Ruth to Elisabeth Järnefelt's in Lojo to escape the epidemic and the letters Sibelius sent her in February and March are overshadowed by pessimism and gloom. On 2 March he wrote to Aino, 'I think very often of you, joy of my heart. If only you could get over it.[1] I don't know what I ought to do. My dearest, don't look back on the past but forward. It is the only way to survive (or better: don't look forward, live in the present). The countryside is so beautiful and besides that you have the children and—I dare scarcely even say it—me.' Some hyacinths that Aino had planted gave him special pleasure, 'I am just sitting among your hyacinths: on one of the window-ledges three are in flower (one red, one blue and the other white), on the other there are three (all of them red). The other four are still not out yet but show promise of interesting colours (dark blue and orchid yellow).' (7 March)

In his grief Sibelius was in no mood for the heated press controversy that was raging about sending the Finnish music and musicians to Paris. Even at the beginning of March it was uncertain whether the trip would take place. He reported to Aino in the same letter, that three professors, Söderhjelm, Neovius, and Lindelöf had spoken out against the trip in *Nya Pressen* and had taken a passing shot at his music. But in any event he settled down to work revising the orchestration of the First Symphony and wrote that he was pleased with the progress he had made. At the same time he was writing a piece for cello and piano for Georg and Sigrid Schnéevoigt and according to Levas, composed it in the space of three hours! This, judging from a handwritten list of opus numbers he himself had prepared, is the *Malinconia* for cello and piano.[2] The title may reflect his feelings at the time of Kirsti's death, or another possible source of inspiration could be Enckell's painting of the same name. As early as 1889, his Cello Fantasy had shown that he was capable of writing extremely well for the instrument and the failure of the *Malinconia* no doubt lies in the fact that he conceived the piano part with the virtuosity of Sigrid (Mme.) Schnéevoigt in mind. The piano's endless, amateurish arpeggio passages, double octaves, and clumsily laid-out chordal progressions shows him striving to match in the keyboard some of the virtuosity for which he was aiming in the cello.

1. It should be mentioned that Aino Sibelius reproached herself for her daughter's death. Some time earlier she had nursed Arvid's child who had contracted typhus and who died. The epidemic took a particularly virulent form in the Kerava area so that Aino had no real grounds for self-reproach.
2. Originally this was called *Fantasy* and is listed as such, Op. 25, in a handwritten list of works going as far as Op. 58. A later list going as far as Op. 67, gives it as *Malinconia* Op. 25. When he later revised his opus list, Sibelius removed *The Maiden in the Tower*, Op. 20, and allotted its opus number to the *Malinconia*.

Jean Sibelius in 1900

Axel Carpelan

However, the combinations seems to have inhibited his imagination and even the cello writing though acceptable cannot be said to achieve distinction. The piece was given by the Schnéevoigts at a concert in March to raise funds for the Philharmonic Orchestra's tour and the programme also included a number of Sibelius's piano pieces. A few days later came the first performance of another new work, *Sandels*, an improvisation for male chorus and orchestra, to words of Runeberg. The piece was coolly received which serves to show that a patriotic theme was not by itself a guarantee of popular or critical acclaim. This same spring Sibelius received a State prize of 2,500 marks in recognition of his work, particularly his pieces in smaller forms.

Kajanus saw that the success of the tour would depend on the emphasis placed on Sibelius's music. Two programmes were drawn up: one with the First Symphony and *Finlandia*, the other with movements from the *King Christian II Suite* as well as 'The Swan of Tuonela' and 'Lemminkäinen's Homeward Journey'. Kajanus and Armas Järnefelt were both represented to two orchestral pieces each and the soloists included Ida Ekman who sang folk-song arrangements and songs by other composers than Sibelius, and in Paris, Aino Ackté. *Hufvudstadsbladet* made it clear that as so many of Sibelius's works were to be included in orchestral programmes it seemed appropriate to exclude his songs so as to represent the widest number of composers: it did however add that 'as encores Sibelius's lovely songs, among them "Svarta rosor", would be given preference.' The second of the orchestral programmes suffered from the lack of any really substantial centrepiece: looking at it from Sibelius's point of view, it was, I think, a pity that 'Lemminkäinen and the Maidens of the Island' was excluded—for apart from providing relief from the minor key, it would have proved more accessible to the admirers of Wagner and Strauss.

Since they were anxious to avoid giving any pretext to the authorities for them to interfere with the tour or ban it outright, the planners took care to avoid using the title *Finlandia*. True, it was used during the tour in Norway and Sweden but outside Scandinavia it was billed as *Vaterland* or *La Patrie*. The Russian commissioner for the Exhibition, Prince Tenishev, kept a vigilant eye open for any manifestation of Finnish separatism. And the entrance of the Finnish Exhibition Hall had to be very clearly labelled 'Section russe'. Needless to say the Finnish promoters did not risk presenting so stirring a piece of patriotic music as *Finlandia* under its proper title but settled for the suitably ambiguous compromise, *La Patrie*.

The orchestra got a dramatic send-off. In order to stiffen morale Kajanus organized an open-air concert with massed choirs: yet again Sibelius's name became a symbol of resistance. His new song, *Isänmaalle* (*To our fatherland*) was given, along with a new piece for wind and brass, *Tiera*, and *The Song of the Athenians*. It was at about this time that rumours began to circulate that Russian was about to be introduced as the official language of the country and in June the Tsar signed a decree to that effect. Sibelius's function on the tour was to serve as a kind of musical ambassador. He travelled with the orchestra as deputy conductor but received no fee and did not conduct once. His appearances on the stage were confined to acknowledging the applause. On 3 July the orchestra augmented to seventy players, set off by boat for Stockholm on the first lap of their journey. On the quayside Sibelius noticed a shortish man of aristocratic appearance. This music-lover distributed small bouquets to all the players though his elegant perhaps foppish gestures and his bowler hat excited some ridicule afterwards. Many years later when he was well away in his cups Sibelius told his friend and patron, Baron Axel Carpelan about the episode and this 'ludicrous figure' having totally forgotten that the ludicrous figure in question was the Baron himself![1]

Sibelius's foreign debut as a symphonist took place on 4 July in the Olympia in Stockholm. This was in fact a circus hall and the pungent smell of horses and hay made an immediate impact. A tent had been erected as a roof but the impresario had omitted to provide an adequate platform for the orchestra itself. It goes without saying that listening to his First Symphony in these grotesque surroundings was a somewhat traumatic experience. What normally sounded rich and colourful with plenty of body, seemed pale and thin. None the less the concert was a success, partly because of the fund of goodwill that Finland possessed in the Swedish capital. Sibelius told Aino 'The acoustic was quite appalling! I have read two reviews both of them good. . . . I was very ill during the night. I drank absinthe with Alfvén, Sjögren and Stenhammar and was quite upset. I felt ill throughout the concert. Kajus[2] and I received an ovation.'

The First Symphony was warmly received by the critics: 'brilliant' and 'magnificent' were among the praises showered on it. It is interesting to see the kind of associations it aroused in the minds of the critics of the day. Karl Valentin wrote in *Svenska Dagbladet* that 'In the Scherzo one was reminded at times of Beethoven's Ninth, in the Andante of Tchaikovsky or Raff, but taking it as a whole, the work is not merely a considerable achievement but to a remarkable extent original and interesting.' *Aftonbladet* drew a parallel between Finland under Bobrikov and Poland in 1830 and compared Sibelius's with Chopin's emergence as a national figure.

The second concert at Hasselbacken turned into a public demonstration of sympathy with the Finnish cause. The programme ended with *Finlandia* and the *Alla marcia* from the *Karelia* suite and during the applause between the encores came shouts of 'Long live the Finns!' None the less in spite of the wave of emotion aroused in the public, one critic made it plain that Sweden's 'learned musicians' having made the acquaintance of Finland's 'eminent talents had to recognize that they had much to learn'. In spite of the generally favourable press, Sibelius could not shake off the impression that everything had 'gone

1. Carpelan reminded Sibelius of the incident in a letter dated 13 April 1911.
2. The affectionate diminutive by which Kajanus was known to his friends. *Tr*

to the devil in Stockholm'. The appalling miscalculation at the Olympia had thoroughly demoralized him and judging from the letter he sent Aino from their next port of call, Kristiania, there is no doubt that the visit had left him with mixed feelings. 'In Stockholm we were given a good but not friendly reception. Many newspapers denigrate me, others are full of praise. In general, the musicians Stenhammar, Alfvén with whom I am on good terms, and Sjögren liked *Lemminkäinen* but not the symphony. They say that it is too indebted to Tchaikovsky. I know that there is much in that man that I also have. But there isn't much one can do about that. *Das muss man sich gefallen lassen*. Sjögren gave a dinner in our honour and was very friendly. There were a lot of other guests; the Swedish composers, Stenhammar for instance, were very formal; at the beginning really unpleasant.'

An odd remark when one thinks that some years later Stenhammar was to become one of Sibelius's few really intimate friends. There may have been a certain tension—relations even between Swedish-speaking Finns and Swedes proper could be strained at times and this, together with Sibelius's hypersensitivity, could have invested the occasion with some delicacy

Sibelius had better fortune in Kristiania where the acoustic of the concert hall was good. One critic describing him in his moment of triumph, wrote 'Jean Sibelius bears a strong resemblance to Strindberg. He has Mongol-like features, ruffled hair and a combative expression, a sarcastic trait about the mouth and small piercing sharp eyes. He appeared in evening dress with a flower in his button-hole and bowed stiffly.' In another letter from Kristiania, Sibelius describes his changing role on the visit. 'At the beginning I was just a private person tagging along but now I live at the same hotel as do the orchestra and eat with them.'

Sibelius was evidently beginning to tire of his purely decorative role and his letters reflect a desire to come home and get on with some work. From Kristiania the orchestra proceeded to Gothenburg where the arrangements for the concert came badly unstuck though matters were even worse in Malmö where the impresario had omitted the elementary step of booking a hall so that everything had to be improvised at the last moment. Sibelius went straight to Copenhagen so that he was not present at either of these disasters but apparently there was some friction between him and Kajanus: the latter jealously guarded the podium for himself. This did not pass unnoticed elsewhere. In Copenhagen the critic of *Dagens Nyheter* wrote that, 'In spite of the advertised undertaking that he would appear, Sibelius did not have the opportunity of conducting the concert. Yet it was his name that was on everyone's lips as they left the hall and the public would not go home until he had been summoned to the podium to acknowledge the applause.' The critic of *Politiken*, one of the most influential dailies, was Charles Kjerulf who had been so critical of some Sibelius songs only a few years earlier;[1] the concert convinced him that Sibelius possessed an exceptional creative talent for, as he

1. See p. 162.

put it, 'Only the finest among modern composers write with such total daring and independence.' Kajanus, on the other hand, did not make anywhere near the same impact in Copenhagen as he had done in Stockholm and Kristiania. Sibelius felt sorry for him: 'Kajanus has had a great deal to put up with and easily gives in to depression. I try and help him as much as I can by at least always appearing cheerful.'

While he was still in Copenhagen Sibelius saw the very last issue of *Nya Pressen*, the publication of which had now been totally suppressed by the Tsarist censor, a concrete reminder of realities at home.

The next port of call was Lübeck where Sibelius's name was not entirely unknown, for already before the orchestra had left Helsinki, a production of *King Christian II* had been staged there with Sibelius's incidental music. The veteran critic Carl Stiehl wrote enthusiastically of his music and Sibelius's buoyant spirits continued to hold in Hamburg. On 16 July he wrote to Aino, 'I don't care about anything else for I have inside me a strange power that tells me to go out alone in the world. I can win a place, I believe, with my music. No, I don't believe, I *know* I can. It's marvellous to be a composer.' After his first Hamburg concert Sibelius wrote a somewhat longer letter to her. 'Yesterday I went to have a look at the harbour here. It is really magnificent and impressive. One's perspective is broadened and by comparison all the pettiness that worries me from day to day seems wholly unimportant. Last night's concert was a success and this morning's papers are full of praise, all except one or two, of course. I've come to realize that in spite of everything one's strength comes from within. One must have self-reliance and the ability to do things oneself. I count more and more on the belief that I really will achieve something. These successes have had a stimulating and encouraging effect on me. Sometimes I get into a silly frame of mind which seems to do Kajanus and the members of the orchestra good. I am thought of as being irrepressible altogether. In actual fact I'm not—mainly because of all that is happening at home and, my darling heart, because of your depression. Try and fight and overcome it. I don't propose to stay in Paris for any length of time. On the way back I'm thinking of going to stay with Busoni in Weimar. Afterwards I shall come home and compose. During the coming winter I shall come back here: with such successes in Lübeck and Hamburg one must strike while the iron is hot and make the most of them. Mrs. Ekman who has sung 'Black Roses' on a number of occasions as an encore had a great success yesterday. She sends you her regards.'

But the real key to success was Berlin and it was the Berlin critics who were the real arbiters of taste. That a Finnish symphony had been praised in Scandinavia would cut no ice in the German capital. There, as in Vienna, they regarded themselves as having exclusive rights to the great symphonic inheritance and looked askance at foreign essays in this genre. And now Sibelius was to discover that the Berlin critics were by no means willing to accept his symphony in terms of the tradition of Haydn, Bruckner and Brahms.

Willy Pastor in *Tägliche Rundschau* took the symphony as a peg on which to hang a number of reflections on the formal problems with which national symphonists had to contend within peripheral cultures like Russia or in this particular case Finland. To start with, he argued, they allow their thematic material to be coloured by folk music and then place it in the wider context of the symphony. But gradually it transpires that in doing this a certain incongruity arises and so they set about modifying classical forms in the light of the needs of their national themes and harmonies. Understandably enough, these attempts give rise to confusion and this is just what has happened in the case of the Sibelius symphony. The composer does not seem to be quite clear as to how the traditional sonata design should be modified to meet the demands of the spirit of Finnish folk music. This view of the young Finnish symphonist grappling with the problems of an emerging national culture was offset by others who saw great possibilities in its future and the untapped riches of Nordic folk music. Ibsen, Drachmann, Strindberg, Munck, Gallén and Grieg had given the north some cultural standing and in many places Sibelius's work encountered understanding and interest. Otto Taubmann in *Berliner Börsen-Courier* found much to satisfy him in 'the fine craftsmanship and seriousness of tone with which the composer developed his artistic argument. Mr. Sibelius's musical language sounds new and unusual from the very first moment.' The *Berliner Fremdenblatt*'s review also spoke of his 'powerful talent' and said that Sibelius found 'compelling expression for the elegaic and the pathetic but succumbed to immoderation in his outburst of energy and suffering.'

However the overall balance of the reviews was decidedly positive. After his second concert at the Philharmonic hall he wrote home in a flush of triumph, 'My pieces had a splendid, altogether colossal success. I can't imagine how it would have been possible without our having our own orchestra here. Of course, there were imperfections but there was plenty of spirit. I have met many well-known people who have been wholly enthusiastic. I'm certain to be played during the coming season in many places. I'm just off to a banquet. Be cheerful for my sake.'

From Berlin the Finns set off for Holland. 'After my Berlin success I am now most disadvantageously placed and have the worst placing on the programme. But that's only fair!' wrote Sibelius from Amsterdam. Neither then nor later on did he care for his work being placed as a buffer either at the beginning or the end of a concert. But otherwise he took to Amsterdam. 'The whole of Holland is very much to my taste. In particular Amsterdam which is a northern Venice. I swam in the Zuiderzee. The cigars are the best in the world.' But in the glowing summer heat the orchestra played to almost empty halls in Amsterdam, the Hague, Rotterdam and Brussels. The critics were on the whole favourably disposed but did not succeed in igniting the interest of the concert-going public. Kajanus scored the greatest success in Brussels where, incidentally, Sibelius was thought to orchestrate like a piano virtuoso! Writing from Brussels, Sibelius told Aino, 'I'm now in a Gallic country for the very first time. It seems sympathetic, far more sympathetic than Germany, but I long for Finland which I love more than ever. I intend never to leave it. If it is necessary I'll be chained to it: I can die for it. . . . In Paris things should go well. You have read, have you, that they have their worst heat wave for a century. Can you imagine having a concert there? But still it doesn't matter as our honour was saved in Berlin. That was of enormous importance for me.'

Sibelius was quite right of course at this juncture in attaching so much importance to Berlin. In Paris the Helsinki Orchestra's concert was one event among hundreds at the World Exhibition. And above all the fashionable musical world whose presence would ensure the success of the enterprise had all left the capital: 'All the Parisians are away at the seaside just now. Foreigners are the only people here', he told Aino on 27 July, two days after his arrival. 'The Exhibition is, if I should be frank, in a slightly *passé* style. One notices this about everything. Our Finnish pavilion is the most artistic (*at this point he goes from Swedish to Finnish*). One becomes really moved. The other countries have pavilions that are full of splendour and ostentation with great display and wealth—our little pavilion is elegant and tasteful, its only display the Bjurböle meteor. Yes, it really is distinguished. Everyone stops in front of it and says, "Ah! Finlande!" It won't be easy to get people to come to our concert. Yesterday, for example, I went and heard the Colonne concert and there were ten (!) people in the hall. The orchestra numbered a hundred.'

Sibelius was afraid that the *entente cordiale* between France and Russia would affect the attitude of the French authorities and the press. 'Would you believe it, but they have printed *Russie* on the concert tickets! That will now be crossed out and instead they will put *Finlande*. Kajus was here this morning and said he was worried about that. One notices Russia's influence here in all sorts of ways, we've had difficulties in getting rehearsal time at the Trocadéro. They constantly make difficulties and keep on altering times. Ackté has been a tireless organizer. Well, we'll see what will happen to our concerts: I am very curious. The pro-Russian papers are bound to heap abuse on us, above all me as I am so nationalistic.'[1] Needless to say, Sibelius's fears were quite unfounded. It was after all a French senator who had led the campaign for the Pro Finlandia petition and French opinion was sympathetically inclined to the Finnish cause. But Sibelius and Kajanus confused Paris and Helsinki and saw Russian influence everywhere.

Sibelius gave his impressions of Paris in a letter home on 26 July. 'Everything is so big and grand and artistic here—but when I think of Italy, then it's another matter, at least up to now. Life is strangely exhilarating yet hard. I react intuitively and that's how I feel it.' Gradually though, he warmed to the French capital. 'My overall impression is that everything here is very old-fashioned. The locks, the doors and the houses are centuries old. Which all gives a very aristocratic impression. The cigars are beneath criticism. The women have horrible faces but wonderfully beautiful figures and feet. Their deportment is

1. Letter dated 27 July 1900, to Aino.

elegant. (*He now changes to Finnish*) I am sitting at a pavement table outside a restaurant while I write this. Just now the waiter came and said that a "lady", who had all the time been eyeing me, would like to meet me at one o'clock. Ah, an assignation! I replied very politely that *je suis engagé*!'

The first concert took place at the Trocadéro on 30 July and the huge mausoleum was barely a third full. The orchestra was swallowed up by the vast stage and sounded terribly thin. But the public liked the Sibelius symphony and applauded between the movements while Aino Ackté '*de l'Opéra*' brought the house down. All Sibelius's fears of political complications proved unfounded. Both the French Minister for Culture and Count Tenishev himself were present and applauded with enthusiasm. Sibelius described the concert thus: 'My symphony received plenty of applause. *Le Figaro* liked the Andante. Armas's[1] Prelude had to be played twice and Kajanus's *Sommarminnen* (*Summer Memories*) also went down well, but above all *La Patrie*. It got a splendid review in *Le Figaro* from Alfred Bruneau. The highpoint of the concert though was Aino (*Ackté*). She is worshipped here to the skies. She had to sing several encores. After the concert we went to Ackté for a dinner party. It was very nice, she sang a lot.'

His music appears to have made a favourable impression on such critics as were left in town. ' "The Swan of Tuonela" with its freely flowing melody on the cor anglais and strange, melancholy harmonies is really a remarkable poetic vision', wrote Gaston Carraud in *Liberté* while *Le petit bleu* thought Sibelius stood head and shoulders above many of his contemporaries. 'He is, truth to say, an original composer, this Finnish Grieg, without however reminding one of the Norwegian master in the slightest. He has a fluent melodic gift, power and sensibility and at the same time he is an orchestrator of the first rank. His way of writing for the wind is wholly his own. Over the broad waves of string sounds, he sets the liveliest of birds fluttering towards the sun: thus we see that it is by no means necessary to be an imitator of Franck or Wagner in order to write real music.'

But even though it had been politically desirable to show the flag for Finnish music, the visit and the bouquets his music received, roused little interest in Sibelius's music in Paris. The key people were away and crucial contacts not made. Obviously the visit should have taken place when the season was at its height. So it seems unlikely that he would have met any of the leading composers of the day, Saint-Saëns, d'Indy, Fauré, Dukas, Debussy or Ravel and none of the leading French conductors. And now Sibelius and Kajanus with some of the orchestra turned on their tracks and returned home from Paris on the Lübeck ferry. Sibelius disembarked at Hangö.

It was at this point that Axel Carpelan entered Sibelius's life in earnest. Already before his departure for Paris he had given him some well-meaning advice about the kind of music he should be composing. The concert-overture,

1. The famous *Praeludium*. *Tr*

Finlandia should be followed by a *Waldsymphonie*, presumably modelling itself on Raff's example; after that, he could let the orchestra rest awhile and settle down at some chamber music and songs. 'Dare we hope,' he wrote in an anonymous letter of 7 June, 'for a Violin Concerto or an orchestral fantasy?' But now Carpelan tried to extend his influence to the practical day-to-day affairs of Sibelius's life. 'You have sat at home long enough, Herr Sibelius. It is high time for you to be on your travels. You can spend the late autumn and the winter in Italy. Everything there is lovely—even the ugly. You remember the important role that Italy played in Tchaikovsky's development and Strauss's. Enough of this, you ought to go abroad—and you shall.' Carpelan regretted that he himself hadn't the means to pay for the journey. But he raised the money for him: he persuaded a Swedish patron of the arts, Axel Tamm to put up 3,000 Finnish marks and raised a further 2,000 from an anonymous Finnish patron. Presumably the former's generosity must have been to some extent occasioned by the success the First Symphony had enjoyed in Stockholm. Sibelius learned of this manœuvre on his behalf in August to judge from the date of his reply to Carpelan's news.

Who was Axel Carpelan? As far as most people were concerned, he was a hypochondriac who had done little with his life, had precious little money and eked out a lonely bachelor existence in lodgings in Tampere. After taking his *studenten*, the school leaving certificate that qualified one for university entrance, he wanted to devote himself to the violin but met with strong parental opposition. His response to their ban was to smash his violin in a fit of rage and frustration and throw the bits and pieces into the stream at Turku. The whole affair seems to have had a traumatic effect on him. He sank into apathy, refusing pleas from his parents to go to university. and retired into a private world of his own, taking refuge in books and music. He began a correspondence with his idol, the Swedish poet, Viktor Rydberg, and another with his countryman, Axel Tamm, a wealthy lover of the arts who for many years made Carpelan an allowance. For all this he lived in something approaching penury and it was only by exercising the utmost frugality and economy that he was able to afford the luxury of spending some weeks in the country during the summer. For a time he paid court to an aristocratic and highly intellectual lady with a fiery, enigmatic temperament, waiting devotedly outside her house for a glimpse of her. She sent him packing in no uncertain terms, brutally telling him to get out of her sight and preferably out of town; this, it seems, he actually did.

As he could not become a musician, Carpelan did the next best thing. He did all in his power to bolster his illusion of being in the midst of musical activity. He had never been outside Scandinavia but was none the less extremely well informed about musical life on the continent; composers, conductors, orchestras, musical periodicals and so on. He was in short an amateur in the truest and best sense of the word, but had little real stamina: he never brought himself as far as doing sustained criticism let alone playing or composing.

But it would be wrong to conclude that he was nothing more than a mere dilettante. At this time he was already in his forties and led a lonely existence, but he had genuine strength, a capacity for idealism and self-sacrifice. In his dealings with Sibelius he showed real flair (the idea of a piece called *Finlandia* was his) and at his best, was a source of true inspiration. His very first contact with Sibelius has a touch of mystery to it and of vision: his approach was anonymous and in a very short time Sibelius's output was to reflect many of the predictions he made in his letter. The violin concerto, a new symphony, a few years later the quartet *Voces intimae*, all of these were spurred into being by Carpelan. It was his idea that Sibelius should go and live in Italy and it was his drive that made the dream a reality. In February 1901 he sketched out in his imagination an idea that Sibelius was to realize only after his death. 'Look, Herr Sibelius, should you not turn your mind to Shakespeare's dramas and in particular to *Cymbeline*, *A Winter's Tale* and *The Tempest*. Tchaikovsky has written an overture to the latter but without altogether succeeding in bringing it off, but *The Tempest* is a subject made for you. Prospero, Miranda, the spirits of Earth and Air.' And when earlier Carpelan had spoken of the 'mystery of the forests, their eeriness, the noise of the forest during the storm' it was as if he had been prophesying *Tapiola*.

Carpelan had drifted through life without much sense of purpose and his new-found friendship with Sibelius gave him a sense of direction. 'It is a source of sorrow to me that I have not made your acquaintance before this and haven't been able to stretch out a helping hand. How else could you have known that in me you have a friend who would stand by you throughout the changing fortunes of life. I understand you so well: although I have no creative gift, I possess a strong feeling for music; yes, indeed, live life at its most intense in music.' The one thing Carpelan expected in return was that Sibelius should take him seriously. He bombarded the composer with his opinions on all sorts of subjects, Beethoven, Goethe, literature, politics, morals, the destructiveness of alcohol, his landladies' ailments, his disgust at a relative's marriage with a Russian officer and so on. Sibelius proved a good listener and throughout their correspondence treated him with great respect, sent him analyses of his works, discussed future plans and made appropriately sympathetic responses to his friend's accounts of his various illnesses by detailing his own rheumatic and influenza symptoms. 'I believe I understand you—perhaps too well', he once wrote.

During the autumn Sibelius composed another new work, an 'Improvisation' to a text drawn from Rydberg's poem, *Snöfrid*, which received its first performance on 20 October 1900 at a concert whose proceeds went to pay off the debts incurred by the orchestra on their European tour. Yet again Sibelius turned to a poem that exhorted his countrymen to defend liberty and, as in *The Song of the Athenians*, *Snöfrid* has a strong heroic element. Perhaps these heroic exhortations may also have a personal significance for he undoubtedly felt at times that he was ploughing a lone furrow battling against everybody and everything. No doubt Snöfrid's words to Gunnar, the hero of the poem, were just the words he would apply to himself.

> If you choose me, then you choose the tempest.

Sibelius chose the most effective dramatic exchanges from Rydberg's poem, together with the epilogue: the orchestral introduction sets the scene of the storm at night:

Ex. 190

The strings whine, the brass howls and there are chromatic outbursts on piccolos while the percussion thunders: in short all the stock-in-trade of storm music and all the equipment of Sibelius's later evocations of storm, even though the sound picture is dominated less by pictorial or onomatopoeic than melodic and harmonic elements. Gunnar's and Snöfrid's journey over the waves is perhaps Sibelius's farewell to the swan of Lohengrin!

Ex. 191

The storm and the first choral episode is an impressive and at the same time poetic evocation but the other more explicitly programmatic episodes, where the hero is lured by the dwarfs' gold, the temptations of fame and so on, are not really of comparable quality.

Sibelius and Carpelan met for the first time in connection with the première of *Snöfrid*; it was the only occasion on which they were to do so before he went abroad. Carpelan had, as we have seen, eventually raised 5,000 marks for this trip and after a good deal of trouble, Sibelius had succeeded in finding someone to take over his teaching commitments at the conservatoire. At the end of October he set out for Berlin with his family with the idea of consolidating the position he had established in the summer.

The season was already in full swing in the German capital. Richard Strauss was at the helm at the Royal Opera, while his predecessor there, Weingartner, still continued to conduct the symphony concerts that the Opera Orchestra gave. Nikisch divided his time and energies between the Leipzig Gewandhaus and the Berlin Philharmonic while Busoni, in the face of some critical hostility, played an increasingly important role in Berlin musical life. It was not easy for a foreigner to accustom himself to the pace of the metropolis or to gain a hearing there.

Shortly after his arrival he went to Leipzig to see Nikisch who expressed his regret that he had not received the score of the First Symphony earlier; now it was too late for inclusion in the present season. However Nikisch did promise to include 'The Swan of Tuonela' in his programmes. Yet again Sibelius learnt the necessity for making and cultivating connections and he remained in Berlin up to the end of January with this end in view. Carpelan could not refrain from pointing out that this delay in carrying out his side of the bargain was causing him embarrassment. 'My position between you and your two patrons to whom I have guaranteed that you will go to Italy . . . is such that I feel impelled to ask you peremptorily: leave Berlin as soon as you can.'

Sibelius hastened to reply: 'I've stayed here in Berlin for the following reason. In the autumn, I had decided to come to Berlin or Leipzig, quite independently of the journey you have so kindly made possible, so as to try and secure a performance of some of my music. I was advised by several people to "strike while the iron is hot". We cannot throw away the good work we have put in by our European tour by not following it up and reminding people of our existence. My presence here has been worthwhile in that Nikisch will perform 'The Swan of Tuonela' at one of his concerts. Besides this the Berliner Tonkünstlerverein is going to put on an evening of Finnish chamber music. You must not misunderstand me if I say that I do not regard myself as having touched the 5,000 marks I have received. May I ask you, my dear Baron, should you consider it necessary, to pass that on to my unknown benefactors. As soon as I can reasonably do so, I shall go south.'

Even if Sibelius did not think he had 'touched' the 5,000 he had certainly borrowed from it. So much so that it was necessary to raise funds elsewhere and in January such an operation was set in motion. One prospective lender gave a somewhat brusque response, 'Come home, it will be less expensive', which roused Sibelius's indignation.

Sibelius sent the 'Spring Song' to Svendsen in Copenhagen and asked him to use his good offices with Wilhelm Hansen to secure its publication. A postscript touchingly adds, 'After our summer trip things have not gone too well, but the future will be brighter if you, my friend, will cast my horoscope.' But instead of Svendsen it was Otto Lessmann, the editor of *Allgemeine Musik-Zeitung* who was to be the *deus ex machina* in Sibelius's fate. He arranged a musical soirée in his home to which he invited some of the most influential figures on the Berlin musical horizon. The programme was of particular interest and distinction. The Bohemian Quartet played a string quartet by Weingartner in the presence of the composer; Strauss, too, was there to hear some of his songs, while Ida Ekman sang novelties by Reisenauer, Dvořák and Sibelius. These included 'Flickan kom ifrån sin älsklings möte'. With this song, as Adolf Paul reported to friends in Helsinki, Sibelius has become 'ein gemachter Mann' and for once he was not exaggerating.

A few days later the Berliner Tonkünstlerverein promoted a concert of contemporary Finnish chamber music. Erkki Melartin, Wegelius's latest favourite was represented by a quartet, Ida Ekman sang some Sibelius songs and her husband played some of his piano pieces, while the cellist, Hutschenreuter, Christian's former teacher, played the Fantasia (*Malinconia*). Sibelius, however, was not present at the concert. He had already set off for Italy. The intervening time had not been particularly happy: indeed, Paul had spoken of his having 'drunk life's sorrows' and this is borne out by a note over one of his sketches on which Sibelius had jotted 'Berlin, 22.1.01. *Memento mori*'

One February evening found Sibelius in the small mountain villa near Rapallo where he had rented a study. The surrounding garden, as he put it in a letter to Carpelan, was one of the most interesting: 'roses in bloom, camelias, almond trees, cactus, magnolia, cypresses, vine, palm trees and a manifold variety of flowers'. His sketchbook rapidly filled with new ideas for the new work. Suddenly he recalled a passage from one of his favourite books, Adolf Törneros's *Letters and Diaries* which he used always to take with him on his travels abroad. 'Jean Paul says somewhere in *Flegeljahre* that the hour just after noon on a summer's day has an unpleasant side to it, and this is not untrue. Between 12 and 1, whether during the daytime or at night, there's a kind of subdued unreal quality, as if nature itself is breathlessly listening for the stealthy footsteps of some supernatural force, and people feel a greater need for company than ever.' Törneros's editor had added a note in which he said that Amiel in *Diary of a Dreamer*, another book that Sibelius had taken with him on his travels, also found these times of day somewhat unnerving. Sibelius evidently shared similar feelings and while in the grip of such musings he had jotted down his own vision of the Stone Guest.

Don Juan.
Sit in the twilight in my castle, a guest enters. I ask who he is—no answer.
I make an effort to entertain him. Still no answer. Eventually he breaks
into song and then Don Juan notices who he is—Death.

On the other side of the page he wrote, '19$\frac{11}{\text{II}}$01 Rapallo, Ligure Villa del Signor Molfino', together with the following music later to be included in the Second Symphony:

Ex. 192

In the enchanted garden when Don Juan is not there.
Balletto in minore
Serenata dell'estero
She bade me send pressed petals from Italy. I sent fig leaves.
'Are they really so small?' said Augusta.

(Augusta presumably refers to the fiancée to whom many of Törneros's letters are addressed.)

Elsewhere Sibelius has made a note: 'Festival: four tone-poems for orchestra'. The enchanted garden round Signor Molfino's villa was working its magic and the villa itself became Don Juan's palace. But his plans for a four-movement tone-poem on the Don Juan theme took another direction. Two months later in Florence, he sketched out the second main idea of the andante of the Second Symphony and here the motive bears the inscription, 'Christus'. Appropriately enough he also toyed with the idea, while in Florence, of setting part of the *Divina Commedia*.

After February had gone the violets blossomed and on 17 March, Rapallo staged a *Battaglia floreale* which culminated in nocturnal bacchic festivities. Sibelius wandered in the scent-laden forests and along the beaches from Rapallo to Zoagli and Chiavari and made outings to Santa Margharita and Portofino. But in this earthly paradise his own struggles and inner conflicts came to the fore. As he had done during his Vienna period, he made Kajanus his confidant and wrote in uninhibited terms. 'You must surely be fed up with my numerous and bewildered letters. . . . Here in the foreign papers they are writing that all sorts of dreadful things are happening in Finland but from our papers at home one gets nothing and nobody ever writes to me. If I believed everything I heard here, there would be no alternative but to. . .! At the moment I am in Chiavari—the sea is raging violently, the waves seem as big as houses. The devil knows how big they really are. Of course, you've altogether forgotten me. If I could have a line about what is going on at home I'd feel much happier.'

When he sees the birds in flight across Italy he thinks of Finland and its fate. 'The Mediterranean rages! Moonlight! All our songbirds are here but they shoot them, and kill them. Lay traps for them! They even give them poisoned crumbs!!! And still they sing and wait for the Finnish spring. Finland! Finland!! Finland!!! They are all here: the willow warbler, thrush, lark, oriole.'[1] Under this card Sibelius scribbled 'Hope you still like my music? Write soon. The almond trees are in blossom.'

After a time news came from home. His brother Christian told him of the new mood afoot in the country: how Plehwe,[2] the Chief Secretary of State had quite illegally tried to dismiss several professors among them Werner Söderhjelm and how the senators in the Government Party had earned the contempt of their countrymen. He also mentioned that *The Ferryman's Bride* had had a success in Helsinki and that there was no conspiracy afoot against him. Presumably Sibelius, as was his wont, had been complaining to Christian on this score. He ended his letter with an injunction to look after his health and cut down—preferably cut out—alcohol and above all, smoking. From Carpelan came an eight-page letter. 'I follow you as an unseen companion to Rome, Naples, etc., intoxicated by their beauty and their rich past.' Sibelius responded with a long letter though he avoids talking about his compositions. 'Now I am living completely in the world of the imagination—nothing disturbs me. I would gladly introduce you, as an understanding friend, to my work but refrain from doing so on principle. In my view compositions are like butterflies, touch them once and their magic is gone. That I am working well you can be sure of. In the summer I shall settle down in the archipelago so that I can get on with my work ready for the autumn, when I am thinking of giving concerts (also in Berlin and perhaps also Stockholm). Several of my projects will not be ready for several years. Next time you shall have a more musical letter. This as you see, is somewhat confused. It's midnight and I have been writing the whole day. The Mediterranean still rages, it is moonlight and "the clouds wander heavy with woe".'

As he surveys the stormy Mediterranean at night, so the lines of Rydberg's *Autumn Evening*, which he was to set the following year, cross his mind and perhaps the musical ideas for the song were already beginning to take root. From Berlin came importunate letters from Adolf Paul who was using the idea of incidental music by Sibelius as a bait to lure the Royal Theatre, Copenhagen, into mounting his latest play, *A Saga of the Wilderness*. The manœuvre did not however prove successful. Both Paul and Ida Ekman promised to keep Lessmann interested in his music and at the next committee meeting of the *Allgemeiner Deutscher Musikverein*, Lessmann suggested that one of Sibelius's works be included at the 1901 Music Festival. Paul passed on to Lessmann the proofs of 'The Swan of Tuonela', 'Lemminkäinen's Homeward Journey' and the autograph of the First Symphony which he dispatched to Weingartner. Sigrid Schnéevoigt gave some of Sibelius's piano pieces at a Berlin recital in March 1901 which prompted Lessman to ask, 'why have none of our concert

1. He wrote three times to Kajanus in the first few days of March.
2. Up to this point the post of Secretary of State for Finnish Affairs at St. Petersburg had always been a Finn. It is a sign of the tighter hold exerted by the Tsarist Government that Count von Plehwe was not only Russian but ominously combined his new post with that of Minister for the Interior.

organizations so far performed anything by this highly gifted and original composer?' Adolf Paul also told Sibelius that the same pieces had provoked the bile of Peterson-Berger in Stockholm but that the *King Christian II Suite* had been well received in Hanover.

Carpelan ceaselessly warned Sibelius against everything under the sun from Neapolitan ice cream to malaria; even Paul warned the female members of the family of the dangers of overripe fruit but this did not prevent Ruth from succumbing to typhus. The doctor kept the truth about the illness from their landlady at the Pension Suisse and, nursed by her mother, Ruth gradually got better, But the marriage was undoubtedly undergoing some strain. The anxiety all this had involved, worries about money, the feeling of being cramped, the incessant toing-and-froing between the Pension Suisse and Signor Molfino's villa, seems to have prompted something approaching a breakdown in Sibelius. One day he suddenly locked the door of his study, put the key in his pocket, left his sketches and the piano he had rented, sent a message enclosing a few hundred lire for Aino, and simply made off to Rome. The card he sent Aino on his arrival reflects something of his pangs of conscience. Writing to her the day after his flight, he said, 'You have no idea how worn out I am by yesterday's events. I went to the post office today but you hadn't wired me. Here surrounded by marvellous art treasures, I wander around waiting for some word from you. If only Ruth were getting better.' Aino wrote him— her letter made a deep impression on him—but, be that as it may, he was soon off on to practical matters, asking her to forward his hairbrush and some linen, and discussing their hotel bill.

He soon came to his senses. In order to compose he needed the solitude of a hotel room, a piano, and the stimulus of a big city. 'Now that I have a good room in which to work,' he wrote to Aino on 27 March, 'I realize what a hell both Rapallo and Berlin were for me. I am working very hard here and —I hope—writing well. And there are so many artistic diversions when my imagination runs dry. I seem to need this stimulus and it also seems that I need total solitude when I am working.' He went to *Rigoletto* at the Opera and heard Palestrina sung in some of the churches. His thirteen days in Rome led to a new musical perspective: momentarily he broke out of the Nordic psyche's fascination for the dark, the powerful and the supernatural. He came to see that Verdi's art embraced an equally comprehensive world as did Wagner's and he came to set greater store by the contrapuntal euphony of Palestrina. The rough Nordic edges were smoothed out: his Wagner crisis and his thralldom to Tchaikovsky assumed a more distant perspective.

In Rome he began a number of piano pieces but he detested the idea of wasting good material on smaller forms. Even if he occasionally 'wastes' a good idea on a song, he could not bear to do so on a piano piece. His next letter tells an altogether different story: 'I'm working. I've now fallen fatally in love with my orchestral fantasy. I can't tear myself away from it'.

And now Sibelius felt he was in a position to collect his feelings about his relationship with Aino. To start with he addressed himself first to the children 'Your papa will probably be staying here for a little while for he has become a changed person in all this beauty and warmth.' Or again, 'Papa must regain his respect in his own eyes and this can only come about through working hard and well.' He then addressed himself to the way in which he had wronged Aino. 'It is because of my thoughtlessness and insincerity that I've been unable to make you happy. Besides this my nature is so volatile. I can see what the trouble is quite clearly and this very fact ought to help to solve the problem But it isn't so easy as that. We shall talk about it when we meet, really seriously, so that I can listen to you and you to me, and so we can understand one another.' He admitted that Aino was right when she said that marriage was something much more than a contract preserving one's rights to posses and so on, but he didn't assume the blame for everything. 'You must also love me: otherwise our relationship will perish.'

Sibelius's compass now pointed north. He took his family from Rapallo to Florence where they stayed for a while. On the way home he was greeted in Vienna by the news that he had been invited to conduct 'The Swan of Tuonela' and 'Lemminkäinen's Homeward Journey' at the *Allgemeiner Deutscher Musikverein* Festival in Heidelberg at the beginning of June. He paid a short visit to Prague to improve his contacts with the Bohemian Quartet whom he had met a few months earlier. The violist of the ensemble was none other than Josef Suk, the son-in-law of Dvořák and already well established as a composer. Suk introduced him to Dvořák whom he found as immediate and unaffected as his music. Dvořák's remark, 'Wissen sie, ich habe zuviel komponiert', remained firmly in Sibelius's memory. What they talked about might have emerged in his letter to Carpelan but the latter's reply gives little concrete information apart from generalities and the assurance that he would keep Sibelius's letter for posterity. Unfortunately however, this is one of the letters that does not survive. Certainly his views on nationalism, on which his letter evidently dwelt, would have left no doubt that he did not want to become a Finnish Grieg or even a Finnish Dvořák.

Sibelius returned home with his family in May but was back in Berlin by the end of the month. Berlin depressed him and he suffered from stage fright at the thought of his conducting debut in Heidelberg. Lessmann took great care of him and showed him much consideration: 'Flickan kom ifrån sin älsklings möte' was published in the Festival issue of *Allgemeine Musikzeitung*, the only song to be so honoured, and Breitkopf und Härtel advertised his work in *Neue Zeitschrift für Musik*. The Festival organizers had told him that some orchestral preparation would be done before his arrival so that his first encounter with the orchestra on 31 May came as an unpleasant surprise. He wrote to Aino, 'Have just come from the rehearsal. They've prepared these pieces scandalously. Thinking of withdrawing my pieces if I can't get an extra session.

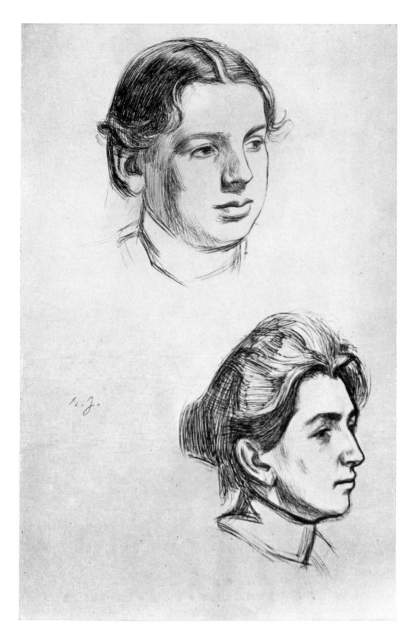

Eero Järnefelt's drawing of Eva (above) and Aino (below) Sibelius
at the turn of the century

Sibelius with his daughter Ruth in Italy, 1901

am on the warpath here. Don't care about anything. But fortunately I didn't
take it out on the orchestra (which applauded after 'Lemminkäinen') nor on
anyone else for that matter. . . . Otherwise I conducted well. Richard Strauss
was complimentary. I think we shall be good friends. I am a new man (*in
Swedish*). I'm keeping completely teetotal and have some self-respect . . . (*in
Finnish*). Lessman will be here tomorrow and then we shall see!'

Strauss's attitude was genuine. What he thought of Sibelius emerges from a
diary entry, presumably from 1901, where he notes: 'Sibelius is the only
Scandinavian composer who has real depth. Though he lacks a total mastery
of instrumentation, his music has a freshness that presupposes a virtually inexhaustible fund of melodic invention.' 1901 was the first year in which Strauss
presided at the Heidelberg Festival which comprised five concerts consisting
exclusively of new works. Whatever Sibelius may have said or done, there
was no possibility of an extra rehearsal time and the final rehearsal which took
place on the morning of 4 June, found him having to stop constantly. The
prospects for the evening did not look very bright. In a long three-hour programme Sibelius's works were given an honourable but demanding place
between some Strauss songs and Wagner's Kaisermarsch which was the
traditional ending of the Festival. Everything depended on Sibelius's capacity
to rise to the occasion as a conductor and in this case he did.

The Berlin papers had sent their critics to Heidelberg for the Festival and
the two Lemminkäinen legends collected numerous plaudits. The *Berliner
Tageblatt* wrote that ' "The Swan of Tuonela" is a highly sensitively wrought
sketch and "Lemminkäinen's Homeward Journey" with its unbroken momentum and inventive sonorities is a brilliantly accomplished piece.' With this
behind him Sibelius had reason to be in good spirits for his homeward journey.

CHAPTER THIRTEEN

The Second Symphony

IBELIUS spent the summer and early autumn on his mother-in-law's estate at Lojo. Most of the time he was busily occupied in his music shed simply furnished with a piano, a writing desk and some stools. He wrote to Carpelan of his plans to write a work based on the Divine Comedy. Carpelan was enthusiastic about this project and cast himself in the role of a Virgil leading Sibelius to the gates of the Inferno! But Sibelius's Dante tone-poem never materialized and he worked instead on the Second Symphony which he had sketched in Italy. In the autumn he cut his last remaining links with the Conservatoire so that the five hundred marks per quarter that Carpelan managed to scrape together from various patrons on his behalf was highly welcome. 'All this you have done for me, undeserving though I am. I ask you to be kind enough to convey my deep gratitude to those noble patrons and patriots. My gratitude to you, too, for all that you have done for my music.'[1] Now and in the future, Sibelius was at some pains to emphasize that he regarded his patrons' generosity not in terms of a personal favour but rather as directed solely towards his music and as such a patriotic duty. To decline such patronage, he wrote, he could not and would not bring himself to do. No doubt this smacks of sophistry but one must regard it as a kind of defence mechanism that salved his pride in the face of charity.

Sibelius kept Carpelan abreast of his symphonic progress. 'I have been in the throes of a bitter struggle with this symphony. Now the picture is clearer and I am now proceeding under full sail. Soon I hope to have something to dedicate to you. That is if you are pleased with the work.' The new symphony, his *Schmerzenskind*, was near to completion at the beginning of November according to a letter he wrote Carpelan (9 November 1901). But it further transpires from his correspondence with Carpelan that he made such comprehensive revisions that the first performance of the work had to be postponed first to January 1902, and then to March. This naturally was a period of nervous strain. A mild bout of influenza prompted fears that he would not live long enough to complete the work.

From Germany there came reports of performances of 'The Swan of Tuonela'

1. A letter to Carpelan dated 11 June 1901.

in Magdeburg and Frankfurt while in Berlin itself Weingartner conducted both
'The Swan', which critics likened to Böcklin's *Isle of the Dead* and 'Lemminkäinen's Homeward Journey'. In London the *King Christian II Suite* had been
included in one of Henry Wood's Promenade Concerts while in America,
conductors admittedly of German or German-speaking origin such as van der
Stucken in Cincinatti, Theodore Thomas in Chicago and Emil Paur in New
York introduced the King Christian music and the Lemminkäinen Legends to
American audiences. Evidently Breitkopf und Härtel were doing their best to
promote Sibelius's music while in Helsinki itself there were a number of new
miniatures introduced during the season. Ida Ekman had sung 'Den första
kyssen' for the first time at a lieder recital, Axel Lindgren published two songs,
'Demanten pa Marsnon' and 'Marssnön' while Wasenius published a Nocturne
for piano.

However there were shadows on the political horizon that undoubtedly
troubled Sibelius at this time. While he had been in Rome he had heard from
Adolf Paul of the plans hatched by Bobrikov and the hard-liners in St. Petersburg to dissolve the Finnish Army as a separate entity. The Russian plan,
launched during the summer of 1901 was to absorb Finnish conscripts into the
Russian army proper thus further undermining the separate identity of the
country. The measure was announced in a decree which unleashed a wave of
protest and a mass address was organized. Sibelius was among the first to sign
it. In the years that followed, the Defence issue further intensified the rift
between the two factions in the country; those who stood by the legitimate
constitution and wanted to defend it by all means short of violence, and those
who were prepared to make concessions as far as was possible, in order to save
the very existence of Finland itself as a national entity and prevent her total
absorption into Russia. In these troubled times Sibelius's music and person became a rallying point for his countrymen and it was with good reason that Carpelan could write that his name and success were a source of strength for many.
Sibelius, too, was well aware that he had a national role to play. It both weighed
on him and at the same time served as a spur. Just before the new year he
worked at even greater pressure to finish the new symphony though this did not
prevent his sending a line of greeting to Carpelan. 'I have a good deal to tell
you but I can no longer keep my eyes open since it is five in the morning and
I began working yesterday at 11. . . . Take care of yourself, glorious friend'.

In January a copyist was engaged on preparing the parts of the new symphony but before the première the composer managed to finish two other
works to fill out the programme, an Impromptu for female voices and orchestra
together with an Overture in A minor that was apparently composed in a hotel
room in Helsinki in the course of one night.

Sibelius conducted the Overture, the Impromptu and the Second Symphony
on the 8th, 10th, 14th and 16th March and on all occasions the hall was sold
out. No previous new work had enjoyed such popular success in Finland. In
an article published after the first performance itself, Robert Kajanus spoke of

the Second Symphony as a musical projection of the current political situation. 'The Andante strikes one as the most broken-hearted protest against all the injustice that threatens at the present time to deprive the sun of its light and our flowers of their scent. . . . The scherzo gives a picture of frenetic preparation. Everyone piles his straw on the haystack, all fibres are strained and every second seems to last an hour. One senses in the contrasting trio section with its oboe motive in G flat major what is at stake. The finale develops towards a triumphant conclusion intended to rouse in the listener a picture of lighter and confident prospects for the future.'[1]

Kajanus's article, it goes without saying, sprang from his own imagination. This emerges from Sibelius's and Carpelan's correspondence and was also touched upon in a letter Carpelan received from Sibelius's Swedish patron, Tamm. 'It does not matter,' wrote Tamm, 'what Sibelius's intentions were. The important thing is that the feelings are so intense and powerful that they can be interpreted in this way. What emerges from this striking atmosphere . . . gains its power from a wider area than the composer himself is aware of.'

The myth that the Second Symphony was in some way a musical portrayal of the Finns' resistance to Russianization died hard. When Georg Schnéevoigt conducted the work in Boston during the 1930s he wrote a programme note for the occasion perpetuating it: indeed part of his notes could have been taken straight out of Kajanus's article. Sibelius wrote to Schnéevoigt as late as 1939 emphatically denying that the symphony had any such programmatic basis, yet even so we find Ilmari Krohn writing of it six years later as the Liberation Symphony providing a set of tags for the main ideas of the work!

With the Second Symphony, and in particular its first movement, Sibelius can be said to begin his real symphonic development. Earlier in *Kullervo* and the First Symphony, he had the example of certain composers, Tchaikovsky and Bruckner among others, as well as a folk tradition, to serve as models, and on this post-romantic style he set his own personal stamp. But his individuality lay in the language he had evolved, rather than in his handling of form. This way of laying a new individual gloss on the practices of a specific earlier tradition is a feature of the romantic artist. If Sibelius had continued along these lines he would have become a Finnish Tchaikovsky or a Dvořák, albeit with Brucknerian overtones. But with the Second Symphony his attitude to tradition can be said to change. He no longer models his thinking on specific symphonic works but takes up the challenge of the symphonic principle as such. He is no longer content to pour new material into predetermined moulds but like the Viennese masters themselves thinks in creative terms of the very form itself.

Sibelius once spoke of the symphonic process thus: 'It is as if the Almighty had thrown down pieces of a mosaic from Heaven's floor and asked me to put

1. *Hufvudstadsbladet*, 11 March 1901.

them together.' In the exposition he examines each of the pieces in turn, in
the development he organizes them into a pattern and in the reprise he sets a
distinctive stamp on each of them placing them in almost the same order as
before, and at times simultaneously. The themes themselves reveal a stronger
organic coherence than is to be found in the works of the 1890s. Several of
the most important motives are related to one or other of two basic formulae
or a combination of them. The first is distinguished by a three-note figure,
rising or falling stepwise and moving diatonically, thus encompassing the
interval of a third. The very opening ideas belong to this:

Ex. 193
a₁:

Ex. 194
a₂:

The other formula tends to open with a characteristically Sibelian sustained
or repeated note, followed up by a group of shorter notes that form a turn
or a similar grouping, usually descending and ending up in a descent of a fifth.
This idea, that opens the third group of themes, is the kind of contour I have
in mind.[1]

Ex. 195
c₁:

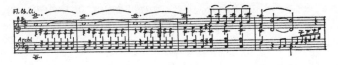

These two basic formulae, their variants and combinations inform the whole
symphonic atmosphere. As far as key is concerned, it is the interval of a major
third that plays a decisive role both in the relationship between movements and
within them. From the tonic D, the music rises to F sharp and falls to B flat, and
sequences tend to follow much the same pattern. These rising thirds often give

1. A number of distinguished commentators on the symphonies, among them Gerald
   Abraham, call this the second group.

an impression of the whole-tone scale. This particular key disposition is not uncommon in the romantic period: a typical example on a smaller scale is the B major mazurka of Chopin, Op. 56, with its episodes in E flat and G respectively.

The scoring is more classical than in the First Symphony: Sibelius refrains from using the bass drum and cymbals and they were not to return in the later symphonies: only the timpani remain. The harp, too, he found incompatible with the symphonic sound world. Only in the Sixth Symphony does he make an exception but even there its use is quite different from the usual romantic swirls, twirls and glissandi. In the brass section he retains the tuba, for the last time in a symphonic context but he handles it with much greater restraint than in the First Symphony.

It is, of course, impossible to pinpoint the exact reason for this development. No doubt his trip to Italy in the spring of 1901 served as one form of catalyst. This was Sibelius's *Italienische Reise* in the same sense as Goethe's. It brought him greater universality of outlook and served to focus his stylistic sense more keenly. His meeting with Dvořák served a different purpose. Here was a master of the previous generation who had successfully infused a strongly national language into the framework of the romantic symphony. Yet for all his admiration for Dvořák's genius, his conviction that the time for national-romantic symphonies was drawing to an end was growing. One might say that Sibelius experienced the romantic crisis intuitively.

In the first movement (Allegretto) of the Second Symphony we encounter a genuine change in the Sibelian climate. Gone are the heavy mists and primaeval gloom of the 1890s: the light is softer and warmer. The opening ideas are already quoted: they are pastoral in feeling and belong to the first basic thematic group we have discussed. First, there is the ascending accompanimental figure on the strings; second, the woodwind theme that answers it which reverses the process so that instead of an ascending figure stepwise we have a descending one. This, if you like, corresponds to the procedure we encounter in Beethoven's *Pastoral Symphony* not least in respect to the harmonic balance between the phrases: notice that they both end on the supertonic.

The last motive of the group, a free amplification of the opening figure on the horn, becomes an important structural element:

Ex. 196

a₃:

The pastoral play continues with this idea, where the rhythm is gradually foreshortened thus:

Ex. 197
a4:

While the flute trills are still to be heard, a new idea on both first and second violins, wafts on to the scene bringing a new perspective. This is the first idea, transitional in character, of the second group:

Ex. 198
b1:

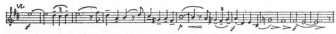

This recitative-like figure, a combination of both basic melodic formulae, hovers between dominant and tonic. In the ensuing writing for the strings, the descending fifth is transformed into an octave, a transformation which we encounter again in the second movement:

Ex. 199
b2:

The dominant is established by a woodwind figure, lyrical in character and serving as a point of repose in this second group:

Ex. 200
b3:

A pizzicato figure which has the same rhythm as the very opening idea shoots off in the kind of sequences that I have already mentioned (A—D flat—F):

Ex. 201
b4:

This brings us to the third thematic group. This, like the development section, is dominated by a pregnant idea belonging to the second category of theme. It brings us to F sharp minor or rather its environs. (The theme itself is quoted on p. 245):

It is accompanied by the opening string figure and the whole has the flavour of a 'thème conclusif', as Marc Vignal puts it, particularly when it recurs a second and third time. The opening string idea assumes a dominant role while the woodwind reply with the descending fifth of the second basic idea:

Ex. 202

c_2:

The 'thème conclusif' could well serve as a second subject if it did not also function so obviously as a climactic, coda-like figure. From that point of view Ex. 200 (b_3) in the middle group is a better candidate but its character is not sufficiently pronounced and it passes by very much like a transitional episode. In this respect, it calls to mind the *Hammerklavier Sonata*: in the corresponding movement, there are two themes, one an expressive lyrical idea near the end of the exposition and another more turbulent figure in the place where one would expect to find a second subject. In Sibelius literature there are no fewer than three suggestions for a second group; apart from the two already mentioned, Ex. b_1 has also been advanced as a candidate.[1] Given the nature of Sibelius's approach to the symphonic problem these attempts at assigning conventional tags to various themes are about as relevant as the medieval conundrum about the number of angels that could dance on the point of a needle.

In the development the themes are seen in a new context and their implications worked out along lines only hinted at in the exposition. The development itself seems to fall into three successive waves. In the first the ideas of the first and third groups dominate; they form a natural alliance. The masculine theme (Ex. c_1) whose undertones of warning have gone unanswered up to this point receives a considered response from the pastoral idea (Ex. a_3) though in a slightly modified form, thus:

Ex. 203

c_1 a_3:

1. The woodwind idea immediately after the pizzicato fig. (Ex. b_4) is regarded as the second subject by several writers, Roiha, Krohn, Abraham, Ringbom and Ekman. Vestdijk also uses this term though he regards b_1 as the real beginning of the second group and c_1 as its conclusion. Törnblom regards the former as belonging to the second group and the latter as a coda, while Parmet suggests the wind figure at fig. B (Ex. b_3). Gray, Tanzberger and Layton stress the importance of all these ideas and avoid talking about first and second subjects.

Perhaps the strongest point of tension comes when the unison violin theme (b_1) is subtly fused with the pizzicato idea (b_4). This is built up sequentially in Beethovenian fashion and as the rhythm becomes more insistent and the fragments smaller it leads to an intense outburst. At this point the third part of the development begins (*Poco largamente,*) and here the combination of c_1 and a_3 produces a splendid effect: the alliance of two contrasting basic motives is at last completely effected. The procedure is repeated in G flat and then D, once again he moves in major thirds, while the climax continues to develop organically: Ex. a_3 rises sequentially, is joined with Ex. b_1, which in its turn is linked with Ex. a_4:

Ex. 204

Not content with this he introduces into the complex, the rhythm of the opening bars (a_1), heard in the lower strings, as well as a three-note figure, first heard two bars before letter D, which is given to the wind. But even now the synthesis is not yet complete: the unison theme (b_1) blazes out in chorale-like fashion on the brass while the strings mounting trills indicate an apotheosis.

After the climax Sibelius draws a double barline and puts a pause mark over it. When the first group's pastoral wind idea (a_2) starts up, one nods to oneself: the recapitulation. But then the thought strikes us, haven't we already heard the restatement of the unison violin theme (b_1) on the brass? Where does the recapitulation really begin?[1] Here, as in the First Symphony, Sibelius telescopes the development and restatement.

Unlike his characteristic large-scale sonata form movements of the 1890s, the first movements of *Kullervo*, the *Lemminkäinen* Suite, and the First Symphony, the reprise is not made the vehicle for greater dramatic intensity. Even in this respect Sibelius is a classicist. When it comes to reshaping the tonal layout of the material in the reprise, Sibelius, as did Beethoven before him, often finds himself at his most inventive. After the double barline he presents almost all the material of the movement in virtually uncut form, but manages to compress it and concentrate it by restating themes from the first and second groups together, contrapuntally. When the pastoral idea (a_2) is given to the wind, the

1. Roiha, Vignal, Tanzberger and evidently Gray take the view that the reprise begins here after the double barline. Having regard to the entry of earlier themes before this, both Krohn and Layton take the view that the restatement begins shortly before letter N. Abraham even includes the string climax from letter M in the reprise.

horn plays Ex. b₃, though now in D major. And at the same time as the pastoral idea continues to unfold Ex. a₂ on the full strings is to be heard thus:

Ex. 205

It is this masterly play with the ideas that brings to light their common origin.

There is no coda. To add one would have been a contradiction of the aphoristic nature of the exposition and restatement.

In the first movement Sibelius smooths over the traditional tensions between the different thematic groups: in the second he makes the most of them. The conflict between the main theme of the Andante and the second subject might indeed reflect something of their very different backgrounds: the one, Death, the stranger who is singing for Don Juan, and the other, the idea over which he had scribbled, 'Christus'. Of course, Sibelius may well have had little thought of the original intention to which he proposed putting his ideas when he introduced both of them into the Andante. But given this reservation, one can however try to match the introduction and the main theme to the composer's annotation for his Don Juan and the stone Guest.

'Sitting in the twilight in my castle.' The timpani roll might suggest the eeriness of the hour, the cellos and doublebass pizzicati, the presence of supernatural steps:

Ex. 206

'A stranger comes in. I ask him more than once who he is.' The pizzicato continues regardless, but the secretive guest remains silent.

'Finally he strikes up a song. Then Don Juan sees who he is—Death.':

Ex. 207

Well, had Sibelius intended to portray the stranger revealing his identity, he could hardly have orchestrated the passage more strikingly. The bassoons sound extraordinarily lugubrious in their parallel octaves while the timpani roll continues and the cellos pursue their ghostlike tread. All this speculation rests, as we have said, on less than watertight foundations: the theme, we know, was originally intended for use in a tone-poem. But something of its programmatic inspiration is possibly still there.

The main theme (Ex. 207) with its stepwise three-note phrases belongs to the first basic category. It is expanded and transformed into an aggressive semiquaver figure to which the cellos make an appeasing cry:

Ex. 208

The exchange is built up in a somewhat Tchaikovskian orchestral dialogue which culminates in a powerful brass outburst with characteristic Sibelian groundswell. After this Death blow, there is yet hope of salvation in the key of F sharp (G flat) major, the theme that Sibelius had marked 'Christus' in his sketch and which has already been anticipated albeit in a rhythmically condensed form in the aggressive semiquaver figure:

Ex. 209

As in *Finlandia*, Sibelius transforms a turbulent motive into one of gentle spirituality. The modulation, the *ppp* strings, the harmonies, the melodic line all suggest the kind of vision of Christ one finds in Leonardo or, nearer to hand, in a Finnish expressionist Sallinen whose *Hihhulit* depicts an ikonlike Crucifixion suddenly illumined by a mystical light. In the continuation of the second group the clarinets and oboes outline a motive that had undoubtedly lain dormant in Sibelius and quietly grown ever since he had composed the song, 'To Frigga'. In it the D major is masked by a flattened sixth and seventh: the theme must be numbered among Sibelius's most inspired ideas:

Ex. 210

This elegiac motive is rounded off by a figure that has an intractable strength to it. Its intervals underline the relationship to the second basic thematic category with its fifth broadened to an octave (viz. Ex. b₂):

Ex. 211

When he answered a query from Carpelan about the form of the second movement, Sibelius spoke of 'a spiritualized development'.[1] He evidently thought of it as a kind of classical Adagio-sonata form without a development section as such. But from the point of view of key structure the movement is highly personal. After having moved from the D minor of the first group to the F sharp major of the second, he begins his reprise in F sharp *minor* instead of returning to the tonic. He was to adopt much the same plan later on in the tone-poem, *Luonnotar*. The main theme, now on the trumpet, assumes a gentler character, nursed as it is by the accompanying string triplets. The ensuing dialogue is all the more violent on this very count and when, after the prolonged struggle with death, the Christ theme returns it is in a very different form: the light of F sharp major is replaced by the darker hues of D minor, the luminous quality of the ikon has given way to a dirge, interrupted only by triumphal fanfares of Death, in a way that reminds one of the Funeral March from *Götterdämmerung*. A subtly harmonized version of Ex. 209, paves the way to the lyrical idea formerly heard on clarinets and oboes, now given to the strings in D minor. This builds up into an eloquent incantation.

The coda offers no consolation. The strings' pleas meet with a harsh response from the brass and the wind and their further protests are tinged with an impotent rage. There can be no equality between life and death, between Christ and the stone Guest. And when the strings bring the movement to a close with two pizzicato chords, it is Death who appears triumphant.

Compared with the scherzo of the First Symphony, the Vivacissimo of the Second has the more vital character both in terms of content and form. Inspired, perhaps, by the example of Beethoven in the scherzo of the Seventh Symphony, Sibelius adds on to the normal ternary pattern (scherzo—trio— scherzo) an additional reprise of the trio, but instead of finishing it off with a final repeat of the scherzo proper and a coda, he replaces it with a transition or bridge straight into the finale. There is no question, however, of a real fusion of the two movements as in the case of the Third and Fifth symphonies the scherzo and finale remain two distinct and independent entities. But all the same the bridge passage performs a more organic function than a normal transition would. It is built on a three-note motive that is heard in the second group and this drives on the music irresistibly towards the finale and forms a

1. A letter dated 31 October 1903.

thematic pillar of the new movement. But not only that: the development of the finale builds up to a climax that recalls this transition thus revealing it in a new symphonic perspective.

The heavy Brucknerian tread of the earlier scherzo is here replaced by rapid forward movement, highly personal accents and surprise modulations, very much in the spirit of a Beethovenian scherzo:

Ex. 212

The main theme is in B flat and its controlled energy explodes on the listener with great force at one moment only to disappear to a pianissimo whisper at the next. The theme with its three-note structure belongs to the first basic melodic category though there is a hint of the second with the initial repeated notes.

The aural perspective constantly changes. One minute the semiquaver movement is in the foreground, next it forms a backcloth against which broader, more powerfully-shaped figures loom:

Ex. 213

Towards the end of the scherzo the strings begin a series of long crescendi suddenly interrupted by *piano*. The transition to the trio is announced, Bruckner-like, by five timpani notes diminishing in level from *p* to *ppp*. The oboe has a lyrical, elegiac tune in G flat major that opens with a ninefold repetition of the mediant, B flat,[1] followed by the fall of a fifth characteristic of the second basic melodic type and then the ascending three notes (G flat, A flat, B flat) of the first:

Ex. 214

1. One may well wonder whether this is not a conscious echo of Gregorian chant. Similar melodic patterns with repeated notes occur both in the complete *Karelia* music and in the tableaux for the Press Pension Fund from which the *Scènes historiques* are drawn (1899) as the accompaniment to the Catholic rituals portrayed on the stage.

Both its pastoral character and its structure recall the opening of the firs
movement just as the fusion of the two basic melodic types (Ex. c_1 and a_3
did in the development. Both of these presumably unconscious themati
correspondences prepare the way psychologically for the finale. Even in th
reprise of the scherzo there is a hint of the finale proper: a rising three-not
figure on the horns to which a minor second is added.

The reprise of the trio is suddenly transformed into a bridge to the finale
the three-note idea comes more to the foreground and after a series of modula
tions we move to the tonic key after impressive dominant preparation.

The first three movements of the symphony leave the listener with a strong
feeling of forward movement. One of the motivating currents is in fact th
three-note figure, a fact that is clearly intimated in the very opening bars. I
is thus no accident that it should be the dynamic force that drives the musi
along into the finale itself. It is the sense of movement towards some kind o
a goal that determines the special nature of the sonata form adopted in thi
finale. It is not aphoristic and concentrated as in the first movement, no
dramatic without development as in the Andante. Here the thematic material
broadly laid out, passes by in well-ordered formation. Continuity is achieve
by this sense of procession rather than through the subtle metamorphosis o
the thematic substance. Everything is more spacious, less dense; the exposition'
different themes build up powerfully in their own right; the developmen
contains both lyrical episodes and a powerful contrapuntal climax, and th
final reprise, apart from the necessary tonal adjustments, is a fairly faithfu
copy of the exposition. As it approaches the coda, the more powerfully th
trumpets and trombones blaze.

The main idea is intoned by the strings to the accompaniment of the trom
bones:

Ex. 215

The trumpets punctuate this with an heroic fanfare-like motive. The mair
group ends with an imposing passage where the three-note figure works it
way over a dominant pedal back to the tonic. This passage appears four time
in all, in the transition from scherzo to finale, then in the exposition, th
development and the restatement where it leads to a B flat major ending: i
cries out, as it were, for a definitive climax.

After an eloquent transition an ostinato figure begins in the lower strings
As in the Andante, the key centre moves to the major third, F sharp, havin
first touched on a Dorian inflected B minor. Over the ostinato scale-passage

he wind intone a lamenting figure.[1] Something of Sibelius's 'Finnish style' emerges in the varied phrase repetitions and the obstinately recurring dominant even if the folk-like flavour as such is not particularly striking. Structurally he theme belongs to the second basic category though traces of the three-note figure can be discerned. If one thinks of the movement as a whole having he character of pomp and procession, this is the point at which the cavalcade comes to a standstill for a moment of solemnity and commemoration:

Ex. 216

The fanfare-like figure returns us to the heroic mood of the movement as a whole. At the beginning of the development we hear both the first and second subjects in F sharp minor; much ground remains to be covered before the final goal is reached. The contrapuntal working-out is considerable (at one or two points I am almost tempted to feel that Sibelius makes heavy weather of this) and the themes resume their onward march in the reprise until the second subject throws off its dark D minor colouring for the brilliance of the tonic major. Now the symphony has reached its final apotheosis. The final motive is thundered out fortissimo and the three-note motive D, E, F sharp rises to the subdominant, G, and the sense of resolution and the triumph of the spirit, familiar in Beethoven's symphonies, is complete.

In Central Europe this kind of finale died out with Mahler and Sibelius though it survives in Shostakovich's symphonies, more as a legacy of Mahler than Sibelius and partly in response to the Soviet aesthetic. There is a quality of defiance and heroism, the *Trotzdem* of Thomas Mann, in this finale. On one occasion Sibelius spoke of himself composing 'in spite of everything and everybody'. One can interpret his attitude in different ways: at times as a kind of nostalgic attachment to '*die Welt von gestern*' where norms and values were unchallenged and which he knew was inevitably drawing to its close; and at other times as a protest against this self same world. In the first movement of the Second Symphony he broke the norms and challenged them; in the finale he clings fast to them 'in spite of everything'.

Immediately after the first performance of the Second Symphony, Sibelius set to work on a cantata for the inauguration of the Finnish National Theatre. This was *The Origin of Fire* (sometimes known as *Ukko the Firemaker*) based on the events described in Rune 47 of the *Kalevala*. The sun and moon have descended to listen to Väinö's playing: Louhi, the Mistress of Pohjola, captures them and hides them in a mountain, and steals the fire from the homes of

1. According to Mrs. Aino Sibelius, the composer wrote this particular theme in memory of his sister-in-law, Elli Järnefelt, who took her own life.

Kalevala. It may not be too fanciful to imagine that Sibelius saw a topical parallel here: Finland deprived of light and fire under the Bobrikov régime. Ukko, the supreme God, fashions a new sun and moon, just as perhaps, the Finnish National Theatre might well be regarded as lightening the darkness with its art. Carpelan was not in favour of Sibelius squandering his valuable time on occasional music and had written to him long before advising against his accepting this commitment. Six days before the inauguration was due to take place, Sibelius wrote to him but his letter betrays none of the enthusiasm or excitement that usually attended him before a new work was due for performance. 'I am still working at my *Kalevala* cantata but at half pressure. Partly, I am somewhat *abgespannt*, and for the rest, God only knows what's the matter.' Sibelius himself conducted the first performance on 9 April 1902 but the work does not appear to have made much impact in the context of so long a programme which also included Erkki Melartin's setting of Erkko's dramatic poem, *Wedding in Pohjola*. The composer subsequently revised the work some eight years later.

The latter part of the spring found Sibelius engaged on more modest assignments: he wrote some songs and planned—at Carpelan's instigation—to arrange some folk-songs for string orchestra. But once the excitement attending the composition and première of the Second Symphony had worn off, he felt a certain restless indecision. He was consumed by a longing for travel and was torn between making a long trip in Finland itself to visit old battlefields or going to Berlin and Paris. When Carpelan sent him his quarterly allowance of 500 marks he made up his mind to go to Berlin. In thanking Carpelan he wrote, 'If you knew what place you occupy in my Frau Musica's heart you would blushingly lower your eyes. For the young lady is 'rather resolute' as you well know. I have played Joseph's role a little but know that it doesn't harm one to undergo some hardship. It weighs heavily on me, nay more than heavily, to know what you are going through all the time. Your fate, dear friend, is one of the most cruel. Listen, you must not die before I do.'

Sibelius set out for Berlin at the beginning of June although he realized full well that it was hardly the best time to go. Breitkopf und Härtel were still in the process of publishing the First Symphony and the Second was still in manuscript so he was hardly in a position to make any useful approach to any conductor. In a somewhat exculpatory letter to Aino, he writes, 'You are surely wondering why I have gone off to Berlin like this but I do so at the bidding of my genius. Even so, one day our happiness will dawn.' While he was there he went to hear Weingartner's new opera, *Orestes* which he thought 'scaled the greatest heights that intellect alone can reach without the aid of inspiration'. After the performance he went to see Weingartner whose charm made a favourable impression on him, and he told Aino, 'There is something noble and distinctive about him. I left the Second Symphony with him and he promised, after studying it, to pass it on to Breitkopf und Härtel for printing.' Weingartner was evidently quite interested in Sibelius as after doing the two

Lemminkäinen Legends in the previous year he had included the incidental music to *King Christian II* in his current season. But Sibelius had to wait three months before he heard from Weingartner whose letter was generally noncommittal. Indeed he did not conduct the symphony until 910 when he gave it in Vienna.

However Sibelius had far more reason to be satisfied with his meeting with Weingartner than his somewhat chilly encounter with Nikisch. The latter received him when he called to pay his respects with far less warmth than in the autumn of 1900 and though Willy Burmester suggested the possibility of intrigue Sibelius was undoubtedly hurt and depressed. But Nikisch's reserve was more than outweighed by Busoni's warmth. The latter was in Vienna at this time but before his departure from Berlin he wrote, 'I am planning a number of concerts of new music in Berlin with orchestra whose purpose will be to introduce little-known music of real merit. You shall in this scheme play a leading part in one of them. Will you do me the honour of conducting *En Saga*? At the beginning of November. The Philharmonic Orchestra. Two rehearsals. I beg you to give your word not to disappoint my hopes. I watch with the greatest delight your German successes which I foresaw as a certainty.'

Naturally Sibelius hurried to tell Aino the good news of Busoni's offer which he gratefully accepted. He had installed himself with his brother and their family at Marienstrasse and occupied himself with correcting the proofs of the First Symphony. As usual he encouraged Aino to be of good cheer and hoped that they would both overcome their bouts of depression. At the end of June he suddenly tired of the stifling heat of the city and returned to Finland. 'Berlin with its reek of beer has become unbearable.'

Some weeks later found Sibelius wandering by himself along the sand beaches of Tvärminne, on the Gulf of Finland, not far from Hangö. The house in which he was staying was owned by one of the coastal pilots and had in its day served both Topelius and Aho as a summer retreat. Sibelius bathed for hours on end and subsequently sunned himself on the rocks under the sweet-smelling pines. One day he rowed out to Storlandstrittan, clambered around on the rocks returning only after midnight through heavy breakers. But when his piano arrived he could not be parted from it. 'It's far worse than his bathing', said his host. 'That only went on during the day but his playing goes on all the time, day and night' He had a Runeberg anthology and some of Wecksell's poems with him and he worked among other things on the song, 'Var det en dröm?' He yearned for solitude and is full of remorse. Aino was spending the summer at Lojo and he wrote to her of his inner conflicts and their mutual problems which they could only work out individually. He speaks of his difficulties in being able to get down to working regularly and hints that he is succumbing to old habits. He expresses himself a good deal more directly to Kajanus, 'I have just come round from a five-day drinking bout with all the detestable consequences.'

Carpelan paid him a visit but his pelasure at this was soon overshadowed by anxiety at his sister's sudden illness. Linda had been staying at Tvärminne during the summer and her health undoubtedly gave him much concern. He already suspected, all too accurately as events were ultimately to prove, that her bouts of intense depression might presage a more serious mental disorder She suffered from acute religious mania: her mother had been deeply religious but had kept a natural grip on day-to-day practical affairs, while Linda longed only for the perfection of the afterlife. Sibelius saw his brother and sister as defining two extremes of the psychic spectrum, poles between which his own volatile temperament moved. In contrast to Linda, Christian was unusually positive in his approach to life, harmonious and balanced in temperament.

In August Sibelius went to see Wegelius at his summer house at Pojo, where Otto Andersseon and Erik Furuhjelm were also guests. Their differences were papered over for the time being, and indeed Wegelius's eyes would light up with pride when he caught sight of his former pupil. Later in the month he returned to Helsinki to prepare for the autumn and spend some time flat hunting. He worked himself into such a lather of indecision going from one flat to another that he became virtually sick with nervous exhaustion. Eero Järnefelt settled the matter by taking the decision out of his hands and renting a five-room apartment in Eriksgatan. Sibelius returned to Tvärminne to get on with his work but things did not work out quite as satisfactorily as he had hoped. He works more at his desk away from the piano but still the ideas don't always take the right shape. 'There's still a part of me that hankers after becoming a violinist and this expresses itself in unusual ways Tinkering and rhapsodizing at the piano which always seems to end up in heavy drinking.'

With the prospect of Busoni's concert in Berlin only two months ahead Sibelius decided to overhaul *En Saga* and sent home to Helsinki for the score and parts. While he was waiting for these to come he busied himself with other projects and one of his letters to Aino notes in mid-September that he had just had a marvellous opening idea for a violin concerto! Busoni wrote suggesting that he might like to replace *En Saga* by the Second Symphony but Sibelius decided against this. He conducted the newly revised and definitive version of *En Saga* for the first time on 2 November in Helsinki and then set off immediately afterwards for Berlin.

At this time the German capital was becoming an active centre for new music Richard Strauss was conducting a series of Modern Concerts with the *Tonkünstlerorchester* which included composers like Mahler, Pfitzner and Wolf while foreign composers were represented by relatively conservative figures like d'Indy and Elgar. Busoni's concerts were with the Berlin Philharmonic and cultivated the international avant-garde of the day: Debussy, Bartók, Nielsen and Delius. His concern to be up-to-date attracted a good deal of critical fire from detractors and it must be admitted that he was not the equal of Strauss as a conductor. In any event the Berlin public booed and whistled the new formless and themeless music and the critics had a field day. The programme of 15 November sandwiched *En Saga* in between two somewhat feeble new works, *The Death of Pan* by E. von Mihalovich and a piano concerto by Ysaÿe's brother, Theophyle: the remaining work on the programme was Delius's *Paris*.[1] After he had conducted his own piece Sibelius was called back to the podium several times and later in the evening he was Busoni's guest at a lavish supper party and drank copiously with Sinding. He reported back to Aino, 'In my view *En Saga* was the best of the new works, I was thoroughly calm and conducted well. They don't really understand my *Saga*, it's too good for them/ it's too refined for them.... The main thing is that I can conduct a world famous orchestra. And that well! Everyone says so.'

The critics poured invective over the majority of the new works and Sibelius got some measure of disapproval but for the most part he fared somewhat better than his unfortunate colleagues. *Vossische Zeitung* found *En Saga* the only decent piece on the programme and Sibelius himself noted that 'they tore everything to shreds except my piece'. It is clear from the tone of his letter home to Aino that he was cock-a-hoop at his success. 'I triumphed over the rest of the programme and have been hailed as an outstanding artist—and that means an enormous amount elsewhere in Europe. . . . And also to know that one has mastered one's art. After this, we can get along anywhere in the world. And do it brilliantly.'

Obviously the ice had been broken for Sibelius in Germany and *Die Woche* printed his picture with the caption '[Jean Sibelius] the most important Finnish composer, whose songs and orchestral works have attracted great attention here.' Just before Christmas, the leading Hamburg critic, Emil Krause reviewed the First Symphony, the score of which had just been published, praising its perfection of form, often brilliant orchestration and touches of genius. This served to pave the way for a projected performance of the symphony in Hamburg in February 1903 under Richard Barth, though this did not come to anything. But there was even more welcome news and on 2 February 1903, Sibelius wrote to his brother in Berlin telling him that Strauss was going to conduct the Second Symphony on 16 February at one of the Kroll Opera concerts. 'I can scarcely believe it's true,' he added. Unfortunately yet again the performance did not materialize.

After he returned from Berlin where convivial life in Busoni's circle had cost him 1500 marks (three times his quarterly allowance from Carpelan) Sibelius conducted the First Symphony in Turku in December 1902. That same month he became the subject of a musical controversy in Helsinki itself. After one concert Elis Lagus, writing in *Hufvudstadsbladet*, complained that the main continental musical currents were being neglected to such an extent that the Helsinki musical public only knew Strauss, Mahler and Weingartner by repute. The review was primarily aimed at Kajanus's programme policy as well as the standard of the orchestral playing but it naturally was interpreted as suggesting that Sibelius dominated the new repertoire at the expense of these continental masters.

1. Not in its definitive form however. Delius revised it in 1907. *Tr*

This stung Carpelan and others into publishing a vigorous reply. Lagus returned to the subject some days later with an article arguing that Strauss and Mahler were played with much the same frequency in Germany as was Sibelius in Finland and that their representation in the repertory would let some fresh air into the Finnish musical scene. He went on to argue that if the merits of these composers were hotly contested on the continent, it could hardly be denied that this had been and still was the case with Sibelius in Finland. Kajanus was anxious to make light of the affair but Carpelan on the other hand took the matter in deadly earnest, wrote a new reply but subsequently regretted it telegraphing Sibelius on Christmas Eve to this effect. The composer spent the best part of Christmas Eve trying to retrieve Carpelan's missive in the capital! In any event it never appeared in print.

This may all seem an insignificant bagatelle in a provincial town. However it was curiously prophetic of a situation that was to arise forty years later when the same arguments were to rear their head: how Mahler was overshadowed by Sibelius, but not in Helsinki but in the United States, and among those who made the point was Thomas Mann. That argument was to assume far greater proportions and consequences.

From the period of 1899 to 1904 come the songs of Opp. 36, 37, and 38. They form the highwater mark of his first period: from now on he concentrates on developing a number of song types, the simple *Biedermeierlied*, songs of an impressionistic character and above all, tone-poems *en miniature* with recitative-like incantations. Unlike Wolf, for example, he made no attempt to mirror all the psychological subtleties of the poem in the keyboard writing; nor did he go anywhere near as far as Wolf sometimes did in concentrating the musical argument in the piano part. In the Sibelius songs the vocal line is clearly dominant and the piano accompaniment more often than not sounds as if it is conceived in orchestral terms and then transcribed. Oddly enough as a result some of his piano writing is all the more successful for his *not* trying to be pianistically effective. His choice of poems show a taste for tragic themes and a strong pantheistic leaning.

All six songs of Op. 36 reflect a sense of loneliness as well as an awareness of the hidden presence of death.[1]

1. Ekman gives 1899 for all six songs but this is true only for the first three. Sibelius sold 'Svarta rosor' to Fazer and Westerlund on 9 September 1899 and as he received a substantial sum in payment (370 Fmks) it is safe to assume that the second and third songs were included in the transaction. Furthermore all three songs appeared between the same covers the following year. 'Svarta rosor' and 'Men min fågel märks dock icke' were both sung for the first time by Ida Ekman on 21 September 1899 and 'Bollspelet vid Trianon' on 31 January 1901. Under the heading 'Works in manuscript' that appeared in a trial number of the magazine *Euterpe* (20 December 1900), Karl Flodin mentions four songs still unpublished, 'Den första kyssen', 'Säv, säv, susa', 'Demanten pa Marssnön' and 'Marssnön'. Sibelius sent the last two to Fazer from Berlin and received a payment of 100 marks for the 'Säv, säv, susa'. So the last three songs of the set in all probability date from 1900.

'Svarta rosor' ('Black roses') is to words of Josephson and tells of a rose-tree whose roots have sunk into the human heart which it tears with its thorns. From its flowering spring deathly white, blood-red, and black roses. The key is C and the black roses prompt a sudden chill as a C sharp minor chord follows the mediant triad (E minor) thus:

Ex. 217

Though key changes reflect the mood of the poem there is hardly any question here of subtle impressionistic pictorialism. The mood of the poem is simply, though expressively, portrayed in the Sibelius setting.

'Men min fågel märks dock icke' ('But my bird is long in homing') contains folklike elements and the piano's opening bars have a strongly Phrygian flavour:

Ex. 218

Indeed the way in which the figure gently rises almost recalls the opening of 'The Swan of Tuonela' and for that matter the song itself begins with a reference to a swan. The music has all the melancholy and pallor of the Scandinavian spring and the open-fifths and organum-like harmonies serve to underline the severity of mood.

In the next two songs Sibelius turns for the first time to the Swedish poet, Fröding whose lyricism undoubtedly had its effect on the composer's treatment of the keyboard part. In no other of his earlier songs has he lavished so successful and unobtrusive a pianistic accompaniment on a text. In 'Bollspelet vid Trianon' ('Tennis at Trianon') he alternates between dramatic recitative and a simple pastiche pastoral writing. The rising chromatic progressions over a dominant pedal somehow convey the bewilderment of the company and the game of tennis continues in an atmosphere of foreboding. 'Säv, säv, susa' ('Sigh, rushes, sigh')[1] is impressionistic in intention if not in technique. The lakeside is pictured in the keyboard figuration and the voice part evokes the character of a folk-ballad.

Ex. 219

Later on a tremolo right hand accompanies the description of how Ingalill broken in spirit, drowns herself.

Ex. 220

It is at this point that one is reminded of a parallel in *Kullervo* where, in the last movement the chorus tells of Kullervo's attacks of conscience and thoughts of suicide over a similar musical device. At the very end of the song, the opening melody is transformed into a heartfelt lament.

The last two songs of Op. 36, 'Demanten på Marssnön' ('The Diamond on the March snow') and 'Marssnön' ('The March snow') are both settings of Wecksell, a Finnish poet writing in Swedish who has something of the intensity of Shelley or in Swedish literature, Stagnelius. He became alas, an early victim of insanity; both poems have as their theme the shadow of Death that hovers over the moment of fulfilment. 'Marssnön' is in $\frac{5}{4}$ and is Aeolian in feeling:

Ex. 221

The song has nothing of the *Kalevala* about it: indeed the outline is more redolent of Russian folk melody one encounters in Rimsky-Korsakov or at times Moussorgsky. In the last song of the group, 'Demanten på Marssnön' we have an example of the Finnish Biedermeier style. The two verses are separated by a short interlude and the key, B flat, is again a favourite of his youth. The

1. This song is also known as 'Ingalill', the heroine of Fröding's poem. *Tr*

ice crystals glistening in the March sunlight and their disappearance when the sun's smile is sweetest inspires him to a cantilena which in some respects anti-cipates the adagio of the Violin Concerto. But the opening harmonic progres-sion is one that we often encounter in his early music:

Ex 222

With the Op. 37 set (1898?–1902)[1] we come to one of the finest lyrical collections in the whole of Sibelius's song output. 'Var det en dröm?' ('Was it a dream?') was written with Ida Ekman's voice in mind and is dedicated to her. There is a smooth legato line and a wide tessitura (B–G″ sharp). The accom-paniment is impressionistic in texture and evokes a dream-like atmosphere while the voice develops a powerful cantilena in B major, almost the equivalent of the big string cantilenas in the first two symphonies.

The only really dramatic song in the collection is 'Flickan kom ifrån sin älsklings möte' ('The maiden came from her lover's tryst'), sometimes known in English simply as 'The Tryst'. As is always the case when he sets Runeberg, Sibelius achieves great simplicity of declamation and directness of utterance. It opens with a Tchaikovskian motive on the piano echoed by an immediate vocal response:

Ex 223

1. 'Den första kyssen' is mentioned as unpublished in Flodin's article (see footnote p. 260) and is in all probability from 1900, not 1898 as Ekman says. He sold the song to Fazer and Westerlund in 1901 but Ida Ekman sang the song from manuscript that autumn, so it was slow to appear. Ekman gives 1902 as the year of composition for 'Lasse liten' ('Little Lasse'), 'Soluppgång' ('Sunrise') and 'Var det en dröm?' (Sibelius wrote to Carpelan in May 1902, 'I am working on a setting of "Soluppgång" by Tor Hedberg. A slight but powerfully atmospheric poem. I have also written a setting of—guess what? Yes, "Lasse liten" by old Topelius!') Fazer bought the two in August the same year. Sibelius mentions 'Var det en dröm?' in a letter to Aino the previous month. 'The Tryst', also written for Ida Ekman, was first sung at a soirée in Berlin in January 1901 so was in all likelihood composed the previous autumn rather than in 1901 as Ekman suggests. On the back of a letter from Kajanus (13 December 1900) Sibelius drafted a letter to Stenhammar, who also set this poem, asking for his per-mission to use the German translation given in Stenhammar's song.

As in the case of 'Svarta rosor' the modulations faithfully follow the changing mood of the poem. When the maiden, at the climax of the poem, confesses her own love and the faithlessness of her lover, the voice takes up the opening motive in its initial form for the first time.

'The first kiss', also to words of Runeberg, begins in a Dorian-inflected B minor. The maiden's reply to the evening star comes in the more brilliant key of D flat major which in its turn is, surprisingly enough, answered in E major. The closing phrase, 'And yet death averts his eyes and weeps', prompts some pregnant chromaticisim:

Ex 224

The progression here is virtually the same as in the last movement of *Rakastava* save for the fact that the texture is enriched by suspensions.

The children's song, 'Little Lasse' to words of Topelius hardly assumes a childlike character in Sibelius's hands. The big, fearsome world is drawn in dark, shadowy ostinato figures in the accompaniment while the voice gropes its way to a simple melody. As is the case with Schumann's *Scenes of Childhood*, this is no music for children but rather the child's word seen very much through the eyes of adult experience. 'Sunrise' to words of Tor Hedberg has great appeal and charm and its neglect is wholly undeserved.

Four of the five songs Op. 38 (1903–4)[1] are settings of Viktor Rydberg. 'Höstkväll' ('Autumn Evening') is an incantation to the setting sun, the gathering storm and oncoming darkness:

Ex. 225

1. Ekman gives 1904 as the date of this set. 'Autumn Evening' was sung for the first time by Aino Ackté in September 1903 and Ida Ekman gave the premières of the second and third songs in the set the following month. Sibelius mentions the last two in a letter to Carpelan (7 September 1903) 'I have relaxed by writing some songs to Rydberg texts, among other things, "In the Night" and "On a Balcony by the sea", but today I return to my main work (the Violin Concerto).' The same day Sibelius sold 'Autumn Evening' to Fazer. The draft of the song is to be found in the sketches of the themes of the concerto. The other two songs were first performed in 1904 and sold to Fazer during the same year.

The familiar Dorian melisma occurs on the phrase 'och molnen vandra med vefullt sinne' ('and the clouds wander heavy with woe'), an idea that came to him one stormy night while he was walking by the Mediterranean. Indeed this phrase of Rydberg's seems to have gripped his imagination since he sets it with one of his most deeply charged and characteristic melodic formulae. After the opening it is as if Nature herself takes command. Over a piano tremolo the singer intones a powerful line in B minor with Dorian colouring:

Ex. 226

In the last verse of the poem a human figure enters the scene and stands transfixed by its grandeur. Sibelius identifies himself with the stranger who observes this awe-inspiring scene and there can be no mistaking the intensity of feeling of the closing pantheistic sentiments.

'På verandan vid havet' ('On a balcony by the sea') is also on an ambitious scale and its language, too, is searching. The opening is chromatic; and then the voice intones a recitative-like plaint over a 6–4 chord of B flat minor:

Ex. 227

There is a strong pull to the dominant in this phrase which could symbolize the longing for the eternal shores of which Rydberg speaks. In each of the poem's three 'flashbacks', the atmosphere becomes more intense. Sibelius reflects this by an upward chromatic transposition. The introduction in which the voice now takes part *mezza voce* and the recitative too is repeated in B minor. Now everything is ready for the most important moment in the song: the silence of nature is represented by C minor. The interval of the tritone (C–F sharp) seems to reach out to the horizon, to infinity, while the trill (F sharp–G) swells to a climax suggesting the distant storm. 'Do you remember a silence', the poet asks, 'when all was immersed, so it seemed, in a longing for infinity: the shores, the heavens, the sea, as if in presentiment of God.' But God, the music seems to say, can only be dimly perceived; the final chord of the sixth gives no sense of certainty or resolution. Looking at the song one wonders whether the interval of the tritone may not be associated in some way in Sibelius's expressive language with mystical experience and pantheistic sentiment.[1]

The other Rydberg poems Sibelius sets in the Op. 38 collection are by no means as fine as either of these and the same must be said for Sibelius's settings. Admittedly some sense of mystery can be discerned in the dark unison passages in 'I natten' ('In the Night') but the bulk of the song is relatively uninteresting. 'Harpolekaren ach hans son' ('The harpist and his son') is encumbered by excessive arpeggio writing in the accompaniment. Nor can one say that the exotic colouring of Fröding's 'Jag ville jag vore i Indialand' ('I would that I were in the Indian realms') is adequately matched in the last of the settings.

In all there are sixteen songs in these three sets, seven of which Sibelius subsequently scored. The two greatest, 'Autumn Evening' and 'On a Balcony by the Sea', gain enormously from their orchestral colouring and the former exists both in a version for full orchestra and for strings alone.

'Eldens ursprung' ('The Origin of Fire') comes close to being one of Sibelius's masterpieces. It is scored for soloist (baritone), male voices, and orchestra. The first version failed to satisfy the composer and he reworked it during the autumn of 1910. His diary entries of the period reflect something of the struggles he was having with it. 'I am battling with "The Origin of Fire",' he notes on 16 September 1910. 'It's all uncertain whether it will be good enough to publish. . . . Why did it have to be that I was such a late developer!' It must have been particularly difficult for Sibelius to break off in the middle of his work on the Fourth Symphony and turn the clock back to the creative struggles of eight years earlier. In any event whatever the revision may have cost him, the work retains its stylistic integrity and belongs in spirit to 1902. A primordial darkness inhabits the opening bars: the clarinet figure confines itself to the compass of a fifth (A–E) only dropping to a G sharp at the end of the phrase:

Ex. 228

The keys modulate in a chain of minor thirds (A minor, C minor, E flat minor) while the soloist evokes the pitch black night of the Kalevala.

> Therefore was the night unending,
> And for long was utter darkness,
> Night in Kalevala for ever
> And in Väinölä's fair dwellings.

1. The Fourth Symphony which is dominated by this interval would seem to lend force to this point. *Tr*

The choral section that follows contains some imaginative passages and the description of how Ukko, the master of the Gods, kindles fire with his sword, has a bold rhythmic profile while Sibelius's usually melancholy Dorian lines generate tension and excitement.

The next verse about the maiden of the air who 'seated on the edge of the cloud' nurses the white flame, is rattled off in a way that almost puts one in mind of the *Nursery Songs* of Mussorgsky:

Ex. 229

And then, when the chorus, having been either unisonal or two-part up to this point, becomes four-part it has a Slav-like colouring that suggests Russian orthodox church music:

Ex. 230

But as is often the case in his choral pieces Sibelius succumbs in 'The Origin of Fire' to stock-in-trade gestures and the final climax is brought too far to precipitate an ending to make a strong effect. The cantata as such was not really his genre.

Like 'The Origin of Fire', the Impromptu for women's chorus and orchestra was also subjected to revision in 1910. It is a setting of an excerpt from Rydberg's 'Livslust ach livsleda', a poem that with some justice may be thought of as having echoes of the 'Klassische Walpurgisnacht' of the second Part of Goethe's *Faust*. Kant, Schelling and a poet from the end of the nineteenth century all suddenly turned up among the Hellenic company. The introductory Andante is prefaced by a chorus of the priests of Bacchus which is not found in the earlier version while in the main section of the work, *un pocchettino con moto* Sibelius makes use of a theme from the early unfinished string trio in G minor. Undoubtedly, there are mild political overtones in the work with the Finns being identified with the Greeks, but in general the work wears the aspect of a tame classicism and lacks real character.

The Overture in A minor, however, is somewhat more interesting. It was thrown together in some haste and much of its weight is centred in the opening fanfares but in the allegro section that follows, a cello theme occurs to which Sibelius was to return later in the String Quartet (*Voces intimae*):

Ex. 231

One of Sibelius's national obligations was to compose songs for various choirs. There are nine such pieces written for male-voice choir *a capella* in the Op. 18 set, all of which date from about the turn of the century. These include 'Venematka' ('The Boat journey') and 'Sydämeni laulu' ('My heart's song'). 'Saarella palaa' ('Fire on the Island') is based on a poem from the collection of lyric folk-poetry known as the *Kanteletar* and moves in parallel 6–3 chords in a kind of organum-like fashion over alternating tonic and dominant pedal points:

Ex. 232

The piece gives an attractive picture of the wedding preparations while the basses intone the words 'saarella palaa'. 'Sortunut ääni' ('What has broken music's power' or 'The broken voice') also comes from the *Kanteletar* but shows its vein of tragic feeling. The $\frac{5}{4}$ melody carefully reflects the speech-rhythm of the poem:

Ex. 233

Quite a number of these songs were first presented by Heikki Klemetti, a conductor of some personality and flair: he gave 'Sydämeni laulu' for the first time in 1898 and 'Sortunut ääni' the following year. In April 1900 he introduced another Sibelius novelty, 'Metsämiehen laulu' ('The hunter's song') to words of Aleksis Kivi. Sibelius matches the poet's revulsion for the city and his longing for Tapiola, the realm of the forest god:

Ex. 234

Another song, written a few months after this was first performed was to words by Paavo Cajander, 'Isänmaalle' ('To my country') and even in the context of a patriotic song Sibelius did not eschew dissonance that served to give the texture a hard and tough surface:

Ex. 235

But perhaps the finest of the series, which Klemetti took with him when he and his choir made a European tour, in 1901, was 'Terve kuu' ('Hail, moon!') this time to words from the *Kalevala*. In this song Sibelius writes polyphonically: the other *a cappella* songs in this set are predominantly homophonic in style. The parts interweave and cross, and up to three different texts can be heard at the same time. In the poem Väinämöinen rejoices that the sun and moon have been set free from their captivity—as related in 'The Origin of Fire'—and are once again in their rightful place. All the spacious and jubilant writing is but a preparation for the magical ending. The tenors wish the moon good fortune on its journey, *pp*, while the basses gradually sink making a striking crescendo at the same time:

Ex 236

In this song Sibelius seems to have captured something of the relationship between man and the cosmos that one finds at the heart of so much of the *Kalevala*.

269

CHAPTER FOURTEEN

The Violin Concerto

O N his return from Berlin at the end of November 1902, Sibelius was drawn into a new artistic circle, the so-called Euterpists. Although there is an obvious parallel between their gatherings and those of the symposium of the previous decade, they differ in one important respect: the Symposium was largely centred on Sibelius, Kajanus and Gallen-Kallela while the Euterpists drew on a much wider circle of artists, nearly all of them belonging to the Swedish-speaking élite of Helsinki society. They had taken over the musical periodical *Euterpe* that Flodin had launched in 1901 and broadened its appeal to embrace a wider range of interests. Their membership[1] was liberal in outlook in that it mistrusted the hard-and-fast attitudes with oversimplified cut-and-dried solutions and forward-looking in that they did not close their minds to expressive means other than symbolism and the imagery of conventional art.

Sibelius was probably drawn to this circle because it was not so exclusively dominated by musicians as the earlier Symposium had been. In a sense he was reliving his youth by returning to the kind of companionship that he had enjoyed so much during his early twenties. Among the Euterpists he was free from professional pressures and in particular the sense of tension inevitable between musicians of different generations. Even though he liked Erkki Melartin and admired his refinement and took enough interest in Palmgren to go to his concert that same autumn, he was never as relaxed or as completely himself in their company as he was among the Euterpists. Here he improvised at the piano while poems were declaimed: Gripenberg's 'Teodora' was one, Björnson's 'Ved Mottagelsen av siste Post fra Finland' ('On receiving news from Finland') was another. The Norwegian poet shared the deep concern common in Scandinavia at the latest powers assumed by Bobrikov that gave him the right of arrest and deportation without any chance of redress.

1. The members included Gunnar Castren, a literary historian, Torsten Söderhjelm, a dramatic critic, Rolf Lagerborg, the philosopher, Sigurd Frosterus and Gustaf Strengell, both architects, and the poets, Emil Zilliacus and Bertel Gripenberg. Many distinguished people in the world of the arts were to be seen at their club premises; Edelfelt, Magnus Enckell, as well as Sibelius's long-standing friend Werner Söderhjelm.

The group was outward-looking too: they did not automatically admire every word of Runeberg; the cosmopolitan outlook of Tavaststjerna was more to their taste than the national-romanticism of the late nineteenth century. They travelled as often as they could, to London and Paris rather than Berlin. Edelfelt in a letter to the poet, Gripenberg, gave a graphic picture of his feelings on returning to Helsinki at this time:

> When we first came into Finnish waters that light summer evening and sailed through the rocks and islets of the archipelago, the conversation and noise suddenly stopped and all we Finns betrayed in our faces, a compound of dread and resignation. Helsinki, the new police, the Tartars . . . absolutely hideous, armed and inescapable, give a new character to our previously quiet and peaceful city.

During these next ten years Sibelius's choice of poets reflects the influence of the Euterpist taste. In his songs, Tavaststjerna is better represented; Runeberg and Rydberg give way to Gripenberg, Josephson and newer German poets like Richard Dehmel. Newer writers like Wilde, Maeterlinck, Anatole France and Hjalmar Söderberg find their way on to his bookshelf and after this period Sibelius's travels took him to England and France every bit as much as to Germany. That did not mean that he fully shared the Euterpists' denunciations of life in Finland, sometimes more affected than felt, even though he no longer enjoyed life in Helsinki itself. During the summer of 1903 the idea of leaving Helsinki and living in the country finally took root and when the family moved that autumn to a new flat in the city they did so in the knowledge that it would be their last.

Word of his brother's activities among the Euterpists with the concomitant Bacchic excesses reached Christian who was in Berlin. His researches had entailed dissecting the brains of alcoholics and prompted by a particularly vivid dream during the Christmas of 1902 he wrote urging him to give up drink. 'For our own sake—and your health—you must turn teetotal. It's absolutely essential,' he wrote and then went on to urge Jean to think of his duty to his country, his art, to Aino who was shortly expecting another child. The letter arrived when Sibelius was in bed with rheumatism and found him feeling, as he put it, 'a bit seedy'.

Perhaps the news that he was to be given an order (knight of the legion of honour) for his contribution to the Paris exhibition gave him temporary cheer. But other matters were undoubtedly weighing on his mind, particularly his rapidly dwindling bank balance. Christian had acted as guarantor for some 3,000 marks in all; not even the most unreasonable demands on his generosity seem to have disturbed the harmony of their relationship. In March 1903 Jean writes apologizing for 'sending so little and so late' in repayment of a loan and promising more soon. 'You are far too polite when you write to me about cash,' Jean told him. 'Just remember what my telegrams are like.' The concert he had given in Turku before Christmas had brought in a mere 126 marks as opposed to the 1,000 he had counted on. He himself had had to pay for some extra players to come from Helsinki to stiffen the orchestra. Also when he conducted at Tampere he had to take a party of reinforcements there from the Helsinki orchestra. The main thing after this was to hold out until his next Helsinki concert.

Christian lost no opportunity of giving his brother encouragement. Indeed he had a sympathy and understanding of people that was out of the ordinary and it is hardly surprising that he should have abandoned pathology for psychiatry as he did this selfsame year. Jean in his turn responded to his various suggestions for soothing medicines or lots of exercise by writing frankly about his problems:

> There is much in my make-up that is weak. Take only one instance: When I am standing in front of a grand orchestra and have drunk $\frac{1}{2}$ bottle of champagne, then I conduct like a young god. Otherwise I am nervous and tremble, feel unsure of myself, and then everything is lost. The same is true of my visits to the bank manager. I have had a great deal of trouble on this score. The worst thing is when I go to concerts given by rivals and imagine that everyone is looking at me to see whether I'm suffering from envy. I get then an expression round the mouth that has done me much harm in the eyes of other people. If I have a few glasses of wine, that's all gone. It's extremely seldom that I feel a real need for spirits. You can see from this that my drinking has genuine roots that are both dangerous and go deep. I promise you to try and cope with it with all my strength.
>
> You will surely do great things though this is not to say that you'll get any credit for it. It's a wonderful world in many ways but not always a just one. It's the surface sparkle that people fall for. But it's this sparkle that I also like. Walking with one's head high, one's cap askew over all life's miseries and difficulties; then everything seems dramatic, not this drab everyday grey!

Sibelius's taste for high life presented its difficulties for Aino. The birth of their fourth daughter left her feeling in a weak condition: Jean was considerate and affectionate, though he tended to linger all too long and all too often at the Kämp or the König. One message scribbled during this spring reads:

Dear Aino,

How are you? Nipsu (the baby) and the others. Send a line in reply. I am at the moment engrossed in a most absorbing discussion.

your own Janne

I shall come home presently.

'Presently' was an all-purpose phrase which would sometimes stretch over several days. But Aino held her head high. Sometimes she would go on her

wn in search of him, but even if she succeeded in tracking him down, it by
o means followed that he would leave his Bacchic revels. On one occasion
e scrawled on a visiting card.

Dear A.
I'm at the Kämp just now. Forgive me for not receiving you.
Your own J.

)nly once, when it was a question of getting the finale of the violin concerto
inished in time, she turned to Kajanus to enlist his help in getting Janne home.
hey took a hansom cab to the König, a typical club-like restaurant for men
nly, in which at that time no lady would set foot, and Aino waited outside
1 the carriage while Kajanus fetched him. Janne took his place by her side
nd they went home. She uttered no word of reproach.

In the new lay circles in which he moved it was assumed that Sibelius worked
t exceptional speed and composed much as a conjuror produces aces from his
leeve, and that his health was uniquely robust. His company was eagerly
ought—indeed people drew lots for the privilege—and he in his turn found it
lifficult to decline invitations. Aino's anxiety mounted and she poured out her
roubles to the only friend to whom she felt she could turn, Axel Carpelan.
Ie wrote suggesting that she should tell his so-called friends and in particular
certain Baron W. the truth about his slow working methods and his far from
obust health and appeal to their better nature and their patriotism. 'Janne can
nly be saved,' he wrote, 'by the efforts of those closest to him; left to himself,
e will go to pieces. He has hobnobbed far too long and often with the dregs of
Ielsinki "culture" for him to be able to drag himself out of their clutches of his
wn free will. When so singular a pearl as Aino cannot tame his wild spirits by
gentle persuasion, then it seems to me that we must mount a proper offensive
—in a war this is the only course that can secure a victory.' Carpelan's plan
vas to make this 'spoilt overgrown child' move from Helsinki and spend the
est of his life in the country away from the temptations of the city. His teaching
t Kajanus's Orchestral School should be no hindrance: he had engaged deputies
o take his classes up to now and so he might as well leave altogether. In any
vent he had drunk his salary from that source many times over. It would be
nore than enough, he argued, for him to come to town once a month, settle
is affairs and go to concerts. After all, Sibelius had moved to Kerava in order
o finish the First Symphony and he had worked, partly there and partly in
taly, on the Second.

Carpelan's reasoning was sound and certainly encouraged Aino to work more
ctively to effect the move. Indeed in August 1903 she was able to tell him
Our plans to live in the country are now much closer realization. This winter
vill be our last in Helsinki.'

Sibelius's outward behaviour may well have been a way of avoiding getting
o grips with the concerto. In April he had written to Carpelan, 'My heart
leeds of all that is happening. It is as if the very ground under one's feet is

being pulled away from under one's feet. But I mustn't burden you with m
troubles. But I need a straw at which to clutch. And don't see one. I would s
love to see you. But don't come if you are not well enough. One must batt
on and trim one's sails to the wind.'

Carpelan did come and found Sibelius poised ready to return to creativ
work. He advised him to go to Lohja and return only for the spring conce
he was to conduct at the Academy, and he saw to it that the interest of Sibelius
patrons did not flag; in June he sent the quarterly allowance of 500 marks t
Lohja.

In the early summer Schnéevoigt invited Sibelius to conduct a programme
his own works in Catharinental/Kadriorg, the coastal resort outside Tallinr
The programme included among other things the First Symphony and as
rousing closing number, *Finlandia* which went under the title, *Impromptu*. Th
previous year, Schnéevoigt had performed *Finlandia* under its proper nam
both in Estonia and Latvia but fear of possible repercussions made him chang
it here. However it is only fair to say that in Finland itself the title had bee
permitted even during the most repressive periods of Bobrikov's régime. On
feature of the occasion that Sibelius must have noted was the absence of Estonian
all the information in the programme was given both in Russian, the offici
language, and German, the language of the ruling élite. The orchestra was a fin
one, composed largely it seemed of members of the Warsaw Philharmoni
while the public (mainly drawn from Baltic Germans and officers of th
Russian Baltic fleet) gave Sibelius a sympathetic reception.

In August Sibelius sent Carpelan the newly published score of the Secon
Symphony with a printed inscription. A letter enclosed with the dedicatio
records that he was battling with the concerto, though he broke off the follow
ing month to compose two Rydberg songs, 'I natten' ('In the night') and 'P
verandan vid havet' ('On a balcony by the sea').

Willy Burmester was undoubtedly the man who spurred Sibelius on t
finish his concerto. Burmester had been the leader of the Helsinki Orchestr
during the mid-1890s and was a keen admirer of the composer. Indeed he late
became related to the publishers of much of Sibelius's early music with hi
marriage to Naema Fazer. In fact it is even possible that the initiative for th
concerto came from him in the spring of 1902, for the following year he wrot
asking if the work was yet finished. In the same letter he offered himself as th
soloist for the following season and suggested that Sibelius should try an
launch it in Berlin where the critics were sympathetic to his cause. Sibeliu
wired a reply offering him the première in November but unfortunatel
Burmester could not manage any time before the following March. Hi
answer showed his determination, as he put it, that 'Sibelius should not la;
behind Strauss in *réclame*.' From this point onwards, however, one can only sa
that Sibelius thoroughly mismanaged the situation and his handling of Bur
mester was totally insensitive. He stubbornly insisted on a première the sam
autumn and this in spite of the fact that the concerto was not yet finished le

alone in the repertoire of a soloist. The news that the concerto was to be dedicated to Burmester had been given to both the Finnish and the foreign press but even that did not stop Sibelius approaching Viktor Nováček,[1] a mediocrity who taught in Helsinki, to undertake the première that autumn. He had even toyed with the possibility of asking Henri Marteau[2] to do it in Stockholm and elsewhere.

The news soon reached Burmester's ears and he was naturally quite upset. He wrote asking for confirmation and assured Sibelius that if the rumours proved accurate he would never perform the work anywhere. Sibelius's reply shows signs of panic. 'I'll agree to whatever you want, but my financial position is so parlous that I must give a concert here either at the end of the year or at the beginning of January. The concerto will be played then by someone here (Nováček for instance) in Helsinki and Turku. When you come in March you will launch it: for any comparison between the two of you is out of the question! So, in March or February (?) we can play it together in Berlin, Symphony II and the concerto and something else. . . . Marvellous! Helsinki doesn't mean a thing!! I'm so grateful that you will do it in so many places.'

Sibelius had finished the first two movements in short score by September and in the late autumn he was in a position to send the whole work (in a violin and piano reduction) to Burmester who responded with an ecstatic letter. 'I can only say one thing: wonderful! Masterly! Only once before have I spoken in such terms to a composer, and that was when Tchaikovsky showed me his concerto.'

In the middle of his work, Sibelius was compelled to act as his own impresario. *En Saga* as well as the Second Symphony had just appeared in print and he wrote to Carpelan: 'As you are so thoroughly at home in the musical scene you would be doing me a great favour if you could draw up a list of those conductors and musical periodicals to whom I should send the Second Symphony and *En Saga*. I shall then collate yours with my own so that we shall have the fullest list possible.' Sibelius also put the concerto on one side for another project: the incidental music to Arvid Järnefelt's play, *Kuolema* (*Death*). The première had been planned for 18 November but Sibelius was not ready with his score in time and the performance was postponed until 2 December. *Kuolema* enjoyed far greater success than Järnefelt's earlier plays had done, thanks largely to Sibelius's music. During the first act the hero dreams that his dying mother dances before him and at this point were heard the strains of what was to become famous later on as *Valse triste*.

In October he wrote to Carpelan that the concerto's première had to be

1. Not to be confused with the better-known Ottakar Nováček who in fact had died a few years before this.
2. A virtuoso well known for his interest in Scandinavian music. He gave the Berwald concerto among other things and was perhaps the leading French violinist before Thibaud. *Tr*

postponed until the spring of 1904, 'because Nováček won't have mastered the solo part before January. He'll study it thoroughly and will do it well. In any event it's not my fault now since I could have had it ready.' *Qui s'excuse, s'accuse*! Sibelius could hardly expect poor Nováček to play it from sight. Just before Christmas Sibelius again wrote to Carpelan about the concerto, the first two movements, he said, were fully scored, and he was about to start on the finale. He wrote this at 5 a.m. and was finding it difficult to keep awake. But perhaps the best picture of his life during this period during the weeks before the concerto's première is to be found in a letter Aino sent Carpelan at the beginning of the new year:

> The first performance of the concerto is now definitely decided for 8 February but that however is uncomfortably soon. Janne has been in the throes of it all the time (and so have I). Again it has been an *embarras de richesse*. He has so many ideas forcing their way into his mind that he becomes quite literally dizzy. He's awake night after night, plays wonderful things, and can't tear himself away from the marvellous music he plays—there are so many ideas that one can't believe it is true, all of them so rich in possibilities for development, so full of life. But if I have been excited by all this, I have also suffered too. As Axel will understand, a woman's temperament can't cope with all the turbulent ups-and-downs of a creative artist's temperament, which changes so violently that I become alarmed. Now, I don't know whether you gather my meaning, . . . but I must talk to someone and indeed ought to have done so before this; and since I have the feeling that I can open my heart to you, I feel happier and can put my mind at rest. Do you know that only a few days ago I thought I would come to Tampere; but now the clouds have parted and I have a glimpse of the blue skies above. Of course I am happy to have been able to be so near Janne all this time—whether my presence is any help to him in his darker moments I cannot say—but it has been a rewarding and satisfying experience for me. I cannot say at the moment much about Janne's work—what the final shape of the concerto will be—but it is well nigh approaching completion. Sometimes he speaks of our partnership and then I feel proud. He is in good health, as indeed am I, save for the anxiety of it all, which makes me nervous. If I had someone to whom I could speak, things would not be so difficult, but there is no one closer than you are to Janne to whom I *can* talk. I believe the artist's inner world to be the most precious and sensitive thing in the world, would you not agree with me? And your friendship for Janne is of inestimable value. Be his friend always as you have been so far. I've much more to say but I will stop none the less. I am afraid that I am tiring you. It has been such a worrying time and as a result I can't write calmly. **Keep** well. Janne sends you his warmest regards. I am sitting at his writing desk—he is at the piano—there's a nice fire. It is night.

But even if the violin concerto was ready there remained the other new works for the concert. As late as the end of January, Sibelius was still working on 'an altogether new piece' that he gave the working-title of 'Fantasy for orchestra' but which was finally christened 'Cassazione'. There was a patriotic marching song, 'Här du mod?' to a text of Wecksell, presumably designed to stiffen national morale.

At the concert on 8 February Sibelius himself conducted while a red-faced and perspiring Nováček fought a losing battle with a solo part that bristled with even greater difficulties in this first version than it does in the definitive score. Apart from the new works the concert also included 'The Origin of Fire' and the whole programme was given three times. In his review of the concerto, Flodin wrote that Sibelius had yielded to the temptation of conventional virtuoso writing and abandoned none of the ballast of the nineteenth-century concerto while Evert Katila, in *Uusi Suometar* compared the Sibelius with Tchaikovsky's concerto and hailed it as a very nearly ideal example of the modern concerto. With some changes, he argued, it could be one of the most significant works of its kind in the repertoire.

After the concert, Sibelius wrote Carpelan, 'I shall go to Turku very soon. (He had a concert there on 26 April.) I do hope it will be a good audience. Here it was worse than ever. *Tempora mutantur.* But I am the same and am full of new ideas. I think I shall soon have something new of importance. I find Helsinki more and more irksome. I either want to be in the countryside in Finland or one of the big cities on the continent. The public here is shallow and full of bile.'

Burmester received the news of the concerto's fate at Nováček's hands and its reception in Helsinki without surprise. The more he worked on the solo part himself, the more he realized its appalling difficulties which he knew Nováček was ill equipped to negotiate. Sibelius's concerto needed a soloist of some substance and Burmester made no secret of the fact that he regarded himself as the ideal interpreter. 'All my 25 years' platform experience, my artistry and insight will be placed to serve this work. Just this very fact will do much on your work's behalf. Don't worry about anything, just follow your own concerns and leave this safely in my hands. I shall play the concerto in Helsinki in such a way that the city will be at your feet.' Burmester made a specific offer: he was willing to play the work three times in Helsinki in October 1904.

So far in their relationship no bridges had been burnt but now the situation was further complicated. Sibelius was himself dissatisfied with the concerto and was unwilling to bind himself in any way to another deadline. He had no intention of publishing the concerto during the summer as he had previously told Burmester. He was deeply troubled by all this and wrote to Carpelan of his intention to withdraw the concerto which would not appear for another two years. The first movement would be completely rewritten and the second also needed a good deal of retouching. Thus the work remained until Sibelius revised it, apparently in one fell swoop. At the end of June 1905 he wrote to his new German publisher, Robert Lienau about the completed new score. Lienau had his own ideas about the first performance of it. His first choice of soloist was Karl Halir, the leader of the Berlin Orchestra and a fine player, though not technically so well equipped as Burmester, while the conductor was to be no less a celebrity than Richard Strauss. Sibelius lost no time; he sent the piano reduction and the solo part only ten days later, and on 20 July promised to send off the complete score. However his conscience was troubling him and in August he replied to Lienau's suggestion. 'I have in fact promised Burmester the concerto but if he is not going to play in Berlin this autumn, it will not be possible to wait longer.' Lienau reacted immediately and some days later wrote to the composer announcing that the date was fixed for 19 October with Halir as soloist and Strauss conducting. Burmester, he added, had agreed to stand down.

One can readily appreciate that for Burmester this was really the last straw. For a second time Sibelius had passed him over in favour of a less eminent artist and he stuck to his earlier threat never to play the concerto. Sibelius's way of handling Burmester throughout the whole affair is, to say the least, puzzling, particularly as Burmester had appeared in Berlin under Strauss. The most likely explanation is that circumstances forced his hand, and that his debts had mounted to such an extent that he was not in a position to fulfil his promises. However, the possibility that subconsciously, he did not really want Burmester to have the first performance, cannot altogether be ruled out. His artistic personality and taste may not have appealed to him though we know he admired his 'wonderful bowing arm'.[1] When the score finally appeared in print, Sibelius asked Lienau to send a copy to Burmester along with many other virtuosi including Ysaÿe. To Marteau he intended to write personally.

The première took place in Berlin as planned. It drew a rather negative response from Joachim who told Lienau it was 'scheusslich und langweilig', a remark that was duly relayed to Sibelius. In view of his admiration for the great violinist he was pained, though more, he put it, 'for Joachim's sake, for he seems no longer in tune with the spirit of our time'. The Berlin press on the other hand welcomed the work as a valuable addition to the concerto repertoire. Its colours reminded the *Deutsche Zeitung* of 'the Nordic winter landscape painters who through the distinctive interplay of white on white, secure rare, sometimes hypnotic and sometimes powerful, effects'. The *Berliner Lokalzeiger* noted the melancholy atmosphere of the first movement, as gloomy and yet fascinating as the Finnish people themselves, though it did not find the movement well held together. 'The *adagio di molto* is related to the first movement but goes deeper and is more unified, a symphonic threnody of compelling lyricism. The finale has greater gaiety even though darker undertones can be discerned.'

1. Burmester had mastered the typical virtuoso repertoire such as Paganini and Wieniawski, and had also made a number of popular arrangements, but as an interpreter of the great classics he was less musically commanding.

But in spite of its comparative success in Berlin, the concerto still failed to conquer Helsinki and when the definitive version was given in March 1906 with Grewesmühl from Riga as soloist, Flodin found no cause to modify his earlier views. 'Even in its revised form the concerto will not, I think, win wide appreciation. With the exception of the *adagio*, the concerto is far too complex, far too busy, dark and dingy, rhapsodic in spite of its tauter form, and above all, it is laden with technical and rhythmic difficulties of such a kind that even the greatest master of the instrument will be hard put to make a successful repertoire work of it that will really catch the public ear.' If Flodin's judgment was eventually to prove wrong, it still took some time before the work achieved any measure of real popularity. At the end of the same year Sibelius visited Leopold Auer in St. Petersburg where Ysaÿe and Taneiev played it through, and reported to Lienau, 'Everyone spoke appreciatively of the work but said that, in general, it takes a long time for a new violin concerto to establish itself.'

Among its early protagonists was a seventeen-year-old boy who in 1910 played the work in Berlin and then presented it to the Viennese public. This was Ferenc von Vecsey, and it was to him that Sibelius dedicated the piece though Carpelan had suggested Ysaÿe! The concerto reached America relatively quickly though Maud Powell's performance at the end of 1906 was at first greeted with critical incomprehension in New York. In Chicago the following January, however, she gave it with such success that the finale was encored. The *Chicago Daily Tribune* reproached the New York critics for not grasping its striking originality; indeed its critic wrote of it as the most original modern work of recent years. It was not until the 1930s that the work really caught on with the public at large. Heifetz was the first[1] to record it and in the subsequent forty years nearly as many commercial recordings have been made of it.

'Dreamt I was twelve years old and a virtuoso.' So reads a diary entry Sibelius made in 1915 when he was in the process of composing his Sonatina for violin and piano. But the entry could just as well have come from the period of the Violin Concerto since he composed neither for Burmester nor any other violinist but for himself, or rather the kind of virtuoso he had dreamt of being.

Unlike Mendelssohn and Brahms, Sibelius did not need to call on expert technical advice. In this respect he was his own Joachim even if he was no longer active as a player. But in his inner self he remained an executant: his activities as a conductor compensated to some extent for the failure of his violinistic dreams but the satisfaction of having direct physical control over an instrument at the level he wanted, was denied him. Naturally in his imagination he identifies himself with the soloist in the Violin Concerto and this may well explain something of its nostalgia and romantic intensity.

1. The first Finnish interpreter of quality to meet its demands was Anja Ignatius who recorded the concerto with Armas Järnefelt in Berlin during 1942. *Tr*

No doubt, too, there was some conflict of interest; the imaginary virtuoso saw himself dominating the horizon while the composer sought to balance his claims with those of a symphonic perspective. In all late romantic concertos the problem of balancing the limited tonal range of the solo violin against the powerful sonority of the post-romantic orchestra was acute.

What, then, were Sibelius models? The Beethoven concerto undoubtedly represented a far-distant and unattainable goal. Mendelssohn, however, succeeded in coming near to it in his concerto and this work which had been a youthful *pièce de résistance* undoubtedly served to give him many ideas; the basic conception as well as the idea, also taken up by Tchaikovksy, of putting the cadenza before the reprise so as to lend it a greater structural significance over and above its usual importance. The Bruch G minor concerto, another work in the Mendelssohn tradition, might figure in the Sibelius concerto's family tree. One thinks immediately of the soloist's dramatic recitative and the characteristic doublestopping in sixths and octaves that are also a feature of the Sibelius.

In all probability Sibelius had made the acquaintance of the Tchaikovsky concerto as early as 1893 in Burmester's interpretation. Tchaikovsky's humanity and sensibility always struck a responsive chord in him and he must have been delighted with the spirited rivalry between the soloist and orchestra in the first movement, by the cadenza's inventive, almost impossible difficulties, and seen how the soloistic element dominated the proceedings, particularly in the canzonetta and the finale.

The Brahms concerto he did not apparently discover until after finishing the first version of his own. He heard it in Berlin in January 1905 and wrote, 'I have heard the Brahms violin concerto which is good. But so different (too symphonic) from mine.' The virtuoso in him resisted Brahms's way of integrating the soloist's role into the symphonic argument[1] though no doubt the concerto's example did not go unnoticed nor its lessons unlearnt. Some months later Sibelius reworked his own concerto, removed some virtuoso passages from the solo part, and strengthened the work's symphonic foundations.

Sibelius solved the diverging claims of the virtuoso and symphonic elements in his own personal way. The solo instrument stands out in relief against the orchestral background whether it carries the lyrical burden of the argument to the orchestra's accompaniment or conversely plays a more obbligato role with decorative passage-work while the orchestra furthers the melodic course of the work. These are the two main kinds of texture that dominate the picture and it is only rarely that the soloist and orchestra open any kind of symphonic dialogue as equal partners. These two patterns together with straightforward tutti and cadenzas, alternate generally speaking in block fashion. Rapid exchanges or the presentation of themes between soloist and orchestra are not a

1. Sibelius never really changed his mind on this issue. During the last year of his life he said: 'Prokofiev's Violin Concerto (probably No. 1) is a symphonic unity where the violin plays a subordinate role. Quite the opposite of my view'.

feature of the piece. These block-like structures have, of course, their dangers for they could work against organic coherence. Miraculously Sibelius turns this very weakness to symphonic advantage since each section performs a form-giving role. Indeed the work could very largely be analysed from its texture changes alone.

Take, for example, the first movement where Sibelius follows Mendelssohn and Tchaikovsky in placing the main cadenza between the development and the reprise. But he carries it a step further: the cadenza actually replaces the development. Originally in the first version of the concerto Sibelius had a cadenza based on the second group, which he placed between the second group itself and the final theme in the restatement. By cutting this somewhat conventional cadenza altogether and composing a new one, based this time on the first group, and putting it in place of the development Sibelius gave the movement a new symphonic perspective. Three large tutti passages play a decisive role in the revised first movement. In the orchestral transition from the first to the second groups in the exposition, some of the material from the former is reshaped and then inserted into the latter. This is by the way an example of Sibelius's attempt to purify his textures: in the first version the soloist had an obbligato part which Sibelius cut, just as in the same way he excised the string accompaniment to the preceding 'little' cadenza. The second tutti—in the reprise with counterplay from the soloist—serves as a closing group. This orchestral transition is matched in the restatement with a kind of symphonic interlude which forms the orchestral climax of the movement. In the first version of the work, this tutti was built up of different material, was shorter and less important.

So much, then, for the cadenzas and tutti. Both in the exposition and restatement, the first and second groups are dominated by the soloist in both a lyrical and virtuoso role. The main theme is not presented on the orchestra, save for a few phrases which appear here and there in solo fashion on the wind. The concerto is distinctly Nordic in its overwhelming sense of nostalgia. The orchestra does not wallow in rich colours but in the rich halflights of autumn and winter; only on rare occasions does the horizon brighten and glow. Against a predominantly dark background the soloist traces a line soaring towards the light, when it is not burning with dark glowing intensity or singing on its melancholy G string. Just how nordic it is, can be seen when one puts it alongside the Glazunov concerto written the same year. The latter offers a quasi-oriental array of colours, guitar effects and a Paganini-like carillon on the soloist's flageolet notes, triangle and harp. He does not hesitate to write for the violins in a high register cantabile and in a dialogue with his soloist or to introduce the main idea of the finale on the trumpets, and later in a brilliantly coloured tutti. Sibelius's writing for the violins on the other hand stresses their lower register and in the wind writing, clarinets and bassoons predominate while the brass command a steel-like strength with the occasional glimpses of warmer, burnished colours. One has to go as far forward as the First Violin Concerto of

Shostakovich to find an example of the genre that explores a comparable sound world.

The first movement, allegro moderato, begins without any orchestral introduction, and against the lightly flickering, undulating background of muted violins, the soloist traces the main theme:

Ex. 237

In the Mendelssohn one might, albeit fancifully, imagine the main theme being intoned by a Titania, and in the Glazunov by the Georgian maiden of Pushkin's poem which Rachmaninoff has set. Similarly in the Sibelius we have the water-nymph from Josephson's painting or the water spirit from Strindberg's *Crown Bride* (*Kronbruden*) who plays the violin in the white summer nights. The tritone, D to G sharp, gives a slightly demonic flavour to the Dorian atmosphere. Gradually the player gets beside himself and his music culminates in a cadenza of almost desperate intensity. The main theme is so ideally suited to the character of the soloist that it is difficult to imagine it laid out for the orchestra. But four segments of it, marked a, b, c, and d, prove to be thematic elements with unsuspected organic power.

In the next orchestral transition the texture changes character from solo-plus-accompaniment to symphonic. It grows from 'c', which continually changes shape, thus:

Ex. 238

And again in the following form:

Ex. 239

The metamorphosis results in the second subject, which is heralded by the bassoons:

Ex. 240

One realizes that this is the second group only when the soloist enters *molto moderato e tranquillo* to confirm, as it were, B flat:

Ex. 241

The soloist's expressive parallel sixths at the modulation to D flat, double octaves *affettuoso* over a yearning *Tristan* chord, the shadow of D flat minor, all this creates a strange elegiac ecstasy. Then, in broken octaves the soloist glides downwards over the most Sibelian of all harmonic progressions which resolve on to B flat minor:

Ex. 242

With the appearance of the final group of themes in B flat minor, the elegiac mood is abruptly shattered. The second subject assumes a more insistent, hard-edged shape, moving entirely within the compass of a fifth:

Ex. 243

It is the descending fifth at the end of the phrase that becomes all important and it is this interval, though in ascending form that begins the final theme on flutes and violins:

Ex. 244

This culminates in an angry outburst where the rhythmic contour of 'a' in the very opening theme is clearly delineated:

Ex. 245

This rapidly undergoes a slight change (the minor third becomes a major one and the tritone becomes a fifth),[1] a pendant is added, and we are plunged into the darkest depths of the orchestra:

Ex. 246

The pendant, incidentally, is clearly derived from 'd'. The climax gradually loses power and from its depths the soloist suddenly brings everything to life with a leap of three octaves, from which height it slowly wings its way down like a bird in flight:

Ex. 247

This G minor passage introduces the main cadenza, which serves, as I have said, as a development. It concentrates on the first two segments of the main theme, 'a' and 'b', to which are added various bird-like cries:

Ex. 248

Throughout the cadenza these cries echo, while the canonic imitation of the 'a' motive sounds both melancholy and searching. This cadenza does not offer

1. Some important motives in the Fourth Symphony have the same basic falling contour.

mpty passage work but does, I suggest, add a psychological dimension to the movement in that the serenity of the opening is seen to have disturbing undertones. The restatement puts much of the thematic material of the movement in new light. The pale colouring of the main theme assumes a darker-hued quality when it appears on the G string and in the subdominant. The following tutti assumes the role of a symphonic interlude where 'b' takes on a new form:

Ex. 249

This idea gives rise to an enormous climax that eventually reaches B minor where the powerful three-note motive (a descending major third followed by a fifth) is thundered out on the trombones. The second theme remains virtually unaltered in B major leading to the tonic major while the closing group is enhanced in impact thanks to the soloist's obbligato, where virtuosity is directly contrasted with the simple insistence of the orchestral writing.

The Adagio is in B flat, a key which drew a special response from Sibelius. Its world was totally unaffected, inward, at one and the same time lyrical and light, yet elegiac and melancholy. This is a world one encounters in the lyric poetry of Runeberg and Wecksell in which Sibelius was steeped. It is no coincidence that Sibelius set Wecksell's 'Demanten pa marssnön' ("The diamond on the March snow') in B flat and that the song begins with a melodic and harmonic turn which reminds one of the main theme of the movement.[1]

The slow movement models itself both in form and spirit on the Nordic romans and indeed could well bear the title Romanza, like the middle movement of the D minor Mozart concerto, K.466. The violin entry is prefaced by a few bars in which the wind weave various lines in thirds. They take some time before finding a firm tonal anchorage but eventually settle in B flat where the soloist begins his long cantabile:

Ex. 250

Its equilibrium is gradually disturbed: the accompaniment is enlivened by scales and pizzicati from violas and cellos, the syncopations thicken and the music moves towards a climax. Suddenly the soloist stops as if to take breath

. Another special instance is the second movement of Rakastava. Tr

and a small dotted figure, already foreshadowed in the pizzacato accompaniment and in the soloist's triplets, is heard, first piano then pianissimo, like some faint half-remembered image, before the soloist resumes his threnody. This passage conveys a sense of stillness, as if time has stopped for a brief moment.

The second theme is expressive, strongly accented, and derives from the very opening idea on the wind:

Ex. 251

The syncopated figure is taken up by the soloist, the melodic line being set against crotchet triplets. In the first version these were tremolo as in Paganini's caprices:

Ex. 252

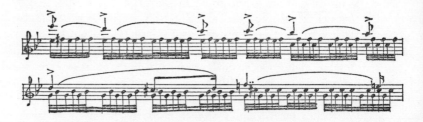

In the reprise the cantabile theme returns once more but with a higher emotional temperature. Sibelius seems reluctant to bring the piece to an end. Certainly the movement bears witness to an inner peace and equilibrium that found scant expression in his day-to-day life at this time. As is the case with many great masters, composition appears to have a kind of autonomy, free from immediate pressures.

When Sibelius was asked about the interpretation of the finale he answered,[1] 'It must be played with absolute mastery. Fast, of course, but no faster than it can be played perfectly *von oben*.' As early as the E major polonaise in the four movement Suite for violin and piano, he had given some signs of his interest in the virtuoso style. In the finale of the concerto, also in the rhythm of a polonaise, he developed his youthful vision of transcendental virtuosity. The movement begins with this proud, chivalrous idea:

Ex. 253

1. Ringbom p. 88 (footnote).

This strongly characterized figure soon explodes in an array of passage work among other things, barn-storming ascending scales in thirds. The second subject is one of the few themes in the concerto to be presented in a conventional fashion on its first appearance. The strongly accented crotchets, the darker colouring and the mediant pedal point almost remind one of *En Saga*, even if the cross rhythms lighten the mood somewhat, hence perhaps Sir Donald Tovey's playful remark about 'a polonaise for polar bears':

Ex. 254

After the orchestral presentation of the theme in an 'objective' fashion, the soloist brings a more 'subjective' view to bear:

Ex. 255

The final theme introduces another violinistic figure: a theme around which classical semiquavers are woven. After this there follows a short interlude that serves as a kind of development; it is primarily based on a dominant pedal point. The reprise returns the first theme in a semiquaver variant which the soloist takes up, dazzling the orchestra and the public with his wizardry. In the second group he seems almost wild with desperation, playing an emphatic obbligato against the orchestra following it with a poetic idea in flageolets.

The concerto poses the question of the relationship between technical display and musical content. In writing of the Chopin Studies, Cortot emphasizes how the pianist must perforce practise and solve the technical problems if he is to master the musical ones, and conversely how technical perfection can be attained only through complete involvement in the music. Similar reflections must have passed through Burmester's mind when he wrote to Sibelius that all his technical knowledge and insight would be completely at the service of the concerto. What perhaps he was trying to say was that the work called on all his powers—plus a little extra, thus stretching him beyond his own limits. Because of this, the listener experiences this concerto not as a compendium of fiendish virtuosity but as an organic musical whole in which every note serves a genuine artistic purpose.

Turning now to the other music of the period we come to the incidental music Sibelius wrote for *Kuolema*. There are six numbers, all of them originally scored for strings save for the fifth which calls in addition for a bass drum and at the very end *campanelli di chiesa*. In 1904 Sibelius scored the *Valse triste* of the first act for small orchestra and two years later he put together two other numbers, the first, a portrait of the young heroine, and the second, a piece called *The Cranes*, under the title *Scene with Cranes*. When in 1911 the play was revived in a more tightly-knit version, Sibelius added two more movements, the *Canzonetta* and *Valse romantique*.

The play is very much of its period. In the first act in particular, one is reminded of Strindberg's *A Dream Play*. Reality and dreams intermingle and in the moment before her death the mother relives a ball scene from her youth: phantom-like figures in evening dress glide noiselessly while Sibelius's music tries to mirror an interplay between this vivid memory and the sense of on-coming death. In the original string version:

Ex. 256

the accompaniment is simpler than in the familiar revised version where the dream-like atmosphere is heightened by the accented passing notes:

Ex. 257

This resolves on to a haunting cadence which leads to glimpses of past happiness. The dance itself comes in the original version at the beginning of the second section:

Ex. 258

In the stage performance the music is silenced for a moment (before the section marked *poco risoluto*), the mother leans exhausted against the wall, while the other dancers withdraw bowing into the background; then she throws herself anew into the dance and the dream ends in a macabre whirling spiral that accelerates more and more and is broken in the play only by Death's knock on the door.

In *Valse triste* Sibelius touched on a responsive chord, much in the same way as Strindberg or Munch had done, and uncovered sympathetic resonances that were in the air at the time.

The *Scene with Cranes*, the second of the pieces that Sibelius arranged from *Kuolema* begins with a movement for strings of some subtlety which is then interrupted by the call of the cranes in the clarinets:

Ex. 259

The interval of fifths and sixths almost foreshadows the famous Thor's Hammer theme (to quote Tovey) of the Fifth Symphony:

Ex. 260

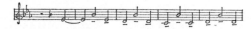

According to a diary entry from 1915, Sibelius associated this theme with the flight of swans. For him the cry of flying swans, cranes and wild geese had a strong poignancy. 'Every day I have seen the cranes. Flying south in full cry with their music. Have been yet again their most assiduous pupil. Their cries echo throughout my being.'

Cassazione, the opening number of his concert in February 1904, was never published. In the spring of the following year he wrote to Carpelan of his doubts about it, at least in its present form, and he subsequently reworked it and in so doing reduced the orchestral forces for which he had scored it. The work is not a cassation in the normal sense of the word. It is in one and not several movements though it has a divertimento-like character; there is some solo writing both for wind and strings here and there and the various sections of the orchestra are set off against each other in concertante fashion. It is worth a mention in passing that the woodwind almost anticipate the finale of the Third Symphony at one point:

Ex. 261

When one plays through the score at the piano one cannot avoid the impression that some of it would have done well as a piano concerto; the introductory theme could have been set out in double octaves, interleaved with virtuoso passage work and with the clarinet and flute dialogue just before the end reworked as a cadenza for the soloist!

Carpelan had incidentally suggested to Sibelius in 1902 that he should arrange some Finnish folk melodies for strings. And the composer felt attracted to the project but made piano rather than orchestral transcriptions which he sold to Fazer and Westerlund in 1903. In his handling of harmony he avoids stereotyped formulae and in fact puts into practice many of the ideas that he had developed for his paper in 1896. Indeed in several of his transcriptions he approaches the kind of harmonization and layout that is characteristic of Bartók in his folk arrangements and other keyboard pieces. Take, for example, the ostinato figure in No. 5, 'Velisurmaaja', ('The Fratricide'):

Ex. 262

and compare it with the third movement of Bartók's Suite Op. 14:

Ex. 263

In each of the accompanying figures there is the opening leap of a ninth; then both rise to the augmented fourth/diminished fifth which functions as a sort of dominant. Eric Blom[1] suggests that this unexpected parallel possibly springs from similarities in the Finnish and Hungarian languages that in their turn are mirrored in the metre and cadential formulae of their respective folk musics. In this connection one recalls the theories of Bartók, Kodály and Szabolci that some of the features, among them pentatonic traits, to be found in Hungarian, Mongolian, and to a lesser extent Finnish folk music could be explained by some common derivation and that the Fenno-Ugrian tribes originated two thousand or more years ago from the same geographical proximity. It is only fair to add that this hypothesis is viewed with considerable scepticism by the Finnish scholar A. O. Väisänen,[2] and in this particular instance the common element might

1. Blom: 'The Piano Music' in Gerald Abraham's *Sibelius, a symposium*, London, p. 106
2. In *Untersuchungen über die ob-ugrischen Melodien*, Helsinki, 1939.

well be called in question since 'Velisurmaaja' has purely Scandinavian prece-
dents.[1] Quite apart from this the minor pentachord is in some respects characteristic of runic song.

However, apart from possible parallels, both Bartók and Sibelius were typical
of their time in that they were reacting against the traditional romantic har-
monizations and pianistic accompaniments given to folk songs and achieved in
their differing ways, simple and stylish solutions. An example of this is No. 4,
'Tuopa tyttö, Kaunis tyttö kanteletta soittaa' ('The beautiful maiden plays
the kantele'). In a routine setting this would have been turned into a G minor
piece; Sibelius's working gives it at first a Lydian-Mixolydian flavour with C as
a pedal point (the so-called Bartók scale):

Ex. 264

Afterwards shades of the minor cross it before it ends in F major. These folk
melodies were an interesting experiment and one wonders how his piano
style would have developed had he continued on these lines.

To return to 1904: by this time the Sibelius symphonies were beginning to
make headway abroad. Stockholm was a useful testing ground, for his Nordic
accents were at one and the same time familiar yet slightly alien for the Swedes.
In the spring of 1901 the Swedish critic, Peterson-Berger had despatched some
of the piano music in no uncertain terms: 'half-talented ravings . . .', 'jaw-jaw
kept going by local patriotism and political sympathy . . .'. After that, Sibelius
read Peterson-Berger's reviews with a mixture of fury and amusement. That he
did not conduct his own work in Stockholm until as late as 1923, even though
he had appeared both in Gothenburg and several world capitals, might well be
at least in part due to what Flodin called, 'Peterson-Berger's butchery'. Indeed,
reviewing the First Symphony after its Stockholm première in October 1902,
Peterson-Berger made his attack a personal one rather than a purely musical
critique. The symphony reflected, 'a moribund, shoddy bohemianism', and
made one long for, 'a fresh wholesome and powerful personality with the
bloom of health on his cheeks and a liveliness about the eyes instead of all this
romantic nocturnal pallor, the blazed eyes of the dreamer-mystic and the bogus

1. 'Sven i Rosengård' in Geijer and Afzelius's *Swedish folksongs*, Stockholm, 1880.

philosophical poses'. (Gallén's Symposium picture had evidently made its mark on him!) A year later Sibelius found an unexpected defender in Willy Burmester, who prefaced a concert with a denunciation of Peterson-Berger's treatment of the composer and ended up by turning him out of the hall. On the other hand, Petersen-Berger could be just as headstrong in his enthusiasms: the first performance in Stockholm of the Second Symphony under Armas Järnefelt prompted him to something like a paean of praise. After some lyrical analogies with the *Kalevala* he goes on to say that one cannot deny that there is a streak of greatness, of genius in this symphony, which he calls 'the strongest and most impressive work we have had from Sibelius up to the present. Its form is generally clear and well-thought-out: it reminds one at times of Tchaikovsky but is individual for all that and frankly more interesting than anything from his pen.'

The symphony came as something of a revelation for Stenhammar. He had visited Helsinki to give a concert at the end of February 1902[1] and had come to know Sibelius better than he had on their previous encounter in the summer of 1900. After the Stockholm première he wrote to Sibelius:

> You are in my thoughts every day since I heard your symphony. You're a wonderful person; you have reached into the deepest depths of the unconscious and the ineffable and brought forth something of a miracle. What I suspected has been proved true: for me you emerge as the foremost, indeed the only major figure at this moment. And now I am waiting for you to make your entrance on the world stage in a clear and unmistakeable form. Give your inspiration flesh and blood, give us a music drama. Take the figures from your wonderful Finnish sagas and present them as the great and simple symbols for the mystic truths that can never be expressed in other than musical terms, but don't attempt to explain what you are doing except by means of the plot. I have also written a symphony now, at least I am calling it a symphony.[2] And according to our agreement which you have perhaps forgotten, it was to be dedicated to you. But nothing will come of this. It is rather good but it is all on the surface. I long to go deeper into myself and you must wait until I have done so. On that great day I shall print your name in large letters first on the title-page, be it a symphony or anything else.

Sibelius did not follow up Stenhammar's plea for a music drama. Presumably his Swedish colleague knew nothing of his misfortunes with *The Building of the Boat* but a lifelong friendship had been forged between the two composers even if it was to be several years before next they met. In Hamburg Sibelius also secured a foothold, for although the city could not boast quite so rich a musical tradition as, say, Leipzig, Munich or Dresden, it was more open

1. As well as being a composer, Stenhammar was one of the leading pianists of his day and later on, of course, became conductor of the Gothenburg Orchestra.
2. His First Symphony. The Second, in G minor, followed more than a decade later. *Tr*

:han they to music from abroad. Moreover the North Germans were temperamentally more receptive to Sibelius's musical language than the Bavarians.
In January 1904, Max Fiedler scored a great success with the Second Symphony.
The well-known critic and writer, Ferdinand Pfohl called Sibelius a composer
of genius and used him as a stick with which to beat Strauss. The only worthy
companion he could find that matched the power of the finale was the corresponding movement of Brahms's First Symphony, no mean tribute in
Brahms's birthplace! But when Kajanus a few days later conducted the same
work in St. Petersburg, the critical reception was little short of contemptuous.
'The Symphony shows that the new music in the Scandinavian countries,
where musical culture is relatively backward, has already, before even reaching
the stage of maturity, taken an extremely decadent turn. How strange it seems
after hearing the unpretentious and direct music of Grieg, to listen to such
unhealthy artificial music.' On the other hand, Kajanus scored a great success
in Moscow with the 'Lemminkäinen's Homeward Journey' and 'The Swan of
Tuonela.'

The same year the Italian composer, Leone Sinigaglia heard *Finlandia* played
in Berlin and was so taken with it that he suggested that Sibelius's music should
be included in the next season of the Turin Orchestra. He was a native of that
city and a good friend of Toscanini. In March 1904 Toscanini made his debut
as a Sibelius conductor in Bologna with 'The Swan of Tuonela' which was so
successful that it was repeated on the spot. He then introduced both 'The
Swan' and *En Saga* to Turin audiences and as Sinigaglia himself told Sibelius,
he could not have been launched in Italy under more auspicious circumstances.
Toscanini also put the Second Symphony into his programmes the following
year but for some unexplained reason, the maestro replaced it with *Finlandia*.
In fact Italian audiences only heard *En Saga*, 'The Swan of Tuonela' and
Finlandia from his baton. When he conducted *En Saga* in Rome in 1915,
Casella called it 'poeticissimo' and rejoiced that in such troubled times there is
a conductor 'di quelle eccelse e misterioso intelligenze di visionari'. Later, of
course, Toscanini added the Second and Fourth Symphonies and *Pohjola's
Daughter* to his repertoire.

The London première of the First Symphony took place in October 1903
under Henry Wood. *The Times* found its musical ideas as full of character as
in the best Russian music. 'Sibelius is often as simple as Mozart. He is also
distinctly modern.' Elsewhere critics[1] did not feel that the finale lived up to the
promise of the opening movement. In America Theodore Thomas introduced
the Second Symphony to the Chicago public as early as January 1904 two days
after a fire at the Iroquois Theatre had occasioned considerable loss of life.
The Musical Courier thought its mood harmonized with the gloom in which
the city had been plunged by this tragedy. In Boston the critics were openly
puzzled by the work. They simply did not like it and Olin Downes was among
them. As he wrote forty years later, 'In 1904 Sibelius's Second Symphony was

1. *Musical Times*, November 1903, and *Sunday Times*, 18 October 1903.

before its time.' All this serves to give some idea of Sibelius's position on the musical map. After the first decade of the century Sibelius was to become a great name in the Anglo-Saxon world. But all this originated with Germany. It was on the successes of Heidelberg, Hamburg and Berlin, and the work of Breitkopf und Härtel and Robert Lienau, that the foundations of his international reputation were laid.

Select Bibliography[1]

Abraham, Gerald (ed.), *Sibelius, A Symposium*, London, 1947.
Ekman, Karl, *Jean Sibelius. En konstnärs liv och personlighet*, (tr. *Jean Sibelius: his Life and Personality*), Helsinki, 1935, and London, 1936.
Furuhjelm, Erik, *Jean Sibelius. Hans tondiktning och drag ur hans liv*, Borgå, 1916.
Gray, Cecil, *Sibelius*, London, 1931.
Johnson, Harold, *Jean Sibelius*, New York, 1959.
Krohn, Ilmari, *Der Stimmungsgehalt der Symphonien von Jean Sibelius*, Vol. I, Helsinki, 1945; Vol. II, Helsinki, 1946.
Layton, Robert, *Sibelius* (Master Musicians), London, 1965.
—— *Sibelius and his world*, London, 1970.
Levas, Santeri, *Nuori Sibelius*, Helsinki, 1957.
—— *Järvenpään mestari*, Helsinki, 1960.
Niemann, Walter, *Jean Sibelius*, Leipzig, 1917.
Parmet, Simon, *Sibeliusken sinfoniat* (The Symphonies of Sibelius), Helsinki, 1955, and London, 1959.
Ringbom, Nils-Eric, *Jean Sibelius*, Stockholm, 1948, and University of Oklahoma, 1954.
Roiha, Eino, *Die Symphonien von Jean Sibelius. Eine formanalytische Studie*, Jyväskylä, 1941.
von Törne, Bengt, *Sibelius i närbild och samtal*, (tr. *Sibelius: A Close-up*), Helsinki, 1945, and London, 1937.
Tanzberger, Ernst, *Jean Sibelius*, Wiesbaden, 1962.
Vestdijk, Simon, *De symfonieën van Jean Sibelius*, Amsterdam, 1962.
Vignal, Marc, *Jean Sibelius*, Paris, 1965.

1. A fuller bibliography will be included in the final volume.

Index

compiled by Terence A. Miller

Page numbers in italics indicate music examples.

INDEX

Joachim Quartet, 59, 200
Joensuu (Finland), 122
Josephson, Ernst (*poet*), 20, 271, 282
Juhlamaarssi (*alla marcia* of Academic Cantata), 151
Jyväskylä (Finland), 218

Kajanus, Robert, 25–6, 29–30: *Aino* Symphony, 30, 58, 151; biography (1952), 137; Chiavari, Sibelius's letter from, 237–8; concerts, 38, 219; and *En Saga* (Sibelius), 129–30; financial situation, 197; Finnish Rhapsody, 30; and First Symphony (Sibelius), 90; his first wife, 102; on Gallén, 137; and Gallén's *The Problem*, 162; Gallén's villa, with Sibelius at (1899), 218; and Helsinki music controversy (1903), 259–60; and Historical Tableaux Music (Sibelius), 220; and *Lemminkäinen* Suite (Sibelius), 293; his nationalism, 106–7; his Orchestral School, 125, 139, 274; performs Overture and Ballet Scene, 90; *Päivälehti* circle member, 100; and Paris Exhibition tour, 223–31; and Paris World Exhibition, 231; his Porkala villa, Sibelius invited to, 218; on Quartet in A minor (Sibelius), 52; relationship with Sibelius, 90, 193, 101–3, 227–8; Scholarship shared with Sibelius, 197; and Second Symphony (Sibelius), 243–4, 293; Sibelius conducts his orchestra, 99; and Sibelius's drinking habits, 273; Sibelius's introduction to, 52; Sibelius's talent, his reaction to, 53; and Sibelius's stress (1896), 184–5; and Sibelius's progress, 32; *Sommarminnen*, 231; and the 'Symposium', 137–8; Tvärminne, Sibelius's letter from, 257; University appointment, 190, 192–4; at Vasa Choral Festival, 151; Wegelius compared to, 29–30
Käkisalmi Castle, 148
Kalalahti (Finland), 18
Kalevala (epic), 17, 72, 75, 96–120: and *Aino* Symphony (Kajanus), 58; centenary commemoration, 167; and 'Drommen' setting, 129; and First Symphony, 217; Hertzberg's prose reworkings of, 185; influence on Gallén, 137, 138; influence on Kajanus, 30, 36, 108; influence on Sibelius, 20, 58, 98, 139; and *Lemminkäinen* Suite, 168, 173; letter to Aino on, 76–7; and 'Marssnön', 262; new edition, 97; and

Volsung myth compared, 109, 119; and 'The Origin of Fire', 255–6, 266, 269; and Second Symphony, 292; 'Terve Kuu' setting, 269; 'Venematka' setting, 136, 268
Kalevala Society, 191
Kalevankatu, Sibeliuses' home at, 124, 136
Kämp's restaurant (Helsinki): and Gallén's painting, 137, 138; and King Christian parody, 207; 'Leskovite' meetings at, 45; Sibelius's meeting with Kajanus at, 102; Sibelius's too frequent visits (1903), 272–3
Kantala (Finland), 18
Kantele (*Finnish instrument*), 108
Kanteletar (folk poetry), 149, 268 (*bis*)
Karelia (Russia), 121, 122–3
Karelia Suite, 164: Ballade from, 178; Busoni sees score of, 161; and *Maiden in the Tower*, 185–6; and Paris Exhibition tour, 226. See also *Karelia* tableaux music
Karelia tableaux music, 145–9, 152: dramatic skill of, 157; and Helsinki 1894–5 season, 162–3; and Historical Tableaux Music, 220–2; piano arrangement, 195; See also *Karelia Suite*
Karelian folk music influence, 118, 122, 145, 211
Katila, Evert, on Violin Concerto, 277
Keller, Gottfried: *Der grüne Heinrich*, 95
Kellgren, Johan (*court poet*), 4
Kerava (Finland), 207, 208, 224
Kexholm Castle, 148
King Christian II Suite, 148, 199–201, 202–4: in America, 243; Hanover performance, 239; Kämp restaurant parody, 207; London performance, 243; and Paris Exhibition tour, 225, 228; Weingartner's performance, 257
'Kiss's hope, The' (*Runeberg setting*), 122
Kistler, Cyrill: *Kunihild* Overture, 159
Kistner (*Leipzig publisher*), 78
Kivekäs, Lauri, 137
Kivi, Aleksis (*poet*), 206–7, 268
Kjerulf, Charles, on Copenhagen tour concert, 227–8
Klavierauzug, 143
Klemetti, Heikki (*conductor*), 269
Klingenberg, Alf (*pianist*), 59
Klinger, Max (*painter*), 161
Knutsson, Karl (King of Sweden), 147
Kodály, Zoltán, 290
Koli (Finland), 122
'König' tavern (Helsinki), 207, 272–3

s—x   305